New Masters,
New Servants

New Masters, New Servants

Migration, Development, and Women Workers in China

Yan Hairong

Duke University Press   Durham and London   2008

© 2008 Duke University Press

Printed in the United States of America on acid-free paper ∞

Designed by Heather Hensley

Typeset in Adobe Garamond Pro by Tseng Information Systems, Inc.

Library of Congress Cataloging-in-Publication data and republication acknowledgments appear on the last printed pages of this book.

Licensed under the Creative Commons Attribution-Non-Commercial-NoDerivs License, available at http://creative commons.org/licenses/by-nc-nd/3.0/ or by mail from Creative Commons, 559 Nathan Abbott Way, Stanford, Calif., 94305, U.S.A.

"NonCommercial" as defined in this license specifically excludes any sale of this work or any portion thereof for money, even if the sale does not result in a profit by the seller or if the sale is by a 501(c)(3) nonprofit or NGO.

Duke University Press gratefully acknowledges the support of the Chiang Ching-Kuo Foundation, which provided support toward the production of this book.

CONTENTS

In this book I focus on rural-to-urban migration of young women serving as domestic workers for urban families in China, examining and challenging some of the keywords—such as development, modernity, *suzhi* (quality), human capital, self-development, and consumer citizenship—that are constitutive of the process of post-Mao reform. Enabled by "reform and opening up," rural-to-urban labor migration is a crucial site where these keywords are mobilized to produce truth-effects. Why? Because migrant labor is vital to the continuation of flexible accumulation and growth, which, on the one hand, allows the state and elite groups to claim legitimacy for the reform and, on the other hand, enhances their resources to negotiate and manage discontented urban laid-off workers and rural residents.

I carried out my main field research, which involved following migrant women from villages in Anhui Province to the city of Beijing, between fall 1998 and spring 2000. I also conducted some interviews in Nanjing, Tianjin, Hefei, and Shanghai during fifteen months of fieldwork. Since then, I have kept in touch with some migrants through reunions, letter writing, and phone calls. The struggles, aspirations, and subjection of these young migrant women articulate the power of the central story as it is structured by keywords, but also mark its limit as a "proper" story. The postsocialist reform has enabled the process of migrant subject constitution and self-representation, and haunted their struggles with its own discursive conditions and contradictions. On the whole, it is unable to produce their lives as proper referents for its keywords.

In chapter 1 I ask how the post-Mao project of modernity has instituted a climatic shift in rural-urban relations that makes migration a compelling experience for rural youth. When the rural becomes the urban's devalorized Other, how do young women respond to the questions of modernity and personhood? In chapter 2 I propose that the rise of domestic service was associated with the outcry about "the burdens of intellectuals" in the early post-Mao reform. The bodies of migrant women, coming through the labor market, were recruited to relieve the bodies of intellectuals, or anyone else who could afford to hire domestic workers, of their domestic burdens. But how do the minds of employers mobilize and govern the bodies of migrant women? Given the constant and numerous complaints from employers about their domestic workers, what kind of sociality do they desire and how do they try to achieve it? In chapter 3 I explore the links between the neoliberal discourse of development and the labor-recruitment process in which migration is represented as pedagogical. How can one describe China as neoliberal when the State is actively involved in what some people have called the new *sihua* (four "-izations") — privatization, liberalization, marketization, globalization — which have displaced the four modernizations (of agriculture, industry, national defense, and science and technology) that were proposed in the late 1970s? How are the population and individuals coded and measured as subjects of development? When consumption increasingly defines identity and status in post-Mao China, I ask in chapter 4, what is its relationship with migrant women whose bodies are locked within manual labor? How does consumption and production form a particular pair of contradictions in the process of women's migration? In chapter 5 I turn to questions of class. When self-development becomes the discourse of individual mobility, and the term *class* (*jieji*) has been disavowed in the official ideology, do migrant women encounter and express "class" experiences? In chapter 6 I explore the subject of self-representation. As the laws of economic development appear to be the laws of nature, what kinds of self-representations are possible? Why do some migrant women negotiate a self-representation aligned with the hegemonic discourse of development when such a self-representation includes poverty, illness, and misery? How do other migrants critique such self-representation and articulate what might be considered a liminal politics of resistance?

My field research was funded by the Wenner-Gren Foundation for Anthropological Research and the International Dissertation Research Fellowship provided by the Social Science Research Council. Many people have contributed to the development and completion of this project. I owe a deep debt of gratitude to my mentors Ann Anagnost, Tani Barlow, Madeleine Yue Dong, Kaushik Ghosh, Stevan Harrell, and Katharyne Mitchell, who played important roles in my graduate training at the University of Washington. Tamara Jacka kindly pointed me to the magazine *Rural Women Knowing All* when I began my field research. Li Zhang generously offered fieldwork advice. Zhongdong Ma provided me with the first important connection to my fieldsite. My friends and colleagues Joel Andreas, Alana Boland, Chris Brown, Beth Drexler, Brian Hammer, Helen Schneider, and Wang Danyu have read and commented on various chapters in the dissertation phase. I must also thank Wang Hui and Huang Ping for encouraging me to publish in *Dushu* and Chen Kuan-Hsing and Ding Naifei for inviting my contribution to *Taiwan: A Radical Quarterly in Social Studies*.

I began to work on the book manuscript while I was a fellow at the Princeton University Society of Fellows (SOF). I thank SOF for its institutional support and am indebted to senior SOF fellows Susan Naquin and Carol Greenhouse for their intellectual generosity. My SOF colleagues Sujatha Fernandes, Anne-Maria Makhulu, Sunil Agnani, and I formed a reading group that provided critical intellectual stimulation and companionship. I am also grateful to Louisa Schein for making me part of the memorable reading-meal group that she organized, and I am thankful to other members of this group—Chen Jin, Li Jin, and Wang Hailing—for both their food and their thoughts. During the years of its development, this project has greatly benefited from discussions with Pun Ngai, Dorothy Solinger, Eileen Otis, Eric Thompson, Tang Can, Liu Huiying, Han Jialing, Joshua Goldstein, Ren Hai, Fan Ke, and Arianne Gaetano. I am also grateful for friends who have inspired me with their support and concern: Nancy Abelmann, Karen Kelsky, Ravi A. Palat, Behrooz Ghamari, Han Yuhai, Zhang Xiaodan, Dai Fang, Pun Ngai, Hsia Hsiao-Chuan, Ku Hok Bun, and Wang Penghui. This book project has followed me to the University of Illinois, Urbana-Champaign, University of Hong Kong, and Hong Kong Polytechnic University. I thank my supportive colleagues at these universities. Two anonymous readers provided invaluable comments that helped refine and reshape the structure of the book. Matthew A. Hale thoughtfully edited the manuscript. Barry Sautman must be credited for his suggestion of the book title.

This project would not have been possible without villagers in Wuwei showing me kindness and migrant workers in the cities sharing their experiences. This book is dedicated to Chinese migrant women workers.

INTRODUCTION

The marginality of her story is what maintains the other's centrality; there is no kind of narrative that can hold the two together (though perhaps history can): an outsider's tale, held in oscillation by the relationships of class.

CAROLYN KAY STEEDMAN, *LANDSCAPE FOR A GOOD WOMAN*

In spring 2001 I served as an interpreter in a meeting between ministry-level cadres from China and U.S.-based economists who consult with the World Bank. I witnessed a remarkable result of two decades of reform in China: the two parties shared the same conceptual language. Many of their keywords lined up quite literally. In table after table, in chart after chart, the universal language of economic development successfully coded the social landscape of post-Mao China as a "transitional economy."

In the process of globalization the peripheries are increasingly coded, evaluated, and disciplined by regulative keywords: development, growth, efficiency, market, structural adjustment, consumer choice, optimal assemblage of resources, global governance, and so on. This occurs through the rapid and dense circulation of capital, knowledge, and technology, and through the uneasy traffic between the universality of global standards and the particularity of "Chinese characteristics." I borrow the term *keyword* from Raymond Williams, who identifies a set of lexical changes since the eighteenth century as a guide to the intellectual transformation that accompanied England's industrialization: "I called these words keywords in two connected senses: they are significant, binding words in certain activities and their interpretation; they are significant, indicative words in certain forms of thought" (1976: 13). While Williams approaches keywords in literary sources through a combination of social history and the history of ideas, I annotate some of the post-1989 keywords in China by locating them in ethnographic instances and examining their discursive functions in shaping everyday experiences. With the ebbing of revolutionary movements, the new global circulation of these keywords bespeaks the force of newly unlimited capital accumulation in the post–Cold War world. This army of keywords collaborates to form a semiotic matrix. Once one takes issue with any particular keyword, the rest come rushing to its aid. They are networked. Intertwined with this sign chain are a series of networked and continually networking local, national, and transnational institutions. Everyday the net is being managed, challenged, negotiated, mended, disrupted, reinforced.

During the meeting for which I interpreted, Chinese delegates, acting like area specialists, periodically reminded their U.S. counterparts of "Chinese characteristics" or "historical constraints." But this did not prevent them from upholding the same transcendental laws preached by their American counterparts. The acknowledgment of Chinese characteristics or historical constraints, which render China a problematic referent for the term *market economy*, makes the keywords not less compelling, but more. A Chinese official keyword at the end of the twentieth century was "advancing with the times" (*yu shi ju jin*). With the passing of socialism, the time of the global capitalist market, expressed through developmental policies, has come to dominate both city and countryside. It commands through transnational organizations and national governments that peoples and areas advance (*jin*), catch up (*gan*), and get on track (*jie gui*). Pheng Cheah, writing on U.S. area studies, urges one to see "how much the discursive formation of Asian studies inhabits the folds of G. W. F. Hegel's text" (2000: 49). In his *Philosophy of World History* Hegel issues a prognostic death certificate to areas or nations (often conflated in area studies) that live automatically, like clocks running on natural time, rather than participating in the time of History (1980: 59–60).

The "reform and opening up," launched in the late 1970s in post-Mao China, created among intellectual elites in the 1980s a powerful sense of crisis about China's time-place in the global order and initiated a process of yearning for the Chinese nation-state to seek valorization in the time-space of capital. Welcoming a big-time opening of the Chinese media market to Hollywood films in 1995, a Chinese film critic described the pedagogical agency of Hollywood blockbusters in China: "A commercial society demands governance by transcendental rules and globally acknowledged ethical behavior. Commercial films thrive precisely on the basis of such ethical values. . . . *Pretty Woman* is . . . revolutionary because it recognizes a business ethic with rational egoism being the cardinal principle of such ethics. . . . It celebrates a love earned with the capital of morality as well as the morality of capital whereby money making has the virtue of subsidizing education and industrial development."[1] In the process of China's embracing the logic of global capital, globe-trotting keywords such as *development* and *growth* have woven a master narrative of market realism that represents unceasing pain, injury, disaster, collateral damage, anomalies, and unrest as the transitional costs of the lofty telos of development, or as historical constraints, implicating the socialist past. Even on a global scale, economies may prosper or crash, but the truth-effects of these keywords remain when they manage to mask the interests they represent and the "interpretive schizophrenia" they suffer (Liu 1999: 770). This was demonstrated in the case of the Asian Tigers, whose government-business cooperation, once credited for creating miracle economies, was attacked as crony capitalism after the 1997 Asian Financial Crisis. The keywords and their global institutional mastermind retain their discursive power, even as they increasingly face challenges outside the five-star conference rooms of their summit meetings.

Catachrestic Keywords and Postsocialism

What vast subterranean reality lies beneath the discursive power of these keywords? Let me introduce the migrant worker Xiang and her letters, which serve as a gateway to her subaltern subjectivity and to a hidden reality that cannot be fully claimed or subsumed by the keywords. I met Xiang in Beijing in 1999, when she was in her second year as a live-in domestic worker employed by a couple, both of whom taught at a university. Xiang, who had a junior-high-school education, loved to read and spent most of her spare time in Beijing perusing literary books and journals from her employers' collection. After she had worked for them for two years, she decided to go to Lhasa, Tibet, thinking that a new place might give her a new sense of being and new life opportunities. During the year that she spent there, she worked as a telephone operator, as a salesperson for a tea company, and as a waitress at a restaurant, with her savings being reduced to pennies between jobs. In 2001 she migrated to Shanghai, where she now works as a shop assistant.

Xiang and I have maintained a correspondence since she left Beijing. In a letter dated April 2001 she relates in detail how she registers and interprets her own life's reality.

> [My friends and I] often talk about our individual gains and losses, happiness and sadness. We also chat about our ennui [*wuliao*]. Nobody is able to cast her gaze [*yanguang*] wider to understand the contour of our bigger environment. As human beings, we accept our parents, family, native place, society, culture—all of which are structures [*kuangjia*] that came before us. And all we have to do is adapt and comply.

> People have the inclination to pursue happiness and avoid the companionship of suffering, injustice, oppression, and darkness. The audience in front of the screen might shed tears for the handicapped, the abandoned, lone resisters, and the impoverished lower classes. But they only do so to congratulate their own superiority and comfort. There are also sensationalized [*chaozuo*] tragedies for consumption. But people can never really understand the much more enormous real reality [*geng pangda de zhenshi de zhenxiang*]. They turn a blind eye to its hazy darkness [*kongmang de hei'an*].

> Myself included. I consciously forget those hardest days I experienced. The small restaurant where I had my first job as a dishwasher in Shanghai is close to the prosperous Huaihai Road. Later I had another job in the area. But no matter how much I like that area, I have never set foot in that restaurant again. There is also an agency for recruiting domestic workers. I slept on its floor for three nights, paying three yuan [forty cents] a night. I seldom even think about that place. All the letters to friends and parents were written after I found the job as a shop assistant. Those other days were thus edited out [*jianji diao*] and forgotten.

What are the "much more enormous real reality" and its "hazy darkness" that "people can never really understand" or "turn a blind eye to"? This "much more enormous reality" lurks beneath the keywords, but it eludes and exceeds their normative symbolic order. While the keywords reign as transcendental laws and mediate for the dominant political and economic interests, this "much more enormous real reality," its darkness, has to be overlooked or kept out of consciousness in order for business and work to go on as usual. Drawing on Jacques Derrida, I adopt the term *catachresis* (literally, the improper or strained use of a word) to describe the violent production of meanings by keywords and their abusive relationship with the "much more enormous real reality."[2]

With "myself included," Xiang hints that her hardest experiences are part of this enormous reality and its hazy darkness, on which she dare not reflect. What is at stake for Xiang's self-consciousness when the hardest days must be "edited out and forgotten" from memory? Is it so that she can struggle on as usual and so that she will not feel her life being consigned to that hazy darkness? Is it because a certain kind of self-representation—how she represents herself to herself and to others—can be enabled and sustained only by conscious self-editing and forgetting? In this sense, is her self-representation a catachresis that mirrors and allegorizes the "much more enormous" catachresis?

Can forgetting be conscious? And what is consciousness if it is conscious of its own forgetting and editing? With the hint of self-critical reflection ushered in by "myself included," Xiang commemorates her forgetting of the hardest days and deconstructs her own self-consciousness and self-representation. This should caution against any representation that takes voice, by way of direct quotation, as unmediated self-evidence and self-representation of subjectivity. If memory is constitutive of identity and self-representation, this kind of conscious forgetting may be an act of leaving memory and identity open to future *re-membering*, a refashioning of self-representation and membership by re-articulating one's memory. The communist-led mass movement of "speaking bitterness" in the 1940s and 1950s exemplifies the rearticulation of difficult experiences of the past in terms of a new vocabulary of class oppression.[3] Peasants, encouraged to speak in public of the past injustice they had suffered, learned to reinterpret their suffering in terms of class rather than of fate as they were mobilized for land reform and social revolution. This enabled the speaker to self-represent as a member belonging to a class collective. In this sense, remembering, or memory opened up to rearticulation, is also a potential process of "re-membering," or forging a new membership.

It is indeed a question of membership that is at stake for Xiang as she tries to forget. In an earlier letter, dated January 2002, she writes, "You see, what I desire forever deviates from the status and role where I'm positioned. I cannot be incorporated into a collective as a *dagongmei*, but I have no way of possessing a knowledge system as intellectuals do. For a long time, I have felt that my two feet are in the air and my heart is empty [*hen xinxu*]." The term *dagongmei*, most typically referring to young, single rural women working in the city, is often thought to be a neologism invented in post-Mao China. In fact, the term was already in use in the late nineteenth century; it was recorded in 1889 in the journal of the late Qing writer Xu Ke (1869–1928), who used it in reference to the news from Guangdong that over 17,000 men and women there were employed by 167 silk factories (Xu Ke 1997: 313).[4] However, the term *dagongmei* might not have had much circulation beyond Guangdong because, during the late nineteenth century and the early twentieth, news reports about women entering industrial-labor relations in Shanghai, Jiangsu, and Chongqing used other terms, such as *nügong, nügongren* (both meaning woman worker), or *funü* (women).[5] The word *dagongmei* emerged anew with a nationwide circulation through the expanding market in the post-Mao era, against the backdrop of the Mao-era industrial-labor relations that guaranteed lifelong employment and various benefits. *Dagong* means "'working for the boss', or 'selling labor,' connoting commodification and a capitalist exchange of labor for wages" (Pun Ngai 1999: 3). *Mei* is a term for sister, girl, and young woman. Although Xiang would call herself a dagongmei, being a member of the dagongmei collectivity presents an existential problem for her, as she explains in response to a letter I wrote to her asking why she could not identify with this category.

> Perhaps the emphasis [*zhongdian*] and referent [*suozhi*] in my original sentence is not the same as what you have in mind. What does it mean to be incorporated into a collectivity as a dagongmei?
>
> First, dagongmei is defined here [in the city] as those who have low education, mainly do physical labor, and have rural household registrations. As carved out by society and the market, the scope of work choice is very narrow for dagongmei. What is the position of dagongmei? They are the

lowest tier of society, the most powerless, and the voiceless. Not only are their freedom and labor cheaply purchased, but they are also restricted in accessing education and rich and high-quality [*gao suzhi*] thinking.

To leave the bookish explanation, I can at least talk about my life as a typical dagongmei. Through some connections, I got a job washing dishes in a fast-food restaurant, earning 450 yuan a month. This wage was a rather good one for those waiting for jobs. Because I'm young, I was favored by the employer [for this job]. Every day [I] got up at 5:30 in the morning, washed vegetables, sterilized dishes, boiled water, and so on. The prep would go on until noon. When it was busy, [I] had to quickly collect the dishes, wash them, and carry them out. Plus [I] had to assist the cook, wash woks, boil water, and fetch groceries. There was one hour for lunch and rest between noon and afternoon. Then prep work started over again. After dinner and cleaning work, [I] could clock out after 8:30. But running around all day, carrying piles and piles of dishes, [my] shoulder and lower back really hurt. I just did not want to go out [in the evening]. There was a bookstore on Huaihai Road and it took five minutes to walk there. But I only visited it twice. I wrote about exhaustion in my diary. But actually for many people this is ordinary. By comparison, I made it seem extraordinary. But when I was exhausted sometimes, I really felt that I couldn't take it any more. This [I] had thought [I] would remember all my life. But now [I] have almost forgotten it. The last day at work [in this restaurant], [my] feet were scorched and blistered by boiling water. [They] were so swollen that I couldn't put on shoes. So [I] finished my last day working there in sandals. Exhaustion plus pain make this a little harder to forget. So busy, so tired, but still no way of asking why [*meiyou banfa wen weishenme*]. Working along with me was a seventeen-year-old girl who had just come to the city. She was full of vigor and joked back and forth with the cook. Some of them chat and laugh all day as if [they were] very accustomed to this kind of life. Being yoked [*tao shang le*] to this kind of life seems as natural as the existence of the sun, the moon, and the stars. . . .

Many times I want to forget my identity/status [*shenfen*] [as a dagong-mei] and try to imagine myself as an orphan or a nomad. This might be literary romanticism, but it is vain and irresponsible. Not being willing to face reality is an [act of] escape. I know it very well, but still I cannot help being "naïve."

Thinking too much like this will lead to a sense of insecurity and uncertainty about things. We make a living by working, but we are not professional women. We are only dagongmei. This kind of independence is not secure.

Several days ago an old classmate, who had not been in touch for a long time, called me to complain about his failure to pass the exam for graduate school. I wanted to tell him my worries to keep him in balance. But after no more than a few sentences, he cut me off and said, "You just need a husband." The implied meaning is that it's hopeless for me to be anything and the only solution is marriage. Putting aside his teasing, actually many, including dagongmei themselves, have really thought that there is no way out other than marriage.

What can be done about the future? That is a question that forbids much thinking [bu rong duo xiang]. We can only focus on the things right in front our eyes and live day to day. I don't worry about the question of marriage. This question is close to being boring. But, frankly, sometimes I really want to put an end to this by getting married. What's the point of struggling on? Don't laugh at me. Just a thought to vent my frustration. Now, [I]'d like to talk about the question of love and marriage of dagongmei. Their choices do not exceed those of their professions. Forget it. I cannot continue on this topic.

Is the future in part claimed by this hazy darkness? It not only forbids hope but also "forbids much thinking," because "thinking too much like this will lead to a sense of insecurity and uncertainty about things." On dagongmei, Xiang speaks both "as a typical dagongmei" and as one who refuses to be incorporated into this group identity. After she defines what it means to be dagongmei both generally and specifically with regard to her own experiences, she expresses her wish to transcend and negate it. "You see, what I desire forever deviates from the status and role where I'm positioned. . . . I have felt that my two feet are in the air and my heart is empty." But her ephemeral transcendence, leaving her neither here nor there and her feet in the air, is enabled by a forgetting and an imaginary flight away from the actual existence of dagongmei, the discursive and material social relations and conditions to which she is yoked.

When Xiang wrote about her refusal to be incorporated into the category of dagongmei, it gave me a chance to query her. I had heard some migrant women critique Xiang's aloofness and distance from other dagongmei when she occasionally participated in activities at the Home for Rural Migrant Women (Dagongmei zhi jia), a Beijing-based nongovernmental organization. "In her mind she places herself above dagongmei. She still has dreams about the mainstream society and wishes to become a member of it. Actually she is quite petit-bourgeois [*xiao zi*]," criticized Hua Min, a migrant woman activist who knows Xiang. *Petit-bourgeois* (*xiao zichan jieji*), a term often used in the Mao era as a political critique reflecting the Marxian class analysis of relations of production, is nowadays shortened to *xiao zi* and used to mean something like "yuppie" or "posh," usually highlighting expensive taste and consumption. However, the "xiao zi" in Hua Min's commentary about Xiang is more akin to its original meaning and is meant to be a serious critique. At stake in the contention is not only what dagongmei is and means, but how it can mean and whether it has a potential transformative agency.

Unlike Xiang, some migrant women have strongly invoked the dagongmei collective and identified themselves as part of it. At the First National Forum on Issues about Women Migrant Workers' Rights and Interests, which took place in June 1999 in Beijing, dagongmei representatives from Beijing and Shenzhen narrated the discrimination and exploitation they had experienced and the pervasive derogatory meaning associated with the word *dagongmei*. One researcher then carefully asked how these women themselves felt about the word and whether an alternative should be used instead. One of the representatives replied, "We *are* [*jiu shi*] dagongmei and it is nothing to be ashamed of." As this representative implicitly critiqued, the politics must go beyond a reform of the signifier. At a casual gathering after the conference, the same representative reaffirmed, "We *are* dagongmei. Only when we are united will we have strength." This desire for affirmation and collective incorporation expresses hope for a politics that works with the social and material grounding of the subject position of dagongmei, and at the same time articulates it as an identity that carries within itself a potential transformative agency. A new dagongmei collective is beginning to be envisioned.

The signification of *dagongmei* for Xiang, as she tries to clarify in the letter, is different. The migrants she writes about do not ask why "being yoked in this kind of life seems as natural as the existence of the sun, the moon, and the stars." They are incapable of querying their own predicament: "so busy, so tired, but still . . . no way of asking why." Although Xiang occasionally finds hope, dagongmei often appears in her writing as a hopeless identity that is unable to break out of the yoke. It is, therefore, an identity that she wants to escape, even temporarily: "Many times I want to forget my status [as a dagong-mei] and try to imagine myself as an orphan or a nomad." When speaking of dagongmei, Xiang shifts between "we" and "they," and between hope and hopelessness, which reflects a problem she has with self-representation, associated with her ability and inability to forget and to escape.

Xiang's signification of *dagongmei* nevertheless problematizes the neoliberal meaning of *dagongmei*, which frames migrant workers as little more than *homo economicus*, rational agents of the market economy and self-development. The massive rural-to-urban labor migration is both a product of the liberalizing processes of the post-Mao "reform and opening," and a condition for its continuation and expansion. In the policy struggles to expand the power of the market, mainstream liberal economists often boost their legitimacy and moral authority through humanistic gestures of celebrating and championing the freedom of migrants, at the expense of urban workers who struggle to make claims to state-owned enterprises.

The hegemony of catachrestic keywords and the contestations about the meaning of dagongmei necessarily raise the question of postsocialism in China today. Many Western academics, journalists, and politicians describe the global condition after the fall of the Eastern Bloc as "postsocialist." Yet Chinese postsocialism seems ambiguous because post-Mao transformation is marked by both a radical reform in ideology and social relations, and by a continuity in the form of a party-state that still claims to be socialist. This ambiguity, sometimes reflected in the ambivalent construction "(post)socialism," has given rise to a variety of enunciations. On the one hand, the Chinese Communist Party and some remaining Cold Warriors in the West appear to be similarly invested in the truth-value in the nomenclature itself, even though this investment serves two very different purposes: for the former, it serves to claim ongoing legitimacy for its rule despite the reform; for the latter, it serves, also despite China's reform, to continually legitimize anticommunist politics against China. For the Chinese State, the strategic investment in the truth of nomenclature enables an ideological separation between the political and economic spheres.[6] With this separation, those keywords that exercise hegemony in economic life can claim to be apolitical and non-interfering with the party-state's claim to socialism, even though they represent the interests of domestic and transnational capital. Writing on post-1989 Chinese politics, Xudong Zhang comments, "As long as the government's legitimacy comes exclusively from maintaining economic growth and social stability, its official ideology will remain a meaningless signifier awaiting appropriation by the newborn economic and class interests and positions in the differentiated social sphere" (2001: 5). For the Chinese State, postsocialism is an enforced separation of the political from the economic and an enforced depoliticization of "development," "productive forces," and "the market." The suspension of the political from the economic is reflected in the former Communist Party leader Deng Xiaoping's adamantly pragmatist "cat theory" of economic development, which discouraged political debate and encouraged cats to catch mice, regardless of their political color.

On the other hand, postsocialism, as Lydia Liu has noted in her criticism of a trend in cultural studies (1999), is taken by some to be a flattened transnationalism which has little place for historicity and for which socialism is irrelevant. Thus China is treated as continuous with the globe to be capitalized and is highly accessible by this form of transnationalism, as long as it knows how to negotiate the culture and the state. The capitalization approach also encourages a near-sighted temporal view in which China seems to have existed only for two or three decades, because in this transnational cognition, only the past two or three decades are relevant and worth considering. This is the explicit view held by transnational capital and by many elite members of Chinese society, but it is also an implicit assumption held by some new students of Western China studies programs who access China as a field only in its late reform period. Socialism is treated as "data" about prior modes of behavior that may have hangover effects, but which present little political or epistemological challenge to analysis.

Chinese postsocialism may have become more frequently invoked, but it has been much less often theorized. In the context of 1980s reform Arif Dirlik (1989) pioneered an examination of postsocialist conditions, conceiving postsocialism as an articulation and response of "actually existing socialism" to its own perceived deficiencies, as well as to the demands of capitalism in the context of socialism's global abatement as a coherent political-theoretical alternative. Yet Dirlik also emphasizes that this process of articulation, premised on the structure of "actually existing socialism," is unlikely to restore capitalism. Dirlik wrote in the early phase of the reform, when more of the preceding socialist structure was still intact. But China's integration with the global market economy in the 1990s effected a much more radical transformation of the political-social landscape. Perhaps to stress the importance of the continuity of socialist legacies, Li Zhang (2002) calls the current conditions late socialist. On the other hand, Ralph Litzinger suggests the need to attend to "a different vision of the stakes of theorizing postsocialist realities" (2002: 34). Lydia Liu points to a "co-authorship of the ideology of business entrepreneurship between the postsocialist official discourse of China and that of the mainstream American media" (1999: 790).

Chinese postsocialism at the beginning of the twenty-first century includes some contradictory structural conditions which can be partially listed as follows: a continued official claim to socialism, coupled with mainstream neoliberal policies that transform China into a market economy integrated into the global capitalist system; rapid capitalization of enterprises (turning state and collective productive assets into private capital) and marketization of essential social services (people in China now refer to education, medical care, and housing as the new oppressive "three big mountains," echoing the "three big mountains" of imperialism, feudalism, and bureaucratic capitalism that oppressed the Chinese people before 1949); collective ownership of farm land, relatively equal but divided land-use rights among individual rural families, and de jure noncommodity status of farm land; large-scale unemployment and loss of benefits for aging urban workers due to the structural adjustment of state-owned enterprises; the new presence of a young army of rural-to-urban migrant workers; unprecedented rural-urban disparity in much of China, as well as drastic regional disparity between the coastal areas and interior areas, including many ethnic minority areas.

Within these sometimes contradictory conditions one finds similarly contradictory articulations of the politics of postsocialism. For example, within China, although the Left has leveled many severe critiques of the state's unsocialist policies and ideology, critics rarely use terms such as *postsocialism*, not so much because it is politically incorrect as because they consider it more strategic to call on the state to make good on its own claim to socialism. On the other hand, as I illustrate in chapter 1, the postsocialist political economy of land ownership and use rights ironically becomes an enabling condition for capitalist accumulation by subsidizing the reproduction of migrant labor power.

In the limited scope of this book I treat postsocialism as an unstable process in which the emerging hegemony of capitalism in China must deal with living socialist legacies, claims, and structures of feeling that surround the current relations of production and sociality. The enforced separation between the political and the economic spheres creates an ambiguous space in which words seem to lose their grounding in previous conditions and are being retooled and recycled for radically different and contradictory purposes. On the one hand, images of Mao are sometimes collected as kitsch, while on the other hand they are used as political symbols by discontented workers in their rallies and demonstrations. Capitalist market relations mobilize and retool keywords from the socialist revolutionary context. Practices such as "speaking bitterness" (*suku*) and words such as "big rear base" (*dahoufang*) are quite ingeniously re-oriented toward a different telos. These words and practices become national or local resources that feed and enrich the authority of the global keywords. At the same time, words are being retooled by migrant women workers for their collective self-expression. In chapter 5 I report on how the migrant worker Xiaohong retools Mao's use of "stand up" to call on the collectivity of migrant women, rather than on the nation. In chapter 6 I describe how the migrant worker Hua Min asserts the political agency of migrant workers and cites the early-twentieth-century leftist writer Lu Xun: "If we do not break out of the silence, we will perish in this silence!" These are different and competing efforts to retool words and to appropriate the legacy of socialist revolution. This, too, is a postsocialist dynamic. To grasp what Litzinger calls "the stakes of theorizing postsocialist realities" is a vast but critical project that requires collective efforts. Some significant work has begun in the realm of culture and gender studies, but there is still much to be done to improve understanding of postsocialism in its multifaceted political-economic conditions and their articulation with old and new forms of collective politics.[7]

How Does Domestic Service Signify? The Master-Servant Allegory

This book is about rural-to-urban migrant domestic workers in post-Mao China and the social relations and discursive power that they experience.

While domestic service signifies as an allegory articulating social relations and imaginaries in Chinese society today, the ability of domestic service to be a trope articulating larger social relations is not unique to postsocialist conditions in China. Therefore, one must first examine how the master-servant relationship serves as a trope in industrial societies.

Common sense might have one oppose the abstract, contractual, modern qualities of relations between capital and wage labor to the concrete, authoritarian, and pre-modern qualities associated with master-servant relations. But Karl Marx highlighted the despotic nature of capitalist relations: "In the factory code, the capitalist formulates his autocratic power over his workers like a private legislator, and purely as an emanation of his own will" (1977: 549–50). This despotism is the will of capital that abstracts and appropriates the worker's living body through "technical subordination" and is, as stressed by Dipesh Chakrabarty, "structural to capital . . . not simply historical" (2000: 666). In this sense Marx saw the master-servant relationship as the essential trope of appropriation: "The presupposition of the *master-servant relationship* [*Herrschaftsverhältnis*] is the appropriation of an alien will. Whatever has no will, e.g. the animal, may well provide a service, but does not thereby make its owner into a *master*" (1973: 500–501). The notion of will here draws on the Hegelian notion of self-consciousness or Being-for-itself that is predicated on the recognition by the self and the other (alien will) of the self's subjecthood. Land and animals thus have no will as such and cannot provide recognition. In the Hegelian master-slave dialectic "the Master's certainty is therefore not purely subjective and 'immediate,' but objectivized and 'mediated' by another's, the Slave's recognition" (Kojève 1980: 16).

Hegel and his followers arguably thought that humanity had reached the end of history with the French Revolution, which proclaimed the universal, rational principles of the rights of Man (Kojève 1980: x–xi). When Francis Fukuyama declared the end of history after the fall of the Berlin Wall, his declaration fulfilled Hegel's observation that history repeats itself. And one may add Marx's further observation that it does so the second time as farce (Marx 1994: 15). Marx's interesting move beyond Hegel is to see this appropriation of an alien will continued in mediated form in the capitalist realm of production relations: "The *master-servant relation* likewise belongs in this formula of the appropriation of the instruments of production. . . . [I]t is reproduced—in mediated form—in capital" (Marx 1973: 501). Beyond the formal political equality of the rights of Man, the master-servant element is found in the capitalist factory, which "confiscates every atom of freedom, both in bodily and intellectual activity" (Marx 1973: 548) and where "the slave-driver's lash" is replaced by "the overseer's book of penalties" (Marx 1977: 550).

Marx, however, is not alone in using the master-servant trope to capture the nature of capitalist relations of production. In fact, by the time of his writing, a legal coding of the master-servant doctrine had already begun to define the modern meaning of "employment" in England. However, while Marx used the trope to criticize the bourgeois view of the rise of freedom and autonomy, the bourgeois legal coding of this allegory defined and legitimized an employment relationship to criminalize labor indiscipline. Daniel Defoe in *The Great Law of Subordination Consider'd* (1724) narrates the story of Edmund Pratt as an illustration of insubordination and insolence of the plebs in the eighteenth century. Pratt is a "journeyman weaver" hired by E——, a clothier, to fulfill an order that he, E——, has received from a third party. Midway through the job, Pratt stops working, preferring to lie "Drunk and sotting in the Alehouse." E—— then approaches the magistrate to demand the arrest of Pratt, only to be told that because Pratt is "not an Apprentice, or a hir'd Convenant-Servant bargain'd with for the Year," he cannot be so compelled to work, nor is his refusal to work punishable. Under the existing law, Pratt can only be sued for damages, which, as judged by Defoe, was "not worth [the clothier's] while." Defoe uses the case of Pratt to illustrate what he sees as appalling social relations in eighteenth-century England. He sounds an alarm in an epigraph: "The Poor will be Rulers over the Rich, and the Servants be Governours of their Masters, the Plebij have almost mobb'd the Patricij. . . . [I]n a Word, Order is inverted, Subordination ceases, and the world seems to stand with the Bottom upward" (quoted in Tomlins 1995: 56). With the Woolen Manufactures Act of 1725 and many acts that followed, the parliament put an end to what Defoe considered "this Deficiency of the Law." Retelling the story, the critical legal scholar Christopher Tomlins states, "By a stroke of law, Parliament made Pratt's employer what a year previously he had not been—Pratt's master" (1995: 60–61). Contrary to the bourgeois celebration of the rule of law and the rise of freedom, Tomlins argues that the history of Anglo-American law in the eighteenth, nineteenth, and even twentieth centuries transformed employees such as Pratt into "servants," not the other way around (ibid.).

Odd as it may seem, as the eighteenth century wore on, the rank of servants saw unprecedented swelling in numbers in England, thanks to the efforts of courts and legal treatise writers. While Sir Matthew Hale, in his 1713 *Analysis of the Law*, categorized "Master and Servant" as one of the "Relations Oeconomical" and found little to say on the subject, in 1743 Richard Burns's *Justice of the Peace and Parish Officer* included in the category of servants "Laborers, journeymen, artificers, and other workmen" (Burns 1757: 229–65). In 1765–69 Sir William Blackstone's *Commentaries on the Laws of England* established "master and servant" as the legal categorization of all employment relations.

In the nineteenth-century United States as well, along with the disappearance of diverse forms of employment relations into a homogeneous wage labor, the master-servant trope emerged as a single legal paradigmatic expression of employment relations. The treatise writer Timothy Walker stated in 1837, "The title of master and servant, at the head of a lecture, does not sound very harmoniously to republican ears. . . . But the legal relation of master and servant *must* exist, to a greater or lesser extent, wherever civilization furnishes work to be done" (243; emphasis added). In 1877 H. G. Wood, a well-known lawyer and treatise writer, published the influential *A Treatise of the Law of Master and Servant*: "The word *servant*, in our legal *nomenclature*, has a broad significance, and embraces all persons of whatever rank or position who are in the employ, and subject to the direction or control of another in any department of labor or business" (2). Wood formulated the "employment-at-will" rule, holding that employment of indefinite duration can be terminated at any time, for any reason, with or without cause. "With us the rule is inflexible, that a general or indefinite hiring is prima facie a hiring at will, and if the servant seeks to make it out a yearly hiring, the burden is upon him to establish it by proof" (Wood 1877: 272, quoted in Feinman 1991: 735). Although the "servant" in the paradigmatic legal coding here is different from that of indentured servitude, the coding of employment relations as master and servant stressed that the employer-master has legally sanctioned property in the service of the servant-employee. The relationship between the master-employer and the servant-employee is one other than equality before the law. Rather, the contract has built-in legal relations of subjection that demand "fidelity, obedience, and sacrifice of control on the part of the employee" (Tomlins 1992: 90).

Since the 1920s, master-servant as the core doctrine of employment has not been dismantled, but many of its specifics have undergone revisions to accommodate labor demands, including an erosion of the employment-at-will rule. However, the conventional master-servant relationship, as understood by common-law agency doctrine, still operates today as the standard by which an employment relation is tested. For example, to define their employee status, university teaching assistants, medical doctors, and many others must pass the employment test, a critical criteria of which is whether one is subject to control and authority by another in the work process, even though this control may not be exercised (Rowland 2001; Frazier 2004). But the National Labor Relations Act, passed by Congress in 1935 to promote industrial peace and stability, and subsequently amended many times, does not regard the "individual employed as an agricultural laborer, or in the domestic service of any family or person at his home" to be an employee for purposes of protection in unionization efforts.[8] The irony can hardly be missed: the domestic-service worker is excluded from the category of employee for unionization purposes even though the master-servant relationship serves as the core doctrine of labor employment.

The rise of neoliberalism in the last three decades has rolled back the progress achieved in twentieth-century common law (the law of contracts, torts, and property) and has instituted what Jay Feinman calls a "regressive . . . revival . . . of the classical law that reigned in the Gilded Age at the end of the 19th century" (2004). Included in this revival is a defense of the employment-at-will rule associated with the master-servant doctrine.[9] In the name of freedom and flexibility, the recent reforms of the Australian workplace-relations laws restore employment at will for businesses employing less than a hundred workers, provoking union leaders to criticize what they consider the regress of workers' rights by a century.[10] In the context of these reversions I return to Marx and finish my quotation of his sentence: "The master-servant relation likewise belongs in this formula of the appropriation of the instruments of production. . . . [I]t is reproduced—in mediated form—in capital, *and thus . . . forms a ferment of its dissolution and is an emblem of its limitation*" (1973: 501; emphasis added).[11]

How does the master-servant relationship allegorize the changing morphology of social relations in China? During the many centuries of dynastic rule, bondservants, together with actors, prostitutes, and beggars, were classified as *jianmin* (inferior people), as opposed to *liangmin*, which included literati, farmers, craftsmen, and merchants.[12] Among jianmin, servants alone were subsumed into their masters' households and thus were not entitled to land. On becoming a servant, one would also usually lose one's family name and have a new name assigned by the master. Neither servants nor their descendants could sit for imperial exams, and thus they could not enter the civil service. Legal codes not only distinguished between jianmin and liangmin but also stipulated more specific differentiations between masters and servants. Servants were severely punished for offenses against their masters and were also subjected to various rules, upheld by local gentries, to compel domestic discipline (*jiafa*) and clan conventions (*zugui*).

The formal, castelike bondservant system was officially abolished by the Qing Dynasty during the late nineteenth century, but it continued informally for several decades. Up to 1949 there existed a variety of domestic employments, including bondservants.[13] A study of labor conditions in 1920 Shanghai revealed the following division of labor in domestic service: *niangyi* (for general domestic chores), *dajie* (a teenage girl for tidying rooms and light chores), *nainiang* (wet nurse), *shutou niangyi* (hair-comber), *timian po* (for facial exfoliation). These women reportedly worked fifteen to sixteen hours a day, with intermittent breaks for rest (Li Cishan 1920: 700–702). A study of labor conditions in Nanjing also found a similar division of labor. Those who worked on miscellaneous chores were paid the lowest and could be dismissed by masters at any time. When there was a contract, the first contract was for three years, the agreement being between the master and the woman's husband, after which she was free to leave (Mo Ru 1920). Lu Xun, in his 1921 story "My Old Home" (Gu xiang), relates three types of domestic employment, measured by length of service: "In our district we divide servants into three classes: those who work all the year for one family are called full-timers [*chang gong*]; those who are hired by the day are called dailies [*duan gong*]; and those who farm their own land and only work for one family at New Year, during festivals or when rents are being collected, are called part-timers [*mang yue*]" (1956: 92).

After the founding of the People's Republic in 1949, paid domestic service largely disappeared. In the first seventeen years of the Mao era, only high-ranking cadres and intellectuals, who were presumably charged with great responsibility, employed domestic service and took it for granted. Ordinary urban families could and did employ domestic labor on a short-term basis, but did not take it for granted as long-term everyday practice. After 1949 domestic workers were no longer called by any of the old terms for servants. The early classical terms *baomu* (literally, "protecting mother") and, alternatively, *ayi* (literally, "auntie") became categorical terms for all domestic helpers regardless of their specific responsibilities.[14] During the Cultural Revolution (1966–76), the presence of domestic servants in elite households came under criticism as a bourgeois privilege and the practice largely ceased. Following the post-Mao economic liberalization, the hiring of domestic workers reappeared in the cities in the early 1980s. In both the Mao and post-Mao eras, rural migrant women were the main source for domestic workers. Placement agencies, which emerged in the 1980s with the rapid expansion of domestic service, addressed domestic workers as *jiating fuwuyuan* (domestic-service personnel).

What does the long history of the servant system mean for most Chinese who grow up in the People's Republic today? Most Chinese citizens may not be familiar with the specifics of the servant system, and many may not even know most of the common historical terms for servants.[15] Yet even in the waning socialist collective memory, representations of servants and their oppression are still among the most poignant hallmarks of the class injustice of the "old society," and the liberation of servants remains the quintessential liberation story. This link was forged through widely known leftist literature of the 1930s and 1940s, such as Cao Yu's literary debut *Lei yu* (Thunder) and Ba Jin's *Jia* (Family), which featured women domestic servants as central characters. One of the classical figures of the oppressed in the national memory of the old society is the white-haired girl in the revolutionary play *Bai mao nü* (White-Haired Girl). This dramatic story of the liberation of the peasant servant girl Xi'er from the persecution of her master-landlord was widely popular in the communist-liberated areas in the 1940s and throughout the Mao era. In this play the experiences of exploitation and oppression were inscribed in the body of the servant girl, transforming her from a youthful woman into a white-haired "ghost." It was in the figure and the body of the peasant servant girl—the lowest of the low—that liberation was most powerfully signified.

The reform of the past three decades in China has made domestic service a contentious allegory of social transformation. For some domestic workers in China today, the "old society" and its class and gender subjugation is a specter that seems to have returned particularly through domestic service. If rural migrants at least initially find modern attraction in collective working and living experiences in Shenzhen factories (Ching Kuan Lee 1998), they have far more doubt about the prospect of working in urban homes and its implication for identity. This is reflected in some of the women's resistance to, or ambivalence about, terms such as *baomu*. For example, Xiang said, "[Baomu] is worse than ayi. I prefer to be called dagongmei." Still another found the term *baomu* "very ugly or shameful [*hao chou*], not as good as *fuwuyuan* [service personnel]." In 1996, when a young woman from Shanxi named Fang Lin was told of an opportunity to work as a baomu in Beijing, her first reaction was "Why? This is like going back to the old society!" But Fang Lin eventually persuaded herself and her parents that she could go to Beijing to work as a baomu. "I told my parents that this is nothing. Isn't it very common now? Newspapers report that even some college students today work as baomu." Fang Lin's doubt seems to have been confirmed by a migrant woman who complained that to be a baomu was to be a *yongren* (servant). The specter of the old society is more clearly manifested in the term *yongren*, which refers directly to pre-1949 arrangements. Although *dagongmei*, *baomu*, and *ayi* are all gendered terms for (migrant) women workers, *dagongmei* is preferred by some migrant domestic workers because, as I examine in chapter 1, *baomu* and *ayi* suggest a particular class humiliation and gender contamination specific to domestic service.[16]

In comparison, *fuwuyuan* was a neologism created in the Mao era to refer to workers in the service sector, such as restaurant servers, hotel workers, and so on. From the Mao-era context that everyone should *fuwu* (serve) the people (*wei renmin fuwu*), the term *fuwuyuan* for some migrant women today still offers the comfort of a discursive legitimacy or a basis for contesting class arrogance. For migrant domestic workers, to be addressed as fuwuyuan implies that they are symbolically placed in a discursive context linked to a modern egalitarian social relationship. *Yuan zai Beijing de jia* (A Home Far Away from Home) (Chen Xiaoqing 1993), a documentary about migrant domestic workers from Anhui Province, included a scene of a young woman, surrounded by her agitated colleagues, breaking down in tears in front of the camera and protesting, "Doesn't our work also serve the people?" The subtext of invoking their work as "serving the people" is to assert the Mao-era discourse of egalitarianism on the basis of the social value of their work.

Is there any need to pay attention to quibbles over the various terms used by migrant domestic workers? Liberalization since the late 1970s and the quick expansion of domestic service means that such service has become an every-day practice in urban China, bringing a significant number of first-generation employers and domestic employees into existence and social relations. At issue is how migrant domestic workers in postsocialist conditions struggle over the meaning of their labor, service, and identities. Both employers and domestic workers bring varied assumptions and locally and globally informed imaginaries into their struggles to define what constitutes "employment" and "service," and to define what desirable and legitimate sociality is.

How domestic service is allegorized points directly to how sociality in general is conceived under "socialism with Chinese characteristics." Employers' mobilization of the bodies of domestic workers to work automatically and affectively constitutes a hegemonic, developmentalist class pedagogy that reflects larger concerns and anxieties about China's ability to actualize the globally normative conditions of "market economy." Contestations over the meanings of domestic service go beyond the specific context of domestic labor to raise questions about the nature of wage labor, market economy, sociality, and socialism. In the conditions of postsocialism, domestic service, far from being a particular, parochial, anachronistic field of its own, is a site where these issues are particularly poignant when the collective memory of liberation and egalitarianism is being submerged by the newly hegemonic ideology of market economy and developmentalism.

Coda

In a letter dated 9 July 2001 Xiang, in a friendly but firm tone, nudged me with a question about my writing: "I have read your article. . . . You must know that I read it at least five times. This kind of academic language is very strange and difficult for me. But I do my best to figure out what you want to peel off and what issues you want to raise. I also speculate whether other readers would take an interest in this topic. . . . But I have thoughts that may be brusque. In my view, theoretical analysis by intellectuals can only be a kind of enlightenment; a greater force should be coming from those who are studied. They should be the number one *duixiang* of your [plural] conversation." The essay that Xiang read and critiqued was a short one I published in the mainland Chinese academic magazine *Dushu* (2001) and on which I partially base chapter 5 herein. Xiang's acknowledgment of "enlightenment" as intellectuals' agency may be an act of courtesy, as intellectuals in China have long asserted this agency for themselves. And it is a qualified one that is humbled in its comparison with the greater social force lying in the transformative potential of "those who are studied." Hua Min, a migrant woman worker activist, issued a similar suggestion when she gave a talk in a research setting: "Please don't just treat us as research materials. We hope you can speak *to* us." Aspiring to social transformation, including that of their own, Xiang, Hua Min, and the dagongmei like them do not literally demand to be spoken to or written for. Contrary to Edward Said's motto of critical intellectuals "speaking truth to power," Xiang and Hua Min demand a reorientation of speaking. This assertion of the transformative power of the subaltern, as well as the urging of intellectuals to reorient their speaking, comes from the legacy of Chinese social revolution in the twentieth century.

In the context of Xiang's critique, the word *duixiang* strikes me. *Duixiang* means a goal or a destination toward which thinking and action is oriented and intended. Duixiang can be things or people and can refer (1) to something to be engaged, studied, or transformed; or (2) to an addressee of love, marriage, writing, conversation, and so on. Xiang's use of the word *duixiang* may at first seem quite ordinary for a Chinese reader, as it is often how the word is used. This word, joining thinking with action, interpretation with transformation, dialectics with affect, is discursively linked with Mao's stress on a dialectical relationship between theory and practice (Mao 1967 [1937]). Its flow into everyday vernacular, including Xiang's casting of it as "in my view," actually bears remarkable witness to a quiet legacy of this revolutionary worldview. In fact the three primary meanings of duixiang given by *Xiandai hanyu cidian* (2001; Modern Chinese Dictionary) are "revolution," "research," and "love" (320). Its multiple and interlaced meanings are embedded in an epistemology radically different from that based on dualist binaries of subject-object or mind-body. Xiang's critique challenges me to enter into a relationship with migrant women in which they are the duixiang of my writing. Contemplating Xiang's use of *duixiang*, I cannot fix it with any one of the meanings, but can only consider how the dynamic move from one meaning to another is the very urge that Xiang and Hua Min try to express.

Writing on the "crisis in anthropology" in relation to the unresolved prob-lematic of ethnographic authority, Michel-Rolph Trouillot suggests, "We need to go out of anthropology to see the construction of 'ethnographic authority' not as a late requirement of anthropological discourse . . . but as an early com-ponent of this wider field that is itself constitutive of anthropology" (1991: 38). If the crisis of anthropology and the problematic of ethnographic authority are rooted in the wider field of history and power, one cannot hope to resolve these problems by making a philosophical acknowledgment of the presence of the other in the grammar of the subject's desire, which is merely a democratic gesture that continues to sustain the centeredness of the liberal subject. Nor can these problems be settled by our striving for more scrupulous textual skills and more sensitivity and innovation within the textuality of ethnographic writing. The duixiang mode of intellectual practice, then, presents a challenge, and a demand, and maybe also an opportunity to experiment a way out of the impasse.

What kind of anthropological practice and writing would this entail? Cer-tainly it is not simply a matter of eliminating jargon and toning down the density of academic language. It is not even "reciprocity" in the act of giving back to the community, because what is to be changed—as urged by Xiang and Hua Min—is not what occurs after thinking and writing, but thinking and writing itself. The duixiang mode of engagement would compel a rethink-ing of the categories of and relationship between the subject and object. The self-adequate writing subject has been imagined, assumed, and debated by anthropologists within the terrain of their textual practices. The self-adequate writing subject seems to prove unable to undo its self-adequacy. This self-adequacy has the rug pulled out from beneath its feet by Xiang's reminder of the inadequacy of intellectual agency alone, however critical it may be.

I have completed this writing project without making dagongmei the dui-xiang of my writing. Xiang's critique has continued to nag me and to reveal the limits and inadequacy of this book project. I share with readers here Xiang's critique and my thoughts on it in the hope that it might provoke further think-ing about our intellectual practices. This book project is primarily a writing project focused on "interpreting the world" to debate issues of development, modernity, neoliberalism, and postsocialism. By examining the migration ex-periences of young rural women working as domestic workers in urban homes,

I look at the processes of postsocialist development in China that have radically reorganized relationships between state and market, countryside and city, mental and manual work, and gender and domesticity.

If, on the one hand, the lives of the migrant women cannot be proper referents for the keywords of neoliberal capitalism, they do not, on the other hand, exist in themselves as proper referents of the subaltern class.[17] Gayatri Chakravorty Spivak constructively comments about the subaltern-studies collective: "The radical intellectual in the West is either caught in a deliberate choice of subalternity, granting to the oppressed either that very expressive subjectivity which s/he criticizes or, instead, a total unrepresentability" (1988: 209). Writing about migrant women is, for me, a process of understanding a variety of life experiences, changing consciousness, and analyzing the women's critiques and self-critiques, while also searching potential politics of the future. It is eminently important to trace how the power of hegemonic discourses works its way into the subjectivities of migrant women, but these subjectivities cannot be reduced to effects of power. Otherwise, Xiang would have not written about the "much more enormous real reality" and its "hazy darkness," with which she struggles between forgetting and remembering. Mapping the morphology of power and subjectivity is always an incomplete project, thanks to the often ignored "much more enormous real reality." This subterranean reality, irreducible to the signification of hegemonic keywords, is part of unceasing everyday life. Its hazy darkness may be a womb where future politics can germinate, when forgetting turns into an active process of re-membering, a rearticulation of memory, and a remaking of membership and identity.

1

THE EMACIATION OF THE RURAL

"No Way Out"

It's like going through a reincarnation and you still choose to be human [*ren*].

A YOUNG, RURAL MIGRANT WOMAN FROM HUBEI WORKING IN SHENZHEN, QUOTED IN CHING KWAN LEE, *GENDER AND THE SOUTH CHINA MIRACLE*

If I had to live the life that my mother has lived, I would choose suicide.

XIAZI, A YOUNG, RURAL MIGRANT WOMAN INTERVIEWED IN BEIJING, IN LI HONG, *RETURNING TO PHOENIX BRIDGE*

Tomorrow, I will be more like a human [*ren*].

XU XUE, A MIGRANT WOMAN, IN *CHINA'S YOUTH*, 1995

When asked why she has returned to Shenzhen after surviving a blaze that took the lives of sixty-eight of her coworkers in a factory there in 1991, the young woman from Hubei expresses her determination to be *ren*, literally "human." The blaze has not diminished her resolve. The second woman, Xiazi, adamantly rejects her mother's way of life in the countryside, as it seems to her to be a life so lacking in meaning that it annuls livability altogether.[1] The third young migrant, Xu Xue, resolutely expresses a hope of being more like ren. These young women invoke a meaning of *ren* that is not inherent within all humans, but is instead achieved through social action. *Ren* is a possessor of socially validated and meaningful personhood or subjectivity. As personhood is often associated with "culture," I adopt the concept of subjectivity in my analysis because it leads to questions of discourse, power, and history, and it facilitates an examination of a historically specific process of subject formation. In the discursive context of postsocialist development in China, these three statements register a dramatic rejection of the countryside as it is considered a field of death for the modern subjectivity desired by young women, who imagine the spaces of hope for such subjectivity to be somewhere else, in the city. What may appear in these statements to be desperate articulations of desire for a new, modern subjectivity encapsulates the ethos of the widespread longing among rural youth to "see the world" (*jian jian shi mian*), and the migration of these youth to the city both enables and is enabled by China's post-Mao efforts at "modernization" and accumulation.

Yet one cannot help noting in the women's comments that the imagining of a new, modern subjectivity is coupled with the idea of death, as expressed by the use of the terms *reincarnation* and *suicide*, as if violence were its necessary companion. Marx long ago revealed the contradiction inherent in primitive accumulation as simultaneously a process of laborers' emancipation from serfdom and guilds, and a history of expropriation and violence "written in the annals of mankind in letters of blood and fire" (1977: 875). But the unprecedented rural-to-urban migration involving more than a hundred million free laborers, whose labor power has fed the engine of China's post-Mao accumulation since the early 1980s, is not based on the forced expropriation of land, as described by Marx more than a century ago. It is, ironically, based on the distribution of once collectively owned and managed land to individual rural households for production and management. Rural reform — the reapportioning of collective land to individual peasant households as accounting units, known as the "household responsibility system" — was introduced as the first measure of China's post-Mao structural adjustment in the early 1980s. This political economy of land, seemingly opposed to the classical model of primitive accumulation, provided a necessary condition for unfettering the mass of peasant labor power to drive a neoliberal, flexible machine of accumulation.[2] It thus begs the following questions: how does the political economy of post-Mao China generate the conditions for a new carnival of accumulation, with its attendant contradiction of freedom and violence?[3] Why was the countryside in the 1990s often invoked by rural young women as a symbolic field of death compelling them to seek a modern subjectivity elsewhere? Pursuing these questions requires one to link the political economy of development and the processes of subjectivity formation, and to track the discursive conditions and contradictions embedded in the struggles and agonies of subaltern subjectivity.

To capture the epistemic discontinuity in rural women's migration before and after the post-Mao reforms, I compare and analyze two cohorts of rural women migrating in the late Mao era of the 1970s and in the post-Mao era of the 1980s–1990s. Although both cohorts are migrant wage laborers, their experiences have been shaped by two modernization projects that hinge on radically different forms of rural-urban relations. A comparative analysis serves two purposes. First, it seeks to reveal the radical shift in rural-urban relations that has impressed itself on rural young women's subjectivity. Second, it places my analysis in conversation with the anthropological discussion of modernities. The experiences of two cohorts of migrant women illustrate modernities in the plural, not in terms of essentialized cultures to argue for a Chinese brand of modernity, but in terms of historicity to examine the tension and discontinuity in social processes, and thus to offer a critique of the teleology of capitalist modernity that has become hegemonic in China and elsewhere.[4]

My interviews in Wuwei County in 1998 included 104 women in twelve villages in three townships. Eighty-eight women I interviewed had experienced migration, among whom fifty-nine had migrated on their own initiative, the rest having migrated with kin.[5] Thirteen were over forty years of age and had migrated by themselves before and during the 1970s. Seventy-five were between their late teens and early thirties, and had migrated at some point between the mid-1980s and the time of research.

"Rural Women," State, Patriarchy: A Small Exodus of Rural Women in the 1970s

Wuwei County lies in southeast Anhui Province, north of the Yangtze River, its southern border defined and often threatened by the river. A base for rice and cotton cultivation, Wuwei has 1.34 million *mu* (1 mu = 0.165 acre) of agricultural land and a rural population of 1.2 million, about 92 percent of its total population. Wuwei was once a base for the Communist New Fourth Army in its resistance against the Japanese during World War II. Local legend has it that some New Fourth Army officers left their young children in the care of local women during the war. Because of this connection, shortly after the founding of the People's Republic in 1949, some of these women were asked by veterans to continue to look after their children who had moved to Beijing. This established the link for later migration.[6] It is estimated that three to four thousand rural women from Wuwei had worked as domestics in the cities up to the 1970s (Wang Shucheng and Li Renhu 1996: 23).[7] In 1993 the number of rural Wuwei women migrants working as domestics reached 263,000.

During the Mao era, women in the countryside shouldered a double burden of gender and rural origins, and the patriarchy and the state played a role in the discursive construction of the subject position *nongcun funü* (rural women). Nevertheless, rural migrants of the period positively claimed a "rural woman" identity through their participation in agricultural labor and asserted that this identity was undiminished by their migration experiences.

Great Aunt was sixty-five years old when I met her in Beijing in 1999. Living with her son and daughter-in-law in a single-room house in the suburbs of Beijing, she looked after her one-year-old grandson and cooked for the young couple while they went out every day to sell processed chicken in the market. A mother of four children, Great Aunt had first come to Beijing from Wuwei more than twenty years before to work as a baomu. Sitting in the courtyard, she told me about her experiences of being a migrant, at one point describing her daily labor in the field and at home during the Maoist collective period.

At that time we had the production team leader and the accountant leading us. The leader blew his whistle, calling out, "Hurry up!" [to summon us to work]. Our production team leader at that time, how should I say it, was a single stick [unmarried]. After he went home and ate his meal, he was all done. But we had to take care of our children, wash them, and then cook. Every morning I got up before dawn: cooking breakfast, washing diapers, feeding the baby, cleaning around the house. I got up before sunrise. After the breakfast was cooked, I ate hurriedly. Then I had to wash rice and fetch water from the river. When I heard the call, I left for the field. Sometimes I hadn't got a chance to really finish eating myself, because I had to feed the baby first, right? And then during the work break, I would hurry home and cook rice for lunch. I got it boiling and almost done, and then I had to rush back to the field. It was the same thing when we came back home around noon. First we lit the stove. Then while the children's father [her husband] made lunch, I fed the youngest baby. After lunch, I would wash dishes and diapers, and then feed the baby again before leaving [for the field]. During the busy season like now [summer], we wouldn't come home until seven or eight o'clock. We worked endlessly, yet we didn't always have enough to eat.

Great Aunt spoke with excitement and sighs of frustration. She also remembered with a hearty smile how her fellow villagers in the production team remarked on her ability to carry full loads of sludge on a shoulder pole balanced above her slender "watersnake-like waist." She derived a certain pride and sense of heroism from this public recognition. She remembered the days of collective labor as bustling with communal activities in the field and in the village, with women's labor contribution publicly recognized and compensated in terms of work points, which gave women some standing in the public arena. In the post-Mao era, when "production responsibility" was contracted to each household, rural women in Great Aunt's village witnessed a loss of the limited ground they had gained in the public arena. With the demise of collective life, rural women's status substantially contracted, and the public sphere came to belong more exclusively to men.

With three small children, Great Aunt's family experienced food shortages during the collective era. To earn a bit more money, Great Aunt went to work for families in Beijing in the late 1970s. The predicament for rural women like Great Aunt during the Mao era was that they were subjected to the double postponement reflected in the discursive category of "rural woman" deployed by the state, whose political-economic policies were formulated to prioritize national industrialization.[8] The Mao-era state was determined to achieve rapid industrialization and nationwide accumulation, which it regarded as a necessary step toward resolving the material and technological gap between the countryside and the city and the "price scissors" (differential) between industrial and agricultural products.[9] In the meantime, to maximize the surplus of industrial output for accumulation and expanded reproduction, the state practiced price controls through a unified procurement system. This system established a state monopoly over surplus agricultural products and kept prices for agricultural products at a consistently low level.[10] The improvement of the peasantry's living standard was put on hold, although the leadership at the time did not imagine that the wait would be long.[11]

For rural women, this postponement was accompanied by a persistent, albeit sometimes restrained, patriarchy in the domestic division of labor and in the organization and rewarding of collective labor.[12] Thus, for peasant women like Great Aunt, the subject position of rural woman in the postliberation period was, on the one hand, highlighted by active participation in collective labor and surplus production for the state's industrialization and, on the other hand, marked by a continuation, although constrained, of the patriarchal structure that circumscribed the nature and value of women's labor. Certainly the gender politics in the Mao era that based gender liberation and equality on women's participation in public labor enabled women like Great Aunt to draw a new sense of pride from their active performance in collective labor.[13] The liberation of women from the burden of housework, however, was expected to be realized through the eventual socialization and mechanization of domestic labor rather than by challenging the gendered division of labor. One may argue that the surplus labor performed by a woman — on top of her own participation in public labor — to put food on the table to enable her husband's full participation in production mirrored the peasantry's contribution of surplus labor to enable the nation's accumulation and industrialization. The final liberation of "rural women" from their burdens was presumed to be contingent on further industrialization, which was to make the expansion of urban-based industrialization all the more compelling in the national agenda and women's labor contribution all the more necessary. Postponement was thus a matter of awaiting the improvement of technology and socialization rather than recognized as a discursive practice.[14]

Writing of the genealogy of *funü* (women) as the principal subject position available to women in Chinese socialism, Tani Barlow argues that "the Revolution restituted *funü*/women inside *guojia*/state (and thus by synechdochic logic, inside *jiatiing*/family) under Maoist inscription" (1991a: 132). Although the discourse of funü was briefly open to a range of heterogeneous subject positions in the early communist base — the Jiangxi Soviet (1930–34) — and it taught and mobilized women to constitute their interest with the state rather than with the family, the gender praxis of the party in the 1940s and in the socialist period at times restituted women in reformed familial relations (ibid.: 145). Reflecting on feminist researchers' critiques that China's revolution did not deliver gender equality, Ann Anagnost questions the relationship

THE EMACIATION OF THE RURAL

between the state and women in socialist gender discourse: "This is not to say that the state's concern for women is not genuine, but the relationship between the ideologies of kinship and the state as they have emerged over the several centuries are so interwoven that their disarticulation was perhaps never a conscious goal of China's revolution" (1989: 317). Although their participation in collective labor and the recognition of their labor contribution in the form of work points accorded rural women a visibility for their work and a limited degree of equality (Davin 1975), the continued presence of the patriarchal structure defined the work performed by women as *nei* (inside) and hence categorically worth fewer points than the work performed by men, which was deemed *wai* (outside) (Harrell 2000; Jacka 1997). During the time of collective labor in Wuwei villages, as elsewhere, the highest number of work points for a male laborer was ten per day, whereas the highest possible number for a female laborer was typically eight, even when she performed the same task as a man. Besides taking part in collective labor, a married woman still shouldered most domestic labor in a family whose head (*jiazhang*) was most often her husband.

It was, then, perhaps no coincidence that in the radical years of the Cultural Revolution (1966–76), the proto-image of women's liberation found in female youth groups, the Iron Girl teams, focused on enthusiastic participation in public labor.[15] The sprouting across the nation of Iron Girl groups, which were modeled after a group of rural adolescent girls of the Dazhai production brigade, became a sign of the liberated productivity of Chinese women outside the domestic closure, on whose base gender equality was claimed (Honig and Hershatter 1988). The rise of the Iron Girls to legendary national honor and prominence displaced and obliterated the funü, who was situated in reformed patriarchal domestic relations, who was working under a double burden, and whose contribution to collective labor was less valued than that of a man.[16] Aunt Lu, who is related to Great Aunt and who also went to Beijing in the late 1970s, came of age during the Cultural Revolution, when she was an activist in the youth performance troupe organized in her village to heighten and cheer on villagers' participation in politics and production. She went to Beijing several years after she married, after her first child was born. In her narrative she portrayed herself as a spirited activist, dynamic and mobile in her community during her teens, and as a burdened woman after she married and became a mother. "You could not have guessed that I was once very active in the village performance troupe, could you?" she asked me, with a trace of nostalgia in her voice. Aunt Lu's question cannot be reduced to a personal nostalgia for her youth. The phrase "you could not have guessed" alerted me to the disjuncture between her life as an activist young woman and her life as a burdened married woman, a disjuncture that was social.

It was in the context of this disjuncture between rural youth and married women and of the double burden borne by married women that there occurred a small exodus of women out of Wuwei to big cities, where they worked as domestics and sought redress by their own means of the problems posed for rural women by the discursive and material practices of the socialist period. Great Aunt left the village for Beijing to get more return for her doubly undervalued agricultural labor, undervalued once by the state as "peasant" labor and again by the patriarchal social structure as "woman's" labor. Almost all of the rural Wuwei women who went to work as domestics in the cities in the 1970s, the late period of the Mao era, were already married and had children. Most of them were illiterate or semi-illiterate. In the 1970s the monthly wage for a domestic was between 18 and 25 yuan (roughly US$10–14). At a time when the annual household income for a peasant family was about 100 to 200 yuan a year, migrant women's earnings were an important subsidy to the family economy.[17]

Yet the income contribution of these women was socially circumscribed, as it was vaguely but palpably associated with the socially transgressive meanings of this particular form of labor. The phrase used to refer to working for a wage as a domestic is *zai ren jia bang gong* (helping out in someone else's home), and it is sometimes uttered with a slightly detectable tinge of embarrassment by such workers themselves. They use these words only when they have to. When they do, their voices seem to lose their usual substantiality and become a bit uncertain. Once the context is established, they tend to use *na* (that) to substitute for the phrase.

Where is the source of the shame that makes these women somewhat embarrassed to speak of their labor? If this shame circumscribed the articulation of the migration experiences of married women, it made it almost unthinkable for unmarried women to migrate before the early 1980s. It is in contemplating the unthinkable that one gets close to understanding the construction of

THE EMACIATION OF THE RURAL

shame. When I asked the head of women's work in a township government in Wuwei why no young women "went out" in the 1970s, and why the small number who did were all married, she replied, "At that time people's minds were closed [*fengbi*] and feudal [*fengjian*]. If girls had gone out, they would have had problems in getting married." When I posed a similar question to a male intellectual based in the provincial capital, himself from rural Anhui, he responded, "Men would find it a problem because they would think, 'How can you serve others before you serve me first?'" The "others" he referred to were men outside the patrilineal descent group and the patrilocal community. A young woman's chastity was not just a matter of sexual purity but was also expressed by the bounded location of her labor performance within the local patriarchy.[18] If a woman performed labor by herself away from kin and home, the sphere of local patriarchy, her chastity could have been called into question because it could not be locally controlled. By performing her paid domestic labor for other people, particularly other men, it was as if she had "prostituted" her labor, challenging her husband's first-order claim to her domestic labor.

These women also experienced a vague sense of shame on the urban front: they embodied a trace of the past in the socialist present. Although the state approved the employment of domestic service for the high-ranking cadres and intellectual elite throughout much of the Mao period, such employment potentially signified a specter of class associated with the old society. The specter of the old society embodied in such employment was the very point of attack by rebels in the Cultural Revolution against the bourgeois lifestyle of high-rank officials. Although the state indirectly paid domestics by allocating an allowance for such employment in high-ranking cadres' salaries, it never attempted to incorporate this service openly into the socialist relations of production and to make domestics into state or collective employees. Domestics were also seen by the state and urban society as attached to the employer family and were not integrated into neighborhood life. Instead, hiring and firing were carried out in the private domestic sphere of employers, invisible from the public relations of production. In the context of urban women's unprecedented participation in public labor in factories, schools, hospitals, department stores, and so on, enabled by the socialist discourse of women's liberation, the small number of rural women in the city working as domestics, who appeared and disappeared now and then around the corners of the residential alleys, could not fit into the new subject position for women produced by that discourse. They were like fragments of the old society within socialism, whose presence was somewhat incongruent with the grand view of public labor and women's liberation, and whose discursive value was their awkward connection with the old society through domestic service.

In both the city and the countryside these rural migrant women were transgressors. In the countryside they had transgressed the sphere of local patriarchy and thus raised anxiety about their gendered personhood; in the city they were transgressors of the proper subject position of "rural woman" as defined by the heroism of agricultural labor, and they invoked the specter of the past through domestic service. These notions of transgression and contamination thus constituted a vague source of shame for these women—vague because it was caught uneasily between the state ideology of women's liberation and the continued presence of patriarchal power that defined what a proper woman was through the spatial circumscription of her labor. In attempting to get a higher return for their labor via migration, these women found themselves in the cornered space produced by a triangulation of discourses: the undervaluation of "rural women's" agricultural labor, the circumscriptive power of local patriarchy to define the propriety of their labor, and the invisibility of domestic service in state discourse.

The state failed to grant these women a subject position from which they could speak back to the local patriarchy about their labor. The state thus colluded with local patriarchy in marking the position of rural migrant women as unclear and unclean, or *bu qingshuang* (beyond interpretive clarity), as one village man put it. The money a woman earned and brought home could be denigrated by her husband or others as bu qingshuang. Women's domestic labor performed outside the proper field of the local patriarchy's gaze therefore seemed to lack discursive accountability, rendering these women ambiguous in personhood.[19] And women could not speak for themselves in this discourse. On the one hand, within the state discourse, rural women could not "speak bitterness" about the double burden piled on their backs and about the double undervaluation of their labor. On the other hand, within the discourse of local patriarchy, these women found it shameful to speak bitterness about their paid domestic service in the cities. The women I interviewed often sighed when reminiscing about their migration: "If it had not been so hard at home, who would have wanted to take the suffering outside?" One woman in her late forties ended her narrative with tears in her eyes: "It's bitter to be outside. Yet with the bitterness we took outside, it is also embarrassing [literally, 'it also makes me look ugly'] to speak of it at home" [*zai wai mian shou de ku, hui lai jiang hai chou*]. The embarrassment in their narratives was counterbalanced by assertions of their contributions to the family economy and by detailed and sometimes sobbing descriptions of how lonely it was to be in the city and how much they worried about their young children at home. Through such recitations, they assertively located the place of their belonging and their identity in the family and the community.

Great Aunt continued to work in Beijing after land distribution to her household in the early 1980s, because her family needed her income to purchase agricultural tools and, later, fertilizer and pesticide to carry out production, and to pay for her children's increased tuition. She later returned to Wuwei and stayed at home for three or four years. In 1993 she once again migrated to Beijing with her son and daughter-in-law, to help them with their domestic work and to look after her grandson. Unlike Great Aunt, most of the early migrant women returned home after decollectivization, when their labor was needed to farm the land distributed to their households. When I was in Wuwei, seventy-six-year-old Grandmother Four, who had found for a number of Wuwei women, including Great Aunt and Aunt Lu, employment in Beijing as domestics in the 1970s, returned to her village for good, having worked as a domestic in Beijing since 1951. When I asked Grandmother Four and several other women whether they found themselves changed after working in the city such that it was perhaps difficult to get back to rural life, they replied, "We didn't have a comfortable life [*xiangfu*] when we were working outside. Why wouldn't we be happy to return to [village life]?" Grandmother Four described returning to her village as a homecoming. The woman in her late forties who was embarrassed at having spoken bitterness as a former domestic worker replied to my question as she picked up her shoulder pole, preparing to leave for the field, "I'm farming twenty mu of land with my husband.[20] Had I changed, how could I have done this?" By giving rhetorical answers to my question, these women subtly contested its legitimacy and affirmed their continued identity as "rural women"—undiminished by their migrancy— proudly demonstrating their linkage with rural life and agricultural labor and production. In fact, I was made to feel that my question was quite improper and misplaced. Perhaps by affirming their "rural woman" subject position so forcefully, they tried to render any questioning about their identity and personhood illegitimate and irrelevant, including questioning from the circumscriptive power of local patriarchy.

The Rise of the City and the Emaciation of the Countryside in Post-Mao Modernity

In Wuwei it is generally acknowledged that young rural women in the 1980s were the pathbreakers for a migration in the 1990s that involved an army of over 200,000 men and women from the county, making Wuwei one of the most active labor-exporting counties in Anhui. Rural young women in Wuwei are credited with inspiring the migration of their menfolk, who saw work opportunities through the information that young women circulated home. The intensification of the work pace and the emphasis on increasing productivity brought on by the urban reforms increased urban demand for paid domestic service. A rhyme circulating in Beijing in the 1980s highlighted Wuwei as the single most important source of domestic workers in the capital: "Beijing baomu chu Anhui, Anhui baomu chu Wuwei" (Baomu in Beijing are from Anhui, baomu from Anhui are from Wuwei).[21] The media in Anhui are fond of contrasting the motivations of those migrating before and after the post-Mao reforms: the older generation sought "survival"; those in the younger generation seek "wealth and knowledge" because their minds have been enlivened and activated (*sixiang huoyue*) by the reforms.[22] Released as "surplus labor" by the breakup of collective farming, young women can now respond to the urban labor market through "push–pull" mechanisms. This interpretation by the media and mainstream scholarship celebrates an epistemic shift from the Mao era to the post-Mao era and an ontological rectification that finally steers the nation onto the normal path to Progress. Just as primitive accumulation was perceived by Marx's bourgeois economist contemporaries only as a form of freedom, the current labor migration is frequently and predominantly perceived by the liberal media and mainstream scholarship as a process in which the individual comes into her own in post-Mao modernity.

Although the post-Mao cities have a tremendous appetite for the cheap labor of young migrants, the presence of large numbers of "low-quality" strangers in big cities has also ignited tremendous anxiety among residents there about the ambiguity and excess of migrants' movements. Migrants are viewed as "blind drifters" (*mang liu*) and "errant waters" (Solinger 1999: 1) that require social control.[23] The figure of the migrant thus functions as a sign calling for a new approach to governance in the post-Mao market economy. Another discursive dimension developed in the mid- to late 1990s, with a significant contribution by some liberal scholars, toward a view of the migrants' movement as a desirable form of labor flexibility and of the migrants themselves as the foremost flexible individual agents of the expanding, ascending, but capricious market economy. This positive perception was offset by a new angst over the lack of such flexibility among the growing number of unemployed urban workers shed by the restructured state-owned enterprises. New social value has thus been invested in the sign of the migrant in contrast with its new negative double, the laid-off urban worker, just as the "dynamic" market economy, growing in volume and volubility, is positively paired against the "inflexible" planned economy.

Rather than framing migration as "individuals" responding to "push-pull" forces, I interpret it as a troubled process of subject formation for rural youth, particularly rural young women, in the reconfigured rural-urban relationship of post-Mao development discourse. The discursive context in which rural young women found themselves in the 1980s and 1990s represents an epistemic shift from that of their forerunners. Migrant young women from time to time opened their stories to me with a despondent judgment of their situation: "There is no way out in the countryside" (*zai nongcun meiyou chulu*). Post-Mao development has reconfigured the rural-urban relationship in its imagining of modernity.

The rural-urban relationship has figured quite differently in the modernization projects of the Mao and post-Mao eras, with Mao-era modernization based on the improvement of national self-sufficiency and post-Mao modernity defined as the nation's reinsertion into the global capitalist market. In the Mao era, cities, especially the former treaty ports, did not occupy an ideological high ground as the privileged locus of production and industrialization, resulting in a characterization of the Mao era by some scholars as anti-urban. Shortly after the Chinese Communist Party (CCP) took over the cities from its rural bases, the Maoist development strategy was implemented to integrate the cities into the national agenda of accumulation and industrialization and to quickly transform decadent, squandering, colonial consumer cities (*xiaofei chengshi*) into hardworking, purposeful production cities (*shengchan chengshi*) (Kirkby 1985: 14–15). Investment and planning policies de-emphasized the growth of cities and avoided focusing resources on existing cities, especially large coastal cities (Naughton 1995: 61). The Great Leap Forward (1958–60) marked a shift away from Soviet-style central planning to reliance on populist enthusiasm in both cities and countryside to move toward the realization of communist society, with the rural "People's Commune" carrying the vital agency (Kirkby 1985: 5).[24] During that period, small-scale industries in the rural communes took precedence over large-scale Soviet-style urban factories (Buck 1984: 5). The "Third Front" construction (1965–71) saw a massive relocation and construction of defense industries in remote interior provinces for national-security reasons, allowing a more balanced distribution of industry throughout the country (Ma and Wei 1997: 219–21). The new oil city of Daqing was touted by the government as a socialist utopian city: a ruralized city or urbanized village, integrating rural, industrial, and residential sectors within its bounds (Lo 1986: 446–47). In the period of the Cultural Revolution the countryside figured as the ideological high ground, functioning as a vast classroom where sent-down urban youth could be reacquainted with the revolutionary spirit of the peasantry. In those radical years the Dazhai Brigade was promoted as the national model and, as Richard Kirkby observes, "It was the farms rather than the factories that dominated the self-advertisements of Cultural Revolution China" (1985: 5). Although scholars debate whether the development policies of the socialist period signified an anti-urbanism (e.g., Kam Wing Chan 1994; Kirkby 1985; Naughton 1995), there seems to be agreement that the development policies at that time unlinked the symbiotic connection between industrialization and the privileges assumed by the city in liberal market economies; both the cities and the countryside were enveloped in "hard struggle, plain living" (*jianku pusu*).

The rural population perceived the difference between the countryside and the city as that between peasants and workers (Potter 1983), which was expressed in their different sources of "rice." Workers in the state-owned industries ate state rice; they were guaranteed food rations and other essentials by the state. Peasants, on the other hand, had to work for their own rice and had limited medical care and educational facilities supported by the production collective.[25] Note the equation of the city with workers during the Mao period. The city signified a secure and desired welfare in the arms of the state; it was also a site associated with modern industrial production.[26] In the post-Mao development strategy that reorganized the relationship between city and countryside, the city commanded a different signifying power for rural young women.

The post-Mao policies of "reform and opening" (*gaige kaifang*) usher in a new form of modernity based on the nation's insertion into the global capitalist economy. The remarkable increase of foreign direct investment in China, the growth of exports from China to the world market, and the rapid expansion of the service sector are underpinned by China's access to cheap migrant labor. This economic reorientation and restructuring underlies the process by which the rural is emaciated in relation to the urban telos. This post-Mao shift in rural-urban relations—the rise of the city and the emaciation of the rural—has taken place in economic, ideological, and cultural dimensions.[27]

Beginning with the Third Plenary Session of the Eleventh Central Committee of the CCP in 1978, the cities began to emerge as the engines of economic growth, occupying the central place in the post-Mao development discourse of constructing a commodity economy (*shangpin jingji*), marking a radical departure from the Maoist policy line. This switch from "production city" to "entrepreneurial city" in China's development strategy (Solinger 1993) paralleled what David Harvey (1989b) has described as a recent transformation in advanced capitalism from "managerial cities" (managing social services) into "entrepreneurial cities" (fostering investment and development)—a transformation of urban governance corresponding to the new logic of flexible accumulation. In 1980 the Chinese government established four Special Economic Zones (SEZs) along the coast to attract foreign investment (a move that may be criticized as a return of the colonial "treaty ports"), and in 1984 an additional fourteen coastal cities were promoted to SEZ status. The system of "key cities" (*zhongdian chengshi*) began in 1981 to allow a special class of fifteen cities (seventeen in 1982) access to a concentration of resources, more autonomy in decision making, and expansion of their commodity economy. In a speech in December 1982 Premier Zhao Ziyang made one of "ten great principles for the development of the economy" reliance on big cities to construct economic centers (Solinger 1993: 208). As Kirkby observed about this tendency toward agglomeration, "There is no reluctance to admit that the chief purpose of this arrangement would be to strengthen the hierarchy of cities and regions. The prevailing view amongst China's economists today is that the institutionalising of such inequalities will accelerate national economic growth" (1985: 225). Beginning in 1983, the administrative hierarchy was restructured so that cities were free from the prefectural government (*qu*) to administer directly their surrounding counties (*shi guan xian*) and their agricultural and peasant labor resources (Kam Wing Chan 1994: 105).

Along with this economic and administrative restructuring, the city has also been renewed as the privileged space of modern civilization or civility (*xiandai wenming*), gesturing toward elusive capital and development.[28] In this discourse, it appears that Modernity and Progress, themselves post-Mao ideological constructs, are given their permanent residence in the city. As Louisa Schein observes, "The city, however conceived, has become an object of increasingly intense desire in the era of reform" (2001: 225). A directive was issued in 1978 channeling 5 percent of the total profits of all urban industrial and commercial enterprises into housing, roads, and other urban infrastructure projects (Buck 1984: 9). Whereas previously all such funds had been distributed to state-owned factories for reinvestment, this new tax money given to the city fueled an urban construction boom beginning in the early 1980s. At the same time, cities also saw a campaign for urban beautification (*meihua chengshi*), with special attention to parks, landscaping, and cleanliness (Buck 1984). Planning of key cities received unprecedented attention. The urban planning of Beijing was attended by four directives from the CCP Central Committee in early 1980. C. P. Lo compares urban planning before and after 1978: "Obviously, a strong emphasis is now placed on the individual character of the city, modernity and the improved livelihood of the people, which contrasts consciously with the uniformity, frugality, and anti-consumerism objectives of the 1950s and 1960s" (1986: 448–49). The urban beautification campaign paralleled the *wujiang simei* (five advances and four beautifications) campaign by targeting urban citizens as subjects of modern civility. It did so through what Foucault termed "biopower," operating on each citizen's language (*yuyan mei*), behavior (*xingwei mei*), mind (*xinling mei*), and agency in improving the urban environment (*huanjing mei*) through the citizen's advancement in levels of civility (*jiang wenming*), etiquette (*jiang limao*), hygiene (*jiang weisheng*), scientific outlook (*jiang kexue*), and morality (*jiang daode*).

At the same time that the city occupied the high ground in the state's development strategy, agriculture's share in state capital investment plunged.[29] State capital investment in agriculture was 7.1 percent in 1953–57, 11.3 percent in 1958–60, 17.6 percent in 1963–65, 10.7 percent in 1966–70, 9.8 percent in 1971–75, and 10.5 percent in 1976–980. It dropped to 5 percent in 1981–85 and further to 3.3 percent in 1985–90 (Kam Wing Chan 1994: 61). Between 1979 and 1990, total state capital investment increased 240 percent from 50.1 billion to 107.3 billion yuan, but investment in agriculture increased only 34 percent from 5.33 billion to 7.04 billion yuan. In the overall picture agriculture's share of capital investment dropped from 10.6 percent in 1979 to 4.1 percent in 1990, and again to 2.8 percent in 1992 and 1.7 percent in 1994 (Li Zuojun 2000: 41), remaining below 2 percent throughout the 1990s. For a brief period between 1979 and 1984, there was a significant increase in agricultural production and rural income, inspired by the rural reform, particularly the raising of procurement prices for agricultural goods and the relaxed state monopoly on agricultural products, but rural income has stagnated since the mid-1980s.[30] The prices for fertilizers and pesticides increased by 43 percent and 82.3 percent in 1985 (over 1983 prices) because of their marketization. The state also lowered procurement prices in 1985 by 28 percent below those of 1984. In 1998 the income from growing one mu of rice was only around 200–300 yuan, and from one mu of cotton around 500 yuan.[31] According to internal government statistics, the Gini coefficient for rural and urban incomes had reached 0.59 in 2002, beyond the 0.4 danger level.[32] A rural township party secretary in Wuwei admitted openly that agricultural production had stagnated since the mid-1980s. Although the urban-rural income disparity narrowed between 1978 and 1985, the gap began to widen again after 1985 and was larger in the 1990s than before 1978 (Li Zuojun 2000: 32–33; World Bank 1997: 15–17). In the meantime, the limited welfare and medical care supported by the production collectives (production team and brigade) were dismantled when production became privatized with the rural reform.[33]

The material production of the countryside as a wasteland in the economic strategy of state investment is symbiotic with the ideological construction of the countryside as a wasteland of "backwardness" and "tradition." To borrow from Walter Benjamin, one might say that "tradition," negatively defined against modernization and development, is a signifier whose signified cannot be fixed, growing like the "piling of wreckage upon wreckage" that the storm of Progress keeps hurling back as its antithesis (1992: 249). China's opening toward Western culture and overseas investment not only opened a new vision of modernity but also furnished a new frame of reference that has reorganized narratives and interpretations of history. The euphoric meaning of the present, previously derived from the present's juxtaposition with the pre-liberation past, vanishes and is now displaced by an urgent sense of crisis when the elite and educated youth refract the gaze of the West to see peasant China as "backward and poor."[34] As a mother commented in the 1980s on how urban youth look at the present, "Instead of comparing China with what it was like before liberation, they contrast it with Japan and the West. They don't appreciate how much better things are now than they were in the old society" (Hooper 1985: 35).

The urban telos appropriates the rural into its system of representation by devalorizing the rural as its moribund other. The 1980s discourse of enlightenment, epitomized in the iconoclastic TV series *Heshang* (Deathsong of the River), links China's backwardness with its agrarian roots and the peasant mentality of its population (Bodman 1991). In the post-Mao cities it has become a crude joke to call someone *nongmin* (peasant), a sign most potently suggesting ignorance (*yumei*), backwardness (*luohou*), and a dire lack of civility (*bu wenming*). The rural base, previously a revolutionary site transforming the petit-bourgeois intellectuals in both the Yan'an period (1936–47) and the Cultural Revolution, is now the deathbed of Chinese tradition.[35] *Heshang* urges intellectuals to fulfill their historical agency in the task of national regeneration. Critiquing *Heshang*, Jing Wang observes that tradition and, synonymously, the countryside are not treated as "an autonomous system of representations" but become "derivative" when they are evaluated in a new epistemology in which a hostile modernity has appeared as dominant and unmarked (1996: 130). The discourse of enlightenment, reconstructing the countryside as the wasteland of tradition while development policies opened up the coastal cities as special portals for overseas connections and investment, harkens back to a semicolonial discourse of the early twentieth century that similarly produced the city and the countryside as the two poles of a primary contradiction in its modernization project. Tani Barlow (1991b) points out that both old and new nationalist enlightenment projects borrowed the authority and power of an imagined Western (read: universal) modernity and produced remarkably similar representations of "Chinese tradition."

The emaciation of the rural is much more deeply articulated in the relationship between peasants and land in many rural areas, where the land of production has practically become a land of subsistence (*bao kouliang*). Labor migration from the countryside to the cities is termed by scholars and the Chinese government as "the transfer of surplus rural labor power" (*nongcun shengyu laodongli zhuanyi*), but the irony is that the migrants, rather than being "surplus" labor, consist mostly of better-educated rural youth, that is, those who are most needed for innovative agricultural production. Those who stay behind to continue farming constitute what is often called the "773861 army": "77" refers to the old (i.e., 77 year olds); "38" refers to women, typically married women ("38" is March 8, International Women's Day); and "61" refers to children (June 1, International Children's Day).[36] In rural areas of Anhui and other provinces, the exodus has caused the de facto abandonment of land (*paohuang*), which has raised alarms.[37] In Wuwei it is common for peasant households to plant only once instead of twice a year, for which the local term is "half abandoning" (*ban paohuang*) or "covert abandoning" (*yinxing paohuang*). Unlike in the early 1980s, grain production has stopped raising incomes. Most people I interviewed said that they farm just for basic subsistence. Private enterprises, domestic and transnational, draw millions of able-bodied migrants to work in sweatshop conditions with no insurance protection. The injured, the debilitated, the ill, and the unemployed are thrown back to the countryside each year in the tens of thousands.[38] The countryside has become a reservoir releasing and absorbing labor according to the capricious needs of the market, supplying a flexible army of migrant laborers for a carnival of accumulation in which Chinese and transnational businesses share in the banquet of profits.[39] When and where the migrant worker wage cannot sustain reproduction of the next generation in the city, such reproduction is carried out in the countryside. The land distributed to each household by the rural reform in the early 1980s was designed to spur agricultural productivity through privatizing production, but in the 1990s production land became welfare land absorbing ill, injured, and unemployed bodies and enabling a cheap reproduction of the next generation of migrant workers. The process of emaciation is a process of violence that appropriates economic, cultural, and ideological value from the countryside, where rural youth can no longer find a path to the future.

The Domestication of Youth and the Conundrum of *Zuoren* (Having a Personhood)

> People [*dajia*, referring to migrants, including the speaker herself] don't understand, but people escape from the countryside like fleeing from death. This really is worth analysis. Why is it like this to such an extent? Even if we die, we want to die outside! It's not that we don't miss home. We miss home. Time and again, we return home, but time and again we come back out. It's not a single person doing this, but a whole generation. Coming out is to meet suffering [*zao zui*], but [we] still want to come out, knowing that there is almost no hope [outside]. (A veteran migrant woman from Jiangsu)

The post-Mao discourse of modernity thus produces the countryside both materially and ideologically as a wasteland stripped of state investment and inhabited by moribund tradition, with the two dimensions mutually reinforcing each other. If Modernity and Progress reside in the city, and if the city monopolizes modern culture, then the countryside is the city's emaciated other. It is in this discursive context that the countryside cannot function as the locus of a modern identity for rural young women, and it is in this context that I interpret the despondent remark "There is no way out in the countryside" to mean "There is no path to modernity in the countryside." As Anthony J. Cascardi argues, "The culture of modernity is given shape as a divided whole that can only be unified through the powers of an abstract subject, or its political analogue, the autonomous state. Indeed . . . the state . . . provides the means through which the divided subjects of modernity can be made whole" (quoted in Lydia H. Liu 1993: 171). Yet one also needs to be attentive to what happens when the post-Mao era severs the Mao-era discursive linkage between rural youth and the state—especially the linkage to rural young women, which used to be the ideological icon of Iron Girls.

What is at issue here is not simply how bad rural life is for young women and how much better urban life is. What is critical is how the ideological and material rise of the city and the emaciation of the rural reorganize how rural youth imagine the future and modernity. To explore this, I analyze the experiences of two young women who went to Beijing, one from Henan and one from Shandong. The narrative of one woman is drawn from my own interview data, whereas the story of the other was published in the magazine *Nongjianü baishitong* (Rural Women Knowing All) (Xie Lihua 1995), a forum where many rural young women have submitted first-person narratives about their experiences in the city. I choose these two cases for three reasons: first, I find that their narratives reinforce the data I have collected from my interviews in Wuwei; second, their narratives demonstrate common problems facing many rural young women today, despite the women's different origins; third, these two young women are particularly reflective and articulate about the problems shared by many.[40] In addition, I selected the narrative published in *Nongjianü baishitong* as a sample of migrant women's self-documentation.

Liu Li's Narrative: Leaving Home

I remember that day to be the 13th. My elder cousin would accompany me to the county bus station. My younger brother stood by the door of our house. I was so saddened that I felt like crying. Tears fell, but I didn't turn my head around. My parents were weeping too. They didn't approve of my leaving home. I'm one of the two junior-high graduates among the girls of my age in the village, and I'm the first one in my village to be a migrant. I came with four girls from other villages. My family's economic situation is not good and I want to help out.[41] People in my village do not allow their daughters to come out. They say that girls who go out will become bad, just like those women on TV.[42] My aunt, my mother's younger sister, who lives near the county seat, helped me persuade my mother, "What era are we in now? Still so old-fashioned and feudal?"[43] But people in my village just think that after daughters grow up, parents should find them a mother-in-law's family [*po jia*].[44] So the parents would save money and prepare new clothes and things like that [for a wedding]. Then there is the marriage and childbirth and raising the family. Just like that. They just think this way. Very feudal. But I don't think this way. I don't want to get married this early. I don't want to be like my parents—their life is going nowhere. . . . What matters to me is that I want to achieve something. I want to live like a human [*huo de xiang ge ren yang*].

"Rural youth" live awkwardly and uncomfortably in the post-Mao era, trapped as modern subjects in a space in, but not of, the culture of modernity. Almost all of the fifty-nine young women migrants I interviewed in Wuwei left home on their own initiative, and almost half of them (twenty-six) did not have their parents' approval to migrate, at least initially. Although some of them were able to change their parents' minds, a fair portion of them simply fled home (*tou pao*), often with friends. Since the post–Cultural Revolution educational reform emphasizing "professionalization" (*zhuanyehua*), schooling, in conjunction with mass media, teaches rural youth to yearn for a resplendent future of urban modern subjectivity.[45] Whatever their educational attainments, the young women of Wuwei overwhelmingly cited as their reason for migrating the fact that everyday life at home was *meijin* (inert) and *meiyisi* (meaningless or boring). They usually did not elaborate on this assessment, seeming to imply that rural life was so devoid of content and meaning that it could offer nothing for description. The description "inert and meaningless" was also given to me as a self-evident reality in the discursive context of rural-urban relations—the city is where everything happens, whereas the rural constitutes only a lack.

In his study of urban Japanese life in the 1920s and 1930s, Harry Harootunian argues that "rather than being an inert experience of facts, everyday life was increasingly seen as the site that revealed symptoms of societies' deepest conflicts and aspirations" (2000: 69). The aspirations of Liu Li and many other young Wuwei women conflict with their experience of everyday life in the post-Mao countryside as a site of inertness—"inert experience" should be taken not as a natural, given fact, but as a product of the discourse of modernity itself, which has redefined "peasant" and rural life in both material and ideological aspects. The inertness and meaninglessness of rural life was expressed by Liu Li as a series of activities setting a young woman on her predictable path of reproduction: "Then there is marriage and childbirth and raising the family." A published letter authored by a young rural woman in 1980 (*Qingnian xinxiang* 1980: 1–2) articulates her strong sense of incredulity that life holds no more for her than reproduction: "My friends tell me not to

THE EMACIATION OF THE RURAL

think about it—this is life in the countryside. It's simply a matter of eating and sleeping, getting married, establishing a household, having children. Is this really how I must pass my life?" (Hooper 1985: 28). Her questions were also a grievance, as she hoped for a reply that would denounce the reality she described. The question was not posed to any individual but to "the abstract subject or its political analogue, the autonomous state," in Cascardi's terms. I interpret the question, implicitly, as follows: where is rural youth's position in and connection to modernity? Where is modernity located for rural young women? Liu Li, in the late 1990s, still struggled with the same question and was determined to locate her life's meaning elsewhere.

Since decollectivization, rural youth have been marginalized in agrarian relations of production, and everyday life entails what might be termed the "domestication of youth." Apart from the three to eleven years they spend in school, young Wuwei women are confined within the domestic sphere, typically helping with household chores but not working in the field. Their parents take care of the farming. Most of the young women I interviewed had never had firsthand experience in agriculture.[46] Whereas during the Mao era rural youth, including rural young women, actively participated in farming and were mobilized for collective projects such as building dikes along the Yangtze River, repairing water-control and irrigation systems, and taking part in performance troupes, since decollectivization they have been domesticated and subjected to parental authority, which has replaced the production team as authority of labor management. The discursive connection between rural youth and the state, embodied in the heroic agency of the Iron Girls, has also been severed. The "inert and meaningless" life in rural young women's narratives today contrasts with narratives of older migrants about their dynamic and bustling lives as young unmarried women in the Maoist collective era.

"Life is just so boring," commented one young man in Henan Province through the magazine *Youth Letterbox* in 1982 (*Qingnian xinxiang* 1982: 30). "There's hardly ever a film. There is just no entertainment. There's nothing to do but wander around the village. What can be done about it?" (Hooper 1985: 28). The only village cinema that I saw in my field site, once the best-looking public building in the village, now stands in desolation from long disuse. The villager who had served as the production team's film projectionist has become a migrant himself, along with his wife. My observation in rural Wuwei coincides with that of C. F. Mobo Gao in rural Jiangxi that "there is no longer any focal point for public life in the village" (1999: 174). Young women's migration could therefore be interpreted as an escape from and resistance to this domestication of youth, by which they embark on an adventurous journey into the space of modernity to fashion a new identity for themselves.

Domestication for many rural young women forebodes an imminent snare that threatens to seal them off from the possibility of a modern identity. Domestication in their natal homes delivers them into their future households through engagement and marriage, trapping them in a snare in which a married woman's place and activity of identity is typically described as "moving around the stove" (*weizhe guotai zhuan*). Youth is thus the only possible crevice in the lifecycle through which a rural woman might take a leap to create a modern identity and rearrange her life. My informants often said that "everything is finished once a woman is married." The sociologist Tan Shen similarly observes how gender defines marriage expectations for men and women in rural China: "According to the gender roles in a traditional marriage, a man's marriage prospect depends largely on his individual achievement . . . but for a woman, the gender role 'designated' for her in a traditional marriage has almost nothing to do with her individual achievement. Her development is to a great extent restrained by her marriage. For many women, marriage means the ending of individual development" (1997: 45). "Youth" is therefore a strategic site for action. The better-educated young women experienced this domestication with greater shock and angst. Liu Li left home not only to help her parents but also because she felt she was in danger of losing the possibility of having a (modern) personhood (*huo de xiang ge ren yang*). Some, echoing Xiazi, articulate the problem as a matter of life and death.

"Rural youth" is itself a modern notion. As Lefebvre writes, "The young man, as a stage in man's youth, is a creation of modern times" (1995: 157). The term *qingnian* (youth) emerged in the late imperial period to refer to boys of gentry and merchant families who enjoyed relative freedom from conventional social obligations and could pursue an emergent modern bourgeois life (Levy 1968). In the early twentieth century, it was through rebellion against the authority of the family, as in Ba Jin's *Jia* (Family) (1972), that elite youth produced by modern education and social movements became conscious of youth as a new social agency. Qingnian, like funü (woman) and nongmin (peasant), belongs to what Barlow (1991a) calls "a discursive constellation" of modern categories by which the Maoist party-state sought to bring particular political subjects into existence and to reorganize social relationships. Displacing the authority of the family, the party-state became the source of reference by which youth could produce and realize their agency. In the communist movement in the 1940s, qingnian expanded from elite boys to include young men and women in the liberated areas. Being the slave of a slave, the subaltern of a subaltern, the young peasant woman has been a particularly important site for party mobilization through her liberation—a process of her transformation from a subaltern in the patriarchal family and old class society into an elated new subject of the party-state.[47] The classic revolutionary opera *White-Haired Girl*, originating in the rural communist bases of the 1940s, plays on this transformation: the White-Haired Girl was turned from a human into a ghostlike wretch in the old society, whereas she was turned from a ghostlike wretch into a human by the new society (jiu shehui ba ren biancheng gui, xin shehui ba gui biancheng ren). The chasm between the field of life and the field of death is not physical death but a discursive boundary that defines livability. Being human (*ren*) for a poor, rural young woman was enabled by a social-political project that created a subject position for her, from which she found a meaning for her life in connection with the party-state.

This subject position later acquired new power and meaning when it became associated with the Iron Girls of Dazhai Brigade, and the post-Mao "total negation" of the Cultural Revolution also involved a thorough discrediting of this former ideal for rural young women. A 1979 cross-talk skit (*xiangsheng*, a comic routine typically performed by two men) ridiculed Iron Girls as impossible wives, and a young woman computer scientist commented in 1985 on their lack of domesticity and femininity: "I do not hope that all women will bare their fangs, brandish their claws and become short-tempered 'Iron Girls'" (Honig and Hershatter 1988: 25). The proud display of their productivity, which had marked them as socialist "new women," now became associated with an unnatural physicality that marked their bodies only as freakish. The Iron Girl, compared with the urban-educated woman of post-Mao gender discourse, was not feminine enough.[48] Gender discourse in the 1980s sought to rectify the gender order by restoring women to their biological destiny of femininity.

Similar discursive shifts took place with "youth." Once hailed as the revolutionary agent wrenched out of the family for social transformation by the Mao-era party-state, youth was now returned to the guidance of parental authority (Hooper 1985: 34) and came to be seen as an unstable object demanding the investigative gaze of "youth studies." With the 1980 establishment of the Research Institute for Youth and Juvenile Affairs within the Chinese Academy of Social Sciences, "youth" was opened up as a site for social normalization and management through the newly restored social-scientific power of physiologists, psychologists, sociologists, educators, and lawyers.

Recalling the words of Liu Li, Xiazi, and the Hubei woman seeking "reincarnation" in Shenzhen, how to have a modern subjectivity has become an issue of whether life is worth living at all in the countryside, where "there is no path to the future." After the new society rescued the White-Haired Girl, a subaltern, from the field of death and enabled her rebirth as a modern subject (*ren*), the problem of having personhood (*zuo ren*) has again become a grave issue for rural young women in the present historical moment. As in the case of the Hubei young woman, who was almost killed in the factory blaze in Shenzhen and yet returned in search of reincarnation—to be ren—the countryside is invoked as a field of death where a woman's modern subjectivity is smothered so that she "always moves around the stove."

A Shandong Young Woman's Grievance Letter

I feel sadness all the way through my bones and I cannot resolve it. After bearing a huge toll on my heart, I came to Beijing stubbornly to look for something. I looked for something and what did I find? . . . When I first saw the wife of that [employer] family and met the gaze (*yanguang*) she laid upon me, I felt that her gaze was not the kind for a human being at all: at best she was buying a high-class commodity. . . . Human dignity means nothing for this kind of job. I just want to sell my sweat, not my dignity and soul. Enough, I really have had enough and cannot bear it any longer. What kind of role am I playing?! Overwhelming sadness. . . . I cannot tolerate it any longer. . . . Dignity and time, the two major elements in my life, are both now broken to pieces. I have stepped from one lowland to another, from one kind of despair to another. . . . I have just learned that one room will be taken away from this family and they can no longer employ me. Perhaps I will be on the street at dawn. (Xie Lihua 1995)[49]

THE EMACIATION OF THE RURAL

This young woman from rural Shandong Province was caught in a conundrum in her pursuit of a modern personhood in the city. She despondently asked, "I came to Beijing stubbornly to look for something. I looked for something and what did I find?" She found that the gaze of her employer stripped her of humanity and dignity to make her "at best . . . a high-class commodity." The sadness that seeped into her bones and that she could not resolve came from her recognition of the overdetermined contradiction at the core of her pursuit of a modern personhood. In the context of post-Mao development the very condition enabling such women's entrance into the city, the center of the new commodity economy, is that they themselves be disposable commodities of migrant labor power. Thus, the very condition enabling their entry and existence in the city fundamentally forecloses the possibility of attaining the modern personhood for which they have struggled. The young woman from Shandong realized that she had only stepped from the lowland of home into the lowland of the city. The city proved not to be a high place of hope; it merely displaced her old despair with a new despair. The conundrum persists: between the country and the city, these young women have no place to pursue a modern personhood. The conditions and contradictions that have enabled and constituted migrant women's search for modernity also overdetermine their inability to become subjects of modernity and development.

Labor mobility cannot be singularly celebrated, as many political observers inside and outside China have done, as a new form of freedom to be realized in the transition from a planned to a market economy. What analysts have overlooked is how post-Mao development has robbed the countryside of its ability to serve as a place for rural youth to construct a meaningful identity. Hence rural young women's invocation of the countryside as a field of death. Migrant women's pursuit of modern subjectivity, situated in the culture of modernity produced by post-Mao development, must be understood in the context of a reconfigured rural-urban relationship in China's restructured political economy. Embedded in the post-Mao culture of modernity is an epistemic violence against the countryside that devalorizes the rural in both material and symbolic practices. The post-Mao shift in urban-rural relations, emaciating of the rural, is constitutive of rural young women's desire for the city. Such women struggle with the impasse posed by the discursive violence of post-Mao modernity itself—a counterpoint to the dominant discourse of development in many Third World countries and beyond.[50]

By examining problems of two modernization projects from the experiences of two generations of rural women, I treat modernity as historically plural. I also hold different modernization projects in tension to forestall a Manichean position of "either-or" with regard to China's transition, on the one hand, or a cultural relativist position with regard to the plurality of modernities, on the other. The Maoist and post-Mao modernities are competing visions that cannot be unified in the multiculturalist notion of culture.[51] By supplanting and negating Maoist modernity as its abject other, post-Mao development has authorized its own vision and practices of modernity as the emancipatory and normalizing process that will earn China a rightful position on the playing field of global capitalism. My focus, therefore, is on examining the epistemological violence embedded in such a modernization project and on unpacking the discursive configuration of tensions, disjuncture, and despair. In highlighting the historicity of modernization projects, I contribute to what Dirlik has called "the identification of alternative modernities, not in terms of reified cultures, but in terms of alternative historical trajectories that have been suppressed by the hegemony of capitalist modernity" (1997: 123).

2

MIND AND BODY, GENDER AND CLASS

The light-comedy series *Twenty-eight Baomu at Professor Tian's* (Wu Pei-min 1999) was widely circulated in Shanghai, Beijing, and many other cities through local cable TV in the late 1990s. Focusing on the domestic space of a well-off home in Shanghai, this series tells the stories of repeated attempts by the Tian family to find an appropriate domestic worker. Highlighting in its title the number of baomu hired, the series sensationalizes and indulges in the abundant availability of feminine labor power, but, at the same time, the scandalous number dramatizes a frustration that the needs of affluent homes cannot be satisfied by quantity alone.

Similarly, in my interviews I have encountered employers who complained, with a mixture of pride and frustration, that the number of baomu they have hired and fired could form a platoon. And it is not uncommon for employers to complain, "Finding a *heshide* [fitting, proper] baomu is harder than finding one's match for marriage."[1] In her story "Purple-Flowered Curtain," the writer Bi Shumin has a computer engineer complain, "To train a smart and under-standing baomu is harder than training a qualified programmer!" (1996: 434). Some of these employers are glad to have an audience to hear out their litanies of complaints about their baomu: they are too wooden to teach; they may be quick learners, but they are undisciplined; they may do their work sufficiently, but they talk back and do not know their position as baomu; they seem docile and simple at the beginning, but they learn to be "sophisticated" and calculat-ing, and allow their travel or holiday plans to inconvenience their employers; they are hardworking initially, but they grow lazy; and so on. Occasionally, when I met an employer at her work unit, our interview would attract the attention of her nearby colleagues, and they would all chime in to vent their own complaints. At one such interview at a university library in Hefei, the original informant was also a little surprised by such a collective show of grievances and humorously remarked, "It feels like we are 'speaking bitterness' here to a Women's Federation cadre." "Speaking bitterness" (*suku*) was a form of revolutionary mobilization of the peasantry in the land reform (1940s and 1950s) that encouraged the oppressed to speak out about their suffering in public and to learn to articulate their suffering as class injustice. At times, the Women's Association (which later became incorporated into the All-China Women's Federation) was actively involved in encouraging rural women to speak bitterness against both class injustice and patriarchy. By invoking "speaking bitterness," these employers implicitly assumed a position of victimhood vis-à-vis their domestic workers and imagined that they deserved the sympathetic hearing of the Women's Federation. In Beijing employers usually arranged to meet me at their homes or in cafés, so I did not encounter there a group of employers. But some employers informed me that during lunchtime at work they sometimes amuse each other by telling stories or mimicking the scandalizing manners of their domestic workers.

The majority of the thirty-five or so employers I interviewed in Beijing and Hefei were professionals, working as university teachers, librarians, publishers, white-collar workers, lawyers, and the like. Most of the employers I interviewed were women between their late twenties and late forties. As hiring domestic service did not become a common urban practice until the 1980s, the majority of employers I interviewed were first-generation post-Mao employers and gained their experiences of employing domestic workers after the 1980s. As of 2003–2004, less than 10 percent of households in Beijing has hired domestic workers.[2]

Most domestic workers—be they rural relatives of their employers, laid-off urban workers, elderly neighbors, or, more often, rural migrants—are the first generation in their family to do this kind of job. The long-standing legally coded social tradition of the servant system, the castelike servant-master hierarchy, and the elaborate division and terminology of servant labor, which existed in China before 1949, were swept away by the Communist Party-led social revolution. If this tradition has an influence today, it exists as a specter of

MIND AND BODY, GENDER AND CLASS

the "old society" that is sometimes invoked by rural migrant women to express their contestation of their labor conditions and to question the meaning of socialism in contemporary Chinese society (Yan Hairong 2006). The reform era has brought a large number of first-generation employers and domestic workers into a discontented relationship in which the lingering socialist legacy conflicts with desires for a postsocialist market utopia. To settle the issue of trust in field research, I made it a working principle not to interview domestic workers and employers of the same households.

The frequent complaints from employers prompted me to ask why it was so difficult to find *heshide* (proper) baomu? *Heshide* can mean (something or someone) meeting or matching what is required and/or being proper to protocols and procedures. In the context of talking about domestic workers the word *heshide* both describes an ideal situation in which the domestic worker suits the needs and expectations of the employer, and expresses an approval of a situation as being the right order of things.

To examine employers' frequent complaints requires one to ask what constitutes propriety, who could make "proper" baomu, and why this propriety is hard to obtain in post-Mao China. To pose this series of questions is not to favor the standpoints and perspectives of the employers. My examination of the employer-domestic worker relationship is not about individual moral qualities of the employers, but about the logic guiding a class relationship, even in cases in which the relationship may seem at its best. I aim ethnographically to grasp the intertwined gender and class problematics embedded in particular contradictions between mind and body, and between manual and mental labor in domestic life and labor in postsocialist China.

This chapter is divided into two parts. In part I, I look at how, in the 1980s, a discursive stage was established that called for the entry of baomu to perform domestic labor in the homes of "overburdened" urban intellectuals. My reading of the 1980s story "At Middle Age" (Ren dao zhongnian) opens up the following questions: how did domestic labor become a burden discursively? Who was burdened? And who could ideally and properly shoulder the burden? Domestic labor is neither self-explanatory nor stable; it is a field of social practices that gains its contour and meaning in the reconfiguration of social differences between mental and manual labor, the countryside and the city, and men and women in the new modernization strategy.[3] In part II, I probe the question of why it is difficult to find "proper" baomu. I examine how the mind of the employer mobilizes the body of the domestic worker, and what mediates the mind of one class and the body of another in the actual practices of domestic service. The problem of domestic-worker employment, particularly the complaints surrounding domestic workers' lack of "propriety," is a knot whose strands intertwine with old and new formations of social difference.

"Intellectuals' Burdens" and Intellectuals' Gender in the 1980s

The rise of domestic-labor employment in the post-Mao era is intimately linked to discussions of the "intellectuals' burdens" (*zhishifenzi de fudan*) in the early 1980s. "Intellectuals" in the Chinese context is a distinctive social group consisting of the educated, including scientists, writers, artists, teachers, medical doctors, and other professionals, as well as technical cadres on the state payroll.[4] During the Cultural Revolution, the meritocratic university entrance-exam system had been abolished and replaced with the direct recruitment of students from the ranks of workers, peasants, and soldiers through a system of recommendation (Andreas 2005). The university entrance-exam system was reinstituted in 1977. A hiatus was thus perceived in the training of national talents, caused by the "ten-year chaos" of the Cultural Revolution. The discourse of intellectuals' burdens prominently featured middle-aged intellectuals who accessed higher education before the Cultural Revolution and who now had particularly weighty responsibilities for making a critical contribution toward the post-Mao project of modernization.

The crushing burdens borne by these middle-aged intellectuals included strenuous everyday domestic labor, poor living conditions, insufficient institutional support for research, responsibility for raising young children, obligations in taking care of elderly parents, and so on. *Fanzhong de* (complex and strenuous) was almost a fixed descriptor of domestic labor, making it a prominent burden. This discourse alerted that the burdens born by middle-aged intellectuals had reached a level of crisis and were responsible for crushing some of the best minds in the country. Nothing better exemplifies this discourse of the burdens than the novella "At Middle Age." First published in the literary journal *Shouhuo* (Harvest) in 1980, Shen Rong's novella depicts the predicament of a woman doctor living with her family in a crowded apartment and burdened by domestic labor, caught between the conflicting demands of mental (professional and technical) and manual (domestic) labor. In the wake of the "scar literature" which swept the national literary scene with the bitterness of urban sent-down youth about their lost years in the countryside during the Cultural Revolution, "At Middle Age" is an ode to the middle-aged intellectuals who unswervingly dedicate their talent and energy to their work and to the post-Mao reconstruction of the nation. Yet it is also a story about a crisis: not a crisis of faith as in the case of the sent-down youth, but a crisis of the body—the body of the intellectual.

The story begins with Dr. Lu Wenting collapsing from exhaustion on an operating table. The narrative then flashes back to detail the demands of her work, her dedication to her patients as an eye surgeon, and her haunting guilt as a failed wife and mother. Although the protagonist is a *woman* professional, burdened by both gendered labor and gendered guilt, the image of her exhaustion and collapse prompted widespread discussions in the media of the burdens of intellectuals as a social problem and inspired the Party Central Committee to issue directives to call this problem to the attention of leaders at all levels and to show concern for middle-aged intellectuals (Gladys Yang 1980: 70). Shortly after the publication of this novella, a film bearing the same title was circulated to draw sympathetic attention across the country (Wang Qimin and Sun Yu 1982). The fame of the writer Shen Rong has since been attached to this particular story.

The social reception of Shen Rong's "At Middle Age" presents two problems. The first problem is why, among the numerous characters in Shen Rong's stories, Dr. Lu, as an exhausted professional encumbered with domestic work and haunted by her own sense of failure in the domestic sphere, became the central figure in the national discourse of the early 1980s. The second problem is why Dr. Lu's gender is elided in the social reception of the story so that she symbolizes intellectuals rather than women. In their edited book on Chinese women in the 1980s Emily Honig and Gail Hershatter observed the reception of this novel: "It was perceived as a poignant depiction of the excessive and unrewarded burdens imposed on middle-aged intellectuals. Despite the explicit description of housework in the story, women's double burden of work and housework was never an issue in the public discussion" (1988: 258). To extend the second problem: when gender is filtered out so that domestic work becomes a burden purely of class rather than of gender, what might be some of the social consequences?

To approach the first problem, one can compare Shen Rong's widely famed "At Middle Age" with her more obscure "Eternal Spring" (Yongyuan shi chuntian) (1979). By examining how the two stories depict radically different relationships between gender, class, and domesticity, one may be able to discern why Dr. Lu became the figure of the new era in the 1980s. In "At Middle Age" Dr. Lu is a mild, unassuming professional who has "no position, no power, but through her scalpel she wield[s] authority" (Shen Rong 1980: 40). During the Cultural Revolution, when her husband Fu's research institute is inactive and he takes over domestic chores, Dr. Lu is relieved of most housework burdens and can focus on her work. With the end of the Cultural Revolution, this temporary, abnormal arrangement is reversed. Both the nation and this family resume "normality": "After the Gang [of Four] was smashed, scientific research was resumed and Fu, a capable metallurgist, was busy again. Most of the housework was shouldered once more by Lu. Every day at noon, she went home to cook. It was an effort to stoke up the fire, prepare the vegetables, and be ready to serve the meal in fifty minutes so that Yuanyuan, Fu, and herself could return to school and work on time" (ibid.: 23).

This re-"normalization" within the domestic order is here sutured to the re-"normalization" of the national political order in post-Mao China, suggesting that both family and nation result from processes of struggle. What becomes normal thus suppresses a history of various openings in what "family" and "nation" might mean otherwise.[5] In order for her husband to be better focused on his work, Dr. Lu proposes a plan the night before her collapse: Fu should move into his institute and leave domestic responsibility completely to Lu herself. Although her tender, loving, and comradely husband resists this proposal at first, he eventually concedes. Only Dr. Lu's sudden collapse the next day prevents this plan from being realized. In a coma, Dr. Lu is haunted by a sense of regret and failure, with images of unfulfilled domestic responsibilities streaming through her mind: her daughter's hair yet to be plaited, running shoes yet to be bought for her son, more research time yet to be created for her husband. "At Middle Age" gives a sympathetic portrayal of this mild-mannered, strong-willed, professionally committed, and resolutely apolitical professional woman who is dedicated to the nation, but who is positioned above politics, especially the politics of the Cultural Revolution. Dr. Lu Wenting's sense of failure as mother and wife is amply empathized in the detailed narrative.

While "At Middle Age" was widely renowned, "Eternal Spring," published by Shen Rong one year earlier in the same literary journal, did not attract much attention. "Eternal Spring" is about a woman revolutionary, Han Lamei, who is resolutely political and has lived a life unburdened by domesticity. The story of this independent revolutionary woman is told by a self-critical male narrator, her former husband and a provincial party leader, Li Mengyu, who is more attached to domestic comfort. Lamei is a rural maidservant rescued from abuse by a group of communists, including Li, and she later, in the 1940s, joins the party herself. While working together, Li and Lamei fall in love, marry, and are separated in a battle in 1943. Rumor has it that Lamei has died in that battle, by falling over a cliff. After searching for her for several years and believing that she has died, Li marries an urban college graduate. He is shocked to encounter Lamei twenty years later and is haunted by grief and regret. He perceives that there is an inexplicable distance between himself and Lamei that cannot be explained away by the lapse of time and the fact of his remarriage. Li's narration of Lamei and their relationship, spanning the next ten years, until Lamei's death, revolves around this mystery of the distance between the two, who were once comrades and lovers.

Puzzled, Li is driven by a desire to find out how Lamei has lived her life on her own. His first visit makes the difference and distance between them apparent and unsettling. Lamei has a small, clean room with bare necessities in a working-class neighborhood, which, to Li's surprise, is not even as good as the room of his family's baomu. He also finds the neighborhood chaotic and alien, although Lamei is quite at home there. That night Li becomes conscious of the furniture, the velvet curtains, and the space of his own study at his home, which he has always taken for granted as necessary to improve his efficiency in work: "This room is quite large. Along the wall on one side stand three tall bookcases with glass doors. On the other side is a set of sofas. Facing the window is a magnificent desk and a leather swivel chair. On each side of the desk is a leather reclining chair. The pendant lamp hanging from the ceiling, the desk lamp, and the floor lamp next to the sofa allow me to read at any corner of this room. Usually when reading and writing reports, I sit in front of the desk. When reading books, I sit in the reclining chair. When thinking, I stroll in the middle of the room, on the polished wood floor" (Shen Rong 1986: 42).

Lamei is never eager to offer any explanation about their distance. In fact, for a long time she is rather reticent when facing Li's many questions about her life and is more voluble and forthcoming when discussing and criticizing problems of policies and their implementations. Even when Li criticizes her for not being a good mother—he learns that their daughter has been allowed to grow up in the countryside with the old couple who had once saved Lamei—she merely explains that the old couple and her daughter grew attached to each other and that it was not a bad thing for her to grow up in the countryside. Lamei's maternal love is only later detailed and defended by the daughter.

Li does not understand the distance between himself and Lamei until he eventually becomes aware of his own failing, a self-critique that gradually develops as he becomes closer to Lamei. As an organic and independent revolutionary who is stubbornly committed to the politics of egalitarianism and liberation, and rejects the privileges and bourgeois domesticity that many cadres of her status took for granted, Lamei becomes the mirror through which Li sees his own failing as a revolutionary who has acquired bureaucratic airs in work and taken for granted the privilege of bourgeois domesticity in his own life.

Lamei's political subjectivity is suggested several times by Li's depiction of her hands. Li recalls several times that Lamei, as a newly liberated seventeen-year-old rural maid, had red, swollen hands from volunteering to make shoes and wash clothes for communist soldiers. Years later, after visiting Lamei at a reservoir construction site, Li finds Lamei's hands to be rough and hard, not at all like a woman comrade's hand. Lamei's hands are signs of her participation in public manual labor. Lamei never stages her Spartan life as a form of sacrifice. She laughs heartily with neighbors, organizes evening classes in the working-class community, and is genuinely cheerful when chatting with an old fruit-farming peasant and taking over his shoulder pole for him. It is Lamei's organic joy as an independent grassroots political subject that Li has learned to appreciate and to hold up against his own failings and alienation.

While Li's official position enables a privileged domestic arrangement that he takes for granted, his wife Shi, a college graduate with a regular state job, focuses on managing the details of everyday domestic life with the help of an old baomu. When Lamei's daughter finally comes to Li's home to visit her father, the young woman, who is "wild" (*ye*) and unrestrained in the countryside, feels terribly confined and constrained by Li's domestic environment, despite the couple's best efforts to make her feel at home. It is through this rural young woman's discomfort and observation that the fastidiousness of their everyday life—the pickiness of their diet, the exquisiteness of their home furnishings, and so on—is further revealed and critiqued. As socialist personhood and womanhood is signaled by her participation in public work, Shi sighs to her husband that "I have this happy family and I have enclosed myself in this golden cage. This is my misfortune. . . . Really, I'm not like Han Lamei. She is a strong-willed soldier, while I am a woman with no achievement [*mei chuxi*]" (Shen Rong 1986: 24). Shi feels that Lamei has an independent political will that she herself unfortunately lacks. Compared with Li and Shi, Lamei is as much admired by the author Shen Rong as is Dr. Lu Wenting.

Perhaps the differences between Lamei and Shi manifest a discursive contradiction in the socialist practices of gender politics. As a rural servant transformed into a revolutionary subject in the early 1940s, Lamei maintains her earliest revolutionary commitment. The 1950s saw a statist closure of earlier, more radical and plural gender politics in the 1930s and 1940s, and relocated the gender of women in reformed and democratized familial and domestic relations even while women widely participated in public labor (Barlow 1991a). When Shi reflects on her situation, she considers herself fortunate because she occupies the center of this democratized nuclear family, with resources enabled by Li's position and without the troubles of kinship hierarchy typical of traditional large families. But this subject position disables her from becoming the independent subject of politics that Lamei embodies and that is still revered in the late Mao era. Shi has to hope that her domestic agency will be transformed into an indirect social agency through her nourishing of her husband and children. Faced with a discursive contradiction between the liberal feminization of domesticity, on the one hand, and the predication of women's liberation on their active participation in public labor, on the other, Shi chooses the former. Lamei does not face this discursive contradiction. Instead, she escapes from domestic labor by being a single mother whose child is in the care of others. She is not unlike the Iron Girls, whose girlhood status temporarily freed them from domestic burdens and enabled them to be heroines of public labor. Only by being in an unusual circumstance does Lamei's subjectivity escape from exhaustion and fragmentation between the dual demands of domestic and activist work. Although admired by the author, the subjectivity represented by Lamei was unusual, rather than typical, even in the representational world of socialist realism.

In "Eternal Spring" Shen Rong also subjects Li, a male provincial-level party leader, to a critical examination of his own relationship with domesticity. Not only does his male gender not absolve him from critique, but the process of his own self-critique with regard to his complicity in privileged domesticity is made more central and his sense of self-negation more excruciating in the story than are Shi's regret and apology. The enclosed domesticity is a site of daily experience and reproduction of privilege and alienation, and it resists politicization until the Cultural Revolution. In Li's reflection the mundane and trivial everydayness of domesticity seems capable of perpetuating itself without his conscious involvement. It is only much later that he becomes aware of his own complicity in its perpetuation. While Shi feels a partial loss and devaluation in her management of domesticity, for the most part Li and their children have enjoyed the benefits of such domesticity without qualms.

Shen Rong's two stories thus represent several radically different relationships between gender, class, and domesticity in the characters of Dr. Lu, Lamei, Li, and Shi. Lamei's final collapse at a construction site and her subsequent death are deeply saddening, but not tragic. In the context of post-Mao modernization, however, Dr. Lu's collapse is staged as a tragedy. Her collapse is a dramatization of the crisis brought out by the double burden: a crisis not only of the body but also of subjectivity. Even in a state of coma, Dr. Lu's mind is still haunted by her failings as a mother and a wife.

The representation of Dr. Lu shouldering dual burdens seems to foreground the contradiction between the feminization of domestic work and the predication of socialist womanhood in public labor and service that found a split representation in the domesticity-oriented Shi and the activist woman Lamei. If Shi and Lamei deal with the discursive contradiction by choosing one side over the other, Dr. Lu is herself split by the dual demands and eventually collapses. Her tragedy could have opened a space to reflect on the long-standing discursive contradiction within Mao-era socialist gender practices. Some feminist scholars in China argue that such a contradiction could be overcome if a different analytical lens of social production is adopted.

Admittedly, the socialist gender politics that promoted women's ability to "hold up half the sky" in public labor powerfully redefined the gendered meaning of "inside-outside" and broke the pre-liberation code of respectability that lodged proper womanhood "inside" the domestic sphere and shamed women associated with the "outside" (Rofel 1999: 66). With the new relations of production, the ability of women to labor without being spatially confined and socially shamed, as well as the real opportunity for women to gain status honors, publicity, and remuneration for their labor, were "the gendered attractions of socialism" that these women embraced with great enthusiasm (Hershatter 2000).[6] Yet the meanings of "work" (*gongzuo*) and "labor" (*laodong*) were nevertheless narrowly defined as productive activities that directly generated surplus and accumulation for the socialist state (Rofel 1999; Jacka 1997). Within this regrettably narrow productivist theory of the value of labor, activities inside the domestic sphere came to be seen as a nonproductive burden to which women were naturally attached and from which women were yet to be liberated via gradual industrialization and socialization.

During the Great Leap Forward (1958–61), attempts were made to create public dining halls and daycare centers, even in some rural areas, in order to socialize reproductive labor and enable women greater participation in public labor. Although motivated by productivist zeal mixed with a belief that such arrangements were appropriate for the transition to communist society, this practice transformed reproductive labor into part of community work that could legitimately claim public attention and resources, and have a value-expression in the remuneration paid for such labor (Davin 1976). This socialization of reproductive labor continued in some places even after the Great Leap Forward. (My paternal grandmother in rural Jiangsu, for example, was charged with the duty to watch over children in the village and was given work points by the production team.) Such experiments, however, were largely discontinued after the failure of the Great Leap Forward. Reproductive labor was again relocated to the domestic sphere and lost its public expression and social support.

The exclusion of domestic work as productive social labor in the Mao era can be traced to the modern concept of economy. The lack of economic value-expression of domestic work has everything to do with the division of what counts as "economic" and "non-economic" activities. Tracing this division to the male-female, outside-inside hierarchy within the notion of *oikos* or "household," Christopher Tomlins, drawing on Boydston (1990), states, "Economy came to be associated with what men did in the household's gendered division of labor. The sign of labor . . . became the wages that were earned on the outside of the household economy. This resulted eventually in a denial that the economy has an inside at all" (1995: 47). Concerning the debate over the productivity of domestic work, Christine Delphy argues that free and unremunerated domestic work is productive. What discursively separates "domestic work" from other work, or what defines "domestic work" as unproductive work, cannot be specific tasks or the totality of these tasks; instead it must be "a certain work relationship, a particular relationship of production," because the same work suddenly has a value-expression when performed outside the home (Delphy 1984: 90). The exclusion of domestic work from the system of value is much less due to its specialization than to its location within a patriarchal relationship of production that situates the work outside of capitalist market circulation.[7]

For most of the Mao era, domestic work performed at home or in the extended family failed to count as productive social labor. Domestic work performed outside the home or extended family existed as wage labor and did have a value-expression, but it failed to be socialized as public-service labor. It was a gendered productivist concept of labor and work that limited socialization and expansion of service work not directly related to production, and discounted such service work as nonproductive. Thus, even service workers who performed socialized public labor, such as workers in restaurants, hotels, and department stores, suffered from less social recognition and prestige when compared to other kinds of workers.

The tragedy of Dr. Lu Wenting could have provided an opportunity for a much-needed reflection on this gendered division of "productive" and "non-productive" labor, and might have opened a way to consider domestic work in a more holistic value system integrating production and social reproduction.[8] This is not to deny that, in the Mao era, men in urban China significantly contributed to domestic work in nuclearized and democratized families, when the overwhelming majority of urban women worked full time, brought home an income for the family economy, and could not be treated as "domestic women." However, the domestic division of labor remained largely intact and was a significant source of domestic conflict. Men were often pressed to do more domestic work by wives contending, "Don't think you are the only one who has full-time work. I, too, go to work eight hours a day. And I'm tired, too!"[9] Surveys in the early to mid-1980s found that men spent 4.25 hours and women 5.43 hours each day in domestic work in urban Jilin province (Jiang Xia 1986), men 2.25 hours and women 3.75 hours in Beijing, and men 3.9 hours and women 5.2 hours in Harbin and Qiqiha'er (Honig and Hershatter 1988: 259).

The second national survey on the social status of Chinese women conducted jointly by the Women's Federation and the State Statistical Bureau in 2001 reports that wives shoulder 85 percent of daily domestic work and that women spend 4.01 hours each day on housework, 2.7 more hours than the time spent by men (All-China Women's Federation and the State Statistical Bureau 2001: 9).[10] Although the survey in 2001 and those in the 1980s were not exactly comparable in terms of scales and parameters, it does seem that women have taken on a greater proportion of domestic work within two decades. It is commonly acknowledged that men in China "help" in housework, and the association of domestic work as women's natural duty is widespread (Zhang Lixi 1998). There is, therefore, a need both to question the gendered division of labor and to critique the productivist concept of labor in order to recognize reproductive labor as a form of social labor.

In the early 1980s, modest attempts at the socialization of domestic work were quietly underway in some urban neighborhood communities that mobilized community resources to establish neighborhood-based service stations and provide a wide range of services, including delivering milk to households, care for the young and old, furniture repair, and so on (Jiang Xia 1986; Croll 1983: 62–63). Yet these community-based attempts at socializing part of reproductive labor, promoted by the Women's Federation, did not challenge the association of women with housework, and this nascent socialization effort seems to have tapered off as an effective social project when the rapidly growing market economy made commodified arrangements, such as paid live-in domestic service, more prevalent.

The questions that the story of Dr. Lu Wenting might have raised did not become questions in the discursive context of the 1980s. Instead, in the national social reception of this story, her gender was muted: Dr. Lu did not stand for women, but for intellectuals. This leads me to examine the reform-era context that shaped the reception of the story and its social reading, for social and political conditions determine what and how questions emerge as "social" questions. Symptomatically, when the author Shen Rong was asked whether she felt like a bad mother and wife, as Dr. Lu felt in the story, she replied, "Yes, I do. Like Dr. Lu, I feel we must make sacrifices to get work done" (Gladys Yang 1980: 68). Yet the interviewer who raised this question ignored the fact that the author and her character shared a specific predicament as women, following up with the comment: "The problems of middle-aged professionals were in her mind for some time" (ibid.: 68). Gender was bypassed.

In the reform context of the 1980s Dr. Lu could not signify her gender and could not problematize the relationship between gender and domestic work because the gender discourse in the 1980s was already shifting. This shift further naturalized the connection between women and domestic work. With the reform era's ontological rectification (*bo luan fan zheng*), which centered on renouncing Maoism, the "socialist woman" represented by the Women's Federation began to visibly lose her ideological ground. She was increasingly seen as an unnatural, distorted creature who grew in a time of "gender disorder" and who had suppressed or lost her gender nature and was "non-woman."[11] The post-Mao gender politics, in the context of the 1980s "new enlightenment" search for humanism, was to reject "socialist woman" and nurture an essentialist notion of womanhood by sexualizing, feminizing, and domesticating women.

In this epistemic sea change, when the socialist woman subject was losing her ideological authority, a debate took place in a number of magazines, particularly in the sociological journal *Shehui* from 1983 to 1984, on whether women should return to being full-time housewives or reduce their outside workloads to part time. A survey of 2,000 readers at the time revealed that 70 percent of the males polled would have liked their wives to "return home" (*hui jia*), but also would have liked to have women's salaries added to theirs (Zhang Lixi 1998: 6). Along with the refeminization and redomestication of women was the constitutive trend in commercial advertisements that represented women much more as consumers than as producers. Advice populated the media about how women could be good wives and mothers (Honig and Hershatter 1988: 167–205).

Maoist "gender disorder" was held responsible for having impeded China's development by messing up the natural gender relationship and familial order. Socialist gender discourse was said to have produced masculinized women and effeminate men who were hen-pecked or "womanishly fussy" (*popo mama*), which was summarized as "the raging of yin and the waning of yang" (*yin sheng yang shuai*). It was argued that because both men and women worked outside and at home, this gender arrangement has exhausted both men and women, and held China back from achieving modernity.[12] Some proposed that Japan could modernize so quickly because it had a natural and rational gendered division of labor: women stayed home and men went out to work. With the overturning of the socialist gender discourse in the mid-1980s, a search for Chinese manhood broke out in media and film circles, making the state the castrator of masculinity (Dai Jinhua 1999; Rofel 1994: 713). This coincided with some women finding the "going home" discussion attractive, as they were exhausted by double burdens. The previously "progressive" Maoist woman who had exemplified national liberation was now seen as a symbol and source of China's backwardness.

Being a mild and resolutely apolitical professional, Dr. Lu Wenting escaped the fate that befell the ridiculed Maoist woman, but in this context she could not signify as "woman" to raise political and philosophical questions about the gendered division of labor and the social nature of housework, regardless of a family's class. Rural women, especially in poor areas, shoulder even more housework than both urban women and rural men (Ye Jingde 1996: 41; Li Hang 1996: 10). However, in the social reception of this story, it was the intellectual Dr. Lu, not the woman Dr. Lu, who was the subject for social concern.

The story thus facilitated a production of the discourse of "intellectuals' burdens." With her gender muted, Dr. Lu, who "had no position, no power," no politics, but was dedicated to the nation and earned authority through her professional skill, became a strategic representation to support the ascension of the intellectual class, which, possessing "intellectual talents" and "expertise," were riding the new technocratic hegemony in the newly designed post-Mao plan of "four modernizations."[13] At the same time that post-Mao discourse has restructured gender relations, it has also overturned the class axis to renounce the "mass line" policies (*qunzhong luxian*) of the Cultural Revolution, which ideologically located creativity and historical agency in the collective force of ordinary people, especially manual laborers. In the process of reform, value differentiation between manual and intellectual work was painstakingly reconstructed, with creativity and agency now associated primarily with intellectual work and intellectuals (Rofel 1989: 244). With mental and manual work becoming respectively located in the minds of intellectuals and the bodies of urban and migrant workers, the modernization effort of the post-Mao state needed to "appropriate the mind of one class and the body of the other."[14] Only in the context of this new discursive differential valuation of intellectuals and workers, mental and manual work, the mind and the body, can one understand the depth of the tragedy and crisis perceived in Dr. Lu: she was split between mind and body, and her intellectual talent was in danger of being burdened or even ruined by exhausting housework. Her tragedy becomes a class tragedy. If post-Mao China predicates its modernization on talented minds (*rencai*), then Dr. Lu's collapse, read allegorically, sounded an alarm for the national future of modernization. The message was that intellectuals need to be liberated from manual domestic work. The liberal wave of "thought liberation" (*sixiang jiefang*) appeared to be the liberalization of ideology and minds, but, in light of the discourse of "intellectuals' burdens," it was also an unspoken separation and liberation of mental from manual labor.

When the problem of domestic work was represented as a burden born by intellectuals, what were the social consequences of this representation? Not only was the government mobilized at all levels to show extra concern for intellectuals not long after the novel was published; rural women also entered the scene en masse to provide the domestic labor highly demanded by urban intellectuals and other elite groups in the early 1980s. This production of the problem of intellectuals' burdens enabled the Beijing Municipal People's Congress and People's Political Consultative Conference to lobby for government attention and bureaucratic resources in organizing and managing migrant domestic workers in the city. The bodily labor power of these migrant women would relieve the intellectuals from the mind-body split.

To be sure, "At Middle Age" did not cause the discourse of intellectuals' burdens; nor was the social effect of this novel fully intended by the author herself. To argue such would be to make the intention of the author a transcendent agent of meaning. Rather, "At Middle Age" shows how the particular logic and forces at play in the post-Mao context determined the social reception of the story and enabled the production and representation of a "problem" in the social field. While Dr. Lu was placed in the discursive limelight, the figure of a Maoist woman revolutionary in "Eternal Spring," published by

Shen Rong only one year earlier, completely fell into oblivion. The ideological sea change instituted by the reform consigned Lamei to a past whose page was being turned. If Lamei could signify at all, she signified the Maoist past to be negated. As for Dr. Lu, her burdens, understood as intellectuals' burdens, and her need for liberation from these burdens, indicated the context in which migrant women surfaced as domestic workers.

An Ideal Baomu: Approaching a Fantasy

In the spring of 1984 a brief report appeared at the most inconspicuous tail end of a Beijing newspaper, announcing that the municipal San Ba Service Company would recruit baomu from around the country. The effect of this news was like exploding the first nuclear bomb on Bikini Island and immediately produced a strong impact among urban residents. (Zhang Meirong and Nan Song 1994, 18)

In the early to mid-1980s the presence of tens of thousands of migrant women working as baomu in Beijing was still far below the market's demand for domestic labor. Efforts that linked the government's hand with that of the market were deployed to quickly expand and regulate the market in domestic labor power. When interviewed in 1999, a manager of a domestic-worker recruitment company described with an idiom that the demand for domestic workers in the mid-1980s was so high that the company never had to worry about finding employers: "They [domestic workers] were like 'the emperor's daughter'—one never has to worry about her marriage [huangdi de nü'er bu chou jia].'" By the late 1990s, there was an extensive network through which recruitment agencies supplied rural young women to urban households.

Yet the complaint has remained constant that finding a "good" or "proper" baomu is harder than finding a wife. In order to understand the complaint, it might be useful to examine what kind of baomu is considered good in the imaginations of some urban employers and how this goodness contributes to a form of desired sociality in the conditions of post-Mao China. Sociality is understood here as interwoven relations of labor, power, and affect. The fantasy of baomu goodness and propriety is exemplified by the fictional character Xiao Ling, who, however, stands in sharp contrast with the masses of migrant domestic workers, whose experiences are epitomized by that of the migrant woman Juju. Juju migrated to Beijing from Sichuan with her aunt when she was just sixteen years old. By the time I met her in Beijing in 1999, she had worked for more than eight years as a domestic worker successively employed by three families.

This [first] family was not too bad, but not too good either. When I first went there, I didn't know very much about how to do housework and looked clueless [*sha huhu de*]. So they were not especially kind to me. For example, they never let me watch their TV. . . . But they did let me eat with them at the same table. You know, some families would not even allow you to eat at the same table; they thought you were filthy [*xian ni zang*]. This family did allow me to eat at the same table. But with many things, how should I say, it was just so different from what it would be like at [my own] home. I wept long and hard several times, because I missed home. My aunt also left Beijing for Shenzhen two months later and left me alone in Beijing. In the evening, the people of this family gathered together, laughing and talking, but I would be alone. Nobody paid attention to me. It's not like at [my own] home. Here nobody cared about you.

Originally they hired me to look after the baby, but they also made me [hand] wash laundry for five adults in the family [including the child's parents, grandparents, and an uncle who was going to college then and was unmarried]. You see, every morning I heated up the milk for the baby, fed him, and then washed diapers. Around eight o'clock, the grandmother would go to the neighborhood committee. And I would wash more diapers, mop the floor, and clean the house. When the baby woke up, I would hold him. Around eleven o'clock, when the grandmother came back and took over the baby, I would do housework. After lunch, the grandmother would put the baby to sleep and then she would go out again. I would wash all the dishes and then do the laundry for the whole family. I would also clean and prepare vegetables and meat for dinner. In short, my day was just full of work. . . .

The baby was just a little over one year old. I have a brother and sister at home, but it's not so complicated to look after a baby in the countryside as here. Here, when the child bumped himself somewhere, his grandmother and mother would immediately say, "Why didn't you look after the baby!" The baby was just starting to toddle around. It's so strange: when you were watching him, he was fine; but just as you stopped watching and started to do something else, he would bump himself somewhere. This child would sleep sometimes for ten minutes, twenty minutes, or an hour, and you would have to rush to handle him as soon as he woke up. While sometimes I was not finished with the work in hand and would have to let him sit for a while, he would bump himself in the meantime. Now I would say, "You ask me to do this and that, but I've got only two hands and there will certainly be one thing that I can't do well." But at that time I did this and that, and wanted them to have a good impression of me so that they would treat me better. But in the end, I still didn't do well and didn't satisfy them. They said that I didn't take good care of the baby and that the laundry I washed was not clean.

After she worked for four months for this family without a day of rest, she was told to pack one morning and was taken back to the recruitment agency. "They didn't give me any advance notice, but of course it wouldn't have done me much good if they had. Because I didn't know my way around in the city and didn't know anyone, I wouldn't have been able to find a job before they sent me back." Juju is among the many migrant domestic workers who form the pale and negative background against which the fictional character Xiao Ling stands.

Xiao Ling, a twenty-three-year-old urban woman from Beijing, is an ideal baomu in the short story "Baomu" (1983), written by a woman, Huo Da, and published shortly after the film based on Shen Rong's "At Middle Age" became a national sensation. Xiao Ling works for a retired head nurse, Ms. Li, and her husband, the elderly Professor Shen. Ms. Li sees the film "At Middle Age" and decides to take over from her intellectual daughter the work of care for the grandson so that the daughter does not become another Dr. Lu Wenting. Ms. Li pities Dr. Lu: "If only Lu Wenting had a mother, she would not have been so exhausted" (Huo Da 1983: 56). But the need to liberate Professor Shen from his frequent, involuntary babysitting prompts Ms. Li to look for a baomu. The process is long and difficult, not because they cannot find one, but because they have to be cautious to "pick one as suitable as possible from potentially dangerous outsiders" (ibid.: 55). Many rural domestic workers who had worked for Ms. Li seem to her like "a pile of dead flesh" (si rou geda), who not only lacked motivation to follow her instructions but were also incapable of learning even when taught face to face. Xiao Ling seems "to have both bodily power [*liqi*] and smartness [*jiling jin'er*] and to be able to work hard and intelligently" (ibid.: 57). Also, unlike previous baomu, Xiao Ling is not intimidated by her numerous and high-standard demands, as indicated by her stern warning, "Cultivating a talented mind [*rencai*] must begin from infant-hood.[15] Nothing—food or anything—can be done carelessly [for an infant]" (ibid.). Every day Xiao Ling buys groceries from the market, serves breakfast, bathes the baby, and prepares a healthy and delicious lunch from scratch. Her work also includes hand-laundering the baby's diapers and clothes, washing and steaming utensils for feeding the baby, cleaning the house, and washing the adults' clothes. She can accomplish all of these in half a day. Before she leaves her half-day of work for this family, she also cooks dinner. She does all these without any need for help or instruction. In addition, she makes a variety of spring rolls and dumplings. The Beijing baomu Xiao Ling proves to be impeccable and never fails to pass the constant strict inspection and unexpected questioning of Ms. Li.

> Xiao Ling is cooking. Li might suddenly ask her, "Where is Uncle's [Professor Shen's] jacket that you washed yesterday? Did you forget to take it in [after hanging it in the sun to dry] and lose it?"
>
> "Oh," Xiao Ling, spatula in hand, without turning her head, gently replies, "in the closet, third drawer on the left."
>
> And sure enough it turns out to be folded neatly and put together with several other jackets that the professor wears when going out.
>
> This kind of inspection, selective checking, and unexpected questioning is not something that all baomu can handle. If a baomu cannot handle it, then she will be asked to leave. It is not that Ms. Li wants to make things difficult for them, it is simply that she does not want to lower her standards (ibid.: 59).

It is not until Xiao Ling passes all these tests and inspections that Ms. Li relaxes her supervision and "the relationship between Li and Xiao Ling could be said to be harmonious." Xiao Ling breaks the record of previous baomu when Ms. Li keeps her after two months have passed. After Xiao Ling's arrival, Professor Shen becomes highly productive in writing his book manuscript. He can leisurely water his garden after getting up, work for several hours uninterrupted in the morning, have a delicious lunch, nap on the couch, and continue his work in the afternoon. With his work done for the day, in the evening he can relax and play with his grandson. "Day after day, he feels his life is full and satisfying. Life is back to its original rhythm." Professor Shen feels grateful: the monthly wage paid for Xiao Ling's half-day of work, 10 yuan, could be spent by his wife in five minutes in a department store, but how much work Xiao Ling does for the same amount! He sighs that her detailed and minute manual work is like "layering countless unremarkable pieces of gravel necessary for the completion of his book" (59). This gratitude prompts him to feel sorry that they treat her as no more than a baomu whose labor is bought with money and that they do not care for her as a child. This patriarchal humanist sentiment echoes that of a well-known early modern writer Liang Shiqiu (1993), who advised through the words of the ancient poet Tao Yuanming (365–427 A.D.) that the way to manage a servant is to treat him as a human, as a child of fellow humans.

In the early 1980s it was almost impossible to find young Beijing women willing to work as a baomu. One may argue that Xiao Ling represents the ideal baomu fantasized by employers and that such a representation is held up as a model of propriety only to reflect the shortcomings of the rural migrant baomu whom Ms. Li had fired one after another. Xiao Ling's superbly efficient and diligent labor and her tolerance of Ms. Li's bluntness and class arrogance produces a desirable sociality—a leisurely and productive life enjoyed by Professor Shen, and a harmonious relationship between herself and Ms. Li.

As this story painstakingly represents the perfect baomu and the ideal sociality provided by her affective labor, performed at an almost impossibly high standard with a meager wage, one is invited to ask what makes her fantastic goodness socially imaginable, even if it is not really possible? Readers do not have access to Xiao Ling's inner world in the story. Although Xiao Ling is narrated and speculated on, she never has a vocal consciousness of her own. How to make sense of Xiao Ling becomes the most interesting question, and it lies at the heart of the story's suspense.

What makes Xiao Ling an ideal baomu? In the context of the early 1980s, when the story was written, even the worldly wise Ms. Li has a hard time understanding the juxtaposition of Xiao Ling's urbanity and her willingness to work as a baomu, which seems both unthinkable and mysterious. So one encounters a historically situated problem, of explaining Xiao Ling during the early transition to the post-Mao market economy. Ms. Li is genuinely puzzled. As an ideal baomu, Xiao Ling is differentiated from migrant domestic workers because she seems to identify with her employer's instructions and never seems to lack motivation to do her job perfectly. How can Xiao Ling be an ideal baomu? What is she? The market logic, which would place Xiao Ling in the same league with rural migrant women as cheap labor power competing for employment, could not be adequate to explain Xiao Ling in the eyes of Ms. Li. At a loss, Ms. Li thinks of a bit of outdated political discourse, the Maoist one of "serving the people." She tries to imagine Xiao Ling as a Lei Feng, an altruistic Maoist hero. Xiao Ling shyly, but firmly, replies that she is not Lei Feng, that she works to make money. The more satisfied Ms. Li is with Xiao Ling's work, the more puzzled she grows about Xiao Ling's identity.

What discursive logic in the early 1980s could make sense of Xiao Ling, if it were neither the market economy itself nor the older logic of "serving the people"? What could be the social explanation for this ideal baomu? In the story it is suggested that Xiao Ling has become a domestic worker because it gives her the time and the schedule she needs to nurse her bedridden mother. The story's author, Huo Da, has Professor Shen comment, "This child is truly good!" (*zhe haizi zhen hao*). In the early 1980s the notion of *suzhi*—which can only be insufficiently translated as "quality"—was growing as a descriptor of populations, but was not as pervasive as it is today and was not yet flexibly applied to individuals. If Huo Da had written this story a decade later, she might have used *suzhi* to characterize Xiao Ling. A decade later, the notion of suzhi would be active in the labor market and in the mobilizing of migrant domestic workers for producing affective labor. Writing in the early 1980s, however, Huo Da coded Xiao Ling's distinction as traditional virtues articulated through the market economy.

Yet the puzzle about Xiao Ling is not yet solved; the story is about to reveal the mark of its times. This otherwise straitjacketed paean to the perfect baomu ends with the climax of Xiao Ling's collapse from exhaustion near Professor Shen's home. Like Dr. Lu, Xiao Ling is hospitalized. But unlike "At Middle Age," in which the narrative focuses on the heroine's consciousness and sub-consciousness, Xiao Ling is almost always narrated through her employers' consciousness. After Xiao Ling is sent to the hospital, the guilt-stricken Professor Shen finds, falling out from her bag, a handwritten book manuscript on a famous Tang Dynasty poet, as well as the breakfast she had just bought for him. The manuscript addresses a subject of Professor Shen's research and challenges his analysis head-on. Professor Shen is shocked by the contradiction.

"Surprise" and "astonishment" cannot adequately describe Professor Shen's feeling at this moment. He doubts his vision. Completely inconceivable! How could it be possible? How could a young girl of twenty-three, a baomu, be associated with this thick, handwritten manuscript? The professor is confused. In front of his eyes appear a grocery basket, a spatula, milk bottles, diapers, a scrubbing board, bubbles of laundry soap, and a clay pot for herbal medicine. How can she have time? She works for two families and has to wait on her own bedridden mother. Unless she were a machine and needed no rest? ("Baomu," 62)

The black-and-white illustration, which accompanied the original publication, dramatizes this moment of astonishment, contradiction, and confusion occurring in the mind of Professor Shen about Xiao Ling's identity. The illustration depicts Professor Shen intensely reading Xiao Ling's manuscript while Xiao Ling flashes through his mind as a baomu washing laundry on the scrubbing board and as a daughter waiting on her bedridden mother, working day and night. Shocking as her collapse might be, the illustration is not about that moment. What appears more astonishing for Professor Shen and the reader is her manuscript, which is also depicted in the illustration. Only the manuscript reveals the true drama of her collapse.

It is revealed here that Xiao Ling, too, breaks down due to the double burden of intellectual and manual work. This moment thus unravels the final mystery of Xiao Ling and brings out the greater significance of her collapse: her collapse as a baomu is only a facile drama, but her collapse as an intellectual is a more profound disturbance. Her final identity is reflected in Professor Shen's emotional response when he hears that she is recovering in the hospital. "'Good.' Professor Shen put down the phone ever so gently, as if afraid of waking up Xiao Ling. The sleep after the completion of a book must be a sweet one. Don't wake her up!" (62).

The illustration of this moment depicts the active and intense presence of Professor Shen, and reinforces several points. First, although Ms. Li has been the main contact for Xiao Ling in this family, and although the plot centers

1. An illustration from the story "Baomu."

on their relationship, Professor Shen is the intellectual center nourished by the labor of both Xiao Ling and Ms. Li. Second, Professor Shen alone, as an authority in his field (*xueshu quanwei*), can appreciate and validate Xiao Ling's identity as a budding intellectual. To enhance the professor's authority, the illustrator even places a nuclear symbol—a common emblem for science and modernization in 1980s China—next to the professor's head, even though its use in reference to this professor of classical literature is a bit out of place. Third, and most important, the intense presence of Professor Shen in this dramatic moment neutralizes Xiao Ling's gender and class difference and transforms the meaning of her collapse.

The illustration features two characters: Xiao Ling and Professor Shen. At one level, their relationship is that between a baomu and her employer. But the new reading intended by the author and the illustrator is the revelation that despite gender and class differences, Xiao Ling and Professor Shen are both intellectuals and are connected as such, at least as far as Professor Shen is concerned. He no longer pities her as a young baomu earning a meager wage; now he respects and cares for her as a young intellectual. The decision to make Professor Shen the character who identifies with Xiao Ling and empathizes with her collapse transforms that collapse into a problem *among intellectuals.* This representation elides and neutralizes differences in gender and class. But what would Xiao Ling think? Huo Da makes no effort to demonstrate Xiao Ling's thought process. Professor Shen's consciousness is the determining perspective that brings the story to a closure.

With Xiao Ling's collapse and the simultaneous revelation about her identity as a closet intellectual, this story unexpectedly echoes "At Middle Age." Ms. Li hires Xiao Ling in order to prevent her own daughter from becoming a Dr. Lu Wenting, but ironically Xiao Ling herself turns out to be a closet Dr. Lu. The title "Baomu" plays with the incongruity of the two identities embodied by Xiao Ling: both a perfect baomu and a young intellectual. The suspense created by the title and the narrative process only intensifies the surprise of her hidden identity. Xiao Ling is a paradox: an ideal baomu and, finally, not really a baomu.

What makes Xiao Ling an ideal baomu? The story pushes to a new horizon Xiao Ling's distinction, which, prior to this dramatic moment, has been coded as traditional virtue articulating with the market logic, when her employers accept the reasoning that a filial daughter would make a good domestic worker. However, as if the author herself felt this explanation to be inadequate, that Xiao Ling could not "just" be a baomu through and through, her raison d'être is further supplemented. Ultimately, Xiao Ling is a perfect baomu, who satisfies all the fantasies that Ms. Li and Professor Shen have constructed, not only because she has traditional virtues and scrupulously exchanges her good labor for a wage, but also because she is like them and is one of them. This painstakingly narrated baomu is therefore so perfect, good, and proper that she cannot be merely a baomu.[16] This supplement—Xiao Ling's intellectual identity—seems finally to explain that perhaps because she is an intellectual at heart (and in mind), she is able to appreciate her employers' labor standards and even make Ms. Li sigh that she herself could do no better. This supplement gives away a contradiction: the carefully constructed proper baomu in the end cannot be proper to herself—Xiao Ling cannot properly be a baomu. Based on the ending, the reader can guess that after Xiao Ling recovers, she will be treated as who she really is and might no longer need to work as a baomu.

Staged as a solution to the problem of intellectuals' burdens, the story

"Baomu" ends up reenacting the collapse of the overburdened intellectual. It sharpens, rather than mitigates, the opposition between body and mind, between manual and intellectual labor. In doing so, the story stamps itself as a product of its time. If Xiao Ling is an ideal but "improper" baomu, the story mirrors a representation that many of those rural migrant women are "properly" baomu, but not ideal baomu. The story's painstaking construction of an ideal baomu finally reveals her impropriety and thus leaves open the gnawing question of who would make a good proper baomu and what logic can render hired labor motivated and affective for the production of the desired sociality. When employers' minds and migrants' bodies are discursively aligned along the split between intellectual and manual work, when modernization appropriates the mind of one class and the body of another, how is the mind to motivate bodies to work?

If family income allows it, almost all families will discuss this: Let's hire a baomu! . . . A mere mention of the word *baomu*—whether it greets the eye or springs from the tip of a soft tongue—is enough to set off a string of associations: warmth, comfort, indulgence, etc. (Guo Chuanhuo 1997: 1)

Handling Domestic Work: From Moral Appeal to Value Management

While the contradiction between body and mind, or manual and intellectual work, underlay the early to mid-1980s concern about intellectuals' burdens, this contradiction shifted with further marketization. The 1990s saw expansive commercialization of social life, rapid growth of the private sector and the new rich, income hikes for intellectuals and state employees, a differentiation of intellectuals through processes of professionalization and *xia hai* (jumping into the sea of commerce), reforms of state-owned enterprises, continued stagnation of rural income, and successive waves of layoffs of urban workers.[17] In this context domestic work as a burden has also undergone significant changes: in terms of rationality, it changed from being a central part of the discourse of intellectuals' burdens, which issued a moral appeal for state concern and social sympathy, to being part of an individualized cost-benefit calculation of time management. In terms of labor supply, although migrant domestic workers are still the main labor force, the sources now include urban laid-off women workers. Employers have grown both in number and in range of professions, even though they are estimated to be still less than 10 percent of the total urban households in Beijing as of 2003–2004.

Everyday domestic life has witnessed a dramatic change in rhythm and structure since the 1980s. The after-lunch nap is gradually disappearing in national urban domestic life. Many people in big cities do not go home for lunch anymore, as many businesses now stay open through lunch and government institutions resume business hours at 1:30, even in the summer, compared to 2:30 or 3:00 before. The amount of time spent on domestic work is therefore significantly diminished. As one baomu-employer who works in a state-owned enterprise noted, "We used to have enough time for domestic work. In some units, people could get off work at 4:00 in the afternoon. There was time to buy groceries and cook. Now it's different. Like here, we are supposed to get off at 5:00, but we might still be here around 6:00 or 7:00. I can't go home and cook. Neither can my wife. The pace of work has intensified because competition has intensified. My wife is not in good health, but she still studies while working. I also need to study. Although my job is O.K., if I want to have a better job, I need to study for a higher degree so I can be more competitive."

The desire to improve one's human capital, driven by China's further integration into global market competition, produced a craze over the Chinese edition of Dryden's and Vos's *The Learning Revolution* (1999) in several large Chinese cities. While "time is money" was a bold and novel idea associated with the special economic zone of Shenzhen in the 1980s, in the 1990s market value has dominated the personal time management that shapes everyday life-process in the present and affects career possibilities in the future.

Here one witnesses a transformation in the way "domestic work" is understood. In the 1980s it was a critical part of the intellectuals' burdens, which, like the late 1990s discourse of the "peasants' burdens" (*nongmin fudan*), called for state attention and policies, as well as broader social sympathy. As a moral appeal, this discourse circulated images of physical collapse, stories of burdened intellectuals, and statistics on the life expectancy of intellectuals as a social group, and so on. In the 1990s "domestic work" entered the sphere of individual rational calculation as the least productive expenditure of time that could otherwise be spent more productively and profitably. It is no longer a heavy burden to be lightened; instead, it has become the least valuable work to be commissioned. As an intellectual-turned-entrepreneur stated about his time management philosophy, "You have to balance yourself in the domestic-work sector, balance the cost and gain, so you know where you stand. I feel that it's worth spending more time on my career than on domestic burdens. So I employ someone to do it so I can focus on my career and have a firmer standing against the competition."

While the time and labor of domestic work has been increasingly subjected to this market-based value regime, where it is considered the least worthwhile of labors, domestic life is paradoxically growing more important for relaxation, leisure, consumption, and reproduction of the self. Intensified business and career competition created by the market machine has incited an increased longing for a peaceful, comfortable, tasteful, quality domestic life (*you pinzhi de shenghuo*). This expectation is enhanced by privatized home ownership and home furnishing that arrived in social life through the government's housing reform in the 1990s. However, the rising standard for cleanliness that accompanies home ownership and furnishing means more domestic labor, discipline, and tension, which directly contradict the desire for relaxation and leisure at home. In short, while the problem of the intellectuals' burdens vanished in the 1990s, another contradiction emerged: one between the new imaginary of domestic life—there is almost no escape from advertisements of sparkling and stylishly furnished homes as objects of consumption and affect—and the rigorous domestic labor and discipline necessary to materialize this domestic ideal.

Mr. N, a middle-aged intellectual who jumped into the sea of commerce as a CEO, tells of the constraints and discipline that have given rise to tension in domestic life.

It used to be more carefree: friends frequently dropped by one another's homes; with newspaper covering the table, we drank beer together and cracked sunflower seeds; if we talked late, we often had friends stay the night. It was very casual like that. Nowadays many families have bought homes and furnished them. Women usually take particular care [about home cleanliness]. When we come home, first we take off our shoes. When we eat, we are especially careful not to let a piece of scrap fall. Now friends rarely visit you at home. Why? It's a lot of trouble to keep from messing up someone's home, especially when the hostess is mindful. Now friends meet in cafés and teahouses instead. The whole thing is upside down—instead of relaxing at home, we are made to be mindful. It's tiring. . . . Except for some nouveau riche whose money comes and goes easily, most people spend their life savings to painstakingly furnish their homes, and they want to take good care of them. So they forget to enjoy themselves. They wipe this, polish that, and become its servants. . . .

You'd think we'd have a good [home] atmosphere. [One day] our daughter was playing piano, when I came home, ready to relax and enjoy watching my daughter play piano. Halfway through she said, "Dad, I'm thirsty." She went to get some water, but she accidentally spilled it on the floor. Immediately, my wife scolded her. "Be careful! Look at you!" So the atmosphere immediately changed, just because of a little spilt water. . . . This is how we're constrained at home, unfree. Many homes that I've been to are like this.

Whereas home ownership brings expectations of leisure, distinction, and affect to a new high, it aggravates the burden of domestic work and intensifies home discipline. Whereas market-oriented individual competition creates the craving for a relaxing and quality home time, the same market principle eschews the value of time and labor necessary to realize this expectation. The labor of a domestic worker is thus necessary to resolve this new contradiction. If, as the CEO observed, home ownership ironically makes an owner the servant of his home, the domestic worker is supposed to take over the subservient labor of serving the home and to make the homeowner the true master. She is supposed to resolve the contradiction between domestic life and domestic labor.

Where Are the Baomu Sourced?

But who will make proper baomu? Although, since the mid-1990s, baomu have become a common sight in urban neighborhoods, only about 5 percent to 8 percent of the households in Beijing's eight urban districts were hiring baomu as of 2003–2004. This percentage is rather small, but numerically it amounts to about 200,000. Urban families have a variety of sources from which to get domestic help: they can hire a domestic worker from family service agencies that supply rural migrant women; they can ask one of their own rural relatives to come to the city and lend a hand; they can hire a local laid-off woman worker or an elderly neighborhood woman; or they might rely on their own elderly parents for temporary help. Yet each source brings its own problems, which begs the question of who makes the proper baomu and what kind of sociality is desired as "proper" by urban employers. An analysis attentive to what constitutes this desired "propriety" also reveals why urban employers are often frustrated and how they sometimes have to negotiate with heterogeneous social relations that cannot be easily reduced or abstracted into wage labor employment.

Grandparents

In *Chinese Women since Mao* Elizabeth Croll queries "whether future generations of grandmothers will be quite so ready to undertake the childcare and domestic labor after a lifetime in production," compared to the then current generation of grandmothers, who had spent much of their life in domestic service and were called on to continue helping their daughters-in-law (1983: 65). By the late 1990s, many young urban professionals and intellectuals knew that they could not take for granted that their parents would help out with childcare and domestic labor, especially if their parents were themselves retired urban professionals and intellectuals. One employer in her early thirties told me that her parents-in-law were both intellectuals and the possibility of them helping her with childcare was never offered or mentioned. There was a tacit understanding that this would just not happen. Her own parents, also intellectuals, had joked long before she had a child that they could not be expected to act like previous generations of grandparents; this post-Mao generation of grandparents might instead engage in part-time employment even after retirement or prefer a postprofessional life of leisure. Another employer said that her parents-in-law "[had] their own life, such as playing the stock market, going to the university for elderly people [*laonian daxue*], watching TV, or going dancing," and they were willing to pay for the expenses of hiring a nanny for the grandchild so as to relieve themselves of the obligation. One man jokingly complained that his parents, retired doctors, "indulge[d] themselves in an easy and comfortable life" and were willing only to supervise a domestic worker who took care of his young child. With intense investment in the only child to prepare him or her for globalized market competition (Anagnost 2004), many urban professional parents today also have reservations about handing their children to grandparents, who are likely to overindulge the grandchildren and will not follow the "scientific way" of childcare promoted in numerous books for new parents. Whether young parents or grandparents hire a domestic helper, many grandparents today are willing to keep a disciplinary eye on the hired helper, but are reluctant to be fully involved in child-rearing and domestic work.

Laid-off Women Workers

It was not until the late 1990s that a very small number of urban laid-off women workers reluctantly entered paid domestic service. Beijing employers often compare the pros and cons of urban domestic workers vis-à-vis rural migrant domestic workers. Laid-off women workers are considered to have higher suzhi (quality) because they more easily understand the lifestyle of their employers and to be "safer" because they have permanent Beijing residence and, therefore, have "roots" in Beijing, unlike migrant domestic workers, who are "rootless." But employers complain that domestic workers from Beijing are about 200 yuan more per month, that they "put on airs," and that "their concern for face" (*ai mianzi*) makes it difficult for employers to order them around. It is not a big secret that urban laid-off workers in domestic service usually conceal the nature of their work from their own families. Because paid domestic work is associated with servility, taking on this line of work for Beijing laid-off workers is like adding insult to the injury of losing the status of being an industrial worker at a state-owned enterprise.

Many employers themselves also feel a little reluctant to order around a middle-aged laid-off worker as they might a young rural domestic worker. The formerly observed Maoist equality is more obviously and embarrassingly breached when Beijingers confront each other as employers and employees in the domestic sphere. One employer emphasized to me that she did not treat her Beijinger domestic worker like she would rural women: "Because she used to work in a state-owned enterprise, she already has a habitual psychology [*xiguan de xinli*]. For example, state units usually distribute benefits in-kind to the employees around holidays. . . . Now when she sees us bringing these benefits home . . . she says, 'We have no *danwei* [state unit] to care for us any more.' So we share some of our holiday benefits with her." Some middle-aged intellectuals who came of age in the Mao era are also not entirely comfortable with the practice of using paid domestic service. One conscientious woman intellectual admitted that she felt a bit nervous and uneasy in the presence of her domestic worker. "It feels like, how should I put it, as if I were sitting on a rickshaw or in a sedan chair, even though I have paid for it. . . . It's a bit like a relationship between the landlord class and the peasant class. . . . So in the presence of my baomu, I feel a bit nervous and always try to busy myself with something. I cannot let her be busy while I appear leisurely." She attributed this uneasiness to the Mao-era education that she received when she was young. The legacy of the Maoist notion of equality is still present in some instances of this employment relationship, carried in the subjectivity of both employers and employees, and it produces a discomfort for both parties in this new relationship. To abate the uneasy feeling, employers supplement this employment relationship with a higher wage or extra gifts, as if the Maoist past requires such sacrifices and supplements.

Elderly neighborhood women are sometimes asked to be temporary domestic helpers as well. Although some of these women may never have had full-time employment themselves, they, too, had their subjectivity transformed during the Maoist decades of mass mobilization and neighborhood activism. A woman with a U.S. master's degree who works as a business consultant at a private firm hired an elderly woman in her neighborhood for several hours of daily house cleaning. She diagnosed that her employee "has no master-servant consciousness [*zhupu yishi*] and has a rather poor awareness of the meaning of 'service' [*fuwu yishi bijiao cha*]." "She does not have a consciousness of 'being hired' [*mei you 'beigu' de yishi*]. If she breaks something in my home, she will complain that my kitchen is too small and chaotic or too dim for her to see!" This employer lamented, "Because she is a Beijinger, I'm more polite with her and more reluctant to give her orders." In the eyes of this employer, this elderly neighborhood woman appears "clueless" about how she should behave in the new employment relationship in post-Mao China and brings an attitude and subjectivity to work that are anachronistic, being a holdover from the Mao era. Employers who are junior in age often compromise with their elderly employees, as they cannot quite ignore how these elderly women's words and judgment influence communal opinions that carry an increasingly limited power in neighborhoods constructed in the Mao and early reform eras.[18]

Some employers choose not to hire neighborhood elderly women because they do not want to be bothered with the "extra" elements in the employment relationship—considerations of the seniority of the employees and compromises with employees' view of the nature of their relationship. An editor in her thirties who stopped employing an elderly woman from her neighborhood explained that she did not want to be bothered with the effort required on her part to "construct a good relationship" (*gaohao guanxi*) with the elderly employee, an effort that included using nice words with her employee (*shuo haohua*) and giving gifts as tokens of appreciation, such as "some apples this time and some eggs next time." The editor complained, "I don't understand why I have to exert myself trying to cultivate a good relationship with you if I already pay you. Neither I nor my husband likes this kind of complication. We just don't want to deal with it." Finding this kind of practice both amusingly outdated and irritating, she said she would rather give her employee a cash bonus once in a while than handle that kind of relationship, which seemed unnecessarily "complicated" in her eyes. Yet she knew that the elderly woman she employed would expect nothing less. Her irritation seemed to come from a frustration that money was not yet a sufficient value-expression of the employment relationship; given the supplements expected by the employee, the employer-employee dynamic did not seem to be a pure and proper one.

These two employers' observations were unexpectedly echoed by a Chinese couple working for the Chinese embassy in South Africa. They were telling me over dinner about their life in South Africa, when suddenly they turned to the topic of baomu in China.

> Instead of bringing our own drivers from China, our embassy should employ local drivers. Local drivers know the local situation and are more obedient. When it comes to a driver coming from China, it depends on his personality [*dei kan ta de piqi*]. If he has a good personality, then it is usually O.K. But if you're occupied with something and postpone lunchtime, the driver will complain. It's the same thing with baomu. In a place like South Africa, their baomu are used to waiting on employers [*xiguan le cihou ren*] and have service consciousness. In China baomu don't have that service consciousness. Sometimes you don't even know who's waiting on whom. You employ a baomu and you have to maintain a good relationship with her. You have to take note of how she feels [*zhaogu ta de qingxu*]. In South Africa things are as they should be. You don't have to worry about working out a good relationship with baomu.

What is problematized here is not just baomu, but the service labor force in China. Service workers have been openly criticized in urban China since the beginning of the reform for their lack of service consciousness and for what has been described as an imperious attitude toward customers. Foreign travelers also contributed anecdotes about the rude behavior of Chinese flight attendants and shop clerks during the early reform era. Two decades of criticism seem to have largely eroded the national collective memory of the political message in the stories of the People's Republic's first premier Zhou Enlai shaking hands and chatting with service workers from street cleaners to night soil workers. Today, new styles of service manners introduced by service businesses from Taiwan, Korea, and Japan have become established in China. Yet the legacy of the past lives on to various degrees among elderly neighborhood women, workers of state-owned companies, and rural migrants. Even if these people do not make explicit and conscious everyday demands for equality, they are not yet habituated to behaving deferentially to the satisfaction of their employers and social superiors. So the criticism of Chinese service workers that measures them against what is held to be the global norm continues. According to employers, domestic service is both where "service consciousness" is considered a most self-evident prerequisite, and where the lack of such consciousness is most scandalous and revealing about problems in China.

This frustration also reflects a widespread general irritation among business circles both in China and abroad at post-Mao China's inability to make a clean break from its entanglement with myriad social relations from the past. The editor and her husband later stopped employing the neighborhood elderly woman, instead hiring a migrant domestic worker. This is but a small, everyday incident mirroring the larger process of desiring and struggling toward a proper market economy on a national scale. Striving for international recognition as a market economy, the Chinese government, advised and supported by its ruling elites, is trying to quickly settle accounts with history, including a recent effort to end subsidies for bankrupt state-owned enterprises that it had previously subsidized, in order to settle accounts with laid-off workers. To quote the exact words used in *China Daily*'s announcement on 3 February 2005, stopping such subsidies is to put an end to this "historical problem."[19]

Rural Relatives

A more common source of help that urban employers mobilize is their rural relatives, who, although often considered to be burdens or nuisances, appear to be quite useful when the family needs a cheap and reliable nanny. Employers who are fortunate enough to have rural connections often find a distant relative to be more trustworthy than domestic workers from the labor market, which seems to consist of throngs of uprooted individuals whose real identities seem illegible and inscrutable due to their haphazard itineration on the market. Employers feel that a domestic worker found through their own rural connections will be much more reliable because her roots and identity are known (*zhigen zhidi*) and can be easily traced if anything happens. A former employer described her frantic search for a domestic worker through her rural connections: "In June 1996, several days before my child was born, we hired a relative from the northwest, where my husband's home village is. We could not trust just anyone [from the market]. We had to find a relative! Otherwise she might mistreat the child or even steal it. So we thought long and hard about whether we could find one from his home village. Later his father brought a twenty-year-old girl to Beijing, a distant relative. It's hard, as if there were too few relatives around and they were either too old or too young."

Among rural relatives, employers compare older with younger rural women in terms of their respective "merits." Some feel that older women are more steadfast, while younger ones in their late teens or early twenties, although more energetic, can be easily distracted by the city's novelties, so that their heart may not be fixed on work. Others worry that older women may be stubborn in their own ways of doing things and that the power balance may tip to the older women's advantage because of their seniority, whereas it is easier to give orders to younger women and initiate them into urban routines. Underlying these comparisons of relative advantages and disadvantages is a speculation about the use-value and affective value of the labor performance that a domestic worker is able to produce in relation to the degree of power compromise that employers may have to oblige.

But employers often face difficulties in turning their relatives into temporary domestic workers, a transformation that employer complaints indicate often fails to occur. Employers usually do pay their relatives, although the payment is "offered" and not negotiated, as both parties feel that negotiation is inappropriate in this kinship context. The rural relatives might even try to decline payment initially, unless their urban cousins insist on paying them: the rural relatives might say that they have come to "help out" and that monetary payment does not fit into the emotive context of their kinship relation. Soon, however, the employers may discover that their rural relatives do not really think of themselves as paid domestic workers. As one employer observed, "Relatives do not earnestly consider themselves as baomu in their heart and mind [*bushi chengxin chengyi dang baomu*]." (The "heart and mind" turn out to be the key sites where "goodness" and "propriety" is defined.) Some young unmarried rural relatives come with a hope that their urban relatives might be able to find them jobs in the city or even boyfriends, and this adds complications to the labor relationship, with which employers must deal tactfully. While employers may complain or keep to themselves their ridicule of such naïve expectations, they may not want to bring into the open their difficulty in fulfilling them.

Employers often find it difficult to directly criticize (*bu hao shuo*) a rural relative-turned-baomu, or to treat her as no more than a paid domestic worker, because the rural relative's complaint might detract from their reputation in their home or ancestral village. An employer recalled that she had had to suggest or remind her elder rural cousin to perform tasks, as she could not give her orders or simply tell her to go packing, as she would have with a domestic worker hired from the labor market. "You have to be tactful about this [*yao jiangjiu celüe*]," this employer said. Older relatives have age seniority on their side, while younger relatives could (although they rarely do) play up their junior status when they are in conflict with their relatives-turned-employers or when they feel the need to protest a certain treatment. A rare case I heard from an employer concerned her younger rural cousin who "acted up like a spoiled child" and, during a conflict, threatened to immediately return to her home village. Indeed, the relationship between a woman computer engineer and her rural cousin was the subject of Bi Shumin's story "Purple-Flowered Curtain." In this story the employer, "who has always been an outstanding engineer, a good wife, and a good mother, is now learning to be a master [*zhuren*]," and she "finds giving orders to others to be an interesting thing" (Bi Shumin 1996: 432). Yet her bumpy relationship with her cousin creates frustrations, which the employer manages with tactful maneuvers through trial and error. In my interviews some employers with experience in hiring rural relatives expressed a retrospective wish for what they thought they had missed out on: a simple, pure (*danchun de*), supposedly easier, and perhaps more satisfying employment relationship. In the eyes of these employers, kinship as a nonmarket social relationship distorted and spoiled the employment experience, but it also saved them from the confusing experiences that many others claim to have had in dealing with the market.

Migrant Domestic Workers

How do employers manage to discern proper and good baomu when they confront domestic-worker candidates in the market? In post-Mao society, where the "sea of commerce" has been engulfing almost every aspect of social life and the market economy is putting almost everything on sale and in circulation, the domestic space is increasingly imagined and guarded as the haven of leisure, relaxation, and a quality life where the self can be refreshed and recharged, leading to a contradiction between domestic life and domestic labor.[20] The haven of affluent homes is ironically more dependent on baomu, who are directly connected to the market. For some employers, the market offers the possibility of the "simpler and purer" labor relationship that they desire, but it is also a site of uncertainty, insecurity, and danger, as well as inauthenticity, where the proper is mimicked and the authentic pirated, and where baby-snatchers and criminals look like authentically proper migrants.

How to certify the good and the proper thus seems to be a hit-or-miss exercise that must nevertheless be conducted with as much prudence and insight as possible. Prospective employers hope they can read the faces and bodies of the "rootless" young migrant women—not that these migrants do not have roots, but their roots and labor history seem ambiguous, suspicious, and contaminated by their very itineration in the market. Employers often consult one another when making such appraisals. One employer consulted a friend who particularly prided herself on her ability to discern people: "My friend assured me [of the baomu she chose], 'In my view, she cannot be a wrong choice. I have a good eye for this sort of thing [*kan ren hen zhun*]. I'm sure she will not be a bad one.'" The CEO Mr. N visited and observed migrant women in a domestic-service company for several days before they selected one young woman: "We [he and his wife] went together and finally settled on one—we had been watching [the candidates] for several days and had been very careful with our selection. We didn't quite approve [of the candidates] [*ganjue bu xing*] and didn't dare to pick any. But feeling is arbitrary and people may feel quite differently."

With goodness and propriety seeming so elusive in the labor market, many employers desire migrant workers fresh from the countryside because they have not yet been contaminated by the market, not to mention that they accept smaller salaries. Big recruitment agencies, very much aware of the demand, organize a regular but limited supply of migrant women directly through their networks, which reach myriad locations in the countryside. Employers who hope to gamble for goodness in fresh labor make efforts to short-circuit the market, snatching up migrant women before they can even rest their feet. One employer described her effort: "I don't feel good about finding a baomu on the market. . . . More experienced colleagues told me that you should go in the early morning on such and such a day and wait outside [the recruitment agency] for the new ones to arrive. Migrants who have been in the city for a while are too slick. So I got to the recruitment agency before eight o'clock and its doors weren't open yet. I waited outside with many others. There was no line or anything. Then the door opened. Boom! We all rushed in. I felt bad—it was as if we were engaged in human trafficking—buying and selling human beings. I had no experience, because it was my first time. So I just looked for someone who seemed docile and had nice facial features, because I was looking for a nanny and an ugly nanny wouldn't be good for the child.[21] Before long, all these migrants were snatched up." This woman employer found a seventeen-year-old girl from Anhui who had come to Beijing for the first time.

This recruitment agency schedules the arrivals of young migrant women on two days each week. They are often chaperoned by cadres from county-level labor bureaus or women's federations. In the city all newcomer migrants must follow the fixed wage set for them by the recruitment agency, and they are not allowed to bargain with employers, while experienced migrants who have a file in the agency are allowed to bargain for their wages. Being cheaper and fresher from the countryside, these young women find themselves awaited and surrounded by eager employers. Often, almost all of seventy or eighty new migrants are snatched up within two hours.

Employers feel that young women fresh from the countryside, uncontaminated by the market, are more malleable and impressionable and can more easily be made to suit individual employers' needs. Both employers and recruitment-agency directors have told me that new migrants are like "a blank slate" (*yi zhang bai zhi*), a metaphor that eerily recycles Mao's comparison of the young People's Republic, mired in poverty, to a blank slate on which a new picture could be drawn and China's new socialist citizenry refashioned. The application of this metaphor to new migrant women, however, assumes that they have no subjectivity of their own and merely await the masterminds of the employers to endow them with the proper training and subjectivity. And such acquired subjectivity would reflect and confirm the authority and authorship of employers' subjectivity and be the hopeful seed of propriety. The original meaning of the blank slate is thus turned on its head, one of many conceptual somersaults of the post-Mao era that recycle earlier ideological formulations

PART II: THE PROPER BAOMU

and make them generate new meanings in new mobilizations for a market economy.

The desire for bodies "outside" the normal circuit of the labor market prompts employers to search for young women from *lao qu* [old liberated areas], poor interior regions that served as revolutionary bases for the Communist Army before 1949 and today as margins and frontiers of the market economy. These areas are now being mobilized as labor-supply bases for post-Mao market development. Recruitment agencies sometimes informally advertise to some employers that a specific group of young migrants are supplied from a certain lao qu. The irony and paradox in employers' desire to short-circuit the market is that the market has to be both present and absent in linking the domestic worker to the domestic space of affluent homes. It is the labor-market circuit that enables the supply of fresh labor power, yet it is also the market that must be short-circuited as much as possible for the commodity to be more desirable and assimilable into the private and secure domestic space.[22]

From "A Blank Slate" to "One Heart and Mind": Body and Subjectivity

The question of why there is a constant lack of "appropriate" (*heshide*) baomu invites one to ask what the desired propriety consists of. If domestic service companies and some employers compare fresh migrants from the countryside to a blank slate, then what picture of propriety would they like to draw? One can find a clue in a letter, addressed to employers, composed by a major domestic-service company in Beijing. The letter is attached at the end of a manual called "A Required Reading for Domestic Workers" ("Jiating fuwu-yuan bidu" 1998). The letter offers earnest suggestions for employers on how to avoid misunderstanding and mitigate tension with domestic workers, and it concludes confidently and understandingly: "We believe that if you pay attention to these points, domestic workers will be of one heart and mind with you [*he nin yi xin yi yi*]" (1998: 277). It is this—the notion of domestic workers who are "of one heart and mind" with their employers—that defines the desired propriety.

"Of one heart and mind" points to the goal of a subjective transformation of the domestic worker: her subjectivity should properly perceive and answer the needs of her employers. "Baomu" offers an exemplary case in Xiao Ling. The final revelation of the story links the enigma of this uniquely perfect baomu with her closet-intellectual identity, encouraging a reading of Xiao

Ling as capable of being a perfect baomu only because she was an aspiring and hardworking intellectual. Although working as a baomu, she was really the same as the family she worked for, of the same heart and mind. While Xiao Ling required no training at all, those whom Ms. Li found difficult to train were damned as "piles of dead flesh," that is, bodies without subjectivity.

Compared with "piles of dead flesh," "a blank slate" also represents migrant domestic workers as pure bodily power devoid of subjectivity. Although both views are based on an erasure of migrant women's rural-based knowledge, "a blank slate" is a particularly useful discursive tactic to encourage employers' agency and authority to inscribe a new form of subjectivity. This commodity of pure labor power is waiting to be inscribed with instruction and training, and it is in need of developing a subjectivity that will match that of its employers so as to render its domestic labor motivated and affective. This training of migrant women's subjectivity, mediated by the notion suzhi (quality), is framed as "improving the suzhi" of migrant women (*tigao suzhi*). The presumption that migrants are ignorant and lacking in subjectivity, characteristics increasingly coded as "low suzhi," is not the creation of urban employers and recruiting companies; it is constructed by the discourse of post-Mao modernity, collectively authored by the post-Mao elites. Suzhi has been linked with a wide range of descriptors and indexes for traits associated with the imagination of modernity and development: formal education, civility, discipline, initiative, cosmopolitanism, and so on. As a measurement of a person's level of modern quality, particularly that of subjectivity, suzhi has expanded and diffused from being a totalizing index of a population to also distinguishing among social groups and individuals. Of course, not all employers are interested or engaged in improving the suzhi of their domestic workers. There are many who think of domestic service as a matter of wage-labor exchange and, beyond giving orders, have little interaction with their employees. The more "enlightened" employers tend to take an interest in the subjective transformation of their domestic workers, and they tend to believe that by doing so they are helping those workers.

Yet domestic-service companies and employers also know that migrant women are not really blank slates. Domestic workers, regardless of their age and experiences, are sometimes instructed by domestic-service-company managers to think of themselves as new learners in the city, to erase their rural-based knowledge and experiences because these have no value or use in the city. If anything, migrant women are told that "prior" experiences interfere with their ability and willingness to learn new knowledge in urban households. It is thus admitted that "a clean slate" is not a natural state of blankness, but rather something that must be actively created by erasing, condemning, and liquidating the value of rural-based knowledge and experiences that migrant women have accumulated.

One male employer in his thirties who hired a domestic worker for his child commented, "In the countryside they raise children just like they raise pigs and dogs." This line of thinking sits well in the context of the post-Mao rural-urban dichotomy in which the rural has become a synonym for backwardness (*luohou*) and ignorance (*yumei*) and is thus outside modernity and progress. The damning comment from this employer, a mild-mannered, college-educated engineer who himself had spent his childhood in the countryside with his grandparents, seems to demonstrate the gravitating power of the post-Mao discourse of urban-privileged modernity. Of course this employer did not think his casual comment was a condemnation of rural nurturing; rather, he thought he was reiterating common knowledge. After all, isn't it true that no urban parents today would consider sending their children to the country-side to be raised by rural relatives, even though that was not an uncommon practice among cadres, as well as intellectuals, in the recent past? This shift of practices, which carries the implication that the future of the nation can no longer be nurtured in the countryside, has come from a profound restructuring of the rural-urban relationship from the Mao era to the post-Mao project of modernity.

This illustrates the power of discourse to code as fact and common sense that which is produced by political and social processes, which, being little questioned, legitimately and actively participate in the expanded discursive re-production of sociopolitical reality. The "fact" that rural childrearing is primitive and stupefying implicitly highlights the modern, stimulating, and value-adding urban nurturing that actively pursues the development of the child's physical, intellectual, and cultural suzhi. The animalistic imagery of "pigs and dogs" suggests a damning, yet deserved, destiny of rural youth as manual laborers on the low rung in social evolution and global competition, seemingly evidenced by the massive rural-to-urban labor migration.

Employers see untrained domestic workers as bodies without proper subjectivity or motivation. If Ms. Li's stark and grotesque metaphor for bodies without intelligence and subjectivity is "a pile of dead flesh," employers in real life commonly complain that domestic workers are rather "like abacus beads — they won't move until you make them move; if you make them move once, they move only once." They have eyes, but they do not see. "Her eyes do not see work" (*yan li mei huo'er*) is a common complaint employers make after hiring a novice domestic worker. As a director of a domestic-worker recruitment agency described a migrant domestic worker, "It seems that after she comes to an employer's home, she does not understand what to do. I think it has to do with her level of schooling. The main thing [to account for this] is her lack of suzhi. She just can't see where work is." Employers who have hired and fired a number of domestic workers complain that they have to train new domestic workers into recognizing work so that they can see it.

To make these untrained and unmotivated bodies work, the minds of employers have to repeatedly act on them. Thus, to train a domestic worker is to foster a proper subjectivity, so that she can see work and respond readily to it. Her "improved" subjectivity is supposed to mediate between the mind of the employer and her own body, thus producing knowing, willing, and affective labor that can anticipate and meet the needs of employers. In this process the worker has to learn and accept new definitions of housework and new standards of cleanliness different from those at her rural home.

While employers tend to see unresponsiveness to work as evidence of a low level of suzhi, ignorance, or laziness, the process of being initiated into the new domestic space is often one of anxiety, disorientation, and frustration for new domestic workers. The domestic space at an employer's reflects a different system of signification that a worker is now suddenly immersed in, but cannot quite decipher. How are household objects related to each other, where are their proper locations, when do they require cleaning and how? What is her relationship with the space and the object in question? Can she enter a certain space without supervision? Which objects is she allowed to use? Here a couch is not just a couch or a DVD player a DVD player. They compose an order and space of domesticity that is alien, illegible, estranging, and dominating, and that negates the knowledge and experiences that the worker has brought with her.

Domestic workers are often forbidden to watch TV when they are alone, and they are not supposed to let their friends visit them when employers are away. Sometimes a domestic worker must make illicit uses of household ob-

jects, away from her employer's radar. In the story "Purple-Flowered Curtain,"
while the domestic worker Xiao Ji, the rural cousin of the employer, is taking
a class broadcast on TV, she hears the key unlocking the door.

> Who could it be? Using her female instinct, Xiao Ji quickly guessed that
> it must be her elder cousin [her employer]. She quickly glanced around: the
> room was very neat; Feifei, an infant in her charge, was also clean from head
> to toe; only a bowl was left soaking in the sink. . . .
>
> "Students, please turn to page 90, . . ." a gentle voice interrupted
> Xiao Ji.
>
> How could [I] have forgotten! Xiao Ji hurried over, turned off the TV,
> and replaced its cover. . . .
>
> Xiao Ji was nervous and knew that it was the master [zhuren] making a
> random inspection of her work.
>
> Luckily, everything was in order. . . . It should be apparent that Xiao Ji
> was a qualified baomu.
>
> But there was an awkward atmosphere in the room. It was an atmo-
> sphere in which only a moment ago one was in a different mood and thus
> could not completely turn around to another mood.
>
> With her usual composure, Ah Ning [the employer] scanned the room
> and noticed that the TV cover was slanted. She walked over and readjusted
> it. She touched the TV screen with her fingertip. It was warm. (Bi Shumin
> 1996: 457)

Away from her employer's radar, the domestic worker Xiao Ji creates a different, yet illicit, ephemeral world in which she can be a student and momentarily and partially escape her subject position as a domestic worker. The escape
is partial because she cannot completely forget her position even when she
is alone, and her sensory antenna are still on guard. A click in the keyhole is
enough to jolt her back to the real world.

In this alien domestic space, the content of labor appears elusive. In my
interview Xiaohong described the learning-to-labor process in which she was
mentally exhausted by her pursuit of "labor."

> Then, *aiya* [sigh], day after day I just didn't know what to do. I couldn't see
> where work was and didn't know what to do. So tiring! My heart was too
> tired! Think of it: you are at your employers' home to do work, but you

can't see work. Wouldn't you feel worried? If you can see work, then you do it and feel settled in your heart. But if you don't know what to do and still have to run around looking for things to do, then it's truly tiring. . . . I was so anxious. One month seemed to last over a year. I felt that time was stretched without limit. When I was in my village, I played and worked all day and my heart wasn't tired. I didn't even feel the existence of time. *Aiya*, after I came to Beijing, a day was just so long. . . . My boss stayed at home for maternity leave. I couldn't see work and yet I was always in front of her eyes. . . . I couldn't just sit there resting. . . . This is why it's so tiring.

What aggravated the ordeal for Xiaohong was the continuous presence of her employer while she was on an anxious wild-goose chase after the elusive content of labor. This ordeal ended when she finally became familiar with the language of the domestic order through which she began to see work with her own eyes.

From "A Blank Slate" to "One Heart and Mind": How One Class Reforms Another

The pedagogical process of working on the blank slate and improving migrant women's suzhi involves one class speaking to another "which has neither the same ideas as it nor even the same words" (Foucault 1979, 276). Insofar as young rural women do not have the same ideas or words, they are treated as blank slates, without words or ideas at all. Learning to labor through this new literacy of domesticity marks an important step toward the further transformation of a migrant woman's subjectivity required for a proper baomu. The transformation of migrants' subjectivity in the city is a constant and fascinating topic for urban media and urban employers. The uninitiated bodies of migrant women and their supposed lack of a modern subjectivity mark both a limit and a task for the national pedagogy of modernization.

It is through these young women's transformation that modernity confirms and parades its universality. Ms. Wang was very pleased and proud to talk about the changes in one particular domestic worker her family hired.

Xiao Yan's change was particularly spectacular! [Of course] all those who have worked for us have undergone significant changes. You just need to compare the picture of her when she first came here and her later pictures.

Simply not the same person! This change is most of all in the appearance of her consciousness [*jingshen mianmao*]. She is from a small place, after all, and didn't know very much. When she first came, she looked like a hick [*tutu de*], and she was timid in speaking. After she came, she quickly learned our habits. She watched TV and watched how we would interact with people. She would mimic us. Then we also often talked to her. I had the best relationship with her [among all the baomu she had hired]. She was quite pure. I often told her that she should learn more things. . . . Sometimes we also talked about her sister's relationship with her boyfriend. I would tell her my views and I always told her how it should be. All of these things must have had an influence on her. . . .

My husband is very good. He would say that Xiao Yan was rather hardworking and had no time for fun. He felt that if this went on for long, she would not be in a good mood and would not do her best in taking care of our baby. So he suggested that I take her out for fun. When we went out together, I would comment on fashion, on how one should dress oneself, and so on. The clothes she wore and things she liked when she first came were very different from when she left. . . . She also became experienced and proper in taking messages and receiving guests. . . . I really liked her. She was like one of the family. She was especially good to our son. Sometimes when I was upset about my work, I would lose patience with my son and even scold him. But she had never been like that to my son. She had always been particularly good to him. I really liked her.

Ms. Wang's narration places her domestic worker in a productive circulation of suzhi and affective labor between employers and their domestic worker. Ms. Wang herself emphasizes how much and how often she had *talked* to Xiao Yan and how her talking had initiated a "pure" "hick" Xiao Yan into a process of suzhi improvement, covering everything from everyday social protocols to topics of consumer tastes, love, and marriage. As Xiao Yan acquired a new subjectivity through mimicking her employers, Ms. Wang found her more capable, efficient, and proper at work. The employers reasoned that their investment in Xiao Yan, which joined suzhi education with entertainment in their outings, was transferred back to them, particularly to their son, by Xiao Yan's impressive acts of patient and attentive labor. Indeed, Xiao Yan's abundant return of affective labor seemed to be a pleasant surprise to Ms. Wang.

In Ms. Wang's narration, Xiao Yan's ability and willingness to perform motivated and affective labor depends on her becoming a willing participant in the
new world of modern domesticity and is thus linked with a transformation
in her subjectivity. After two years, Ms. Wang, through her family connection
with the head of Xiao Yan's home county, found Xiao Yan a job as a cook in
a middle school in the county seat and said that Xiao Yan had written to her
once or twice a year after going home.

For the domestic worker to be of one heart and mind, the pedagogical
work does not necessarily shy away from talking about both the interest of
an employer and that of her domestic worker. Ms. D's relationship with her
domestic worker Leilei shows how the issue of interests is dealt with and how
the language of one class speaks to the other and attempts to bring the other
into "the family." Ms. D was a single mother. She had been a physician, but,
after living abroad for several years, she returned to work for an insurance
company—a new line of business in post-Mao China. Ms. D had a close
relationship with her eighteen-year-old migrant domestic worker, Leilei, who
had not finished her junior-high-school education and had been working for
Ms. D for a year. During my research in Beijing, Ms. D had a number of can-
did discussions with me about her relationship with Leilei. Ms. D. was more
reflexive, thoughtful, and conscientious than many of the employers I have
interviewed about the employment relationship. Not only did she encourage
Leilei to read in her spare time, but she also had many discussions with Leilei
about life philosophy, such as the need to eat bitterness, the need to strive for
success, and so on. "She does not understand everything. It's not possible that
at her age she knows how to deal with everything. At my home, whatever she
doesn't understand, I have to teach her."

A situation arose that presented Ms. D an opportunity to talk Leilei into a
new perspective on progress and alliance.

Her best friend in her native place gave her a call and asked her to go back
for her engagement ceremony. It seemed they had various kinds of customs
there. It seemed that one must attend the engagement ceremony, otherwise it would not be possible for one to attend the wedding. She muddle-
headedly [hu li hu tu] agreed. She had never had experience with this sort
of thing. Later two friends of hers would get married and invited her to
attend their weddings. She asked me for permission to leave. I told her that

she had a job here and she could not just go back for anyone. I asked her, "What do you think?" She said, "I don't want to make this trip back either. The New Year is coming. So I don't want to make two trips home." I said, "Yes. First, let's not think from [the perspective of] my need whether you should make this trip: from the perspective of this job, you should not and cannot make this trip. But from the perspective of your life, think about it: since your friends will get married one after another, it's not appropriate that you attend some of their weddings and not others, right?" So I told her how, when I moved away from an earlier circle of friends, I was no longer able to participate in things related to that circle. . . . Now she and I can often think alike. I feel that she has gradually assimilated herself into this family and life in Beijing. . . . So she easily accepted it [my advice], because she is in this situation—she has left her earlier circle of friends and can no longer participate in it.

Leilei's initial agreement to attend her best friend's engagement was dismissed by Ms. D as a muddle-headed decision. According to Ms. D, Leilei's logic was a lack of logic, and her thinking was a lack of thinking. It was not enough for Leilei to give up her plan on the basis of the practical inconvenience of making two trips home in a short span of time. Ms. D earnestly conducted with Leilei what could be called "thought work" about the trajectory of individual progress.[23] Using herself as an example, Ms. D positioned Leilei in an irreversible progress from her association with her native place to an association with this family and life in Beijing, a progress that asserted "this family and life in Beijing" as primary and teleological. This logic thus framed Leilei's continued friendship and obligation to her rural friends as potentially detrimental to her progress and, therefore, better left behind. The first perspective, Ms. D's need and dependence on Leilei's work, was tactfully set aside, only to be reinforced a moment later when Ms. D's thought work on individual progress demonstrated to Leilei that her own interest now coincided with that of Ms. D's. This life philosophy, shared by Ms. D with Leilei, brought Leilei closer to Ms. D's needs and interests—to being "of one heart and mind," and so like one of the family.

Yet transforming migrant women into modern subjects is a precarious project of interpellation that needs to balance the double meaning of the subject: "subject to" as submission to an authority, and "subject of" as self-knowledge and identity. A danger always looms that a changed subject might become so ambitious as to act more in the sense of "subject of" and not enough in the sense of "subject to." Ms. Wang, for example, told of a distant rural relative who had once helped with her housework. "She really would like to live in Beijing and wanted to open a store. She has an especially untamed ambition [*tebie you yexin*]." Compared to Xiao Yan, her favorite baomu, this distant relative seemed to allow her identity as "subject of" to predominate over her identity of "subject to." Ms. Wang criticized her relative for having an untamed ambition or, literally, "wild heart" (*yexin*), because she seemed to have developed an improper self-knowledge as a "subject of" modernity that was insufficiently disciplined by her subject position as a baomu. Thus, the migrant woman has to be transformed and motivated in such a way that she will not perform labor like a passive abacus bead, but her interpellation should gravitate toward "subject to," so that she knows her social station.

Training migrant domestic workers involves balancing between the double meanings of the subject. It is thus a nuanced business for professionals and other elite groups to balance between maintaining their own class privilege and encouraging class mobility. In this sense, the notion of suzhi improvement is both a discourse of universal mobility acting on every individual and a hegemonic process of a class speaking to and acting on another class in everyday practice. "Subject to" is not only subjection to the power of discourse but also subjection of domestic workers to professionals and intellectual elites as speaking agents of power.

What is the proper subjectivity that a trained domestic worker should have? Ms. D felt satisfied with what her influence had produced: in her perspective, Leilei had matured considerably and had almost completely changed in how she talked and thought. But Ms. D recalled with amusement that once, when asked what her dream was, Leilei thought hard about the question and replied slowly, "That we have a new home, free from cockroaches." Ms. D was both amused and surprised by its triviality, "That's the dream you have?" Compared to the domestic worker that Ms. Wang criticized for having untamed ambition, Leilei demonstrated that her subjectivity and even her dream was derivative of her employer's—not only derivative but also diminutive. Yet one also wonders whether Leilei's pause and slow speaking reflected an effort to craft an answer that would both carefully place her own subjectivity within bounds that her employer would deem proper and undermine its gravity.

"One of the Family?" Managing a Commodity with Affect

But an employment relationship that requires labor power to be a commodity, as well as to have affective value, sometimes gives rise to the possibility of affect compromising the commodity nature of this relationship. Thus, affect is necessary, but needs to be carefully managed so that it does not contradict and compromise the commodity nature of the relationship. The following letter from Leilei's mother to Ms. D presents this contradiction, which prompted Ms. D to be more careful with managing the boundary.

> Hello Sister D,
> First of all I wish you good health. This is the third letter that I'm writing you. Probably you didn't receive any of the two letters that I had sent you before, because Leilei didn't write down your address for me correctly. . . . That's why the knit trousers that I mailed to Leilei were recently returned to me. . . .
> With pen in hand, I have so much to tell you. I'm really grateful that you're so kind to our Leilei and care about her as if she were your own daughter. Last time Leilei returned home and told us how well Aunt D has been treating her. When she was home, she kept talking of your home in Beijing just like her own home. You're just so very kind to her. She told us that Aunt D took her to many places that she had never been before, and she had a chance to see many new things. She told her grandparents and all her good friends how well you've treated her. Our whole family is so happy for her. In our mind you are truly noble and great. We cannot thank you enough for the true feeling you have shown our Leilei. We will not forget your kindness all our lives. . . . After our Leilei left, we began to raise two chickens to treat you when you come back with Xiao Fei for a visit. I wonder whether my wish will be satisfied. . . .
> Leilei's mama

The characters of Leilei's mother's handwriting were large and not very smoothly connected, filling several pages and suggesting a hand not used to writing. While showing the letter to me, Ms. D admitted that she felt flattered, surprised, and amused by the hyperbole used in the letter and that she certainly was not as good as described in the letter. She speculated that maybe Leilei wanted to raise her own status among friends and relatives by bragging about her employer to folks at home. "Maybe one can say it is a kind of like dependent growth [*yifu xing zengzhang*]?" While Ms. D used an economic term to construct her theory of Leilei's unreserved praise, the letter did prompt her to think more of her responsibility as Leilei's employer. "In essence she works for me and I pay her. . . . But she is a young adult. As her employer, I have some responsibility in training her, teaching her some skills, and improving her suzhi."

I pointed out to Ms. D the difference between her language of responsibility premised on an employment relationship and the sentimental and familial language of Leilei's mother. Ms. D agreed and said that she intended to keep a distance and did not want to be drawn into the affect offered by this letter. This incident triggered Ms. D's memory of her relationship with another rural family some years before. At the time, she had worked as a physician for a public hospital, and a rural patient had initiated a series of gift exchanges. The former patient had visited her whenever there was a chance, often bringing her fresh home-grown produce. However, Ms. D saw a difference in Leilei's case: "I feel that the employment relationship is the foundation of our interaction. Had it not been that I need to employ Leilei, we would not have been together." Leilei's strong exhibition of her identity with Ms. D's family both satisfied Ms. D and somewhat unsettled their employment relationship. Ms. D was aware of this contradiction and decided to resolve it. When Ms. D's sister came to visit them from Canada, the sister, who was rather unhappy with Leilei, played as Ms. D's double to speak to Leilei, as Ms. D imitated for me the tone and words of her sister's lecture to Leilei: "My sister is very good to you. Yes, that's apparent. But have you ever thought about why she's good to you? First of all, it's because you have made contributions to this family. You do your job well and she pays you. Second, the feelings that have developed are a secondary matter, a different matter. My sister does not have to be so good to you, right? She doesn't have to employ you. She can just as well employ someone else, whoever does a good job."

This statement was prompted by Ms. D's sister's observation that Leilei did not act like a baomu—for example, Leilei lay in her bed reading during the day. The lecture was intended to remind Leilei that her labor power was a disposable commodity and that the primary commodity nature of her labor power should not be eclipsed and compromised by affect. While employers often like to foreground affect in order to deflect the employment relationship (the cliché is "We treat her as one of the family"), in this case, because Leilei appeared to believe that she was indeed one of the family and behaved as such, she was reminded that affect was secondary and depended on her proper performance of labor. Although Ms. D did not approve of the harshness of her sister's language, she shared with her sister the conviction that the commodity character of Leilei's labor power was the primary aspect of their relationship, which could be supplemented, but not unsettled by affect.

If Ms. Wang managed a productive circulation between affect and labor through her domestic worker Xiao Yan's transformation, here Ms. D encountered the prospect of a different circuit of affect. The letter from Leilei's mother expressed the wish that Leilei's identity with Ms. D's family would be the beginning of a reciprocal relationship between the two families. Leilei's mother's invitation was a symbolic goodwill gesture of this reciprocity. Ms. D was wary about participating in a circulation of affect that would subject the market logic of employment to the moral and affective logic of Leilei's family and rural community. So she mused to me that she was not against visiting Leilei's family hundreds of miles away and that she could become more familiar with Leilei's family through the visit, but she paused, then commented, "Usually this kind of relationship between me and Leilei shouldn't involve me visiting her family as if we were relatives [*women zhe zhong guanxi shi bu yinggai zou qinqi de*]. So, China is very strange. I feel it's as if her family has adopted us as relatives." Ms. D was ambivalent: she had had a good relationship with a rural family before, but she was always conscious that now her relationship with Leilei was one of employment and that she needed to keep the authority to discipline, pay, and eventually terminate the relationship. By suggesting a Chinese inflection to the affective exchange, Ms. D translated her dilemma into a national allegory and made it part of a common problem that market logic in China is often entangled with heterogeneous logics and practices, and that it seems to have difficulty existing purely and properly. Ms. D and other employers share with some economists in China and elsewhere a fantasy about the ontological purity and self-adequate propriety of market logic. This fantasy purges from the market logic its close entanglement with politics and its suppressions and transformations of heterogeneous forms of sociality.

The common complaint that "it is hard to find a good or proper baomu" expresses the problem of how the mind of one class, mostly first-generation employers, mobilizes the body of another, first-generation domestic workers, in the post-Mao restructuring of sociality. This process of restructuring sociality is intimately tied in with the changing relationship and division between the countryside and the city, between manual and mental labor, and between men and women. This is the context from which domestic workers have emerged en masse to perform domestic labor for affluent urban households.

The labor power of the domestic worker is a special commodity not only because it is a source of surplus labor but also because it is a commodity with a subjectivity that is capable of affective labor. Generally, migrant women are the preferred source for domestic labor, and young migrant women from poor interior regions have a special currency because their subjectivity is conveniently seen as a blank slate, presumably waiting for transformation by the mastermind of employers. The modernization and pedagogical project taken up by some employers is to discursively mobilize the bodies of domestic workers through transforming migrant women's subjectivity. With such a transformation, a migrant woman's subjectivity mediates between the mind of the employer and her own body. Therefore, the subjectivity of migrant women is the very lever, the very process through which the mind of the employer class mobilizes the bodies of another class and transforms the bodies of migrants from a reservoir of raw labor power to a spring of affective labor needed for the production of a desired "quality" lifestyle and sociality.

The desired propriety of the employment relationship depends on a carefully managed balance that joins commodification and affect and maximizes affective labor. Self-consciously enlightened and urbane employers recognize that affect is necessary, but that it needs to be circumscribed and disciplined by the primary commodity nature of the relationship. Obstacles to achieving and stabilizing this ideal appear numerous, including the continued legacy of the Mao-era past that sometimes lives on in the consciousness and subconsciousness of both employers and domestic workers, heterogeneous social relations that bring rural or communal logic of affect into the employment relationship, and various contingencies of personalities and individual aspirations of employers and domestic workers.

With the availability of the labor of domestic workers, have intellectual and professional women been largely freed of their association with domestic work? To some extent. Yet they are not discursively freed from the gender question of domestic work that was displaced and represented as a class question. Baomu, as a domestic coolie whose labor is taken for granted and is least valued, stands as a double of and a substitute for intellectual and professional women or their mothers-in-law, who feel sometimes that they, too, serve the family like baomu—and unpaid ones at that.

With large numbers of women being laid off in the economic restructuring of the state-owned enterprises and more rampant gender discrimination in the hiring process from the 1990s onwards, more women have been reoriented to the domestic sphere as full-time or part-time housewives. The twenty-eighth baomu in the TV serial *Twenty-eight Baomu at Professor Tian's* turns out to be Professor Tian's own daughter, who has recently been laid off. This domestication of women has prompted some women to support "remuneration of domestic labor [for housewives] [*jiawu laodong baochou hua*]" as a way of visibly articulating the value of domestic labor (Zhang Meirong and Nan Song 1994: 58–62). Yet this proposal met strong resistance. One contributor to the discussion charged that discussing this issue was "fomenting discord" in conjugal relations: "You say, 'I do domestic work at home, which should amount to no less than five hundred yuan.' If your spouse is understanding, he might say, 'Fine, [I'll even] give you a hundred more.' . . . But if your spouse is not so understanding, he might say, 'Five hundred? A baomu is no more than three or four hundred. Don't you think you're asking too much?' Lo and behold, you've degenerated yourself to the position of a baomu" (Xun Da 1996: 30).

The warning in this message is clear: women who dare to demand remuneration for their domestic labor risk being compared to and treated as baomu. Whether "remuneration of domestic labor [for a housewife]" alone is an effective strategy to articulate the value of domestic labor is itself a debatable question that deserves a more extensive discussion.[24] What should be of immediate concern is the chiasmic play of gender and class; because the gender question of domestic labor gave way to a class question in the 1980s, class now comes to trouble the gender discussion of domestic labor and punishes this discussion by reducing it to class: women who dare open up this discussion are seen as putting themselves in the position of baomu, thus appearing to fall down a rung on the class ladder. Gender discussion of domestic labor is thus still haunted by the occlusion of gender by class. It is in this sense that even professional women who have a class solution to the problem of domestic labor are still not freed discursively. Any serious discussion of the value of domestic labor must, therefore, address the discursive value of domestic workers and undo this occlusion by bringing together the issues of gender and class.

The *Eastern Time-Space Program* (Dongfang shikong) of Chinese Central Television conducted a survey, which was reported in a show titled "It Is Not Easy to Be a 'Good' Baomu," airing 16 March 2005. The survey revealed a significant discrepancy between the expectations of employers and domestic workers.

When asked, "What is your biggest concern when hiring a baomu?" a total of 4,573 employers answered in the following distribution.

1. moral fiber (*daode pinzhi*): 57 percent
2. health: 24 percent
3. domestic common sense (*jiazheng changshi*): 16 percent
4. other: 3 percent

Employers were also surveyed on whether they could meet the expectations of domestic workers. A total of 5,741 persons responded to the following questions.

If a baomu demands to take one day off work a week, do you think it is reasonable?

reasonable: 49 percent
unreasonable: 51 percent

If a baomu demands to eat at the same table with your family members, do you think it is reasonable?

reasonable: 40 percent

unreasonable: 60 percent

If a baomu demands that you pay for her medical-care insurance, do you think it is reasonable?

reasonable: 17 percent

unreasonable: 83 percent[1]

3

SUZHI AS A NEW HUMAN VALUE
Neoliberal Governance of Labor Migration

Labor export is a social university [*shehui daxue*] that improves the quality
[*suzhi*] of peasants in all respects.

JIN YUANJU, "TIGAO NONGMIN SUZHI DE SHEHUI DAXUE" (A SOCIAL UNIVERSITY
THAT IMPROVES THE QUALITY OF PEASANTS), *ANHUI RIBAO*, 16 JUNE 1998

On a hot afternoon in July 1999 in the northern city of Tianjin, a dozen or so
young rural women are gathered inside a small waiting room of the municipal
family service company. Sitting on a narrow wooden staircase or standing
with their bodies leaning against each other, they are waiting for urban families to employ them as domestics. Outside, in the courtyard, more women
seek refuge in the shade as they, too, wait to be called. The room occupied
by the waiting women connects to an air-conditioned office via a sliding glass
door, which remains closed to keep out both the heat and the women outside.
Through its panes, however, the office staff inside keep an eye on the women,
whom the manager privately refers to as "smelly hicks" (*lao ta'er*).

Following the staircase up to the third floor, one can find the office of the
general manager. Here, the new wooden floor is smooth and gleaming. An air
conditioner hums quietly in one corner of the room, the abundant coolness in
the office testifying to its power. On the wall facing the manager hang several
red silk banners awarded for good performance by the municipal government
and the city branch of the All-China Women's Federation under the leadership
of the Chinese Communist Party. The office is very quiet.

This family service company, the largest among two hundred or so in the city of Tianjin, is officially attached to the Women's Federation although it is financially responsible for its own profits and losses.[1] However, in view of its hybrid private-public character, the company is expected not only to be economically profitable (*jingji xiaoyi*) but also to achieve a "social effect" (*shehui xiaoyi*): the migrant women who find employment here will rid themselves of poverty and develop their *suzhi* (quality), while also serving an important social service in easing the housework burden of the urban families who employ them.

The mission of this company points to the dual process of labor migration: labor migration critical for China's development is not only part of an economic process of exchange of labor power for wages, but is at the same time a social process that enables rural women to gain suzhi. The quick creation of a vast migrant-labor force within one decade, from the 1980s to the 1990s, has nurtured the expanding market economy while also presenting a grave challenge to social management for stability and, therefore, to the expanded reproduction of the market economy. Hence, the imperative to achieve a "good social effect" is in the mission of companies engaged with migration labor. This strategic mission belongs not only to these companies; it is also promoted by state agencies, their cadres, and elites generally.

Suzhi functions as an intangible but crucial operator in the process of migration and in the strategic mission of the state and its affiliated agencies. It was first officially designated a political keyword through a resolution passed by the sixth plenum of the Twelfth Party Congress in 1986, nearly a decade into the reform era. Entitled "A Resolution by the Central Committee of the Chinese Communist Party on the Guiding Principles of Socialist Spiritual Civilization," the resolution stressed "the moral suzhi and the scientific and cultural suzhi of the Chinese nation" and the agency of suzhi in history: "Human suzhi is a product of history, but also has an impact on the making of history" (Sha Lianxiang et al. 2001: 2). About two decades into the reform era, it was more centrally and comprehensively linked with the project of modernization by the Fifteenth Party Congress report presented in 1997 by then president Jiang Zemin, which called for "cultivating millions of high-suzhi laborers and skilled technicians to meet the demands of modernization."[2] Following this report, the most prominent party newspaper, *People's Daily*, carried an editorial entitled "Concentrate Efforts on Improving the Quality of the People of the Nation."

> The Chinese nation once created a brilliant culture for mankind. However, as a result of being backward and underdeveloped over a long period, the quality of the people in our country can hardly meet the requirements of modernization, and it has seriously restrained the economic and social development of our country. Especially today, when science and technology are developing rapidly and vigorously, the competition of comprehensive national strength intensifies day by day, and peace and development have become the main themes of the times: comprehensively improving the quality of the people of the nation has naturally become an urgent and important task before us. We must, from the strategic high plane of the long-term development of the country, and proceeding from the stern reality of international competition in the twenty-first century, deeply understand the important significance of improving the quality of the people of the nation, and comprehensively implement the task of building the culture put forward by the Fifteenth Party Congress.[3]

What is suzhi? How is it linked to the "culture" of post-Mao construction of a market economy? The editorial defines national suzhi as "the general level of the physique, intelligence, ideology, and ethics of the people of a country in the course of transforming nature and society." At the level of everyday speech and popular media, *suzhi*, for which "quality" is in many respects an inadequate translation, refers to the somewhat ephemeral qualities of civility, self-discipline, and modernity. Suzhi marks a sense and sensibility of the self's value in the market economy. As such, it is often used in the negative by the post-Mao state and educational elites to point to the lack of quality of the Chinese laboring masses. Improving the suzhi of China's massive population has become vitally important in the planning of governing elites for China to become a competitive player in the field of global capital. Organizations such as the family service company facilitate the exchange of labor for poverty relief and suzhi improvement. They form, therefore, a critical link that joins value transfer in the economic domain (surplus value) with that of the cultural domain (the value of personhood).

Suzhi is a key political-cultural-economic operator in the discourse of development, particularly in poverty-relief campaigns and labor migration. I propose that suzhi is a new form of value that represents human value to the teleology of development, and that alongside structural adjustment for the market economy, "national quality" (*guomin suzhi*) articulates a structural adjustment in the sphere of human subjectivity. A serious critique of China's engagement with neoliberalism must tackle structural adjustment in these two interrelated spheres, particularly the often overlooked sphere of subjectivity.

The Phantom Child of Development:
Suzhi as a New Form of Human Value

The Fifteenth Congress of the Chinese Communist Party in 1997 was a highly significant landmark in China's drive toward a market economy, as it elevated the private sector to the same level as the state sector in the "socialist market economy." The emphasis on suzhi by the Fifteenth Congress signaled that a certain logic of development, with suzhi at its core, had reached a new summit of discursive power. Suzhi began its prominent career in the early 1980s in the context of the post-Mao eugenics discourse of striving for "superior birth and nurture" (*yousheng youyu*).[4] Stringent population planning had zoomed in on the rural population as an object of intense anxiety for political and intellectual elites. In this light, the rural population appeared as a tumorous mass—large in quantity, low in quality—encumbering the national body that strove to join the world of global capital through its policies of "reform and opening."[5] Such representations have become ubiquitous since the mid-1980s, when, for example, Chinese Central Television's 1986 "New Year's Gala" included a minidrama ridiculing the peasant "over-birth-quota guerrillas" (*chaosheng youjidui*) who hid to evade official birth control. The image of abject poverty among rural households, further burdened by "too many" children, marks rural people not only as low-quality and intractable, lacking modern civility and discipline; but, perhaps more important, rural people are seen as lacking a *consciousness* of development that the post-Mao Chinese state has been striving to foster through reform and opening.

Within the two decades of reform, suzhi has permeated official as well as everyday speech. For example, one constantly hears statements such as "We must urgently improve the suzhi of the Chinese population." The low suzhi of peasants is so frequently invoked that a reader complained in a letter to the editor of the nationally distributed newspaper *Nanfang zhoumo* (Southern Weekend), "The low suzhi of peasants has become an excuse for many things not getting done or not getting done well."[6] Despite this complaint, the letter does not argue with the deeply entrenched premise that development depends on the improvement of peasant suzhi. Rather, it goes on to complain that one of the reasons why peasant suzhi is low is because those who occupy official positions look down on peasants and thereby prevent them from improving their suzhi. An article in a prestigious party magazine (Liu Xiuming 1996) suggests a more sympathetic view of the rural population, making the point that peasants were the foundation of Chinese civilization and should be treated as the basis for planning development. However, by the end of this article, the author returns from his reverie on the glorious historical achievements of China's peasantry to speak in a more pragmatic tone: "But [we] must admit that, generally speaking, the suzhi of Chinese peasants is not high. The grave concern is to educate the peasantry. And this adage should be applied to the fullest extent to include all political, economic, and cultural aspects" (ibid.: 41). The lesson to be drawn from history and current reality is that the peasantry should not be despised as the antithesis of Development, but that they should be placed at the very center of policies directed toward Development.

I use "Development" with a capital D to refer to a certain discourse of developmentalism promoted by organizations of North-dominated international capital, such as the International Monetary Fund (IMF) and the World Bank.[7] Since the 1980s, the state and elite groups in China have increasingly committed themselves to the idea of globally integrated, market-oriented national development. In the aftermath of the 1989 social movement, pro-market developmentalism has become a more forceful and explicit ideology in state-orchestrated reforms that have radically transformed social and economic life at all levels of Chinese society. It is through this commitment that the post-Mao state defines and builds its legitimacy.

Although *suzhi* as a social keyword lies at the heart of the discourse of development in post-Mao China, what suzhi is eludes precise definition. At a national conference in 1987, scholars disagreed on its exact meaning, but were able to propose four possible definitions (Li Shuqing 1988). The first of these divided suzhi into "hardware," or embodied physical quality, and "software," which referred to a wide range of cultural qualities (*wenhua suzhi*), including psychological quality (*xinli suzhi*) and quality of thought (*sixiang suzhi*). The other three proposals offered at least three alternative sets of categories that could be used to evaluate population quality. Despite all these efforts, the meaning of suzhi eludes grasp. Nonetheless, the conference report states authoritatively that "suzhi [however defined] is for the most part higher in the city than in the countryside, higher in Han areas than in minority areas, higher in the economically advanced areas than in backward areas" (ibid.: 60). On the international level, the commonly heard view is that "the quality of the Chinese as a whole is too low."[8] And populations in the developed First World have higher suzhi than those in the Third World. What suzhi is, therefore, appears to be most confidently stated in terms of a differential.

The phrase "for the most part" in the statement above reveals the hegemonic status of this truth claim. However, this statement betrays a strange logic. The use of suzhi as the key to understanding China's "backwardness" — in particular, the low level of "development" in rural and minority areas — is, in the final analysis, measured and indexed in terms of economic Development. Attempts to define suzhi in this way are, it would seem, tautological. The telos of Development appears at the origin — as the lack of Development — to explicate and reaffirm Development as the endpoint of a necessary process. Suzhi is, therefore, nothing more (nor less) than Development's phantom child. As Development hardens as the "indisputable logic" (*ying daoli*) that reorients postsocialist China toward global capitalism, suzhi has likewise solidified its substantiality in the social space.[9] It becomes an indisputable mapping of the demographic and cultural landscape that explains various levels of Development in the political imaginary of the Dengist state. The teleological promise of Development to improve the suzhi of the Chinese masses masks this tautological relationship. It evangelizes an idealist interpretation of the politico-historical processes that have produced the *difference* between "developed" and "underdeveloped" areas, the First World and the Third World, and the differentiation of the "Four Worlds" emerging within the Chinese nation-space.[10]

The efforts to treat suzhi as an already existing object for scientific analysis, exemplified by this national conference, presume that suzhi has a substantive existence. It has indeed become a field of study and a subject of learning reflected in many academic articles and media commentaries and editorials, as well as monographs.[11] The analysis aims at a positivist classification and measurement, representing suzhi as a quantifiable materiality, despite its apparently indefinable character. Statistics about suzhi include distribution of educational attainments within the nation, as well as among rural households over a number of years. Such statistics also take in national and regional percentages of illiteracy, the distribution of skills among rural laborers, and percentile correlations between levels of education and production and consumption choices made by rural households. Statistical comparisons are also made between "traditional peasants" and "modern peasants" with regard to their dependence on land, relations with people inside and outside the community, skill levels, willingness to take risks, and respective responses to social transformation. There are surveys that investigate the level of modernization of individuals (*geren xiandaihua*) and use a five-point scale to measure twelve indexes of modernization (*xiandianhua zhibiao*): consciousness for competition, efficiency and timeliness, attentiveness to information, planning, confidence, political participation, trust, personal autonomy, willingness to take risks, spirit of innovation, desire for achievement, and ability to collaborate (Sha Lianxiang et al. 2001: 145). These indexes, dividing "traditional" from "modern" peasants, recode and replay the binary descriptors of Orientalist national characterization of "Chinese" vis-à-vis "Westerners."

The most quantifiable index of suzhi is, perhaps, the evaluation or appraisal of embodied labor through wages. Other articulations and quantifications of suzhi include various kinds of psychological and practical ability tests and IQ tests offered by popular publications.[12] Since 1995, schools (both public and private) and universities have been revising their curriculum for suzhi education (*suzhi jiaoyu*).[13] For example, Nanjing Normal University now issues a suzhi diploma in addition to its regular academic diploma to enhance opportunities for their graduates in the job market.[14] What such practices suggest is that the development of suzhi is by no means limited to rural people; it is a general project for improving the "quality" of the population as a whole, although clearly operating differently at different levels of socioeconomic privilege, not to mention suzhi's packaging as a profitable commodity. In June 1999 the Central Committee of the CCP and the State Council issued "A Resolution to Deepen Educational Reform and Promote Suzhi Education on All Fronts." The opening statement of this resolution reads as follows: "In today's world, science and technology are progressing by leaps and bounds; a knowledge economy [*zhishi jingji*] is emerging; global competition for national strength is increasingly fierce. Education is fundamental to the comprehensive formation of national strength, which is increasingly measured by the suzhi of workers and on the development of a pool of talented human resources. This places a more urgent demand on educating and training the new generation for the twenty-first century."[15]

According to the text of this resolution, educational infrastructure and methods lag behind the new demands being made on them and therefore "cannot meet the need for improving the quality of the people of the nation." Yet even amid all the fanfare surrounding educational-reform policies to improve suzhi, once again no definitive meaning is given. Despite its indefinability, the notion of suzhi thrives as a social fact, provoking quantitative and qualitative measurement.[16] The catch-all nature of suzhi is mocked by a rhyming couplet popular among educators: "Suzhi education is a basket; anything can be placed in it" (suzhi jiaoyu shi ge kuang, shenmo dou keyi wang li zhuang).

The rhyme quite ingeniously suggests that the discourse of suzhi may have to be suitably empty and indefinable for it to function as a catch-all discursive basket. But this is no ordinary basket; it is a magical one that reframes whatever goes into it, creating strange bedfellows. In addition to labor and education, much more has been put into the basket: history, peoples, culture, economy, and ideology. It is quite stunning to see how recent publications retroactively represent suzhi as a universal form of human value embedded in various kinds of social, political, and economic theories. For example, *Zhongguo nongmin suzhi lun* (On the Quality of Chinese Peasants) includes quotations by Marx on humankind and Lenin on knowledge, which are placed in the section titled "Marxism-Leninism on suzhi"; quotations by Mao on the peasantry and Deng Xiaoping and Jiang Zemin on suzhi from the section "Statements by Three Generations of Leaders of the Party and State"; a section called "Theoretical Analysis of Human Capital in the Field of Economics Abroad" includes the eighteenth-century Scottish economist Adam Smith on the profitability of vocational training, the nineteenth-century German economist Friedrich List on the "mental capital" of the human race, and the twentieth-century American economist Theodore Schultz on human capital (Chen Qingli 2002: 10–25). Never mind that other than Deng Xiaoping and Jiang Zemin, none of

SUZHI AS A NEW HUMAN VALUE

those listed here ever spoke or wrote on suzhi. But this kind of ideological drag show is not author Chen Qingli's individual invention; it is routinely practiced by party ideologues.[17]

In such an analysis, not only does suzhi claim to be a universal form of human value found in wildly different social and political theories, but it also makes itself a universal value operator that rearranges the relationship among these theories and retools them for the new teleology of Development. It is not by negating any of these theories, but by retooling all of them and making them "speak" the language of suzhi—the author literally puts the word in their mouths—that suzhi claims to be the universal form of human value and a catch-all discursive basket.

So, what is suzhi? What does it do for Development? As a post-Mao key-word, *suzhi* becomes "real" through a phantasmatic production. As a catch-all discursive basket, suzhi, empty in itself, is a mode of expression that aspires to shape all expressions. Suzhi, therefore, behaves much like value in Marx's analysis of commodities. Empty (*Inhaltlos*) in itself, value is a form through which things are made commensurable.[18] As value makes commodities (e.g., labor power) commensurable for market exchange, suzhi is a form of human value that renders human subjectivity commensurable for Development. The representation and valuation of human subjectivity through suzhi is achieved through the processes of abstraction and radical suppression of heterogeneity existing among individuals and populations, much as "value" operates as an abstraction and reduction of the radical heterogeneity of concrete and individual aspects of labor.

Its deployment as a form of value-coding inscribes, measures, and mobilizes human subjectivity as the powerhouse for productivity and Development. In Gilles Deleuze's and Félix Guattari's conceptualization, a code establishes relations among "incommensurable flows of different qualities" and "expresses the apparent objective movement according to which the economic forces or productive connections are attributed to an extra-economic instance as though they emanated from it, an instance that serves as a support and an agent of inscription" (1983: 247). The invention of suzhi as value-coding establishes a seemingly improbable translation or transvaluation between human subjectivity, culture, and consciousness on the one hand and the rate of Development on the other.[19] It reterritorializes consciousness and culture into the sphere of Development and holds them directly responsible for unleashing its forces. As suzhi evaluates heterogeneous human subjectivities in terms of their capacity for Development, human subjectivity acquires the character of value (worth) and is coded as such. As Deng's words already attested, "The national strength and the stamina of economic development more and more depend on the suzhi of the laborers" (Zeng Min 1989: 165). This reification of human subjectivity is an idealist move.

Discovering Suzhi Poverty

The notion of suzhi, applied most frequently to the peasantry and rural migrants, has been central to the production of "new peasants" (*xin nongmin*) as the subjects of Development that began in the 1980s. These "new peasants" first took the form of rural households designated as "specialized households" (*zhuanye hu*) that, emerging as private commodity producers in the dismantling of the rural collectives, were willing to specialize in production of a single commodity for the market. In the early 1980s, when market mechanisms were first being developed, many specialized households were among the group able to "get rich first," functioning as showcases for the achievements of rural decollectivization. In 1983 the *People's Daily* commended the new peasants for their "commodity consciousness" (*shangpin yishi*) and for "having broken away from the ideological bind of small peasant self-sufficiency and recasting their gaze from their small plot of land to the vast market inside the country and abroad."[20] The task of the party leadership at all levels was to set the peasantry on the path to the market through ideological campaigns and policy designs and to lead, push, and pull the peasantry to being "commodity producers" in the market economy. Studying the meaning of "quality" for the women's movement in the reform era, the anthropologist Ellen Judd observes that the movement to improve women's status, promoted by local Women's Federations, focused upon improving "the quality of women's labor power, and upon the extent and character of their participation in the market economy," and the goal and strategy to attain higher status for women was "operationalized in the language of exchange value—women would have higher status where they produced more value [*jiazhi*], as measured directly through the value of their economic products" (2002: 24–25).

Yet the campaign to lead the peasantry to market seems an arduous task

of transforming their anti-market, "traditional," and "feudal" consciousness, which is perceived as deeply rooted among peasants in backward areas,
"severely prevent[ing] the development of a commodity economy."[21] The *An-*
hui ribao, a provincial-level party newspaper, points out six manifestations of
this traditional feudal consciousness: (1) viewing wealth and commercial activity as morally dubious; (2) contentment with merely having sufficient food
and clothing and therefore not interested in innovation and competition; (3)
egalitarian (*pingjun zhuyi*) sentiments that encourage the expropriation of the
rich (*chi dahu*), striking fear in those who get rich first; (4) small peasant self-
sufficiency which directs surplus income to the sphere of household life and
festivities rather than using it to expand production; (5) a clan consciousness
that favors nepotism and the hiring of incompetent relatives; (6) gambling and
superstitious belief in deities and ghosts.[22]

The logic that collapses, unifies, and inscribes these diverse beliefs and
practices as aspects of a "traditional feudal" consciousness is that they all act
as impediments to the development of a modern commodity economy. These
beliefs and practices are represented as facing backward and as not yet epistemologically advanced to the modern. This logic bypasses any possibility that
some of them may be "forward looking" expressions of grievance and resistance against effects of the market economy.[23] The invocation of "feudal" here
is a strategy that justifies the need for liberalization and enlightenment and
thus calls on the market economy as the cure, never as a problem.

By 1992, the party secretary of Fuyang Prefecture in northwest Anhui,
one of the more "backward" areas in the province, took pride in the local
achievement of a well-established network for commodity circulation in which
the "peasantry revolves around the market and the market revolves around
prices."[24] In his article entitled "Leading the Peasantry to Market," the party
secretary Wang Zhaoyao described an important lesson from his experiences
of governance: "A great deal of practice has revealed to us that only by pushing
peasants to market and developing a rural market economy can there be comprehensive economic development and prosperity."[25] Wang's view was echoed
by many headlines appearing in the provincial party newspaper throughout
the 1980s and 1990s on the transformation of peasant consciousness in connection with the market economy.[26] In the words of the head of Lixing County,
Cheng Fengjun, with regard to the "correct handling of the relationship with

the peasantry," the primary task for the government was to connect the peasantry to the market through "thousands of methods and hundreds of tactics [*qianfang baiji*]."[27] These pushes and pulls to bring the peasantry to market is a process of reterritorializing the peasantry into the spheres of Market and Development. The "new peasants" are constructed as subjects of the market who, having developed a commodity consciousness, have advanced on the path of Development by producing for the market.

In the face of widespread rural poverty, the discourse of development sponsored by the party-state and the elite is unable to grasp how continuing poverty is integral to the process of marketization, and how coastal cities and enterprises of all capital forms build their economic success on the backs of interior rural areas that supply cheap resources and labor. Instead, the discourse transforms this problem of continuing poverty by recoding it, signaled by two neologisms: *wenhua fupin* (cultural poverty relief) and *suzhi fupin* (suzhi poverty relief). These strategies of poverty relief are commended by government officials and the official media as a theoretical breakthrough and "a vital reform in our country's poverty-relief strategy."[28] In a seminar attended by Anhui provincial leaders and researchers from cosmopolitan Shanghai, a research report states, "Poverty is not just caused by poverty in material resources, but is more importantly caused by poverty in social resources [*shehui ziyuan*], that is, poverty in the cultural level of society [*shehui wenhua*]. The bottom line is this: poverty is ultimately caused by poverty in human subjectivity itself [*ren zishen de pinkun*].[29] To be thoroughly rid of poverty, our poverty-relief strategies must undergo a fundamental transformation from attending to poverty [*fupin*] to attending to human subjectivity [*furen*] and implement the strategy of 'cultural poverty relief.'"[30]

Through this recoding of the problem of poverty, not only are culture and subjectivity reterritorialized into the field of Development; they are now placed at its very center as the objects for improvement, and they are held directly responsible for holding back economic forces. This new poverty-relief strategy also reconfigures "cultural work" at a time when local state-sponsored cultural centers (*wenhua zhan*) find themselves in deep crisis.[31] Newspaper commentaries, such as "Today's Culture, Tomorrow's Economy," written by the chief of a cultural center in a small city, highlight the ability of "cultural work" to contribute to building a culture of Development.[32] In the context of

SUZHI AS A NEW HUMAN VALUE

economic transition, the author of the article, having described the desolation of cultural work in terms of severe cuts in government funding and the corresponding decline in cultural workers' morale and public recognition, ponders how to redefine the function of cultural work so that it can be linked with the market economy. This instance is indicative of what is taking place more generally in the wider cultural sphere.[33] According to this line of thinking, for the work of culture on the grassroots level to have a viable future, it must be linked to the telos of Development. The goal of cultural work is to "shed the light of modern civilization on every rural corner . . . to improve the general suzhi of the peasantry."[34] The cumulative work in the field of culture today— culture as a "noun of process" (Williams 1976: 77)—can be transvaluated as greater productivity and profit in the field of economy.

The new poverty-relief strategies of the 1990s therefore push the function of suzhi to yet a higher level of idealism. "Cultural poverty relief" is to generate a desire for Development in the consciousness of the peasantry. Development is now conceived as something that should not come from the top down, but should be internally generated. This shift is expressed as requiring rural people to change themselves: from being the objects of poverty-relief actions (*yao wo tuopin*) to being subjects who act on their own desire to leave poverty (*wo yao tuopin*). The project of producing these desiring subjects is aptly described by one newspaper commentary as "producing [new] human beings" (*zao ren*).[35] The transformation of consciousness, then, is now the key to solving the problem of Development. It is this discursive link between suzhi, poverty relief, and Development that mobilizes the peasant subject for labor migration to the city.

Suzhi–Value Flow and Value Predications of the Subject

Since the 1990s, the massive movement of 100 million migrant laborers has come to be seen by local governments in the sending provinces as a quick means for poverty relief. The benefits of migration encompass not just the monetary remittances sent home but also the accumulation of suzhi for those who leave, ultimately to return after years of labor in the city. In Wuwei County of Anhui Province, for example, it is estimated that about 230,000 migrants earned 326 yuan monthly (approximately US$41) per person in 1997. This is close to an average monthly income among domestic workers in Beijing.

In terms of suzhi, migration is supposed to bring benefits that cannot be measured in monetary terms—it is supposed to effect a transformation from "traditional" to "modern" subjectivity, producing a power for Development that has been compared by some analysts to the power released by nuclear fission.[36] The spectacle of migrants driving back from Beijing to Wuwei County for the lunar New Year in over a hundred private cars provides a stunning materialization of this power. As noted by one commentator, "Labor migration enables a transformation of peasants from the despised 'country bumpkin' [*tu laomao*] to 'Human' writ large [*da xie de ren*] in those who have truly realized their full value as human beings."[37] This idea of "full value" registers the idea of "the human" as a potentiality that can be exploited as a new frontier of neoliberal capital accumulation.

Because of this promise of transformation into Human writ large, labor mobility is celebrated as the third liberation of the peasantry. The first of these was the 1949 national liberation, which carried out land reform in the countryside, and the second was the post-Mao reform beginning in 1978, which broke up the rural communes and established household-based production. In the post-Mao culture of modernity, prosperous and bustling cities are seen as a "comprehensive university of society" (*shehui zonghe daxue*) where millions of peasants can go to develop their suzhi at no cost to the state. With the erosion of basic education in the rural areas as a consequence of the dismantling of rural collectives, migration is celebrated as a substitute to fill the void.[38] The hopeful vision of migrants transformed by their experiences in the city, returning home with a small fund of saved cash, the latest market information, and internalized principles of the market, motivates local governments to describe migrants as akin to "students studying abroad" (*liu xuesheng*), mirroring the idealized accumulation of suzhi through transnational mobility to the West that is available only to the educated elite.[39]

I will examine labor recruitment to bring into view how the accumulation of suzhi functions as an "intangible operator" in the labor contract and how the extraction of surplus value is both eclipsed and facilitated by the coding of labor mobility as suzhi mobility. The family service company, established in 1992 in Tianjin, made a great effort to advertise its services through local media (radio, TV, and newspapers) both in Tianjin, to attract urban customers, and in poor rural counties, to attract women migrants. The company's director spoke of these efforts not as a commercial activity but as a form of "social education" (*shehui jiaoyu*) that would bring order to the labor market. From the view of urban clients, the focus of this "social education" was on the labor security and social stability that occurs when the "black" labor market, whose illegality is defined by its lying outside the regulative control of the urban government, is replaced by a more dependable labor source. Before the establishment of the Family Service Company, there was a large underground labor market. Hundreds of migrants used to gather in the open space beneath the bridge pilings in the city, looking for employment. This unregulated labor market came to be associated with social disorder and criminality.[40] In such places, migrants bargain with employers over wages in an unequal relationship of power. Abusive treatment and labor conflicts between buyers and sellers of labor power have no formal means of redress, resulting in desperate measures of revenge and retaliation; in recent years, a number of abductions and murders have been associated with the informal labor market. There have also been cases of migrant women being physically abused by their employers or not getting paid for their labor, as well as cases of employers being robbed. To urban clients, the labor-recruitment company promised to provide an organized, "clean," sustainable, and reliable source of labor power.

The cleanliness and security of this labor source is guaranteed by mass recruitment directly at the site of origin by the local labor bureau or, more often, by the local Women's Federation as a branch office of a nationwide network. "Cleanliness" refers here to whether a domestic has "clean hands and feet" (*shoujiao ganjing*), that is, whether she has been known to steal or embezzle. Yet labor recruitment at the origin also evokes the "bottled-at-the-source" practice of drinking-water companies. After recruitment, these women are always escorted by one or two of their county's Women's Federation cadres, crossing hundreds or thousands of kilometers to urban labor markets. They are hand-delivered to the company and to their urban clients, who consume these women's "fresh" labor power. In contrast to official and popular representations of rural-to-urban labor migration as a "blind flow" (*mangliu*) and the historical association between itinerant lumpenproletarians and water transport (*jianghu*, literally, "rivers and lakes"), this regulated stream of migrant women is bottled at the source.[41] Following a securely channeled flow, both bottled water and migrant labor power are supposed to be free of contamination by suspect influences. Yet once they have acquired urban experience as domestic workers (ostensibly realizing their anticipated development as knowing subjects), these women are viewed as no longer pure, trainable, uncontaminated labor power and therefore are no longer so desirable. The image of drawing young women from interior rural areas as pure water from its source thus portends their own eventual disposability.

The company also advertises and encourages sustainability and security of labor power by awarding "good domestic workers." In the first two years of its establishment the Family Service Company, emulating the status honors of the Mao period, selected "good domestic workers" and "good employers," and held ceremonies once a year as part of its publicity effort. A major family-service company in Beijing has a similar annual practice, but it selects only "good domestic workers" and not employers.[42] An important criterion for a "good domestic worker" in both companies is that she must have worked continuously for one family for at least one year, which means, in the words of the director, "She has staying power" (*neng dai zhu le*). "Without this criterion, the whole selection would have been meaningless," the director in Tianjin stated. The ability to stick it out with an employer therefore becomes a necessary measure of the desirability of migrant labor bottled at its source. Urban households of the rising middle class rely on the adaptability and docility of migrant women. However, the longer they stay in the city, the more knowing they become and the more likely they are to quit or change jobs due to homesickness or dissatisfaction with their working conditions.

Moreover, thanks to its affiliation with the nationwide network of the Women's Federation, the labor-recruitment company can also attest to the security of its labor flow: a migrant's whereabouts—should she suddenly abandon her contract and her urban employer—can be traced. This ability to keep tabs on workers supplements the public-security gap left by the loosening of the Mao-era household-registration system and eases the anxiety over the rootlessness of migrant labor and its potential to create social disorder. This company prides itself on not having encountered any serious mishap since its establishment. A telling example testing the security of the labor-source system was a recent incident in which a migrant woman disappeared with her employer's beeper and mobile phone. The company had a record showing that her home was in Henan Province and that she had been employed not by a family, but by the owner of a small restaurant. I was told that the woman worked in the restaurant for some days and felt it "was inappropriate [*bu heshi*] for her." So she left suddenly, taking her employer's beeper and mobile phone with her.[43] The company contacted the Women's Federation cadre of the woman's home county who had accompanied her group to Tianjin. The county-level office had a record of the township and village origins of all its migrants and the errant woman was quickly located. With the help of the women's cadre in her township, the young woman was found at home with the beeper and mobile phone intact. The issue was thus settled, with the employer's property returned, the integrity of the company restored, and very likely the woman's local reputation irredeemably damaged.[44]

Yet the effort to channel clean and secure labor resources to urban households is not an easy task when the labor bureau or Women's Federation is unwilling to collaborate. As I was told by a labor bureau cadre in Wuwei, "There have been many incidents [*chushi*] with migrants in the cities. . . . If they are paid too poorly, given bad food or lodging, bullied, or bad things happen to them, they or their parents would come to us, when we were still involved in organizing their migration. But we really could not follow through on these problems — now we have a market economy. So, if they go on their own, they go at their own risk. We will not be blamed."[45]

The labor-recruitment companies in both Tianjin and Beijing have found themselves in the position of having to find their labor supply in poorer and more isolated areas, where there are fewer communally based networks for migration. But this presents yet another problem, as the manager of the Tianjin company complained: "The poorer the area, the more conservative the people. The problem is their unwillingness to come out." On hearing this, a U.S.-trained economist was puzzled: "But don't they want the money?" The company's field recruiters were not, however, defeated by this lack of desire. Greater efforts were put forth to incite the desire for Development. Local television and radio stations were mobilized to publicize the benefits of migration. The linkage between Development and suzhi improvement was thus deployed, to persuade both cadres and peasants that labor migration was the only way to effect positive change in their local areas, not just through the monetary remittances that the migrants would send home but also through the change it could effect in local consciousness. Recruiters represented these benefits as a form of "mutual aid"—a sentimentalization of Marx's ironic description of the labor contract: the owner has the means of production and the worker has the labor. The logic of capital in its restless search for ever cheaper labor is thereby represented as a *gift* of Development through which the worker is educated by the owner, as poor areas are by more prosperous ones, and the Third World by the First World. These benefits supposedly outweigh the poor wages earned by migrant workers, who receive instead the opportunity for suzhi improvement.

The Tianjin company made a concerted effort in its first year of operation to produce a positive demonstration of suzhi improvement through domestic labor. All the young migrant women recruited that year were assigned to work in the homes of municipal officials, retired cadres, and managers of joint ventures. According to the director, "The working conditions and domestic environment in these homes are superior. Most of these people are quite cultured. So a domestic would not only do housework but would also experience a giant leap in consciousness. . . . The effect was indeed obvious." A young woman from rural Henan was sent to work at an elderly cadre's home. When she first arrived, "She was simple, naïve, and a little clueless [*shahuhu de*]." To be *shahuhu* is to be oblivious to one's environment and one's relationship with, and position in, that environment. As Dorothy Solinger observes, rural people are often seen "as uncouth, even nearly imbecilic, an embarrassment to polite Chinese society" (n.d.: 24). To perceive a young woman as having an "imbecilic" character is to imply that she appears to have no consciousness of her self-in-the-world, that she does not recognize her position in the order of things and her own inadequacy: "It is not until they come to the city that they come to know themselves."[46] Migrant workers must learn their lack of suzhi in order to desire it. Through the pedagogical role of the state and its agents, the subjectivity of the migrant worker has to be transformed such that she comes to "know" her place in the suzhi hierarchy. To paraphrase Louis Althusser's (1972) formulation of ideology, the discourse of suzhi functions ideologically by setting the migrant worker up to recognize her "imaginary relationship" to the conditions and terms of her labor.

The cluelessness of the young woman from rural Henan seemed to be most effectively captured by her reported expression of wonder at hearing a train whistle—a sound she had apparently never heard before—arousing pity among those urbanites hearing her tale, who in turn found themselves even more dissatisfied when confronted with this detail attesting to the nation's failure to achieve a timely Development. The macrological desire for national Development was thus micrologically invested in transforming this young woman, who worked four years for the same family before returning home to marry. The manager, commenting on her transformation in the city, said, "Now when you look at her, although she still has that kind of . . . what do you call it . . . about rural people, yet in the way she speaks, she has a certain refinement now, and her air of awareness shows that she has learned a lot, at least in these respects, at the same time that she was doing the housework." Although some ineffable mark of rurality remained on her, at least as a knowing subject of Development she recognized her deficiencies and was on the right track, unlike other rural young women who, in the eyes of the director, "learned nothing else but cosmetics and bright red lips."[47] Women who exemplify the latter are on the wrong track because they take suzhi improvement as a purely cosmetic matter—in both senses of the word—without gaining consciousness of what they lack. But the young woman from Henan had undergone a transformation into Development, accruing just enough suzhi for her to showcase Development on her return to the village, a fate preordained by the structural limits in the city of how much suzhi she might accumulate.

When the young woman returned to Henan, she became a living demonstration of suzhi improvement through labor migration, facilitating the next round of labor recruitment in her area. The company found this publicity strategy to be very effective. The demonstration of the young woman's transformation, and the transformation of other women like her, has further opened the way for the flow of rural labor power to the city. The labor mobility of migrants is coded as a form of accumulation of suzhi that will lead to self-development (*ziwo fazhan*) and class mobility. What this coding makes invisible is how the labor power of migrant workers creates surplus value for capital accumulation.

To effectively critique this idealist characterization of the subject, it is helpful to think through the relationship between value and subjectivity. Gayatri Chakravorty Spivak (1988) links the question of value with the predication of the subject, that is, with the logic and criteria determining the ways in which subjectivity may be thought or experienced. In the context of the idealist predication, the value of the subject is defined in terms of consciousness and its fulfillment. Spivak approaches the materialist predication of the subject through labor power as a way to critique the idealist predication of the subject centered on consciousness in the spheres of "Truth," "Beauty," and "Goodness" (i.e., the cognitive, aesthetic, and ethical value domains). She defines consciousness not as thought, but as "the subject's irreducible intendedness towards the object" (ibid.: 154). In the idealist discourse of suzhi the subject is defined and measured by her "intendedness" toward Development, the desire for which propels the rural migrant to the city as waged labor.

What effects are produced when the subject is predicated on suzhi, or when the value (worth) of the subject is defined in those terms? Suzhi codes the value of the migrant subject in terms of lack: she is marked and defined by her lack of suzhi. Development is her salvation. It elides her productive activity, which is what actually produces the wealth of cities, the accumulation of capital, and economic growth. Moreover, with "suzhi improvement" beckoning more and more migrants to receive the city's civilizing education, this idealist predication of the subject facilitates the channeling of an ever-greater quantity of labor power toward the city—an arterial flow feeding a vampiric accumulation.

Speaking on migration as suzhi education, the director of the Beijing company remarks, "How much money would the state have to invest to propagate this kind of education [now enabled by migration]? This kind of change in the migrant, the suzhi education, cannot be measured by money. When they [migrant women] return home, they will practice improved child nurture on their own. [This is] more effective than any amount of persuasion on the part of family-planning cadres." Return migration is represented as enabling a circular dynamic in the production of suzhi. Suzhi acquired in the cities can be brought back to the village so that the rural household can also become a theater of suzhi production. Migrant women will transfer their suzhi development to their children—the next generation of workers—through their improved maternal agency. Their proximity to urban families will teach them to practice better techniques of birth and nurture (*yousheng youyu*), thereby laying the foundations for raising the quality of the rural population.

The way in which suzhi and its lack code the value of migrant labor takes one back to the idealist and materialist predications of the subject. As sug-

SUZHI AS A NEW HUMAN VALUE

gested by Ann Anagnost, "Suzhi is in a sense an inverse image of 'value' insofar as it is premised on value as something that must be added to the body, rather than inherent in the body's capacity for labor" (2004: 193). Postsocialist China is ideologically overdetermined to predicate its development on suzhi, rather than on the labor theory of value, as the latter necessarily raises the specter of exploitation and Marxian conceptions of class, the tacit disavowal of which is the raison d'être of the post-Mao market reforms.

Neoliberal Governmentality: Suzhi as Neohumanism

In his seminal lecture "Governmentality" Michel Foucault (1991) uses this term to discuss the rationality, tactics, and techniques of governance and de- lineates a transformation of governmentality from the sixteenth century to the late eighteenth. Pivotal to this transformation was the "introduction of econ- omy to political practices" (ibid.: 92) and the eventual emergence of political economy enabled by the shift from the family to the population as the model and field of governance. How does the operation of these labor-recruitment companies prod one to rethink the mode of postsocialist governmentality through its relationship with the market economy, in which the promotion of suzhi has been central? I propose a consideration of the question of gov- ernmentality in terms of the value-predication of the subject and the state. The question of value, especially the value-predication of the state, was not explicit in Foucault's discussion of governmentality, so some scholars have applied his theory in ways that peg the question of the subject to the state and reduce the problem of governmentality to social technology. If one introduces the question of value-predication to one's thinking of governmentality, then one can link the question of technology with a critique of the state, ideology, and power.

This rethinking of governmentality through value-predication of the state and the individual subject is more imperative when one examines China's metamorphosis from a socialist-planned economy to a postsocialist market economy. Although specific policies shifted as the state leadership steered the direction and pace of reform, it is in the presumed universal idea of a market- oriented and capital-driven Development that the post-Mao state defines its historical mission, legitimacy, and agency. This commitment to Development has not only compelled a shift from "politics in command" to "economics in command," fostering the marketization and privatization of everyday life; it has also redefined the role of the state in relation to the market. This predication of the post-Mao state and its wrestling with collective Mao-era legacies through a process called "crossing the river by groping for the stones" underlies Chinese neoliberalism.[48]

I now examine neoliberalism as a form of governmentality in the sphere of labor recruitment and discipline, basing my discussion on the genesis of the two aforementioned companies and their operation of labor recruitment through government institutions. With post-Mao economic liberalization, the hiring of domestic workers began to reappear in the cities in the early 1980s. The Beijing company, established in 1983, was first organized on the initiative of the local People's Congress and People's Political Consultative Conference—both being political organizations with high concentrations of political and intellectual elites (especially the latter)—to address a "crisis" in the domestic-labor market: domestic workers were in short supply and those who were available were undisciplined. These initiatives led to several meetings organized by the municipal government to address the problem.[49] It was decided then that the Women's Federation should take charge of creating and supervising the family service company.

Employers' complaints particularly targeted migrant women from Wuwei. The number of migrant women working as domestic workers in Beijing during the period 1982–88 numbered approximately 50,000–60,000 (Wang Shanping 1992).[50] Wuwei County alone supplied over 10,000 domestic workers in the early 1980s. Most rural Wuwei women migrants were young and unmarried, and they moved to the city in a chain migration through kinship and village networks, earning 18–25 yuan (US$10–14) per month in the city.[51] But in the mid-1980s many Beijing employers began to shun rural women from Wuwei, or even from Anhui Province as a whole, as they found these domestic workers "ganging up with their *laoxiang* [people from the same native place]." The director of the Beijing company explained the problem with the unregulated labor market: "The reputation of Wuwei domestic workers really stank then. Their connection with each other was kinship-based. . . . They would strike or quit on the spot. The salary for them was of course very low. And they jumped from trough to trough [*tiao cao*] too frequently for even a slightly higher pay of 1–2 yuan. Nobody was there to regulate this or put a stop to it.

And if one of them had a problem with her employer, they tended to gang up with her against her employer."

Incidents of collective action were attributed to the creation of an "Anhui gang" (*Anhui bang*), the term *bang* being clearly associated with the power of unruly gangs and gangsters in preliberation China. The circulation of this term in the 1980s signified a desire to ridicule as well as to signal alarm at the power of domestic servants from Anhui. Kinship and place-based networks played the dominant role in bringing migrant women to Beijing in the 1980s and in providing mutual aid among migrants. But such networks often operated on the basis of exclusiveness and according to a resource-based hierarchy. According to my interviewees, Liyang County of Jiangsu Province was also a major supplier of domestic workers in Beijing in the early to mid-1980s. Women from Wuwei and Liyang had exclusive place-based networks, with women from Jiangsu Province often looking down on women from Anhui Province.[52] As a migrant from Jiangsu described this exclusive relationship, "None of us had any friends from Anhui. For a long time as soon as I saw them, I looked down on them. I had never worked together with women from Anhui and had never interacted with them. For instance, if two women [from Jiangsu] were chatting, as soon as they spotted an Anhui woman [another domestic also working in the neighborhood], they immediately would say to each other, 'Here comes an Anhui person. I'll talk to you later.'"

Within the kinship and place-based networks, experienced migrant women who possessed certain resources were likely to act as leaders for younger migrants, or *baomu tou* as they are called by employers (rarely by migrants themselves). The "head" is tacitly recognized because she has a relatively secure position and good relations with her employers. This means that if a young migrant woman suddenly finds herself unemployed, the head, who is herself a live-in domestic, may be able to provide temporary lodging for her without raising her employers' ire. The head might also be able to find employment for her and negotiate a wage with a potential employer. Women with the ability to do these things have usually been working in the city for a longer period of time and are experienced and well known in the neighborhood. Other families from the neighborhood may come to the head for help in locating a suitable domestic worker. As her reward, the head enjoys the respect of, loyalty of, and occasional gifts from the migrants she has helped.[53]

For example, migrant women from Liyang in the early to mid-1980s all knew about Grandma Wangfujing (Wangfujing popo) who achieved an almost legendary stature as a head. Grandma Wangfujing was so called because she lived in the famous Wangfujing area of Beijing (a shopping district near Tiananmen Square). All had heard of her and talked about her, but only a few had met her. My informant explained that only the most well-established Liyang migrants, such as her cousin who was also a head, would have the honor to meet her. Grandma Four from Wuwei, a strong-minded woman in her late seventies who had spent a good part of her life working in the city, was another such figure. She brought dozens of women from her village and nearby villages to Beijing, giving them help and advice and, when necessary, a scolding. In the early to mid-1980s a growing number of potential employers relied on old trusted domestic workers in their neighborhoods or in their friends' neighborhoods to supply new domestic workers.

It was in the context of widespread dissatisfaction among urban households over the shortage of labor and the propensity of migrants to "gang up" on their employers that the family service company in Beijing was founded to organize a contract-based system of employment. The company in Tianjin was formed to address a similar set of concerns. The network of the Women's Federation and other government organizations provides an important linkage through which labor power in the countryside is connected to these urban companies. Both companies in my study were connected with Women's Federation offices and the labor bureaus of sending counties, and they relied on their organizing work and their local credibility as government agencies to deliver migrant women. If local governments in poor rural areas are unwilling to organize labor migration due to fear of the lack of security associated with the urban market, companies attached to the Women's Federation seem to provide the security and credibility needed to counterbalance the insecurity of the market. The company in Beijing was able to establish over a hundred outlets of labor supply from eleven provinces due to the promotion of labor migration as the most efficient and cost-effective project for poverty relief and suzhi improvement. This idea is promoted by the Poverty-Relief Office of the Central Government and by lecture tours to poverty-stricken areas organized by the Central Committee of the Communist Youth League. In the organization of labor transfer, the government thus functions as an enthusiastic matchmaker between the labor power of poor areas and the urban labor market, and as a regulator of the violence, capriciousness, and insecurity of the market.

In the 1990s contract-based domestic service companies, straddling market and state, significantly displaced chain migration on the basis of the kinship and place-oriented networks that had united, disciplined, and regulated domestic workers and claimed their loyalty. In place of these networks, domestic service companies have appointed themselves as the modern institutional locus of identity for the young women to whom they promise to open the pathway to suzhi improvement. In this process the notion of suzhi, the phantom child of Development, has facilitated a balance between economy and stability by appearing as a guardian angel from the *future*, from the teleology of Development, as a supplement for the *present* of these migrant women.

With the reform state predicated on Development, post-Mao governmentality is the constant mediation and balancing of economic growth and the specter of social disorder. Central to this mediation is the project of constructing a market economy in which the market is not taken to be a natural formation, but is both a system and a subjectivity that must be actively produced, facilitated, and managed. The production of "the new peasant" involves both an acute production of market consciousness among the peasantry and an indictment against the so-called feudal practices and consciousness that do not follow market principles. The construction of a regulated domestic-labor market, involving the networking of government institutions and the promotion of suzhi improvement, is a displacement of the socially dangerous free labor market that might detract from stability and growth.

This active production of a market economy in postsocialist China thus puts into practice, as it were, the neoliberal vision of the market analyzed by Foucault.[54] The Ordoliberalen, a group of jurists and economists in postwar Germany, rejected the classic liberal vision of the market as a quasi-natural entity capable of self-regulation, along with the corresponding liberal practices of laissez-faire government.[55] The neoliberal vision conceives that "the market is not a natural social reality at all; and what is incumbent on government is to conduct a policy towards society such that it is possible for a market to exist and function" (Gordon 1991: 41). What makes this conception of market neoliberal, differentiating it from both Adam Smith's laissez-faire liberalism and Keynesian corporate liberalism, is not so much its recognition that the market is not natural or self-regulating, but what this recognition entails for governmentality and social politics: "For the *Ordoliberalen*, the major problem of social politics within this framework is not the anti-social effects of the economic market, but the anti-competitive effects of society" (ibid.: 42). Just as neoliberalism compels the idea of market "into a personal moral code" on this side of the Pacific (according to an article in *Fortune* magazine [Magnet 1986: 68]), the ascendance of neoclassical economics as an imperative worldview "has acquired the force of ethics" in China, as Wang Hui has observed (2000: 94–95).

In the process of post-Mao neoliberal restructuring the notion of suzhi forces the ethics of the market on the individual subject and codes its worth for Development. The president of a well-known company, a representative of the National People's Congress who received the status honor of "excellent entrepreneur," writes for *Anhui ribao* about the agency of the human subject in relation to the market and capital: "It is the human subject (*ren*) that directly and ultimately determines the effectiveness of capital. Therefore, the human subject constitutes an important part of capital and is its most active, driving, and dynamic element."[56] One can see how the suzhi level of the human subject is directly linked to the productivity of capital. The author continues, "Without a high-suzhi human subject, capital cannot increase in value." Just as the root cause of poverty has been discovered to lie in the poverty of human subjectivity, one now learns that human subjectivity greatly affects capital growth and is in fact its crucial ingredient. With the "capitalization of the meaning of life" (Gordon 1991: 44), one encounters this unprecedented attention to, and exaltation of, human subjectivity as the most important agent for market growth and Development. The exaltation of the power of human subjectivity is what I call "neohumanism."

By coining the term *neohumanism*, I wish to continue Marx's critique of humanism as constitutive of a society "where the commodity form is the general form of the labor-product" (Marx 1977: 152). Heterogeneous use-values produced by heterogeneous human labor can be exchanged because everything sensuous that marks the heterogeneity of things and labor has been extinguished and violently abstracted in its translation into exchange-value. A "phantom-like objectivity," in the form of "congealed quantities of homogeneous human labor" is what effects an equivalence and makes exchange possible (ibid.: 128). The irony is that it is the "phantom-like objectivity" in the universal commodification of human labor that furnished the epistemological foundation for the very idea of humanity and humanism. As Thomas Keenan points out, "[Humanity itself] arrives only with the domination of the commodity form" (1993: 171).

In China's market reform, suzhi abstracts and reduces the heterogeneity of human beings by coding their value (worth) for Development.[57] Suzhi as a new valorization and abstraction of human consciousness for market and development mirrors the valorization and abstraction of human labor in commodity production. In *Capital* Marx points out that a commodity "has value only because abstract human labor is objectified or materialized in it" (1977: 129). While labor is simultaneously individual, concrete, heterogeneous, social and abstract, value is the abstracted and homogenized human labor expended in production, a radical reduction of heterogeneity to equivalence through abstraction. The subsumption of labor under capital enables the dominance of abstraction and reduction of labor articulated through the universal equivalent: the money form of value (Elson 1979: 164–165).[58] Therefore, the hegemony of the notion of suzhi demands a subsumption of subjectivity to the discourse of Development; it is an abstraction and reduction of heterogeneous subjectivities into a presumed universal equivalence. Suzhi is therefore a value-articulation of subjectivity and is a new form of human value. This valorization and fetishization effects an "idealist predication of the subject" while rendering a "materialist predication of the subject" less visible. In fact, the cultural production of the post-Mao concept of suzhi is central to the economic production of surplus value extracted from rural migrant workers. The promotion and deployment of the notion of suzhi as such a value-predication of the subject is central to a neoliberal governmentality that has rearticulated the relationship between the state, the market, and subjectivity in Development.

Furthermore, in this conception of valorization, the human subject is ironically no longer presumed to be the inviolable, autonomous, self-knowing subject of the liberal Enlightenment tradition. Rather, the notion of suzhi in the neoliberal economy compels a conception of the human subject as lacking, in need of constant adjustment, supplementation, improvement, and continual retraining (*zhongsheng xuexi*). As the notion of suzhi codes the value of human subjectivity as a crucial productive force for Development, suzhi is the concept of human capital given a neoliberal spin to exceed its original meaning of stored value of education and education-based qualifications, to the capitalization of the meaning of subjectivity itself.

The way in which neohumanism both fetishizes the agency of the human subject for Development and renders the human subject inherently unstable would appear to share a similar epistemological position to a poststructuralist decentering of the Subject, but it is, in fact, its nightmarish mirror image. A poststructuralist critique thus cannot be singularly focused on the project of decentering the Enlightenment Subject, nor should it celebrate this decentering as a triumph, but should take care to locate it in the context of a post–Cold War decentering of capitalism.[59] In the context of the instability of the human subject in Development, the decentered subject is not the agency of poststructuralist critique alone, but is perhaps unwittingly complicit with a globalized neoliberal logic. With the dismantling of old borders and the opening of new frontiers after the Cold War, fiercer global competition has tremendously upgraded the sensitivity of capital for more nuanced regional differences in terms of productive potential measured on a global scale. Identity has entered into productive processes and calculations of profitability, and can be cultivated and outsourced along with other means of production.[60] The abstraction, fragmentation, volatility, and potential of human subjectivity has been integrated into the productive forces in the discourse of Development, and this very integration constitutes the rise of suzhi as a new form of human value in neoliberal governmentality. Labor recruitment and migration is not just a managerial and statistical process of labor streamlining, but also an ideological and productive process of making new laboring subjects.

A Rhyme

My parents both retired several years ago in their hometown, a medium-sized Chinese city in Jiangsu Province. Their pension, about 2,000 yuan a month each, is based on the level of their salaries at the time of their retirement. While their pension cannot allow for "advancing-with-the-times" consumption, they are nevertheless basically content with the modest living to which they are accustomed. They are in their late sixties and worry most about how the coming medical-care reform will affect them. As of now, their old work unit, a provincial university, covers 90 percent of their medical expenses. The much-discussed medical-care reform is to "push us to the market" (*ba women tui xiang shichang*), as my mother calls it. Insurance companies, rather than the state unit, will take charge of the management of medical care. In our weekly telephone conversation, we frequently discuss the upcoming reform. My parents pass on to me the latest rumors about the starting time of the reform and the latest speculations on the schemes to be implemented. In our hometown, both the water supply and the grain supply, which had been owned and managed by the state, have already been privatized. My parents report that many workers cried when the biggest textile factory in the city was privatized. The privatization of medical care in this context seems imminent. To be more self-sufficient, my parents have grown anxious and conscious about "healthful" food, becoming experts about foods with medicinal values. They collect tips from books, newspaper clips, and health programs on TV. My brother, who spent more time living with them recently, complained that our parents have become so meticulous and particular that they just don't seem to know what and how to eat anymore.

One day, while my mother was on the usual subject of the medical care reform, mixed with tips for my health, she related a rhyme that she had just heard from her friends:

Chenji shi lingdao de	One's achievement is one's superior's
Laoban shi renjia de	One's spouse is someone else's
Qiancai shi ernü de	One's money will be one's children's
Fangzi shi sunzi de	One's apartment will be one's grandchildren's
Zhi you shenti shi ziji de	Only one's body is one's own

This rhyme reflects a popular sentiment of anxiety and crisis generated by urban transformations. One's social and familial relations have become unbound and been carved up into ownership by various others. After layers of stripping, one finally achieves the status of one who owns nothing but one's own body as an asset and liability.

A Parody: An Obituary for Comrade Reagan

A friend in Beijing forwarded Ronald Reagan's obituary to me. I later came across different versions on the Web. Due to its multiple existences and variations, the piece fits the definition of folklore proposed by my former teacher, the folklorist Alan Dundes. It demonstrates how a connection between neoliberalism in China and in the United States is drawn at a popular level, and provides an opportunity to criticize neoliberalism in China.

Written in the familiar language of official eulogy for Chinese Communist leaders, this obituary assigns President Reagan, who was known to have promoted neoliberal policies in the United States, Chinese characteristics: "Reagan Thought" includes "liberating thoughts," "seeking truth from facts," and the theory of "three represents," which are associated with the post-Mao leaders Deng Xiaoping and Jiang Zemin. Indeed, while Deng Xiaoping called for the country to "let a few people get rich first," Reagan was similarly determined that "more than anything else, [he] want[ed] to see the United States remain a country where someone can get rich" (Phillips 2002: 333). Xue Yong, a supporter of Deng Xiaoping's legacy, recently examined the timely resonance between Deng Xiaoping's reform and Reaganism in the early 1980s. Xue states in his article published by the *Southern People Weekly*, "What did Deng Xiao-ping mean for Americans? He came to power a few years before Reagan and helped Americans hear the voice of Reaganism even before Reagan came to power."[1] For critics of neoliberalism, it would be hard to miss the sarcastic and poignant critique of market-oriented reform and its ideological justifications in China in the following eulogy for the neoliberal leader Reagan.

June 6, 2004

The Central Committee of the Republican Party of the United States, the Joint Chiefs of Staff, the Congress, the Senate, and the Federal Government of the United States, proclaim with profound grief: Comrade Reagan, the great bourgeois revolutionary, statesman, thinker, the long-tested leader of the party and the state who enjoyed high prestige, passed away after failing to respond to emergency treatment, in his California home at 1:12 p.m. on June 5, 2004.

Comrade Reagan was born into an ordinary middle-class family. Through his own individual struggles, he became an outstanding actor. Via this route, he entered the field of politics and was elected the governor of California in 1966. While he was governor, Comrade Reagan immersed himself among the masses, understood the situation from all perspectives, surmounted all kinds of difficulties, brought about the rise of California, kept high the rate of economic development, quadrupled the income of the people, transformed California into the biggest economic power in the United States, and was thus deeply loved by people of all ethnic groups in California.

At the end of the 1970s, the United States, under the leadership of the Democratic Party, had a devastated economy and declining international status. Supported by a group of highly respectable old comrades, Comrade Reagan, at the senior age of sixty-nine in 1980, rose again to take charge, saved the party, saved the United States at the moment of crisis, and thus opened a brand new chapter in American history.

After becoming president of the United States, Comrade Reagan issued a call to "advance with the times and strengthen the United States," and reinspired the ambition of the American people. He promoted the plan of strategic deterrence (also called "Star Wars"), implemented a Reaganism that employed a multiple-layered shielding system with flexible response, improved the power of the U.S. military, eventually succeeded in wearing down the Soviet Union, won final victory in the Cold War, and brought about the end of history. Peoples of the world who love peace will forever remember Comrade Reagan.

Comrade Reagan upheld the principle of "seeking truth from facts," devoted himself to simplifying the governmental structure, and facilitated the transformation of the functions of the government. He unswervingly carried out economic reform, deepened the reach of the capitalist market economy, and led the United States out of deflation. While the economy was growing, he managed to keep a low inflationary rate and comprehensively improved the standard of material life. People thus obtained real benefits from the reform. At the same time Comrade Reagan called on people to liberate their thoughts and advance with the times, he put forward the important "three represents" theory that the party should represent the advanced productive forces, represent the advanced culture of humanity, and represent the interests of the widest range of people.

During his terms, Comrade Reagan defended the territorial security and dignity of the United States. He liberated Grenada, successfully led a self-defense war against Libya, and gave long-standing support to the just cause of the people of Cambodia and Afghanistan against foreign invasions. With the altruistic support of the United States, the people of these two countries won their final victories.

Comrade Reagan was also dedicated to friendship between the United States and China. Before his election, Comrade Reagan had severely criticized the Carter administration for its soft approach to Beijing, but, considering the greater interests of opposing the Soviet Union, he found an ally in China and built a wide united front. This played the most critical role in wearing down the Soviet Union and bringing an end to the Cold War. During his presidency, Comrade Reagan also visited China many times and made an outstanding contribution to mutual understanding between the United States and China. He had great prestige in the hearts of the Chinese people.

The eight years under the leadership of comrade Reagan were eight years of progress and development. The United States earned worldwide attention for her achievements on all fronts, including economy, politics, military, science and technology, and culture.

Comrade Reagan also set himself as an example for the rejuvenation of leaders and cadres. In spite of strong appeals on the part of people of all ethnic groups to revise the Constitution to allow another term for his presidency, Comrade Reagan determinedly left the presidential office and the chairmanship of the Joint Chiefs of Staff and enabled a smooth transition to the forty-first generation of leadership.

In 1994, when Comrade Reagan suffered from Alzheimer's, he was still full of revolutionary optimism and fought a long fight with the disease. When he was critically ill, leaders of the party and the state, such as George W. Bush, Colin Powell, Donald Rumsfeld, and Arnold Schwarzenegger, paid him warm visits at his hospital.

The life of Comrade Reagan was a life of honorable struggles. The passing of Comrade Reagan is an incomparable loss to the whole party, whole army, and the people of various ethnic groups throughout the country. The people of the United States are immersed in a profound grief. We must turn our grief into strength, inherit the legacy of Comrade Reagan, hold high the banner of Reagan Thought, unite closely around the forty-third generation of leadership of President George W. Bush, and carry on the war against terror until the final victory!

Comrade Reagan lives forever! (boxun.com)

4

A MIRAGE OF MODERNITY

Pas de Deux of Consumption and Production

出门拎个蛇皮袋	When they left they carried "snakeskin" bags
回来皮包加皮鞋	When they returned they had leather bags and shoes
不说再见说 "拜拜"	Instead of *zaijian* they say "bai-bai"
乡邻误认 "小老外"	Village neighbors mistake them for "little foreigners"

"DAGONGMEI DE BIANQIAN" (THE TRANSFORMATION OF DAGONGMEI),
ANHUI RIBAO, 9 MARCH 1996

One winter day around the lunar New Year in 1996, at a long-distance bus station in Anhui, two migrant women returning home in their new and fashionable winter coats and carrying luggage printed with Latin letters were caught by a knowing photographer. By 1996 the Anhui government leaders at all levels frequently discussed, encouraged, celebrated, and reiterated the modernizing and transformative effect of labor export on the appearance, consciousness, and practices of its five million migrants.[1] To be sure, the provincial media aired many social problems associated with labor migration and migrants, such as the urgent need to upgrade the supervision and management of birth planning among migrant women, and the national transportation overload created by millions of labor migrants returning home for the Spring Festival (Chinese New Year). However, the dominant view in this sending province also affirmed labor migration from interior areas of Anhui as an indication of the dynamism of Development pointing toward the eventual connection of interior areas with the market at large. It was in this context that the camera encountered the two migrant women at the bus station, and thus it quickly grasped a familiar message in their image. The photo, taken by Chen Xiuchen, accompanied by a rhyme written by Xing Xianman, was submitted to *Anhui Daily* (see figure 2). On March 9, tens of thousands of readers of *Anhui Daily* saw what the camera had captured for them: two migrant women circulating from cosmopolitan cities to interior Anhui embodied an image of modernity in transit.

The rhyme accompanying the photo (and opening this chapter) highlights the message—"The transformation of migrant women" (*dagongmei de bianqian*)—in a way that intends both to amuse the readership and to share with them a privileged "more modern" position. The transformation of migrant women is signified by their new image as consumers. The sturdy "snakeskin" bag to which this rhyme refers is a kind of thick plastic bag, rough and tough like dried snakeskin, that was originally used to hold or transport large units of chemical fertilizer or pesticide, but it is often cleaned and reused by rural households to transport anything. The varied use of such bags, including carrying luggage or food for long- or short-distance travel, is a sure sign of rural bricolage and down-to-earth labor. The transformation of rural migrant women is captured as the make-do "snakeskin" bags give way to leather bags and shoes purchased from urban shops. The rhyme in Chinese plays with the word *skin* (*pi*) for both the "snakeskin" bags and the leather bags and shoes, contrasting migrant women's pre-migration image as down-to-earth laborers with their postmigration image as cosmopolitan consumers. Apart from the urban commodities that bespeak this transition, the women's use of the word *bai-bai*, a Chinese transliteration of "bye-bye," is an amusing sign of their contact with the cosmopolitan world and creates the comic scene of their misrecognition as "foreigners."

The rhyme accompanying the photo betrays the authorial conceit of the provincial elite in constructing a comic and upbeat story surrounding migrant women's return. The humor is rendered on two levels. First, the rhyme juxtaposes the peasant woman and the foreigner (read: white Westerner), two figures usually situated at opposite ends of the tradition-modernity spectrum. Second, the rhyme posits the prospect of confusion for villagers who cannot

出门拎个「蛇皮袋」，
回来皮包加皮鞋，
不说再见说「拜拜」，

乡邻误认「小老外」。

摄影 陈秀春
配文 邢献满

市井万象

打工妹的变迁

2. "The Transformation of Dagongmei," *Anhui Daily*, 9 March 1996.

differentiate between modern-looking migrant women and foreigners, and who fail to discern and locate transformed migrant women within a global hierarchy of modernity. The little tale told by the rhyme implies that returning migrant women can function as a valued sign of modernity only when they circulate back to the countryside, inviting the reader to smile knowingly and to share the author's privileged position: the reader is certainly more modern than villagers and would not mistake returning migrants for foreigners, the presumed ultimate authentic sign of the modern. Discernment and knowingness are necessary conditions for shared amusement between the author and the reader and confirm them as urban-based and secure cosmopolitan subjects watching the circulation of migrant women back to the countryside and interpreting their return as the advance and imitation of cosmopolitan subjects.

If the image of returning migrant women functions as a sign of mimicking subjects-in-transformation, "the sign is always a product. What the camera in fact grasps is the 'natural' world of the dominant ideology" (Johnston 1974: 28). More than that, the production of meaning depends on its circulation between dominant ideology, spectators, and image performers. How, then, do images of consumption function in migration? How do migrant women themselves participate and understand their own implications in performing these images? How do returning migrant women come to embody signs of mimicking consumer subjects who seem to have disarticulated themselves from their former identity as down-to-earth laborers? If consumption is indeed a new site that expresses both distinction and social mobility, then how does the body of the migrant woman negotiate this consumption and production? My itinerary of analysis journeys from Quanyang Township, Anhui, to Beijing, and then back to Anhui.

A mirage of modernity relies on a sort of pas de deux, a dance between consumption and production that incites and disciplines young migrant women. It excites them as longing consumer subjects in the countryside, but subjects them as providers of labor power for urban consumption. The bodies of domestic workers, inextricably grounded in labor, are caught in contradictions of production and consumption that are specific to their subject position. Through my ethnographic study of one labor export station in Anhui and a training session for domestic workers in Beijing, I argue that the process of migration, caught up in a pas de deux of consumption and production, is a process of re-collecting the self through these contradictions. The contradictions of production and consumption come into sharp focus in a verbal battle waged by Anhui readers against a Shanghai columnist who penned a satire of migrant women in the city. Not surprisingly, migrant women are largely erased in this battle putatively waged on their behalf. Migrant women become further erased and symbolically disowned in the provincial campaign for a new image of Anhui.

From Quanyang to Beijing: A Mirage of Modernity
through Consumption

I begin with the story of a migrant woman pioneer in her township. Jiao Xiumei, a thirty-one-year-old woman, had already become a famed local entrepreneur of a labor-export station when I visited her in 1998 in Quanyang, a town in northwestern Anhui. Compared with central-eastern Wuwei County on the bank of the Yangtze River, northwestern Anhui, adjacent to Henan Province, is even more interior, poverty stricken, and backward in the eyes of provincial elites. If Anhui is often considered a peripheral member of the prosperous Eastern China (*huadong*), northwestern Anhui seems more decidedly outside huadong's cultural landscape. In 1987 Xiumei was among the first group of rural women to work in Beijing as baomu, work organized by the Quanyang Township Labor Office for the largest family-service company in Beijing. Xiumei's father, then a cadre working at the township labor office, used to escort women recruited from villages in the township en route to Beijing. The two-day journey covered over a thousand kilometers, first by bus to Hefei, the capital of Anhui Province, and then by train from Hefei to Beijing. The township labor office stopped organizing labor migration in 1989, since expenditures by chaperon cadres on the trips made the venture unprofitable for the labor office. Xiumei then began taking a dozen or so women with her each time she returned to Beijing after a home visit. "From 1989 to 1992, we made only five thousand yuan in three years, as initially Xiumei didn't charge much in fees," Xiumei's mother told me. In 1998 the labor-export station charged 180 yuan per person as a registration fee and had its own sleeper bus to drive recruited women directly to Beijing, a twenty-four-hour trip that took place two to three times a month on average. On arriving in Beijing, migrant women would each pay another 110 yuan to the Beijing company.[2]

By 1997, the labor-export station had cumulatively sent about six thousand rural women from villages in Quanyang and its neighboring townships to Beijing as domestic workers. In 1997 alone, this station delivered a total of 635 women to Beijing and made a profit of 20,000 yuan, according to Xiumei's father. Among 110 such labor-export stations that organize the labor mobility of women for Beijing's family-service companies, this station is prominent for its large and steady volume. It has been visited by provincial and prefecture leaders and covered by national and regional newspapers, including *People's Daily*, *Zhongguo funü bao* (Chinese Women's News), *Laodong bao* (Labor News), and *Anhui Daily*. In 1994 Jiao Xiumei received the status and honor of "a star entrepreneur" (*chuangye zhi xing*) at the regional and national levels. In a 1997 work report on the labor-export enterprise, Xiumei's father, quoting the former party secretary of the prefecture, wrote, "Labor export is a factory that requires no space, no physical plant, no machines, little investment, but which has quick returns, high profit, no risks, and no smokestacks" (Quanyang 1997).

The ground floor of Xiumei's parents' two-story house functions as a registration office. The door opens to the south and faces the main dirt road. On entering the house, one sees a map of Beijing, which occupies the center space of the wall facing the street. Under the map is an old couch. To the east of the map is a desk with a telephone. This is the desk where rural women report their personal information to Xiumei's mother or father, who then fills in the registration forms. Next to the desk on the eastern wall hangs a large monthly calendar titled "Glamorous Looks" (*yan zi*). The picture for October features an urban beauty's profile from the shoulders up; she is smiling seductively, her face turned toward the viewer. Next to the calendar, newspaper clippings about this labor-export station are posted on the wall. A pictorial report by *People's Daily* is entitled "Take Beijing's Civilization Home" (Ba Beijing de wenming dai hui qu) (5 February 1994); a pictorial report by *Beijing Youth Daily* is similarly titled "Anhui's little baomu take Beijing civilization home" (Anhui xiao baomu ba Beijing de wenming dai hui jia) (30 January 1994). Both pictures feature groups of migrant women, in their holiday clothing, gathered at a bus station and ready to return home for the lunar New Year. An undated and untitled picture from the *Chinese Women's News* features a similar scene. On the same wall hang annual honor lists for "excellent domestic workers" (*youxiu jiating fuwuyuan*) sent by the Quanyang labor station to Beijing. Each year the Beijing company bestows this honor on a select minority of workers. Over the years a total of 267 women from this labor station have been given this recognition. To the west of the map, against the western wall is another couch. Next to the couch, against the southern wall is a desk that often attracts the attention of rural women arriving for registration. The desk is covered by a large piece of glass, under which lie photos of visiting officials and of Xiumei and her parents on a trip to Shenzhen. One photo shows the three of them standing in front of the Luohu Customs Building, the gateway to Hong Kong; another shows Xiumei and her mother standing beneath the sign "To Hong Kong" near the Shenzhen–Hong Kong border; yet another shows the "star entrepreneurs" from the 1994 conference that Xiumei attended.

I first met Xiumei in her parents' house. Xiumei lives with her husband, who is a local schoolteacher, their five-year-old son, and her father-in-law. They reside in a two-story house in the northern part of town, a five-minute bike ride from her parents' house. In addition to making biweekly trips to Beijing, Xiumei runs a small restaurant on the ground floor of their house, with the help of her husband and father-in-law. Xiumei's hair is partially permed and tied in a ponytail, and her face is dark-skinned and broad. She speaks quickly, and her voice carries well in the local dialect. She is the middle child of five siblings. When she was in fourth grade, Deng Xiaoping's rural reform decollectivized their farmland. Fourteen mu (2.3 acres or 0.93 hectare) of land and an ox were distributed to her family. Her father worked as a cadre in town, and her mother as a village schoolteacher, raising the children alone. Since the family needed labor to attend to the land and the ox, Xiumei was told to quit school and help with farm work. Because Xiumei had little formal schooling, which her mother, a retired schoolteacher, regrets to this day, her parents were proud of their open-minded decision to send Xiumei to Beijing as a migrant in order to make up for her lost education. Xiumei shared this with me as we walked along the town's main dirt road, which led to a park that her mother had urged us to visit.

It was dusk. There had been a sudden blackout, and Xiumei's mother had suggested that we walk to the park, rather than sit in the dark at home. The main dirt road had apparently been leveled. It was scheduled to be turned into an asphalt road, but construction had been idle for quite a while due to shortage of funds. There was not much in the way of township or village enterprises. By dusk, traffic had quieted down, and domestic pigs, dogs, and chickens had begun to walk around freely, sharing the street with children, occasional bicycles, and residents. The park on the edge of town had been built recently, with bushes arranged in circular patterns and a new pavilion standing tall in the center. An important image of Quanyang's modernization, the park had apparently cost hundreds of thousands of yuan. While Xiumei's mother urged her to take me there, Xiumei was not proud of the park: "In Beijing what kind of park would one not have seen?" Over the years, she had visited all of Beijing's parks. What Xiumei did not speak of during our conversations, but what her mother later related to me in detail, were the difficulties and frugality that Xiumei had experienced. For example, before they had their own long-distance bus, Xiumei ate only instant noodles on her trips to Beijing and walked for miles to a suburb of Beijing in order to get free lodging in a factory dorm. Her mother sympathized with her daughter's difficulties, and she presented them as evidence of her daughter's virtuous ability to "eat bitterness."

In Xiumei's account of other migrants whom she sent to work in Beijing, there was a similar omission of the hardships.

Nowadays the lowest wage one can earn as a family-service provider is 260 yuan. The average pay is about 350 yuan. A good wage is about 400 or even 500 yuan. There are bad families as well as good families. Bad families make you eat leftover food. Good families can be really good to you. One woman we sent to Beijing worked for a nun from Taiwan. They didn't go through the [Beijing] company for the formal procedure [registration and contract]. So I told the nun that "if she steals from you, don't come to me," and I told that woman that "if she doesn't pay you, you can't come to me either." As it turned out, things worked out well for the woman. I heard she receives a new towel every month. What kind of family can be so nice as to give you a new towel every month? Another woman received two watches and two necklaces from her employers. They first gave her a watch. She lost it. Then they gave her another one. The first necklace they gave her was worth 800 yuan. Then they said the first necklace wasn't so good and gave her another one. They also gave her clothes.

Xiumei's decision to remain silent about her difficulties and highlight her own and other women's experiences of acquiring luxury goods did not appear to be motivated by a particular individual vanity. The migrant women I interviewed in Beijing and Wuwei were also more inclined to talk about their consumption experiences in the city—their visits to theme parks and other tourist sites—than about their work experiences. Xiumei's choice of omission and focus appeared to reflect a discursive predilection that assigns differential values to diverse experiences and allows certain experiences—certain kinds of consumption, for instance—to appear as valuable and representable self-expression. Critiques of representation and self-representation must consider the role played by social formations of value as a sorting device that determines representability—how experiences enter the realm of recognition and representation.

As Richard Wilk writes about the Caribbean country Belize, "A global standard has become an ever-present (and perhaps internalized) significant other by which the local is defined and judged" (1995: 127). Using nationally representative sample data of sixty villages in six provinces of rural China, Alan de Brauw and Scott Rozelle (2003) find that rural-to-urban migration

A MIRAGE OF MODERNITY

has the effect of significantly encouraging rural households' investment in consumption rather than in production. In their examination of consumerist culture in China, particularly rural China, Chen Xin and Huang Ping (2003) poignantly describe a sign chain of consumption: "Villages chase after townships, townships counties, counties cities, small cities big cities, big cities foreign countries, Hong Kong, and Taiwan. . . . Just like elite consumers, youth positioned between the city and the countryside form the links of this chain." Consumption has become a routine exercise of the value orientation of the self. Not surprisingly, the pictures of Xiumei and her parents as tourists in Shenzhen represent Xiumei's success through their consumption in the most enterprising city in the country, which Xiumei's mother seldom fails to mention to rural women who stare at those pictures while waiting to register. "Taken in Shenzhen last month!" She would project her voice from one desk, where she was sitting and filling out forms for one group of women, to the other desk where women gathered around to see the photos. The apparent glamour of the family trip to Shenzhen obscured the actual exhaustion and frugality of what had been an unsuccessful business trip: arrival in Shenzhen in the morning after a full-day-and-night train ride, an unsuccessful meeting that very morning with a domestic-service company in the city, a quick tour of the city in the afternoon, and departure in the late afternoon for another full day's train ride home.[3]

With the emergence of a wealthy class—1 percent of China's population now owns 40 percent of its wealth—the media have increasingly shifted the spotlight to images of this population's lifestyle as a sign of the times.[4] The morally dubious image of the nouveau riche (*baofa hu*) in the 1980s gave way to the respectable image of "successful figures" (*chenggong renshi*) in the late 1990s. The literary critic Wang Xiaoming describes the chenggong renshi thus: "It is usually a middle-aged male with a slightly protruding stomach and dressed in well-ironed attire. He is very rich and drives a new BMW to his office. He may have studied in America and cultivated a Western style. Before hurriedly stepping out of his front door on his way to sign a contract with a foreign enterprise, he does not forget to kiss his beautiful wife" (1999: 71). As Ni Wei suggests, the myth of "successful figures" lies in "the dense interweaving of global transnational capital (economic, cultural, and ideological) with the current political, economic, and cultural mediators in China" (1999: 80).

If "labor" in socialism was "a cultural arena in which women and men crafted the meaning of 'liberation,' proved their socialist moral worth, expressed their nationalist sentiments, and received their rewards" (Rofel 1999: 122), labor no longer represents the focal point in post-Mao identity formation. Heroic deeds of production no longer take center stage in the social arena and are increasingly devalued socially and economically.[5] The glorious figure of production has been displaced by the glamorous figure of chenggong renshi, whose myriad connections with production, exploitation, stock manipulation, and the buying and selling of state property are often shady, secretive, volatile, or speculative. The commodities, recreational activities, and services that he tastefully enjoys are signs of his success. Consumption activities move into the social limelight, while production activities—where, how, and how much one works and gains—are relegated to the background as irrelevant, private experiences. Before the 1990s, most urban Chinese worked in state-owned enterprises, had secure employment, and frequently compared salaries and benefits among themselves. These comparisons were not taken to reflect an individual's worth, but how their respective employing units were doing collectively. At that time, such discussions were so commonly and casually practiced in China that Chinese college students majoring in English were specifically told to refrain from doing so when conversing with foreigners. However, after ten years of accelerated marketization, it has become a norm among urban well-to-do Chinese themselves to discreetly avoid talking about their financial situations. Hence Wang Xiaoming entitles his critique of representations of chenggong renshi as "The Myth of a Half Face" (1999)—how deals are made and wealth generated is obscured from the public.

For the post-Mao reform, commodity consumption functions as a strategic site that stimulates and captivates the imagination and desire for modernity, progress, and recognition among elites and masses alike. In the novel *Taiyang chushi* (The Birth of a Sun), the writer Chi Li describes an urban couple, Zhao Shengtian and Li Xiaolan, shopping in their native city of Wuhan. The young, lower-middle-income couple, a factory technician and a librarian, decide to buy Nestle's Nan 1 milk powder for their baby, in spite of the fact that its exorbitant price will make a serious dent in their modest income. Their purchase of the milk powder causes a sensation.

> On hearing that these two customers wanted ten cans of Nan 1, the sales clerk immediately became humble and respectful. He eagerly told them,

A MIRAGE OF MODERNITY

"This kind of superior milk powder usually goes well with superior fruit-juice powder." He took out a bottle of fruit-juice powder—imported directly from America, not from a Sino-American joint venture—and placed it next to the ten cans of Nan 1, as a handsome stallion that could be matched only by a golden saddle.

"Here is the label. Look: specially designated by the American National Aeronautics and Space Administration—"

Zhao Shengtian read aloud the rest, "The drink of the age of space, the enjoyment of a new epoch."

"Absolutely right! Would you want to buy it, *xiansheng* [sir]?"

A crowd had formed around the counter, watching the scene. People were all watching "xiansheng."

This was the first time that Zhao Shengtian had been addressed as "xiansheng" in public. Li Xiaolan was quite proud of it. She answered, "Sure." (Chi Li 1992, 104)

This scene took place at a time before the rationing system had been abolished. The introduction of global brands in department stores represented a new civil society of commodity circulation that interpellated the technician Zhao Shengtian as a xiansheng, a respectable consumer subject, and Li Xiaolan as one of the "global mothers" (*quanqiu muqin*), who "all trust Nan 1." Earlier in the novel, during an unexpected meeting with his ex-girlfriend, Zhao Shengtian freezes while searching for a cigarette. When his ex, a nouveau riche woman, pulls out a "More," he realizes that the "Double Happiness" in his pocket is "a poor and lower-middle peasant [*pin xia zhong nong*] within the family of cigarettes" (ibid., 69). He decides not to pull out his Double Happiness, instead claiming that he has quit smoking, attempting to hide his embarrassment.

The family of commodities imitates and acquires the language of class, gender, and distinction from the classed and gendered human society. Once the family of commodities possesses this language, it maps its system of distinction onto human subjectivity and makes its language of commodity relations a master language that bespeaks the relations of social hierarchy. Hence the cigarette has the fetishistic power to secretly shame Zhao Shengtian. In the anonymous space of the department store, ten cans of Nan 1 avenge him, make him a *valuable* customer, and endow him with recognition, civility, and courtesy. The working-class technician's wife is apparently even quicker to sense the effects of Zhao's recognition and answers the sales clerk on his behalf. Ephemeral as it is, this scene reflects a trend of the rising prominence of the consumer subject in post-Mao modernity, a trend that can be indexed by the changing definition of the "three big items" (*san da jian*) for household consumption: a watch, a sewing machine, and a bicycle in the late 1970s; a television set, a washing machine, and an air conditioner (preferably foreign brands) in the late 1980s; and home ownership, a car, and a computer in the late 1990s. This indicates a rising threshold of visibility for the consumer subject, which increasingly plugs the urban Chinese population into global consumption trends. As Louisa Schein suggests, "A general culture of consumption—an acute commodity desire linked to social status—has saturated all sectors of Chinese society, regardless of what specific changes in actual consumption patterns have taken place" (2001: 226). In 2000 it was said in Beijing that the passport to the globalized twenty-first century consists of a car, English-language ability, and a computer.

Consumption is therefore increasingly portrayed as a "global" experience signifying China's "getting on track with the [First] World" (*yu shijie jiegui*). Paul Fussell's *Class: A Guide through the American Status System* has been translated and published by the reputable Chinese Social Science Publishing House (1998). The importance of this book, the translators tell the reader, is to rearticulate the question of class through "taste," which displaces the Marxian legacy of the tension-fraught and struggle-inducing discourse of class (Fussell 1998: 1). Although the first printing issued only 10,000 copies, 180,000 nonpirated copies of this translation were sold and seven pirated editions of the book appeared in 2000.[6] The same year, urban readers saw the Chinese publication of Peter Mayle's *Expensive Habits*, with 20,000 copies produced for the first print run. Titled *Youguan pinwei* in Chinese, Mayle's book had neither a foreword nor an introduction, which is usually employed by translated books to help readers overcome the cultural gap. Its translator and publisher confidently wrote off the problem of the cultural gap and presumed an adequate interest and curiosity in the topic in late-1990s urban China. Along with these books were two others: *Jieceng* (Class: An Analysis of Chinese Styles and Taste) by Chen Shaogong, a U.K.-based Chinese; and *Gao ji hui* (High-Class Gray: A Portrait of the Urban Chinese Middle Class) by Yin Yiping, the editor of

A MIRAGE OF MODERNITY

a new magazine called *Shishang* (Fashion). Three thousand and ten thousand copies of each book, respectively, were printed for the first run.

However, the mobility and expansion of cosmopolitan consumption also deterritorializes its opposite, "hickness" (*tu*). When global consumption renders the national border porous and enters China's interior, the "hickness" usually rooted in the rural spaces similarly leaves its rural boundary, expands to the city, and leaves the urban Chinese feeling like "hicks" in the context of the new globalized sphere of consumption. Therefore, in Chi Li's novel *Lai lai wang wang* (Back and Forth), the character Kang Weiye, an urbanite and president of a company in Wuhan, feels embarrassed that he is "a bit like a country bumpkin" when he spends the night in a hotel suite with his savvy cosmopolitan lover after an exquisite dinner accompanied by French red wine and Kenny G's saxophone music (1999: 84). In the sublime space of cosmopolitan consumption, tu creeps in and secretly plagues certain elite urbanites' identity as cosmopolitan subjects.

Since the late 1990s, consumption has become linked to citizenship as a critical part of the national economy. The fall in commodity exports due to the global economic downturn is supposed to be absorbed by expanding internal demand in order to sustain the breathtaking economic growth rate on which the creation of jobs and social stability depends. "Stimulating internal demand" (*ladong neixu*), a hot phrase with the media and economists in the late 1990s, mobilized spending by both government and citizens, and it was the major economic motive for creating week-long holidays for the first time on National Day in 1998 and May Day in 1999.[7] In the September 1999 issue of *Focus* (Jiaodian), a Shenzhen-based magazine, the chief editor announced, in the essay "To the Readers: It Begins with You," that the state was to give civil servants a pay raise.

> But have you thought of this: the state takes out 16 billion yuan directly and 90 billion yuan indirectly [for raises and welfare increases] and puts money in our pockets. The state certainly does not intend for the money to sleep in your pockets, or to be saved in the bank. The state hopes that you will spend it all. It has been fifty years since the founding of our country and there has never been such a strong state desire: to spend money is patriotic. If everyone spends, money will circulate in all spheres, markets will be energized, and the whole national economy will enter a positive cycle.

Therefore, you should be aware that your attitude toward consumption and your spending habits are already not only your own individual business. When you decide to spend your savings on an apartment, when you take out a loan from the bank to buy a car, when you lead your family out of stores, hands full of shopping bags, are you aware of this: when you enjoy the bliss of consumption, you also enjoy the pleasure of patriotism, since you are supporting the state.

Each of our destinies is now more closely linked to the state than ever. Let it begin with you. Let us go forward into consumption! And let us use the money the state gives us to help the state. (Hua Guoshun 1999: inside cover)

Never mind the rise of national debt and the hollowing out of state properties through sales, theft, and consumption.[8] Persuading the masses to consume and adopt a new attitude toward consumption is a difficult task since they want to hold on tight to their wallets in order to assess whether they will be affected by policy changes in healthcare and other forms of social welfare.[9] Consumption is touted as a form of "social contribution" in this distorted production-consumption linkage; the overheated economic engine cannot stop and must be kept running at a high speed lest it be besieged and stalled by the mounting wreckage that it has created in its own wake: massive and growing unemployment, an increasingly defunct welfare and pension system, an alarming Gini coefficient of income disparity that has reached 0.45, and increased social unrest and instability.[10] The contemporary economy tries to outrun its own problems. What is hoped to keep the economy running ahead of its own shadow is deficit spending, which can help generate employment and cover up growing patches of disillusionment and discordance with an illustrious portrait of "the well-off society" (*xiaokang shehui*). State-owned banks have lowered interest rates repeatedly to incite consumption and promoted low-interest loans on cars and houses. Thus, consumption is not only a strategic and privileged site which the post-Mao state has mobilized as sensual and sensory evidence for its vision of progress; it is also a life-buoy that helps the state keep the deflating economy afloat in the context of global economic downturn. Considering the intimate connections between the post-Mao state and consumption, I argue against the thesis that consumption is a space autonomous from the power of the state (Davis 2000). Furthermore,

A MIRAGE OF MODERNITY

consumption is not a democratizing space, but constructs a new hegemonic and oppressive "system of recognition," hierarchy, and exclusion (Baudrillard 2001: 22). The anthropologist Louisa Schein has warned that "anthropologists need not be complicit with a prevailing interpretation in social analysis—that the expansion and strength of the market is in direct inverse proportion to the strength of the Chinese state" (2002).

If the figure of the "successful person" is usually male, and if his entrepreneurial tendencies often place him on unstable political and moral grounds, then the consumer, a continually thriving, celebrated, forefront figure in the post-Mao imagination of modernity, is often associated with middle-class women.[11] While the middle-class woman accrues gender value through consumption, the working-class woman has seen her gender value depreciated in production: urban women workers find their labor cheapened and marginalized in the labor market, and migrant women emerge as the cheapest of China's cheap labor.[12] Set against the depression and impoverishment of millions of urban women workers laid off and depreciated in the labor market, the glamorous figure of the middle-class consumer now graces TV screens, as well as shopping centers and restaurants. She dwells in private homes in gated communities and inhabits the front pages of colorful shopping guides distributed to pedestrians on the street. She magnifies her self-fulfillment on the larger-than-life billboard and through conspicuous consumption at holiday tourist sites. She multiplies her image on the covers of numerous magazines wheeled on mobile carts selling popular books, magazines, and newspapers, enticing pedestrians in Beijing as well as in rural Anhui. Her image circulates to county seats and villages on New Year's calendars and county-library current-magazine shelves. She adorns the walls of rural young women's bedrooms and is mimicked by migrant women. Glittering in rural markets, she and her associates are the symbolic figures of cosmopolitan culture in the countryside.

In this context, it is hardly surprising that Xiumei and other young migrant women portray their consumption experiences as meaningful migration experiences to a visitor such as myself—a cosmopolitan subject in their eyes. This discursive predilection enables consumption to emerge from myriad experiences of migrancy, becoming a valuable and representative event as it contributes to self-recognition as a knowing modern subject. Xiumei might have shared stories of her various hardships and frugal practices among her close friends and relatives, but she probably did not consider them worth mentioning to outsiders. I am not suggesting that Xiumei is particularly calculating and unusually selective in her self-representation. Instead, I contend that a discursive predilection functions on the level of habitus that informs the interpretive subject—Xiumei as she makes sense of her experiences and interprets them within the dominant system of values and meanings—of what is important and worthwhile in her self-representation and what is better left unsaid to outsiders, including myself and many rural women recruited by her labor-export station.

To many rural women who come to Xiumei's labor-export station to register for migration, the image of Xiumei, as a transformed modern subject with high suzhi and consumption experience, mediated the urban culture of modernity for them. When the township organized women for migration for the first time in 1987, many women applied, but few went. The rumor that recruited women would wait on handicapped soldiers injured in the Sino-Vietnam war (1978–79) discouraged many young women applicants from going. The image of the disabled adult male body seemed to expose an awkwardness and contaminating meniality associated with domestic labor. Moreover, the rumor had a temporary power to deter migration because it assumed the centrality of this kind of labor in shaping the reputation and social recognition of the person undertaking it, particularly when it involved young women who were doubly located in the labor market as well as the marriage circuit. A problematic identity in the labor market would affect a woman's value in the marriage circuit.

However, rural young women in Quanyang Township soon found not only that the rumor was false but also that labor seemed to give way to consumption, which surprised them as an exciting new ground for identity. The rumor evaporated when Xiumei and a few others came home from Beijing for the lunar New Year, their clothes and speech having acquired a "foreign air" (*yangqi*) in the local idiom. Many of those who had stayed behind found the new image of Xiumei and several other migrants appealing. To many young women who had experienced life in the countryside with despondence and melancholy, the return of migrant women opened up a new possibility of life and subjectivity attuned to the times. The women staying behind did not discover or invent the power of consumption to liberate themselves from the power of the rumor. Rather, consumption came to them via the circulating bodies of migrants with a discursive force that seemed to offer new grounds for identity and recognition. As Xiumei told me, "Now people have accepted the idea of migration. Here every village has at least dozens of people going out. Women in their twenties and thirties have almost all experienced going out."

Consumption experiences for migrant women in the city include visiting parks or other tourist sites with friends, shopping for and putting on makeup, going out for snacks (*xiao chi*), taking pictures at tourist sites, window shopping at department stores, discussing their favorite popular music or movie stars, and bicycling on weekends to supermarkets or "small commodity markets" (*xiao shangpin shichang*, which are concentrated spaces with dozens of vendors). Domestic workers observe firsthand urban domestic consumption in employers' homes. A survey of 172 migrant domestic workers in Beijing found that 51.16 percent consider their most important personal change after coming to the city to be "knowing a lot of new things that [I] didn't know before" and 25.58 percent considered it to be "learning to dress well" (Sun Xiaomei 1993). Although "learning to dress well" is not considered the most important change by the majority, it is likely to be considered important by most migrants. A research team studying female migrant workers from Hunan to Guangdong also noted that migrant women "attach importance to dressing" (*zhuzhong chuan*) ("Wailai nülaogong yanjiu" ketizu 1995: 80).[13]

In my own field research I noticed that migrant women implicitly contrasted themselves with male migrants by remarking that male migrant workers, especially construction workers, undergo little change in the city. As one put it, "You still see them squat there eating their meals at construction sites, baring their chests, and watching TV together in large crowds. It's as if they still live a village life in the city. That's why some of us migrant women are not attracted to this kind of male migrant." Writing on the power of images of women in post-Mao China, Harriet Evans states, "Feminine beauty, romance, and consumer capacity are visually enmeshed in public display of desire" (2000: 217). The figure of the middle-class feminine consumer parades a new way of "having a gender" (ibid.: 221), along with new values and the bliss of femininity that she realizes through commodity consumption. Some commercials advertising beauty products for women play with what could be called consumer feminism, in which "being a woman is truly good."

In this social context, consumption is a stimulating and mediating force behind young migrant women's pursuit of a new self. This is especially visible in young women's increased interest in clothing and personal image. While migrant men's freedom and mobility is not predicated on marriage, the custom of patrilocal residence means that women's futures, freedom, and mobility depends greatly on the families they marry into. Once married—most likely to men from their native places or to migrant men they meet on their own—a woman either returns home to the countryside or migrates with her husband or other family members. Unlike her husband, she can seldom migrate on her own. The stakes in marriage are usually higher for rural women than for men. Similar to the sentiments expressed by migrant women in Beijing, some migrant women in Hunan explicitly wish for boyfriends to be less "hick-headed" (*tu tou tu nao*), but men have not expressed the same desire for their female counterparts ("Wailai nülaogong yanjiu" ketizu 1995: 82). Because of their higher stakes in marriage, migrant women appear to demand more modernity of their potential marriage partners. For women, the contradiction between their pursuit of modernity and their frustration over a lack of modernity in the bodily habitus of certain male migrant workers—an ironic reversal of the more common designation of women as the embodiment of tradition—forebodes a potential problem: that their quests for personal development and new self-expression do not mesh well with courtship.

Migrant women are caught in the contradiction between production and consumption. Although domestic workers are not conventionally seen as producers, their labor power in fact produces use-value for direct domestic consumption. Their lived experiences offer a poignant critique of the contradiction between consumption and production, a contradiction that incites, disciplines, and obliges them into the process of migration, but simultaneously ridicules and disavows them, thus rendering them doubly exploited—in labor as well as in the realm of representation. Eighteen-year-old Rong, after dropping out of high school and quarrelling with her mother, became one of many who traveled to Beijing on Jiao Xiumei's bus in 1997. When I met Rong in Beijing, she spoke Mandarin with a very colloquial Beijing accent, much better than I could manage.

I wanted to go out because they [returned migrants] said how nice and comfortable the outside was, and I wanted to experience it. Moreover, I thought I could earn my own money and would be free to spend it.

A MIRAGE OF MODERNITY

At home parents put constraints on you. If you want to buy things, you need to ask them for money and give them a good reason, and even then you don't get much. So I only thought about the convenience of earning and spending my own money. I didn't think very much and just wanted wholeheartedly to get out. I was young and simple-minded. . . . At the beginning, I also imagined that Beijingers were really cultured [*you wenhua*] and had high suzhi. My mother even cried when I left. My elder brother is the stubborn one in my family, but even he couldn't stop me. My mother didn't want me to go out; she wanted me to finish school. On my last visit home, my elementary-school teacher saw me at home. Since she thought I should have been in school, she asked, "Are you on break already?" I didn't want to tell her that I had quit school and replied, "I'm indeed on a long break." Hahaha. . . .

Her wry laughter came only minutes after Rong had described the stress of her work in Beijing: "Sometimes you hope that others won't find fault with you. You always hope so and always try to think how you can do well to satisfy them . . . because you want to keep the job. So there is an intense pressure on my heart."

Rong's tale of migration began with images relayed by returned migrants. To understand how images motivated Rong, one must go beyond seeing images as merely skin deep. Images reflected by returned migrant women project a depth of interior subjectivity and incite a desire in the spectator to inhabit and embody the images both subjectively and corporeally. Feminist film critics refer to "the *performative* and *corporeally* experienced aspects of film" as a way to understand the relationship between the spectator and the women on screen (Donald and Lee 2001: 134). This alludes to the process of spectators recomposing themselves in relation to images, as Sobchack writes of the image effect: "Regrounded in our bodies, we have dimension, gravity, and the enabling power [of the images] to regain our sense of balance and to comport ourselves differently—first, perhaps, *before* our images, and then, one hopes, *within* them" (1999: 60). The *qi* (airs, spirit) in the *yangqi* (overseas [Western] airs) of returning migrants like Xiumei refers not only to their new bodily appearance but also to the new spirit they embody. This spirit is a new subjective interiority articulating with the "modern" Zeitgeist. Bearing witness to its triumphal power, the new subject seems to be on her way to self-fulfillment.[14] The metaphor of qi suggests mutual resonance between superficial image and the interior spirit or subjectivity that one possesses (or is possessed by). So one cannot dismiss the importance that migrant women attach to clothing and personal image as a mere matter of vanity. Rather, one should consider the power of consumption in mediating self-conception. As Xiaobing Tang describes the dominant image of the consumer in post-Mao China, "The subject of the dramatically fulfilling world must dominate our view because the mirror image functions by invading our self-conception" (Tang 1996: 118).

Rong recomposed herself vis-à-vis the image of returning migrants and decided to rechart her life path against her parents' will. In Quanyang the images of returning migrants as embodying modernity have enabled migration and effectively exorcised the local rumor that had made menial labor seem the most likely prospect of migration. During my research in Wuwei County, a returned migrant woman admitted that her main reason for becoming a domestic worker in Beijing in the 1980s was to buy a red *huaxueshan*, a winter jacket made of synthetic fabric, considered stylish and fashionable in the cities at that time (compared to the more conventional and heavier handmade cotton-padded jacket). The charm of the red huaxueshan motivated her journey. "*At the time* it was fashionable." She nudged me and laughed over her fixation on the huaxueshan—now the very name of huaxueshan is considered passé or perhaps even hickish.

Yet the power of images in representing a new subjectivity does not necessarily complete its project of transformation. I visited Xiumei in her small bedroom above her restaurant after our initial meeting in her parents' house. The bed, wardrobe, and dresser were probably purchased as a set for her wedding. There was a bouquet of plastic flowers in a vase on the wardrobe, collecting dust. Cardboard boxes of children's drinks and food supplements were stored beneath the bed. There were clippings of female models glued to the surfaces of furniture: the corner of the pink, heart-shaped table mirror, the front of the wardrobe, and the wood frames of the bed. One of the images featured a blond woman, which Xiumei had obviously cut from a package of Lux soap. These images found their way onto the surface of furniture through a bricolage recycling of fragments over time, creating an effect different from systematic interior design, which produces the interior as an inner space of the

A MIRAGE OF MODERNITY

self through a mastery of the semiotics of commodities.[15] Sometimes, Xiumei's bedroom doubled as a sitting room for visitors. Inviting me to sit on the bed while she changed her blazer, Xiumei murmured, "Actually I don't like wearing fashionable clothes. When I wear them, it feels kind of hard to step outside." I later learned from Xiumei that all the marriages in her family (hers and her four siblings') were arranged. However, the discursive predilection that delimits what one may reveal to the public and what one must conceal as personal and unpresentable, forced these aspects of her feelings and experiences to remain inside as fragments of herself. The circulating re-presentable images of Xiumei that rural young women encountered were images of Xiumei in the photos taken in Shenzhen and at the 1994 conference of star entrepreneurs. There, the person of Xiumei appeared as a frequent traveler between Beijing and Quanyang, and as a confident veteran migrant whose clothes were clearly more fashionable than those of rural women.

On the Urban Labor Market I: "What Are You Here For?"

The imaginary of migration as mobility, freedom, and "Western airs" renders the conditions and relations of labor invisible and insignificant. If the return of the first group of migrants as modernized consumers dispelled the widespread anxiety in Quanyang about the menial nature of domestic labor, how, then, do migrant women, who arrive in the city to be laborers, find their subject position in the circuit of production and consumption? My ethnography followed the workers to the city, where, on arriving, they received a "practical training" lecture by a company manager. I was allowed to sit in on the training. Every week the manager addressed groups of migrant women from various provinces. Since its establishment in the early 1980s, this company had recruited more than 70,000 migrant women into domestic service. On the day I was there, about seventy migrant women were present.

Standing poised, the company manager glanced at the throng of women settling on the floor, sitting or squatting. Most of the women were in the city for the first time and were much younger than the manager herself, although a few seemed older. The manager spotted one older-looking woman in the corner and asked, "How old are you?" Her voice was loud enough for all to hear. "I'm forty," the woman answered in her dialect. The company only recruited women under the age of thirty-five. The manager questioned the woman further, without diverting her glance: "Are you really just forty?" The tone of the question was authoritative and disbelieving, as if the manager could see through the woman. A moment of silence passed; the woman in the corner did not respond. The crowd was still settling down, but some women began to pay attention to the conversation. Turning to the group, the manager asked, "Can all of you understand what I'm saying?" After pausing for a moment, she said, "You should all be able to understand." Then several young women wearing makeup caught the manager's attention. She said disapprovingly, "Many women from your place like to wear makeup. No other place is like this. Do you know what you are here for?" A few young women around me giggled at this question. One made faces. The manager continued, "You don't need me to tell you. You know what you are here for." With this remark, she launched into a loquacious lecture in her Beijing-accented Mandarin (the company refers to employers of domestic workers as *yonghu*, that is, customers, consumers, or, more literally, users).

Now the market is not as good as it was before. Customers are more particular. Up until several years ago, demand was so much higher than supply that employers would want you as long as you were a human. Now it's the opposite—now five or seven domestic workers compete for one customer. Therefore, only those who excel can survive. You need to be extremely good-tempered to do your work well. A girl from Gansu province was hired to look after a sick granny. That granny had a bad temper: she slept during the day and was up making trouble at night when this girl needed sleep. One night the granny kept asking the girl to help her use the toilet. In the end, the girl lost her patience and beat the granny badly. She was sentenced to a year in prison. Although this is one case out of tens of thousands, we still have to exercise caution. You would have to bear it even if the patient spat on you or poured urine on you. It is with courage that you come here and this courage should now be applied in your work.

The manager then narrated some scenarios about accidents caused by the negligence and ignorance of domestic workers, such as the explosion of a gas stove, the washing of a baby in the washing machine, and so on.[16]

You should always use your head to ponder how to do things carefully and well. If you're lazy and gluttonous, then conflicts between you and your customers will surely arise. Don't be self-centered or think only of your own position. You should think from the customer's point of view first in order to understand how to resolve conflicts. Like in a family, it's impossible for a pot and a bowl to avoid colliding. There are quarrels even between children and parents and between wife and husband. It's impossible to avoid conflicts. But you should consider how to bring contradictions to a minimum. If a conflict grows out of control, [it] will affect you and affect the reputation of this company. If you know how to be accommodating, know how to say soft words [*shuo ju ruan hua*, to be apologetic], and have the courage to acknowledge your mistakes, then big problems can turn into small problems and small problems turn into no problem at all. The only thing you should not tolerate is harassment [*saorao*] by male customers. You might say, "Aiya! Don't all these things make domestic workers inferior?" Well, only if you look down on yourself.

Tomorrow when you meet the customers, you are not allowed to bargain with them. You should stick with the standard wage. If a customer picks you out, hurry up and sign a contract with him or her. If you're picky and bargain, you will be the one left out, while others find their customers. Beijing customers believe that good ones are likely to be picked first and those who stay behind must be bad. Once you're left behind, it will be hard for you to find a customer.

"Do you know what you're here for?" is a rhetorical question whose answer is supposed to be self-evident in the context shared by speaker and audience. For the giggling young women, who had probably come to Beijing for the first time, the answer seemed too obvious. The mere act of posing the question appeared ludicrous to them, as it seemed to grossly underestimate their sophistication. Yet they might have been unaware of the role that this rhetorical question would play in defining their subject position as "baomu" in the city. The manager of the company was therefore intent on disciplining these women by teaching them the market calculus on which their existence and livelihood in the city depended. Though not answered directly, this rhetorical question was pedagogically addressed throughout the whole lecture.

The long litany surrounding "what you are here for" serves as an existential qualifier, qualifying the conditions of existence for migrant women in the logic of market calculus. By introducing migrant women to their structural position on the market at this specific point in time (the market in 1999 was different from what it had been several years prior), the manager sought to instill discipline: she taught the migrant women exactly how they should behave on the labor market and in relation to customers, in order to ensure their employment and the company's financial survival. Many of the new migrant women may have been unaware of or unprepared for their predication as commodified labor power. These young women emerged from a context in which anxiety surrounding the rumor about the nature of domestic labor had been dispelled and replaced by consumption as an enticing sign of modernity and a defining marker for the self. Thus the manager posed the question in order to signal a new context—a new regime of labor and subjectivity—that many of these young women were now entering. The expectation that they must endure being spat on and even showered in urine ironically reinstated the centrality of menial domestic labor, at one point discarded along with the rumor, as their existential qualifier in the city and indicative of their subject position as baomu.

Referring to employers of domestic labor as *yonghu* (customer or consumer) shifts the terms of representation of the contradiction between employers and domestic workers. To be sure, employers of domestic workers have a double identity: they are both employers and consumers of domestic labor power. The yonghu-consumer reference used by the company latches onto the growing discourse of consumption and consumer rights in post-Mao China, thereby giving this post-Mao industry a modern flavor and distancing it from the suspicion of old-society exploitation. On the one hand, the yonghu-consumer reference downplays the employment relationship and eclipses the productive character of domestic labor; on the other hand, it re-presents the contradictions between employers and domestic workers as a legitimate and sovereign consumer demand about the quality of a commodity—the labor performance of domestic workers—and renders this demand more compelling and deserving of satisfaction.

Domestic labor is a dual performance of labor and subjectivity. This means the labor performance required of a domestic worker is not merely physical labor in its quantifiable nature but also labor performed from a specific subject position. One may therefore call it *subjected* labor.[17] In order to teach subjection the training lecture assumes that new domestic workers are self-centered, so the first corrective measure involves a form of self-discipline and endurance. Conflicts between employers and domestic workers are likened to those in a family between children and spouses. However, the manager refuses to acknowledge the crucial difference in power relations: unlike conflicts between family members, a domestic worker in conflict with her employers bears sole responsibility for conflict resolution. She is supposed to manage and keep contradictions to a minimum, always striving to be accommodating and apologetic at critical moments—to say "soft words."

Domestic workers often endure various grievances and humiliation while working for employers, including being forced to eat leftovers, deprived of food, suspected first when any valuable item appears to be missing in employers' homes, and so on. Such humiliations and mistreatments occur frequently enough that a domestic-service company in Nanjing decided to establish a "baomu grievance reward" (*baomu weiqu jiang*), rather than change its rule that forbids domestic workers to contradict their employers. The most these companies are willing to do is to encourage employers to adopt a more "modern" relationship with their domestic workers and to respect their workers' dignity (*renge*).[18]

It is not that problems with employers are unknown to these companies. The director of the Beijing company complained to me about certain employers' lack of empathy for domestic workers and about sometimes having to speak up for a domestic worker in front of her employer. However, it is the sternly conveyed position of this company that domestic workers are responsible for ensuring a good relationship with their employers. Small wonder that some domestic workers complain that "the company always favors the customer" in conflict arbitration. "Jiating fuwuyuan bidu" (A Required Reading for Domestic Workers), an unpublished manual distributed by the company to all domestic workers to teach them hygienic habits and domestic work skills, also contains "a letter addressed to customers." Written in a gentle and respectful tone and using the honorific "you" (*nin*), this letter implores employers to treat domestic workers with a sense of equality, beseeches their patience in teaching domestic workers, and offers tactful messages to help promote harmony—for example, by recognizing a common humanity that domestic workers share with them.

Subjected labor not only helps to reproduce the employer family and its domestic life on a daily basis; it also reproduces the family's self-representation, including its class relationship with the domestic worker. Does this subjection make domestic workers a lower class? The manager answers this question by citing a liberal notion of the individual that treats the value of the self as autonomous and sui generis: "Only if you do not look down on yourself." The manager warns migrant women that they are capable of (and responsible for) adjusting how they feel, regardless of how they are treated. In other words, the urban society, the company, and the employers are exempt from any responsibility regarding migrant workers' feelings. Consistent with the biologized notion of womanhood in post-Mao society, the only integrity and right that the company firmly encourages the worker to maintain against her employers is her right to sexual integrity, which underlies the value of migrant womanhood, but also presumably sustains one's confidence in the level of morality in post-Mao society.[19]

To perform subjected labor, the self of the domestic worker must be familiarized and disciplined into her new specific class position. This is not an easy task, as many employers are frustrated that their domestic workers do not fit in as baomu and seem instead to turn the social order upside down. I have heard many employers complain, "We want to hire a baomu, but what we get is a *xiaojie* [young lady]" or "It is not even clear who waits on whom." Certain employers who hire urban women as domestic workers have similar complaints. In the training lecture, the domestic worker is presumed to be self-centered, which makes her in need of discipline. Her sense of self has yet to be molded to fit a new labor regime, and she has yet to become familiar with her role in a new class relation.[20] Many new young migrant women feel uncomfortable, tense, and alienated when they first arrive in their employers' homes, even though they typically address their employers in familial terms (grandpa, grandma, uncle, aunt, sister, brother). Li Hong described her process of becoming familiar with her subject position as a domestic worker: "When I first came to Beijing in 1997, I wasn't used to anything. It's not that I was particularly unhappy here, but I just couldn't smile. My face was always tight and I couldn't bring it to smile. Sister Liu Ying [her employer] was nice to me. But I just couldn't smile and couldn't find my own position here [*zhao bu dao ziji de weizhi*]." When I talked to Li Hong in the garden of a guarded and gated residential complex where she worked in late 1999, she said she could now smile more easily and had finally found her position. She told me that her cousin, who had come to Beijing recently to work for a family in the same residential compound, was as lost as she had once been. It was hard for her cousin to smile, too.

The difficulty Li Hong and her cousin faced was connected to a regime of subjectivity, specific to domestic workers. They could not smile, since they felt lost and in limbo; they did not know how to inhabit the baomu position and did not know how to navigate these new social relationships. Their inability to smile was a sign of the intense confusion of their subjectivity. It was not until Li Hong finally familiarized herself with her new position and learned to inhabit that position that she managed to smile. The process of disciplining was also a process of becoming familiar with her new subjection in the city. Only through this dual process did she learn how to act in her new class context and, ironically, only then did she acquire the sense of freedom *to act as a domestic worker.* The journey of the self, departing as a rural young woman and arriving as a domestic worker in the city, can be an intense and confusing process of reconfiguring oneself by learning one's position within a new class relationship. Li Hong was indeed relieved to emerge from the limbo of estrangement and confusion. When she finally found her subjective position as a domestic worker, she gained a certain ease and freedom in her job—freedom as a domestic worker.

This regime of classed subjectivity facilitates good performance of subjected labor, but the latter still requires more. Desired domestic labor is labor performed from a subjected position that also incorporates a double vision. As the manager explained, a good domestic worker should not only have her own perspective but also be able to see things from her employers' perspective. Developing an ability to switch between points of view is a measure to correct the worker's presumed self-centeredness. Here, the domestic worker is expected to undergo a different process of self-recollection. This process forces her to shift her point of view to that of her employers, as if momentarily standing in their position and having a view of the picture as they see it, and then to use that vision to guide how she should act and perform better work as a domestic worker. The everyday satisfaction of her employers' expectations and her conflict management skills depend on her possession of this type of double vision. One experienced domestic worker prided herself on her intelligence and ability to think ahead of her employer: "This job is difficult. It's both manual and mental labor. You have to think. It's like she [the employer] is a *xiaojie* [lady], while I am a *yahuan* [maidservant]. In all the traditional plays, which yahuan is not smarter than her xiaojie? So I have to be smarter than her. I have to anticipate what she needs and think of things that even she has not thought of." The greater her ability to switch between perspectives and anticipate her employer's desires, the more she can approximate the ideal of being "of one heart and mind" with the employer, which is touted as the ideal employment relationship in the company's manual.

While labor performance occupies a central position as the existential qualifier for rural women in the city, the manager did not forget to discipline migrant women on the importance of image and consumption.

> Another thing is about wearing makeup. We are not against you wearing makeup, but it's not appropriate for this situation. Customers don't like to see you wearing makeup: eyebrows thick and black like worms, eyes as shadowed as a giant panda's, lips as bloody red as if you had just eaten a dead mouse. But some women from Anhui don't especially care about their image. You wear an undershirt under your shirt in the summer, but you don't button up your shirt. When you walk, the unbuttoned shirt flaps around. Your customer will think, "If you can't even put yourself together, how can you clean and organize my home?" So you must look neat, but do not try to stand out. On your day off, you may wear light makeup. Among the "excellent domestic workers" we have here, some are good at it and have good suzhi. On their day off, you can't even tell by looking at them whether they're here to hire a domestic [*qing ren*] or to look for a fellow migrant [*zhao ren*].

Managers divide migrant women into two categories: those who seem overly concerned with their image and exaggerate their makeup, and those who are oblivious and clueless about their appearance. Migrant women are ridiculed for both excess and lack. The manager's message implies that employers find both types of migrant women to be inappropriate and offensive commodities, since their appearance detracts from their value as domestic workers and therefore turns them into commodities of low suzhi. Proper consumption and appearance reflects a migrant woman's level of suzhi and enhances her value as a domestic worker. In the eyes of the manager a migrant woman's ability to pass for an employer is the highest level of suzhi she can attain.

On the Urban Labor Market II: Use-Value and Semiotic Value for Consumption

The morning after such a training lecture, the market is exclusively for the new migrant women, until most of them find employment. The salary scale regulated by the company for new migrant women is 260 yuan per month, and new migrants are not allowed to negotiate for a higher wage. At such a price, new migrants are in demand. Some new migrant women accept wage offers of 200 yuan or even less. At about ten o'clock, two hours after the company opens, only three of the seventy or so new migrant women who arrived the day before still await employment. Experienced migrant women who are between jobs are now allowed to enter the meeting room. Soon it is filled with over 130 of them. The salary for experienced domestic workers ranges from 300 to 400 yuan and is up to negotiation between individual employers and individual domestic workers. The migrant women sit on long benches in the room, talking, with their luggage next to their feet. Most are in their late teens and early twenties. A small number of them appear to be in their thirties or perhaps forties.

Employers come and go. At any given time, about a dozen or so potential employers stand against the walls or walk slowly from row to row, silently observing the migrant women or whispering comments to their friends or spouses. Some even wear sunglasses in the room to allow themselves the leisure of scrutinizing the roomful of women without the potential discomfort of the workers returning their gazes. Compared to the earlier commotion, when the new workers were quickly snatched up by employers, the process now is slow and prudent. Employers are much more cautious with experienced migrants, not only because they are more expensive but also because they are considered likely to be "slick" (*you*) — glib, flippant, and too knowing. Occasionally, an employer goes over to talk to one of the women who might be an appropriate candidate.

I am sitting on the bench next to Rong, who is awaiting employment. Around us are women from Henan, Sichuan, Gansu, and Shandong. Two urban women in their thirties or forties are standing nearby. I can hear their not-so-hushed whispering:

"I need someone with good hygiene. The one a moment ago—just the look of her already makes me uncomfortable, gives me headache."

"Those from Henan like to steal. You have to keep your eyes on them and can't let them out of your sight for even a moment."

"Some look too wooden."

Then they spot me—the only bespectacled one with a small notebook in hand among the hundred-some women seated on benches. One of them looks at me suspiciously and asks, "You aren't for hire, are you?" "No," I reply. Annoyed, they turn to Rong. She is wearing a long sleeveless dress with black and green stripes and a white short-sleeved shirt. She isn't wearing any makeup. The following is the conversation between these two women and Rong. In brackets are Rong's comments on the exchange that she tells me after the two women leave.

"Do you wear this dress when you work?" one woman asks.

"No." Rong replies. ["I went to visit a relative yesterday and stayed overnight there. This morning I came straight from there to the recruiting station. Otherwise, I would have worn pants."]

"Can you make stuffed buns [*baozi*], buns [*mantou*], dumplings [*jiaozi*], noodles, and pancakes [*jianbing*] from scratch?"

"I can make dumplings and pancakes. I can also cook standard dishes [*jiachang cai*]." ["Actually, I can make stuffed buns, buns, and noodles from scratch. But buns don't cost much to buy on the street. Why do I have to make them from scratch? I don't want to tell them what I can do because I don't want to do it."]

"How long have you worked?"

"Two years."

"What's the longest time you've worked for a family?"

"One year."

"How long did you work most recently?"

"One month."

"Why?"

"Because the child in the family I worked for liked to tell lies."

"Is it he who liked to tell lies, or you?"

"Perhaps it's me. I can't tell whether it's he or me." ["What can I say if they ask me in this way? The more I try to explain, the less they would believe me.]

"Are you married?"

"No."

"Do you have a boyfriend?"

"No."

"Impossible! Girls of your age where you're from [the countryside] all have boyfriends." ["They are trying to determine how long I can work for them before I go home to get married."]

"Yes. Where I'm from there are women of my age who even have children. But I am exceptional."

The conversation ends here, and the two women leave. No job for Rong.

This morning few found employment. The company closes for a short period at noon. All the employers are asked to leave and come back again. The director of the company gives all the women a half-hour-long talk. He asks one woman to count the number of migrant women in the room and asks all of them to ponder two things: first, given the ratio between potential employers (30 plus) and domestic workers (130 plus), why so many potential employers left this morning without finding anyone suitable; and consequently, how domestic workers should behave themselves.

This scene reveals the structure of interaction between seated domestic workers and standing potential employers: all the domestic workers were on display for potential employers' careful inspection. When domestic workers walk around in the room, they tend to walk hurriedly, sometimes hunching their backs, and to sit down as soon as possible. When, once in a while, a few of them stand up to stretch, they stand next to their seats. They inhabit and move through the market space in a manner different from that of the employers, who stand and walk around slowly, pausing intermittently, observing the seated from above.

Employers double as consumers and scrutinize migrant women as special commodities of labor power as bearers of use-value and semiotic value. They demand consumer satisfaction for the use-value of the hired labor—the ability of a domestic worker to do housework efficiently. For example, Rong was once tested for her use-value and failed a potential employer's test. When asked how she would wash bean sprouts, Rong replied, "In a basin." On hearing this, the potential employer immediately turned away. A few women around Rong puzzled over the question and suggested that one should perhaps rid sprouts of their tails before washing, which might have been the question's trick.

Employers also demand a semiotic value from the commodity: how the domestic worker places herself socially in relation to her potential employers, and to what extent her self-expression might enhance the social distinction of the consumer's self-identity and self-representation. In other words, not only must domestic workers produce use-value for consumption, a necessary condition for their employment; they must also present a certain personhood for consumption. The two urban women who examined Rong not only questioned her cooking skills but also expressed particular concern about her semiotic value. In fact, their questioning began with Rong's dress. These two urban women, who had already rejected the appearance of the woman "a moment ago" as a nuisance, apparently also found Rong's dress to be a sign of her transgression and slickness, indicating that she did not know her position. Throughout the rest of the conversation, the two women tried to discipline Rong by openly second-guessing most of her replies. In this interview, Rong failed to present a domestic worker personhood for consumption by her potential employers: regardless of her labor skills, Rong's self-expression threatened to disturb rather than enhance the women's self-distinction and self-representation. Rong's Beijing-accented Mandarin and urbane dress, rather than being a positive sign of her improved suzhi, as the manager would have suggested, marked her as negative in semiotic value on the labor market. She was deemed unable to perform properly subjected labor for consumption.

Migrant women have triple identities in the urban labor market: they are producers, consumers, and objects for consumption. Contrary to the claim that consumption is a liberating force leading to democratization (Davis 2000), in the post-Mao domestic labor market the consumer-employer is not a liberating agent, because she ensures her and her family's class distinction and reproduction through consuming commodified domestic labor. Nor can the consumer–domestic worker be a liberated subject, because her consumption is constrained by her wage and disciplined by her association with labor. Her meager wage does not allow a level of consumption that could elevate her to the celebrated visibility of the consumer subject. Even at a level of consumption she could afford, the domestic worker has seen her consumption disciplined by the employer on the basis of her association with labor. Xiaocui, a woman in her thirties, was an hourly employee and the mother of a ten-year-old child. After working as a domestic worker for more than ten years, she had acquired a reputation of competence and generosity with her labor power (*bu xi liqi*). Yet, even her highly rated use-value cannot exempt her consumption and image from being scrutinized by employers with disciplinary power over her. Sitting in her small one-room basement apartment, where she lived with her husband, Xiaocui's mood was somber.

> I, too, hope to make myself good-looking and put on a little lipstick. But if I do so, employers will be shocked: "How can you be like this?" If I wear a pair of one-inch-heeled leather shoes, employers will say, "You wear this kind of shoe? Aren't you a laborer [*gan huo'er de*]? Then you don't work today. Just go home and come back tomorrow with different shoes." I thought, "But wearing these shoes should not affect you. If they get dirty from work, I would not ask you to clean them for me. I come to work and I finish my work. Isn't that enough? Should I come to your home barefoot? You can't ask me to come in rags, because I have to take the bus and I can't wear rags on the bus. Otherwise, what would others think of me? When you go out, you dress neatly, too. I'm not wearing any revealing clothes. I just want to be like you and dress cleanly and neatly." The bottom line is that they look down on you as a domestic worker, even if they often deny it. This is so, isn't it?

Outside employers' homes, on the street, on the bus, and in other public spaces, Xiaocui and other migrants are still subject to disciplinary and evaluative gazes. Police and security personnel cast eagle eyes on them, scan their appearance and body language for signs of rurality, and throw many of them out of the city in periodic sweep-cleaning efforts that prepare a civil and clean image of the city for significant national holidays and international events. (When Beijing celebrated its successful bid to host the 2008 Olympic Games, many labor migrants feared that they would be driven out of the city.) If the police and security force disciplines via violence and coercion, civil society disciplines the migrants through cultural hegemony, particularly through a civilizing and modernizing mission. The following joke circulated in Beijing in 1999: "To fulfill its duty for blood donation, a company employed a number of migrants to substitute for its urban employees in this task. In order to avoid the suspicion of the doctors, these migrants were carefully disguised. Under the supervision of an organizer, they took showers, brushed their teeth, manicured their nails, put on new clothes, and were warned 'no talking and no fighting.' The organizer was confident in the disguises. But at the time of blood donation, the organizer found a scene he hadn't prepared for: these migrants, all clean and neat, were indeed quiet without brawling, but they all squatted on their chairs, patiently awaiting their turn."

The punch line of this joke reveals an unexpected omission of the civilizing work: the organizer had forgotten to discipline the migrants against squatting. This joke demonstrates how deeply the low suzhi of the migrant is engrained, exhibited by his or her rural bodily habitus. The joke also replicates the self-identity of civil society as civilizing agent. Chuckles at this failure to conceal the migrants suggest that civilizing and disciplinary powers should be applied at a new level. However, this suggestion simultaneously naturalizes the exploitative power over the "surplus population" of migrants whose bodies are disciplined as disposable lives to produce surplus values in labor, blood, and representation. A satire by the Shanghai columnist Wang Weiming of migrant women "running amok" in cheap "flip-flop" sandals on the streets of Shanghai further illustrates civil society's power over migrant women in public spaces.

Between the Village and the City: Migrating in Contradictions

During the process of migration, young migrant women find themselves twice caught in contradictions between labor-production and consumption. In both instances, the spatial segregation of production and consumption fosters the invisibility of labor. In the first instance, labor seems invisible to migrant women heading to the city: the city is a prospect of modernity, civility, and consumption that offers possibilities of a new personhood. However, they arrive in the city to find themselves predicated in the specific class position of domestic worker—as laborers and objects for consumption. In the second instance, labor is made invisible to relatives and friends at home: when they communicate with people at home or travel home, migrant women's laboring experiences in the city are largely obscured, and they are seen as a mobile image of the modernized subject, again mediated through consumption. Both instances of contradiction are enabled by a spatial segregation between production and consumption.

The migrant woman Hua Min reflects on this second instance of contradiction, in whose formation she participated.

> This has to do with all of us who have come to the city. That is, we report only good things to our parents at home, no bad things about our lives in the city [*bao xi bu bao you*]. I used to tell them how nice things were outside. I also see young migrants today doing the same. If some of them have an opportunity to be photographed with a celebrity, they will immediately mail the pictures home. Folks at home will say, "Aiya, your daughter is in the same picture with this celebrity!" and so on. "Her life seems very nice, interesting, and meaningful [*you yisi*]." There is no way life is like that for us in the city. But after I visited some place for fun, I would write home about this new experience, telling them that last time I did this and this time I visited this park. I didn't tell them about bad things that happened to me in the city, partly because I didn't want them to worry about me, and partly because folks at home wouldn't know what things were like outside, and it was difficult to communicate. . . .
>
> Then folks at home also become snobbish. If you appear successful when you return, they'll be nice to you, ask you about this and that, and seem to care about you, even though they may be jealous. But if you don't seem to be doing well in the city, you'll see the whites of their eyes [looks of scorn] when you return. . . . So this puts you under a lot of pressure. When I return home for a visit, I make an effort to dress up my husband and myself.

While relegated to the role of a domestic worker in the city, Hua Min relays an image of a self appropriately stimulated by urban novelties and comfortably engaging in modest consumption activities. Like many migrants, she finds it easier to report good things than to "speak bitterness" about her labor experiences. Such reports of hardship would worry her parents and might even prompt them to request their daughter's return. Moreover, to speak bitterness without inviting disdain and criticism of individual incompetence (*mei benshi*) requires a structural and discursive analysis of the hardships. Speaking bitterness is encouraged only when it is linked to the teleology of self-development.

Many migrants have acquired structural analyses of their subject positions, as exemplified by Hua Min's narrative, which also reflects her understanding of her structural predication in the city as a domestic worker. However, it remains difficult for her to share such analyses with people at home who have not experienced migration directly.

Hua Min thus finds herself caught in the second round of contradiction in whose making she participates: in spite of her experiences as a migrant worker in the city, she feels compelled to erase the traces of those experiences and fashion a respectable self-image through consumption when she returns home. It is therefore no accident that cameras often catch images of returning migrants as new subjects of modernity-cum-consumption. The images hide the fact that, for migrant workers, post-Mao modernity remains a strange pas de deux of production and consumption, performed on a stage that stretches from the city to the countryside. One perceives the dance differently, depending on one's position on the stage—whether in the city or the countryside. This pas de deux incites migrant women, traps them in paradoxes, and engages them in the same dance when they traverse the space from the countryside to the city and back.

Politics of Regional Identity and the Erasure of Rural Migrant Women

About half a year after the publication of the celebratory picture and the tongue-in-cheek rhyme on "The Transformation of Migrant Women," many Anhui readers responded with anger to a Shanghai author who referred to migrants from Anhui as "country bumpkins" in an article entitled "Women in Cheap Sandals Running Amok on the Streets."[21] Written by a Shanghai columnist and published in the Shanghai *Youth Daily* (Qingnian bao), the article so infuriated an Anhui reader visiting Shanghai that he submitted it for reprinting in the Anhui-based *Xin'an Evening News* (Xin'an wanbao). This satiric article stung many Anhui readers since it sorely reminded them of Anhui's identity as a "regional periphery" (Skinner 1985), a poor cousin, in spite of its geographic location in Eastern China.

> The attire that covers [migrant women's] loitering bodies under the summer sky is rather sexy: the short and belly button-revealing top accentuates their bodily curves and the super-short skirt beneath renders their buttocks especially voluptuous. The top also has three English letters DFA. Heaven

knows what brand or meaning they signify. Next, it is these details that catch people's attention: a handbag slightly out of fashion and red finger-nails. One can detect blue veins on the backs of their hands. The nail polish has partly peeled off and the patches show some sadness and sorrow. Yet what will attract your utmost attention are their poor-quality slippers. To be precise, this is a pair of "flip-flops," as they have no backs. They wear these flip-flops in and out of the subway, around commercial buildings, and on the streets. These women are running amok in the world in flip-flops, but they all think this is the greatest fashion statement of the summer of 1996.

After some analysis, we discovered that many of them come from other places—some are born in Gaoyou, Jiangsu, and others grew up in Hefei, Anhui. They come here straight from Gao Village or Ma River Village.[22]

This article, written by Wang Weiming, an editor of *Life Weekly* (Shenghuo zhoukan), the weekend supplement of *Youth Daily*, criticizes rural migrant women in Shanghai for having "no interest in understanding the history of the city; nor do they even care to know today's protocols held by residents of Ma Le Villa or the etiquette observed by men and women relaxing in Baile-men."[23] Wang continues that these women "treat Huaihai Road as the thresh-ing ground of their home village and think of Paris Spring as the big bathhouse at home." "What is most awful," in Wang's eyes, is that while walking around in flip-flops, these women fancy they have acquired an urban taste, "which in our eyes is completely off the mark." He warns that "in the city of Shanghai you can be bold and unconstrained, but not crude, and certainly not cheap or vulgar."[24]

The voyeuristic male gaze that examines the bodies of these migrant women relishes their curves and voluptuousness, then has its "fun" spoiled by noticing signs of low-quality consumption that detract from the feminine value of mi-grant bodies: an unfashionable handbag, protruding veins, peeling nail polish, and a pair of poor-quality sandals. Migrant women's consumption—especially their cheap sandals and peeled nail polish—not only fails to cover up but actu-ally becomes a telling sign of their migrancy and class. In this city of leisure men and women, relaxing in the tasteful Paris Spring and Ma Le Villa, can hide or forget their heterogeneous relations of production and homogenize themselves as consumer subjects. In this same city bodies of migrant women are an inextricable sign of manual labor that haunts even consumption, transforming the act of consumption into a sign of manual labor and vagrancy.[25] The migrant worker is branded by her consumption as an inappropriate consumer, a poor mimicker of fashion, a person with decidedly low suzhi. Migrant women, predicated as producers of value and surplus value, are evaluated through the lens of consumption as low-value bodies. Wang Weiming's article ends with his famous indictment: "From your posture that moves around in cheap sandals, we can read only two characters: *bazi* ["bumpkin" in Shanghai dialect]."[26]

Within a week, angry Anhui readers had submitted to *Xin'an Evening News* numerous critical responses to Wang's article. Some readers retaliated with a list of flaws of the Shanghainese (Jiang Xiao, 12 August; Chen Ping, 16 August; Hou Lu, 19 August). Others accused Wang of having a vulgar colonial mentality and a lack of Chinese identity; Wang's appreciation for Paris Spring and Ma Le Villa—signs of colonial consumption—greatly offended these readers (Jin Guo, 14 August; Zhang Kun, 14 August; Zhang Jihua, 19 August; Jiang Weiyang, 13 August; Nian Sun, 13 August; Zhao Chenggong, 16 August; Han Han, 9 August; Shan Ren, 9 August). Others pointed out Wang's disdain for the working class and stressed the contribution of migrant labor to the development of Shanghai (Wang Guijie, 16 August; Zhang Junzhong, 16 August; Liu Zuci, 8 August). Finally, some readers admitted that migrant women were indeed backward and low quality, but that they merited being improved through reason and education rather than through virulent satire (Shan Gang, 12 August; Chen Xianwen, 16 August).

What incensed readers most in Wang's article was the way he juxtaposed Shanghai's taste and modernity with Anhui's provinciality by associating the former with foreign-sounding names and the latter with ignorant, low-class migrant women. Many images of returning migrants had been published in the province as a way to celebrate their transformation into subjects of modernity. Until the mid-1990s, provincial readers and elites in Anhui seldom had reservation about celebrating migrant women's improved consumption as a sign of modernity. Moreover, as the photo of returning migrant women and its accompanying rhyme reveal, readers of the provincial newspaper were expected to share the rhyme writer's secured self-identity as a cosmopolitan subject. The scathing satire in Wang's article treats migrant women as a metonym for Anhui. Many Anhui urban readers thus found themselves humiliated by association and considered their own position as secure modern subjects challenged by the gaze from Shanghai. They were conspicuously reminded of Anhui's lack and, by extension, their own lack.[27]

Apart from a minority of readers who brought up the issue of migrant labor value, most readers had no problem accepting that consumption has the discursive value to define identity. What disturbed them was the intimate association of urban fashion with Western names, which the columnist Wang Weiming treated as if they belonged to Shanghai. The tactic of debunking the association of modernity with Westernness is a call for a "Chinese" identity. The journalist interviewing Wang Weiming questioned him forcefully: "We are all Chinese. Why should you use foreign names and things to reflect our fashion? Do you think this is a healthy national mentality? This is a question many readers want to know."[28] The problems of how migrant women are caught in specific contradictions of production and consumption and why the discourse of consumption should code the identity of individuals did not emerge in this debate. Although Anhui readers fought with Wang about his representation of migrant women, what seemed of greater concern was that their own wounded cosmopolitan identity and the identity of Anhui were at stake. Migrant women were largely erased in this battle putatively waged on their behalf.

The symbolic violence against migrant women did not begin with Wang's article in Shanghai. It was already under way in the provincial campaign for a new image of Anhui that would symbolically disown migrant women. Beginning in the mid-1990s, the Anhui provincial government and local elites slowly grew dissatisfied with the negative image of Anhui circulating nationally through the migrant bodies of refugees fleeing floods and droughts, traveling Fengyang County "flower drum" (*huagu*) singers, and rural migrant workers. In a column called "Re-inspecting Ourselves through the Lens of Reform" (Yong gaige de yanguang chongxin shenshi ziji), two journalists described the fame of *hui shang*, Anhui merchants renowned in the Ming and Qing Dynasties. Frustrated and angry, they asked, "Progeny of the Huishang, What Has Happened to You?"[29] Similarly, "A Cross-century Call: Constructing a New Image of Anhui," written by the chief secretary of the Anhui provincial party committee and published in the *Anhui Daily*, bemoaned that "in some people's eyes, Anhui has become a synonym for poverty personified by floods of refugees and baomu."[30] The article called for a scientific redesigning of Anhui's image to correct the distorted portrayal that had discouraged investments in Anhui. Citing unnamed "international" research, Ji told the readers that "every dollar an enterprise invests in its image will reap more than two hundred dollars in return; as for a region, investment in the research, design, and construction of its image can bring immeasurable economic and social profit."[31] Corrective measures included designing a new image of Anhui, redefining the meaning of "Anhui people," and building up the image of Anhui as a sign with positive value to attract outside capital.[32]

On 10 August 1994, half a month after the publication of Ji's article, the *Anhui Daily* launched a forum called "I Am an Anhui Person" and invited discussions around several topics: what kind of spirit should Anhui people have? What kind of image should be constructed? What kinds of practical actions could one take for Anhui's rejuvenation? The twenty-episode TV series entitled *Hui Shang*, about Anhui merchants in the Ming and Qing Dynasties, received official and popular attention in 1997 and encouraged a new generation of Anhui businessmen to strive for similar achievements.[33] The same year, a seventeen-episode TV series called *Anhui People in the Special Economic Zone* (Anhui ren zai tequ), about successful Anhui figures in Shenzhen, was hailed as an exemplary effort to "construct a new image for the outside and enhance confidence on the inside."[34] In 1998 *Anhui Daily* initiated another forum, calling for articles about "the region's image and the development of Anhui." One article in the forum summarized the problem of the province's image in three characters: poor (*qiong*), hick (*tu*), and low (*di*). "Poor" referred to the large number of Wuwei baomu who had appeared in Beijing since the 1980s; "hick" reflected Anhui's unsophisticated infrastructure and the image of its people; "low" referred to self-esteem.[35]

Reconstructing the image of Anhui involves dissociating its image from refugees, street performers, and migrant women, and associating it instead with past successful merchants and historical figures and with present brand names. The new image of Anhui would symbolically disown refugees and migrants. In the forum "I Am an Anhui Person," one contributor shared his or her feelings after visiting "an exhibit of Anhui's achievement" in Beijing: "I felt a sweetness in my heart . . . a happiness that Anhui people do not just come to Beijing as baomu."[36] The same contributor also shared his or her recent experience in the Gobi Desert. Exhausted in this desolate place, he or she suddenly saw a bright-colored vehicle appear on the horizon. On recognizing the familiar characters on the vehicle as an Anhui brand name, "Yangtze Refrigerators," he or she writes, "I couldn't stop the tears from welling up in my eyes. I was so happy, my Anhui, to see this brand name of my province in such a desolate place! I was so moved, my Anhui, to see this 'old friend' in such a strange place. My Anhui, do you understand my tears?"[37] In the sentimental tears shed for a brand name, a new identity of Anhui was born, purged of its association with refugees and rural migrant women.

5

SELF-DEVELOPMENT AND THE SPECTER OF CLASS

I had a realization: I should not be as I was before. I began to have a kind of . . . self-consciousness, a consciousness that I should change myself. Before this, when I worked for employers' families, it was common sense among us [domestics] from the same native place that we would embezzle. For example, I would record fifteen cents for vegetables that cost ten cents. I followed the examples of my *laoxiang* [people from the same native place] and so became accustomed to this. At the time, the kind of suzhi we had didn't make us feel shameful about what we did. On the contrary, it made us feel that we ought to do it.

XIAOHONG, A MIGRANT, INTERVIEWED 25 JUNE 1999, BEIJING

Migrants encounter many problems, but the biggest enemy is still ourselves.

MIGRANT GIRL, ADDRESSING A GROUP OF MIGRANTS, 17 OCTOBER 1999, BEIJING

How could Xiaohong—a migrant from Anhui who had worked as a domestic in Beijing for several years—have had such a realization and such a desire to change herself, a change that would dislodge her from a practice that, in recent ethnographic writing, has been celebrated as "everyday resistance"? What is the larger discursive context that enabled her to disavow her previous practice as a sign of her and her fellow domestics' deficiency in suzhi.

Xiaohong's *desire* exists in relation to the discourse of self-development (*ziwo fazhan*) that has emerged in the reform-era discourse of Development to forge a new laboring subject. The case of Xiaohong allows one to see how the power of Development is expressed in the self-conception and self-evaluation of the individual migrant woman. When compared to the Mao-era workers of state-owned enterprises, whose primary identity focused on their relationship with the socialist state through planned economy, the discourse of self-development promotes new laboring subjects that have a symbiotic relation with the market. It nurtures a conscious technology of modern selfhood that aligns the self with market logic and Development.[1] Migrant women's acquisition of suzhi, deemed foundational to their self-development and transformation into new subjects, is supposed to represent a kind of surplus value in the process of exchanging labor power for a wage in the market. But the discourse of self-development through an acquisition of suzhi has a profoundly negative implication for class consciousness and collective social agency.

However, Xiaohong's self-critique and self-negation in hopes of elevating her suzhi does not automatically render her a frictionless instance of interpellation into an ideologically defined subject position. While the state calls on the whole nation to advance with the times (*yu shi ju jin*), it is understandable that migrant women workers struggle to avoid being abject casualties of Time and thus throw themselves into self-development. However, they also experience a tension between their lived reality and the discourse of self-development. This tension arises from a contradiction between the discourse and the everyday subterranean experiences that it cannot easily subsume.

Self-Development: Accumulating Suzhi as Surplus Value

Numerous media reports and social-science research papers in China hail the progress of rural migrants from seeking survival (*qiu shengcun*) in the early 1980s to seeking self-development (*qiu fazhan*) in the 1990s. As the feminist scholar Li Xiaojiang observes about the Chinese women's movement during the reform process, "If the catchword of the Chinese women's movement of the 1980s was (social) enlightenment, today's objective is (individual) development" (2001: 1278). Underlying the notions of "progress" and "enlightenment" is a Malthusian loathing of "survival" as merely remaining physically alive, as a process outside Progress involving no modern consciousness of the self, in which an unproductive life-cycle and struggle achieves a zero-sum outcome at best, and at worst consumes resources and detracts from national

THE SPECTER OF CLASS

development.[2] Such a notion of survival is constituted by Development as its own outside and is Development's trope of self-authorization.[3]

In 1998 Anzi—formerly a migrant working woman (dagongmei), now an entrepreneur running Anzi Sky, a club with over a hundred employees—emerged as a model of social mobility from among tens of thousands of migrant women in Shenzhen. Chinese Central TV popularized Anzi's story of transformation and included her as one of two women among "twenty distinguished figures in the twenty years of reform," half of whom were entrepreneurs (CCTV 1999). The media's introduction of these twenty figures to the masses was an important program in the 1998 national grand celebration of the twentieth anniversary of post-Mao reforms. Anzi's inclusion among the twenty was indeed a political gesture legitimating the role of the new self-enterprising laboring subject in China's postsocialist development.

Dagong signifies the new flexible terms of the labor relationship that are profoundly different from the socialist mode of labor relations. Dagong means that the labor relations are stripped of the welfare benefits (housing, medical care, pension) and lifelong employment once guaranteed by the Mao-era *danwei* (work unit) mode of employment.[4] The figure of the dagongmei, an icon of the capitalist mode of exchanging labor for wages in the post-Mao market economy, does not stand alone in the discourse of the 1990s. Her emergence is coupled with the abjection of urban laid-off workers, who are associated with moribund state enterprises and the Maoist past, and whom the state and elite consider to be deeply "dependent" on the Maoist social welfare that is being dismantled. Lisa Rofel, in her study of women workers in China's state-owned enterprises, argues that while these workers were previously recognized as heroes of socialist progress, they now signify "an internal lack, potentially hindering China from reaching modernity, because they bring the past into the present in their very existence" (1999: 106). This negation of urban workers as others brands them as obstacles to development, which postsocialist reforms must overcome. Young migrant workers from rural areas represent the new laboring subject favored by flexible accumulation. The honor accorded to Anzi exemplifies the state's gesture to introduce the new self-developing subject into the symbolic-economic order of postsocialist development.

While migrant workers are excluded from the diminishing urban-based social-welfare system, migrant workers are told that this exclusion gives them an advantage of "self-sufficiency" over their urban counterparts. At a meeting at a nongovernmental organization called Home for Migrant Women (Dagongmei zhi jia) in Beijing, a long-term advocate of migrant women's rights told the workers, "Your position is superior to laid-off urban workers, because they are used to eating state rice and are dependent. You are each a small boat and easy to turn around. In addition, you have *da houfang* [rural bases] in your native places." Though they are said to be deeply rooted in "traditional consciousness," young migrant women are considered better fit for the "training and tempering" of the market and have greater potential for self-development than urban workers, who seem hopelessly stuck in their Maoist "welfare" mentality. In this sense, individual migrants are construed as "small boats" that can sail in any direction the wind of capital blows. However, the fact that rough winds easily knock over small boats remains unsaid.

Migrant workers' connection with their da houfang, their rural base, renders them even more desirable than urban workers. In modern Chinese history, the phrase was born from the Chinese Communist Party's strategy in the 1930s and 1940s to mobilize the vast interior rural areas as support bases for the Chinese revolution that eventually overtook the cities. The origin of the phrase stands worlds apart from its current use in the age of flexible accumulation, but the invocation of da houfang egregiously continues the strategy of positing the rural interior as a base for carrying out social transformation—this time as a postsocialist "market revolution." The migrants' connection with their base is supposed to grant them greater flexibility as laborers who can spring forth from and retract back to their native places effortlessly and tirelessly according to the ebb and flow of a capricious market.

Migrant workers are looked on as the most favored laborers of the expanding market economy, as well as the most promising agents of self-development and social mobility. An article on the transition of Wuwei County girls from young domestics to entrepreneurs in Beijing appeared in *Ban yue tan* (Biweekly Forum), a Party magazine widely circulated among cadres of all levels. The article, entitled "Wuwei: Baomu xiaoying" (Wuwei: The Baomu Effect), celebrates the transformation of rural girls from Wuwei from being domestics for urban families in Beijing to being entrepreneurs who have crossed the rural-urban boundary. A total transformation of their beings accompanies such spatial mobility: "Shortly after they left for the city, these smart and hardworking girls quickly became a generation of new human beings [*xin ren*] combining the culture of the city and the country. When they left the fields, they carried in their bodies a rustic air [*tuqi*] and bodily or labor power [*liqi*]; when they returned they not only brought back capital, information, technology, and market experience but also new ideas, new concepts, and the ability to explore the market economy, none of which folks at home have" (Wang Shucheng and Li Renhu 1996: 24).

The authors summarize the important lesson: "The outside world is broad and wide. If you leave the narrow farmland, you can change everything. Getting rid of poverty and backwardness is up to your own effort" (ibid.). As compared to the small number of migrants before the reform who sought only the means of "survival" through waged labor in the city, the article tells the reader, post-Mao migrant women are able to break away from "traditional consciousness" and elevate themselves, through self-development, from being low-paid hick laborers having nothing to sell but their labor power to becoming new entrepreneurial players in the market. The city is "a vast classroom whose market economy trains and tempers rural girls." This pedagogical call to temper oneself in the classroom of the urban market is an ironic reversal of Mao's call, three decades before, urging urban youth to "go to the vast countryside to learn from peasants." According to this representation, migrant women's identity, previously bound with the timeless physicality of the inert backward countryside, is now a repository of qualities associated with mobile capital, information, and technology on a national or even transnational market scale.

Zhao Yueming is one of the most showcased models of self-development in Wuwei. The story of three generations of baomu in Zhao Yueming's family has been repeatedly reported to demonstrate the transition of rural women from survival to development (e.g., Yue Jie 1998; Yu Jie and Wang Lei 1998). Zhao Yueming's maternal grandmother and mother began to work as baomu in Beijing in the 1970s and 1980s. Zhao Yueming—then a teenager—and her father followed Yueming's mother to Beijing. Zhao Yueming and her father both worked on a chicken farm in a Beijing suburb. In the 1990s her father returned to rural Wuwei and contracted to run a township chicken farm. Later, the whole family resettled in Wuwei to manage the chicken farm. Most of the reports emphasize the dramatic transformation of Zhao Yueming from baomu to entrepreneur and contrast her with her mother and grandmother in various headlines: "Sandai baomu de meng—hukou, zhuanqian, chuang shiye" (Dreams of Three Generations of Baomu: Making a Living, Making Money, and Making an Enterprise); "Nainai dang baomu, mama dang baomu, ta dang baomu lu bu tong" (Grandmother and Mother Were Baomu, but She Struck Out on a Different Path as a Baomu). Zhao Yueming told a township woman cadre and myself that she had never worked as a baomu in Beijing. A reporter from the provincial newspaper *Xin'an wanbao* interpreted Zhao Yueming's denial as shying away from the problematic reputation of this line of work and insisted on entitling his report "Sandai baomu: Jiongran butong renshenglu" (Three Generations of Baomu: Radically Different Life Paths).[5] Although these reports differ in details—the role of Zhao Yueming's father in establishing the enterprise is sometimes mentioned, sometimes omitted—in all cases Zhao represents a new generation of domestic workers whose development in the 1990s was enabled by the market economy. Out of the tens of thousands of rural migrant women in Wuwei, no more than a handful of women are repeatedly pursued by media as women who *made it.*

Ziwo fazhan (self-development) is a neologism derived from *fazhan* (development), and the discourse of "self-development" often links the Development of nation-states or regions to the self-transformation of individuals through participation in the market.[6] One observes a similar totalizing and individuating effect with the notion of suzhi. The desire to get on track with the world through the catalyst of the market economy and transnational capital both enables and compels the state and its educated elite to "refract the evaluative gaze of the global capital that sees Chinese labor as cheap but undisciplined by modern standards of labor quality" (Anagnost 1997a: 214). One commentator reflects on Development: "If [rural] people do not change, no change can be sustained. . . . [F]or real change to take place, it will have to begin with reforming the [rural] people" (Dong 1999: 3). Regional and national Development is thus crucially conditioned by the formation of a subjectivity "through which people come to see *themselves* as developed and underdeveloped" (Escobar 1995b: 12, emphasis added). As reforms and Development gain currency, the notion of suzhi increasingly both totalizes and individuates the populace, compelling people to see themselves each as developed or underdeveloped in terms of their adaptability to the market.

The refracted evaluative gaze is cast not only on labor but on anything and everything potentially linked with investment, subsuming them under the

THE SPECTER OF CLASS

catch-all "investment environment" (*touzi huanjing*). Large street banners and billboards linking the population's level of civility (*wenming*) and the city's image (*chengshi xingxiang*) with the potential to attract capital investment betray this evaluative gaze. In my hometown, Yangzhou, a sign, strategically located on the newly built boulevard extending from the long-distance bus station to the downtown area, speaks volumes: "Chuchu shi chengshi xing-xiang, renren shi touzi huanjing" (Every place is [part of] the city's image, every person is [part of] the investment environment). China's transforma-tions—previously staged under Mao-era socialism as due to the triumph of the collective national will through the mass mobilization of labor for public production—are now believed to be truly predicated on the catalyzing power of capital. The disciplinary gaze of transnational capital refracted through such a sign both totalizes and individuates the citizenry. It also makes them respon-sible, through their elevated level of civility and internalized self-discipline, for the presence or absence of capital.

With "liberating the productive forces" as the goal of the reform, "econ-omy" is liberated from "political economy" and increasingly lords over the political and the social.[7] Market and capital—which had profoundly negative political connotations in the Mao era—now claim to be free from political and ideological predications. The migrant woman's transaction on the market is portrayed by the *Biweekly Forum* article as a win-win situation, a more than equal exchange: the process of transaction produces a desirable surplus value by endowing the migrant with modern suzhi. The actual exchange of labor power for a meager wage is rarely mentioned, and the imagined gain of suzhi as surplus value surpasses the significance of the wages. Once trained and tem-pered by the market, the labor-power-selling hick girl will be transformed into a modern subject with good suzhi: a disciplined and self-motivated worker, a "white-collar lady" (*bailing liren*), and ideally—in the archetypal form and spirit of the modern subject—a successful entrepreneur. The migrant woman worker will become an entrepreneur when she emerges as a player from her training in the market. Therefore, the accumulation of this particular surplus value, suzhi, when invested, can produce the entrepreneur. The discourse of self-development thus calls for a neoliberal technology of the self where "the individual producer-consumer is in a novel sense not just an enterprise, but the entrepreneur of himself or herself" (Gordon 1991: 44).

The win-win logic of individual development through the market process parallels a similar imaginary for regional development in the slogan "Ni facai, wo fazhan" (You make profit, I develop), a slogan, commonly seen in hinterland areas, that expresses a hope for regional development through the magic touch of capital—if only investors ("you" in the slogan) were to appear. The microtale of self-development and the macrotale of regional and national Development mirror each other. The positive projection of China's development in anticipation of China's entry into the World Trade Organization replays this logic: just as individual development requires tempering in the market, it is believed, the development of the national economy, particularly domestic industry, needs tempering through full participation in the global market economy, painful and bitter as the process may be in the short term.[8]

"Even Clinton Is a Worker [*Dagongde*]": Doing Away with Class (*Jieji*)

The logic of self-development and social mobility would have been discursively impossible had there not been a reconfiguration of the concept of class in China.[9] In post-Mao development, the term *jieji* (class) and its derivative *jieji yishi* (class consciousness) are signs that stand for the Maoist past and are held responsible for the excessive waste of Chinese energy on unproductive and irrational political struggles during the Cultural Revolution. The negation of the Cultural Revolution by the Dengist State signified the beginning of a revision of the concept of class. Now, a model of scarcity explains the notion of jieji, which compels the presence of exploitation, class domination, and antagonism. That is, the backward productive forces of the past created constant class struggles between the ruled and ruling classes over scant resources that could never have satisfied everyone. The well-known writer Liang Xiaosheng, self-identified as a plebeian intellectual (*pingmin zhishifenzi*), champions this line of argument in his popular book *Zhongguo shehui ge jieceng fenxi* (An Analysis of the Strata in Chinese Society) (1997). The very title of Liang's book explicitly invokes and displaces Mao Zedong's well-known 1927 *Analysis of the Classes in Chinese Society* (Zhongguo shehui ge jieji fenxi) (1967 [1927]). Liang's introduction to his strata analysis celebrates China's progress from backward to more advanced productive forces, and from a society organized by jieji (class in the Marxian sense) to one organized by *jieceng* (strata, or status groups in a broadly Weberian sense [Weber 1978]). Facilitated by an increased division of labor and a more complex social structure, jieceng society places a marked emphasis on mobility, functional coexistence, and harmony among strata.

In Liang's book the notion of "jieji consciousness" is "a primitive consciousness of humanity, involving sensitive reactions and simple reasoning, resulting in violent and desperate actions" (1997: 3), and it is associated with Chinese peasant uprisings of the past.[10] Liang's description implies a "natural" connection between "peasant" and "rebellion": the violence and physicality associated with "uprising" bleeds into the image of "peasant"; the primitiveness associated with the word *peasant* mirrors the crudeness and backwardness of class struggle (ibid.: 3). Jieji thus comes to signify not only social antagonism but also the specter of physical violence associated with peasants' hungering bodies eking out an existence. Liang's book advocates that in postsocialist developmentalism the "primitive" and "violent" structure of jieji connected with subsistence and survival should be displaced by the advanced and civil concept of "strata" associated with wealth and development.

The concept of jieceng appeared in President Jiang Zemin's speech of 1 July 2001, in which he invited private entrepreneurs to join the Communist Party. Jiang's speech immediately gave cause for leftist party members and overseas observers to question whether this invitation was tantamount to a formal disavowal of the Communist Party's self-avowed class basis. In the heat of this controversy, *Dangdai zhongguo shehui jieceng yanjiu baogao* (Research Report on Contemporary Chinese Social Strata) was immediately published, validating and substantiating the concept of jieceng (Lu Xueyi 2002). Based on research conducted by social scientists from the Chinese Academy of Social Science, the book maps Chinese society into ten strata. While acknowledging and criticizing polarization between rich and poor in post-Mao China, this book also rejects, as did Liang, the concept of jieji because of "its association with serious social conflict, turmoil, and struggles" (ibid.: 6). The social structure mapped through the lens of jieceng is represented as an achievement of the post-Mao reform that "conforms to the development of human civilization [*renlei wenming*]" (ibid.: 65). The conditions for the emergence of such a social structure, it is argued, should be further legitimized (*hefahua*) and solidified (*wendinghua*) (ibid.: 34).[11] The redefinition of class from jieji to jieceng thus underpins the postsocialist vision of a civilizational and developmental progress toward a refined, normative, and orderly society. The invocation of "civilization" here hardly emphasizes China's particularity, but rather stresses and assures that China has moved toward a universal telos of Development and progress by "getting on track with the world." As private entrepreneurs spawned by the post-Mao reform have contributed toward such a civilizational progress, the book argues for a theoretical justification to enable the Party's overt open-door policy to private entrepreneurs.

Here one witnesses what may be called a postsocialist drama of class equalization in official representations of model workers: with a small number of migrant workers, such as Anzi, joining the rank of entrepreneurs, some entrepreneurs also symbolically join the ranks of workers. While the working class slid downward on the social scale and experienced relative or absolute poverty in the recent reform efforts, entrepreneurs symbolically won spaces among the ranks of workers.[12] The All-China Federation of Trade Unions (ACFTU) honored four private businessmen with labor medals during the 2002 Labor Day celebration and named them "model workers," a title previously reserved for state-sector workers.[13] Staged by a peculiar politics of modeling, this two-way mobility created yet another win-win exchange for the (migrant) workers and private entrepreneurs: it is a win-win symbolic exchange for a small number of migrant workers to become entrepreneurs and for a small number of entrepreneurs to have the honorary status of workers. No matter how farcical or ironic this ideological manipulation may seem, its rhetoric is far from nonsensical. Underlying these instances of mobility is a theory of self-development, a neoliberal conception of the self that grants each individual an enterprise in him or herself.

It might be easy to laugh off the drama of class equalization achieved through apparent manipulation of the politics of modeling, but when I encountered it in a different context, I paused. The occasion was a weekend meeting that took place, at the Home for Rural Migrant Women, between migrant women workers and several young journalists of the newspaper *Dagong zhoukan* (Dagong Weekly). These enterprising journalists stated that they were college graduates who had decided to work for the newspaper in order to give voice and draw attention to all who were engaged in *dagong* (wage-labor, usually by migrants in the private sector). They also shared that they had no permanent residency in the capital and considered themselves also to be wage laborers (*dagongde*). The young man who appeared to be the lead journalist reassured the audience: "The essence of dagong is a fluid labor relationship [*liu-dong de laodong guanxi*]. Since the 1980s it has become fashionable [*shishang*]. In my view, it represents a more advanced labor relationship. But people are still embarrassed these days if they are called 'dagongde.' It is a matter of how our society comes to accept it and how people come to accept themselves. Maybe after a few decades people will no longer dwell on this issue and will treat it with ease and accept it as natural. In our editorial office, we joke that even Clinton is a dagongde."

Most migrant women in the audience indeed appeared to be heartened by this journalist. Compared with the daily discriminations they experienced as migrant workers, this statement assured them that they were in fact pioneers of the times who would find greater social acceptance in the future. But this statement also tells a story of class equalization, enabled by a universalist spin given to the term *dagong*. Taken out of the actual social relations and stripped of its class specificity, *dagong* becomes a free-floating sign that can be applied to anyone. What the journalist has done to *dagong* parallels what the official union, ACFTU, has done to "labor." If Clinton can be considered a dagongde, then one does not have to stretch one's imagination any further to think that entrepreneurs can be awarded labor medals. Everyone is equally a dagongde, as much as everyone is at least an owner and entrepreneur of himself. Based on the equal status of dagongde and the equality of ownership of the self, both migrant workers and entrepreneurs appear to be workers and entrepreneurs of themselves.

Eating Bitterness for Self-Development

The state and its elite are aware that the training and tempering provided by the market in the city neither necessarily produces the much-needed suzhi in rural migrant women, nor does it automatically transform them into replicas of Anzi. Cautionary tales and sensational stories of migrant women who lose heart and turn to make quick money in unproductive and dishonorable businesses are featured in newspapers, magazines, and tabloids as frequently as success stories. The danger lurking behind these tales of migrants is the improper transaction of *liqi* (labor power), which not only fails to produce requisite subjects for development but also contaminates the suzhi of the Chinese masses and threatens postsocialist governmentality. One success story about a migrant woman who eventually acquired a Beijing accent, permanent residency, and a Beijing husband described her as finally achieving *zhengguo* (literally, "the right fruit"), originally a Buddhist notion indicating one's arrival at an enlightened stage of being.[14] The path of self-development, like the path to nirvana, is fraught with temptations, contradictions, and obstacles; only those who pursue it with perseverance and accumulate enough good karma or suzhi will achieve the higher state of being. In order for this transformation to occur, they must accept certain understandings about themselves, which enable them to desire surplus value in suzhi as a displacement for fair wages.

Here we approach an understanding of the sort of knowledge of the self that Xiaohong acquired and that enabled her to desire a change in her self. We broach a technology of the self, a process in which the self is both object and subject of change (Foucault 1979: 170). Through the desire for change, the technology of the self thus appears to be an expression of free will emanating from within oneself, a will that internalizes the disciplinary gaze on the self and takes the self as its "biggest enemy." When one recognizes the self as one's biggest enemy, the need for radical change in the self replaces the potential demand for social change: self-antagonism takes the place of social antagonism. The migrant thus channels her agency inward toward the self and ensures its transformation, so as to endow it with suzhi. This remolding and reorientation of agency is signaled by the reemerging popularity of Samuel Smiles's *Self-Help* (1999) in Chinese bookstores, advertised as a second bible, one that purportedly changed the destiny of millions of poor people around the world. Since its original publication in 1859 in Britain, *Self-Help* has been widely circulated, instilling self-discipline and the habits of industry and perseverance among the working-class population both in Britain and its colonies.[15] The cover design of the Chinese edition includes lines from the "Internationale," a song familiar to most Chinese people during the Mao era.

> There has never been a savior
> We depend not on spirits or emperors
> To create happiness for humanity
> All depends upon ourselves.[16]

Self-Help and the "Internationale," worlds apart from each other in political orientation, are now only words apart, conjoined on the same page. The agency for social revolution called for by the "Internationale" is reoriented toward self-development.

I now present two scenes in which the self of the migrant woman is constructed, negated, and developed, a process that implicates domestic-service companies, cadre activists, as well as migrant women themselves. Before migrant women can be spurred on to a path of self-development, they must learn a truth about their selves, but they are then encouraged to negate this truth.

Scene 1: Encountering the Truth about One's Self

One day in 1999, at a domestic-worker recruitment agency, 130 rural women from Henan Province—most of them in their late teens and early twenties—arrived straight from the train station. They had boarded the train at 10:40 the night before in Xinyang, Henan, and arrived in Beijing around noon the next day. Before a training session began, they had half an hour to wash their faces and eat boiled eggs, buns, or instant noodles, which they had brought with them for the trip. Some of them had been in Beijing before as migrant workers, but the majority of them were first-time visitors to the city.

In the language and accent of the capital city the voice of the supervisor conveyed the authority of her managerial position. Her Beijing identity made her a knowing cosmopolitan vis-à-vis the migrant women, and her authoritative voice revealed to them knowledge about themselves: "We planned to have sixty, but now you are many more than that. There are about 150 still waiting in the meeting room for employers. It's not easy to find work now. . . . Whatever you were at home—a vagrant or a young lady (*xiaojie*)—whatever you might have had at home, once here, you have to relearn from scratch. Because you're new here and you know nothing, you have to follow your employers. Don't take it for granted just because you have children yourselves or you've taken care of your siblings before. You're here and you have to start anew, from the beginning."

The supervisor's message *constructs* the migrant women as a repository of invalid values and irrelevant identities in the eyes of the market. Their identities and experiences become irrelevant and must be actively erased when they enter the labor market (although, at times, their former identities as filial daughters or caring sisters may be invoked to inspire endurance of hardship). The enabling condition for the transaction of labor power for suzhi is that migrant women engage this "truth" about themselves and become motivated to transform themselves. Their past knowledge and experiences of childcare must be actively unlearned, erased, and forgotten; they must liquidate their past to become a blank slate receptive to teaching and training.

I use the word *construct* with some reservation. As Judith Butler has eloquently cautioned against turning the notion of "construction" into "linguistic monism" (1993: 6), construction is not "only and always" linguistic play and practice. The Development discourse that produces the material reality of the "developed" and "civil" coastal cities and the "isolated" and "backward" interior areas also produces the material forms of both cosmopolitan and migrant subject positions, as well as the particular power relationship in their encounter. Before the particular speech act of the supervisor treating migrant women as learners in the city, values and practices associated with rurality had already been liquidated and denounced by urban-biased development programs. Yet this speech act renews the liquidation effort, as new and veteran migrants in the city do not feel wholly at home with post-Mao urban-based "modern civilization." It is through the cosmopolitan position of the supervisor and the subaltern position of the migrant women that the discourse of postsocialist Development exercises its power. The negation of migrant women's experiences and knowledge affirms urban affluent citizens as coherent subjects of Development and as a force of stability, the post-Mao reforms having violently destabilized old structures of identity and security.

Scene 2: Witnessing the Living Truth of Self-Development

She really made it just step by step. She ate all the bitterness she had to eat: she worked fourteen hours a day as a typist to earn money; she studied accounting while half starving all the time; there were times when she worked for several months without pay and earned money by selling her blood to a blood-donation station, and so on. This kind of accumulation (*jilei*), this kind of training through eating bitterness, and this kind of training through hardship became the foundation for her success.

Xie Lihua, chief founder of the Home for Migrant Women and chief editor of *Rural Women Knowing All*, a magazine targeting rural and migrant women, offered lessons to migrant women who had come to hear a talk by Yang Feng, a migrant woman from Gansu who, after having worked in Beijing for ten years, now owned two beauty salons worth a million yuan (US$120,000). Dressed in a pink, stylish, three-piece business dress, wearing minimal jewelry and light makeup, flanked by her two younger, fashionable-looking managers, Yang Feng appeared illustrious in the meeting room filled with migrant women. For two hours, she narrated her story of eating bitterness and the vicissitudes she had encountered; she paused, several times, only to weep. She was living proof of how self-development ultimately leads to success.

Xie Lihua's concluding remarks aimed to drive home the concept of self-development by using the trope of eating bitterness as a necessary and enabling foundation for success.

Many of us cannot suffer through this kind of training. I have received many people here, including dagongmei. But many cannot eat this kind of bitterness. Once I received a girl from Shandong. She was a high-school graduate. She couldn't find any other job when she got here. So she went into domestic service. She complained to me, "In the employer's home none of them treat me like a human being. Even the little five-year-old boy in my charge could order me around and look down on me." She considered it unjust. I told her, "Yes, you walk into the city and you expect the city to receive you with smiling faces? But it's not like the city can't function without you. Now that you have chosen to dagong, you need sufficient preparation and capacity to bear this kind of hardship and bitterness. If you lack this preparation and if you were a precious baby [*baobei*] at home, then you may as well go back to being a precious baby at home."

Xie Lihua then instructed the migrant workers to always honor their profession (*jingye*) by doing their work well. She explained the meaning of jingye: "Whatever Yang Feng does, she does with the spirit of jingye. . . . Even ten days before her childbirth, she still works for others. Don't think that you can play tricks or be lazy when you work for others. If you don't cultivate good suzhi through this kind of training, it does you no good for self-development. If you set yourself up as a good example, all your people will follow you when you're a boss someday. No matter what you do and for whom you do it, you should do it well and honor the contract."

Yang Feng's spirit of continuous self-development culminated in selling her blood to finance her accounting studies. If the Wuwei girls described in the *Biweekly Forum* article accrue surplus value of suzhi by selling their bodily power (liqi), Yang Feng builds the foundation for her suzhi by selling both her liqi and her bodily fluid. The economy of the body and the economy of suzhi are thus linked by the desire and will for self-development.

Yang Feng's story, delivered in a low-key but emotional and personal manner, acquainted the audience with the immediacy of the truth of self-development through eating bitterness. Yang Feng's narrative performance of speaking bitterness, presented as a subaltern coming to recognize herself as a subject of Development, is a sign of Development itself speaking. Xie describes Yang Feng's vicissitude of eating bitterness as a form of *jilei*—which often refers to the accumulation of capital, funds, or experiences of value—thus further illustrating the theory of self-development wherein each individual acts as an entrepreneur who develops him or herself as an enterprise through gradual accumulation of suzhi as surplus value.

In describing Yang Feng's narrative as performance I do not mean to suggest that she literally acted according to a prepared script. Instead, I identify her speech as belonging to a genre of practices called *chiku* (eating bitterness) and *suku* (speaking bitterness), both of which were used in revolutionary mobilization and the education of peasants, workers, intellectuals, and students in the 1940s and 1950s and again during the Cultural Revolution. Young urban intellectuals and students were mobilized to eat bitterness by living and working among peasants in the liberated rural base during the Yan'an period (1940s) and in poor and difficult rural areas during the Cultural Revolution. Only by shaping their lives around the bases of revolution could these intellectual youth cultivate a true class feeling toward the masses and transform themselves from petite bourgeois into proletarian revolutionaries. For these intellectuals and students, eating bitterness was a way of embodying and materializing their revolutionary enthusiasm and of producing and proving themselves as subjects of the revolution.[17] For poor peasants and workers in the 1940s and 1950s, the public act of speaking bitterness symbolically transformed them from being subjects of the subaltern realm in the old social order to being subjects of liberation in the new socialist order. Speakers learned to organize and articulate fragmented and disparate experiences into a coherent whole. It was by identifying, speaking, and denouncing bitterness, or hardship and its causes, that the speaker could articulate a new subjectivity in opposition to past adversity and realign herself with the revolutionary present. Such an exercise "incites desire by offering a historical imagination of overcoming" and organizes "the meaning not just of certain aspects of life but of life in its entirety" (Rofel 1999: 141). It enables the speaker to "speak" her way into the socialist nation-state as a coherent and liberated subject whose life has achieved belonging, integration, and extension in the unfolding of the time of the nation-state.

THE SPECTER OF CLASS

Yang Feng's speaking bitterness is also a story that incites the imagination and desire to overcome, but it is performed at a time of postsocialist flexible accumulation, structural adjustment, privatization, and working-class fragmentation. In speaking bitterness Yang Feng stitches her fragmented and indeterminate experiences into a coherent and linear story that unfolds toward the telos of self-development. Unlike the bitterness spoken before, the bitterness to be experienced today is understood as the agency of the market, playing the role of a necessary evil that tests the will for the individual self's transformation and furnishes the necessary foundation on which the subaltern can build herself into a modern subject. In speaking bitterness, Yang Feng does not place herself in opposition to bitterness, but champions it as a catalyst that tempers her and integrates her subjectivity into the logic of Development. Althusser's metaphor of interpellation (1972) seems to be completed instantaneously in a painless moment. When a pedestrian is hailed by a policeman, the pedestrian's act of turning around to respond denotes him or her as a subject of power. However, the interpellation I analyze below is constituted through a series of discrete intersubjective moments of hailing and responding.

In championing Yang Feng's speaking of bitterness, Xie Lihua referred to another kind of speaking bitterness as improper. A Shandong girl who wrote to Xie complained about being treated as a commodity and being looked down on by her employers. She spoke her bitterness in order to protest and register her grievance with the state cadre—a speaking of bitterness haunted by the specter of the Maoist past and therefore in need of exorcism. Coming from a state cadre and advocate for the rights of rural women, Xie's stern advice for migrant women not to act like "precious babies" in the city was remarkably similar to the warning issued to new recruits by the Beijing company supervisor. The market logic of Development prohibits the Shandong girl's form of speaking bitterness: "Now that you have chosen to dagong, you need sufficient preparation and capacity to bear this kind of hardship and bitterness." Postsocialist discourse cannot legitimize this kind of speech because its rejection of bitterness questions the logic of Development and raises the specter of social antagonism.[18]

On arriving in Beijing, the young migrant women in scene 1 were told that the size of their group had far exceeded the targeted number. Scene 2 reiterated that the city and the market could function quite well without any of the individual migrant workers. It is no coincidence that both scenes warned the migrant women of their excessive numbers. Indeed, popular and official reports in the media, as well as scholarly works, frequently refer to the hundred-million-strong population of peasant migrants as the "excess labor-power population" (*shengyu laodongli renkou*). "Excess" is already inscribed as a constitutive part of dagongmei consciousness, a part of their subjectivity that spurs them onto the path of self-development. A feeling of anxiety and trepidation common to all migrant women was expressed by a veteran migrant woman with seventeen years of migrant life: "We are really afraid of being abandoned by society [*bei shehui paoqi*]!" It is in the imminent terror of falling into abjecthood that governmentality, working through the discourse of suzhi for self-development, deploys its power, but also reveals its limits. Xiaohong's self-development begins with an awareness of her deficiency in suzhi and a desire for a change that would distinguish her from her cohort. At the end of her story, however, the specter of class unexpectedly returns and throws Xiaohong back into the collective "we" from which she had tried so hard to distance herself.

The Specter of Class and Xiaohong's Dialectical Return to "We"

Xiaohong begins her reflection by recognizing her low suzhi, which she considers herself to share with her cohort in the collective "we." As her story unfolds, her individual "self" gradually emerges in a triangulated relationship between herself, her employers, and her cohort. She speaks of her change, through which she first disconnected herself from her cohort.

> When I first came out here [at the age of seventeen], I looked after a child for a couple. The couple was rather good to me in the hope that I would in turn be good to their child. The child was only one year old. They had another nanny before me. She had just left for a family who gave her a slightly better salary, but she remained close by in the neighborhood. When I worked for that family, they [the previous nanny and her friends] often came to look me up—after the couple went to work, I was the only one at home—because I'm their *laoxiang* [from the same native-place]. She used to *chuan* [roam or conspire; literally, "string together"] among laoxiang. She told me bad things about the couple. But she was double-dealing, because later she was knitting a sweater for the couple's child as a gift. I feared she might be a bad person and didn't want to deal with her. . . . So I told the

couple that she had said bad things about them. I was childish then, myself. They seemed to see through her immediately. They felt that I was good and that I was unlike them and did not chuan with them. So the child's parents then were really good to me. Then several [laoxiang] got angry because I stopped interacting with them. When I went out sometimes, they would stand in my way and wouldn't let me pass. Sometimes they called me names. Actually I didn't fight with them, I just didn't want to be with them. So they were angry. It became like they were against me, but the employer couple stood on my side. So, it seemed that I had a closer relationship with the couple. From then on, they [laoxiang] were displeased because they saw that I wasn't on their side. From then on, I disconnected myself from them and devoted all my time to the child, teaching it to read and write.

Chuan is a verb or an active noun often used by urbanites to name migrant domestic workers' habit of visiting each other and getting together. The term is derogatory, implying that the act is done either stealthily or excessively, in a way that might have transgressed the line of legality or the code of civility. Since employers usually frown on or directly forbid live-in domestic workers to gather in neighborhood playgrounds or to visit one another at their employers' homes, domestic workers often must meet stealthily in the absence of their employers. The fear that domestic workers will compare wages and working conditions, and gossip about their employers adds to urban employers' anxieties. The increasingly desired privacy of the urban middle-class home becomes potentially porous as the figure of the peripatetic domestic worker crosses the line between inside and outside, home and market. As often happens, employers fear that their domestic workers might begin hinting for better wages as a result of information exchange with other domestic workers, or, what is worse, that they might become a discontented and centrifugal figure in the employer's home, which is supposed to represent a place of security, intimacy, and privacy in the postsocialist market ideology.

Xiaohong's reference to her laoxiang's visits specifically as chuan, and her developed distaste for such behavior, suggest her awareness of chuan as it appears objectified in discourse. Drawing on Valentin Volosinov's notion about signs arising "only on interindividual territory," Dorothy Smith suggests that naming objects is a dialogic production of objects for discourse. In naming objects, she continues, "there is an alignment of the individual consciousness via the utterance" (1996: 186). Xiaohong, by acting out against her perception of chuan, develops a positionality in a triangulated and relational sequence of actions among herself, her employers, and her cohort. Once she has spoken to her employers about her cohort's chuan, all three parties shift and adjust their actions in relation to each other according to Xiaohong's move. What I extrapolate from Smith's proposal is the pivotal importance of Xiaohong's "naming": it triggers a series of actions by her employers, her cohort, and herself around chuan, which coordinates her consciousness with that of her employers' and marks her off from her cohort. Xiaohong's interpellation was not a solo performance, but one that took place through a series of responses and actions, by all three parties, that her recognition of chuan had necessarily set into motion. Critiquing recent poststructuralist writings that resurrect the unitary subject by representing the interpellation of a subject as a solo performance of "citing" discourse, Smith stresses "the social" in the process of interpellation.[19] She uses the social to emphasize interpellation as a dialogic and intersubjective coordination that involves multiple subjects. Thus, "the social," involving multiple subjects, rescues interpellation from a more determined and enclosed process of "citation" involving a singular subject, and it opens up self-development as a problematic, open-ended relational process relying on the interplay *among* subjects. "Interplay" among subjects is a source of instability. Xiaohong, looking back on her experiences years later, talking to me in her Beijing home when she was unemployed, smiled and took responsibility for the "naming" she had done years ago: "I was childish then."

Xiaohong's consciousness of her low suzhi and her determination for self-reformation coalesced a year later, when she had a chance to work in the home of a famous writer. She recalled this experience in an article published in the *Rural Women Knowing All* (Min Xiaohong 1999). "I already had that desire [to change myself] before I went to the writer's home," she told me. In the article, she narrated in detail the emergence of a self in her process of self-development, while working for the writer.

> When I came to the writer's home, I respected and admired writers as if they were like saints. I didn't want them to look down on me. When the writer's wife totaled up the bill after my first grocery purchase, it turned out that there was a one cent surplus [in the employers' favor]. So the wife and I looked at each other in the eyes and smiled. From then on, she never

checked the bills and trusted me greatly. It felt so very good to be trusted! Finally I knew what was meant by *ren'ge* [integrity, personhood, self]. I gazed appreciatively on [*xinshang*, normally referring to works of art, landscapes, etc.] my new self [*ziwo*]. Later, even after leaving the writer's home, I decided that I would never embezzle again, regardless of whether others trusted me or not. For my self [*wo de ziwo*] is always keeping watch over [*zhushi*] myself [*ziji*], and I cannot do things that will make my self look down on myself. (Ibid.: 30)[20]

Xiaohong's narration of the emergence of a new self (*xin de ziwo*) begins with "I shouldn't let them look down on me" and ends with "I cannot do things that will make my self look down on myself." What begins as an external source of disciplinary gaze directed from the outside "they" turns inward and transforms into an internalized disciplinary gaze directed from the newly formed self. If the notion of suzhi consists of the state and its elite "refracting the evaluative gaze of global capital" on Chinese labor in order to measure their quality and discipline (Anagnost 1997a: 214), the emergence of a new self in Xiaohong enables a transmission of that disciplinary gaze from global capital—refracted by the writer and his respectful wife (as the icon of Chinese elite) through the discourse of suzhi—to reach her subjectivity. When Xiaohong and the writer's wife "looked at each other in the eyes and smiled" after the first account inspection, the mirroring of the gaze and the smile of recognition between Xiaohong and the writer's wife is a meeting of desire and principle; it is an identification of the two. In this meeting of gazes and in these smiles, which follow the suspense of the accounting, the employer, who represents the disciplinary gaze and the reality principle, recognizes Xiaohong as a domestic worker of good suzhi who deserves trust. Such recognition pleases Xiaohong since it fulfills her desire. The Lacanian notion of desire as "a perpetual *effect* of symbolic articulation" allows one to trace the itinerary of desire back to the discourse that incites and disciplines it (Lacan 1977: viii; emphasis added). When Xiaohong and her employer meet in the space of the gaze and the smile, desire and principle meet and identify with one another: desire embraces the reality principle and principle fulfills desire.

This moment of the mirroring of gazes and smiles is a significant factor for the birth of Xiaohong's new self, which appears to be her new ideal ego. One may argue that the emergence of Xiaohong's new ego involves a mechanism similar to Jacques Lacan's psychoanalytic formulation of the "mirror stage" in the formation of a child's ego. The mirror stage is a symbolic moment when a child takes a "jubilant assumption of his specular image" (Lacan 1977: 2). The child (mis)recognizes his or her mirror image as a coherent and bounded self and reaches out to it for this phantom image, as if about to cohere with it. The gaze and smile of the writer's wife reflects back to Xiaohong an image that she has desired, with which it pleases her to identify. The significance of this moment gradually sinks in, until she finally feels the emergence of this new ideal ego, which she appreciatively gazes on as if it were a work of art. In demonstrating the formation of Xiaohong's ideal ego, I am not suggesting that Xiaohong remains childlike. Rather, I am suggesting that the formation of the ideal ego is an open-ended social process that reaches beyond childhood. I am also suggesting that a historical process specific to China's postsocialist project of Development (or modernization) enables the discourse of suzhi and self-development to incite Xiaohong's desire for a new self through what Rofel calls the "historical imagination of overcoming" (1999: 141).

Furthermore, Xiaohong's new self or ideal ego actually embraces and introduces the reality principle (the disciplinary gaze) onto her ego (ziji). The formation of her new self occurs when her desire merges with the reality principle. The disciplinary gaze, first attributed to the writer and his wife, later comes from Xiaohong's new ideal ego. In her narrative, the reality principle (ascribed to the realm of super-ego in Freudian psychoanalysis) and desire (ascribed to the realm of the ego) dance, identify with each other, and finally melt away in Xiaohong's new ideal ego, which becomes a source of both discipline and joy. She simultaneously gazes on the new self as a work of art and remains under its disciplinary gaze. Freudian psychoanalysis posits only a rigid and oppositional relationship between ego and super-ego, and between desire and reality principle. The interaction between ego and super-ego supposedly incites displeasure. Yet in Xiaohong's articulation, "myself" (ziji) and "my new self" (xin de ziwo) supplement one another, and such a meeting of desire and principle incites pleasure.[21] Xiaohong herself certainly does not maintain a clear division between ziwo (my self) and ziji (myself); later, she uses ziji literally to refer to both the self that disciplines and the self that is disciplined. From the gaze of the writer and his wife to the gaze emanating from Xiaohong's new ideal ego, the hegemony of the discourse of suzhi and self-development generates a new structure of feeling in Xiaohong and incites complex sensations, including desire and pleasure.

During the moment of shared gazing between Xiaohong and the writer's wife, exploitation seems to have vanished: Xiaohong joyfully (mis)recognizes and (mis)identifies with the image reflected back at her from her counterpart. This mirroring of gazes, like chuan, entails an intersubjective recognition: at the moment when her employer recognizes a good domestic in Xiaohong and trusts her, Xiaohong desires suzhi and accepts the disciplinary authority of the writer's wife. Agony ensues when Xiaohong's pleasurable identification with the mirrored self is violently disrupted. Things take a sharp turn for the worse after the writer's wife smiles at her in a different context.

> The reason why I left the writer's home was because there was too much work at this home. I was busy all day like a work machine [*ganhuo jiqi*]. After a day's work, I was completely exhausted physically and mentally. I proposed to leave. The writer's wife told me to wait till they found a replacement. A week later, the writer's wife told me that they had found a new domestic and expected me to leave that very day. While I was waiting for them to look for a replacement, I was foolishly working like before [without looking for a new job]. In the end I was driven out without a place to go. The face of the writer's wife had that same consistent, benevolent smile, but this time it made my heart feel icy. Before I left, she said she wanted to check my luggage. She said this was the usual rule: whoever leaves has to be checked. She was afraid that I might steal books from them. I was unwilling in my heart, but agreed to it with my lips.
>
> How I hated myself for being so cowardly! Why did I dare not say "No!" Many years since [then] I have considered myself tragic. We girls coming out from the countryside are too deeply poor, unknowing, and self-abasing. We long for respect from society. But if we don't stand up for ourselves, who can we depend on? We girls who worked as domestics have felt more deeply [about this] than those girls who are vegetable vendors or workers in restaurants and stores. We enter into the basic cells of society [the family and the domestic scene], where beauty and ugliness between people, and civilization and benightedness in the space between city and countryside collide without any disguise. The process leading from collisions or clashes to merging involves pain and awakening. (Min Xiaohong 1999, 30–31)

The specter of exploitation surfaces after Xiaohong finds herself becoming "a work machine" (ganhuo jiqi). Xiaohong is no longer even a breathing human body producing labor power (the *qi* in *liqi* means breath or life-force, but the *qi* in *jiqi* means tool—an inanimate object). Is there a place for Xiaohong's subjectivity when her "I" becomes a "work machine" and even her body is lost in this metaphorical transformation? The experiences of the body are absent, or present only in an exhausted state: "I was busy all day, like a work machine. After a day's work, I was completely exhausted physically and mentally." Xiaohong has no choice but to leave. The experience of eating bitterness becomes an impossible foundation for self-development, as that very experience threatens the presence of her subjectivity.

Xiaohong expresses her agonizing sense of irony on seeing "that consistent, benevolent smile" that could perform opposite functions. The same benevolent smile that had inaugurated Xiaohong's bliss at her new mirrored, ideal ego now turns Xiaohong's heart to ice. The same smile that once recognized Xiaohong's desire for good suzhi and drew her into a shared consciousness now appears as a sign of domination: with complete ease and without any advance notice, the employer drives her out and demands to inspect her luggage. Xiaohong can now retrospectively recognize the presence of the first smile in the second smile, and comprehend the first smile in light of the second. The second smile shares discursive conditioning with the first smile and functions as its double. Drawing a worker in and then throwing her out are both consistent with the logic of hegemony. The "heart," the abode of consciousness and subjectivity, is turned to ice by the smile. Once Xiaohong understands the second smile, her self can no longer cohere with the ideal ego, and her path of self-development is derailed. She opens the next paragraph with a tremendous sense of agony: "How I hated myself for being cowardly!" The wound has refused to heal for many years: "I have considered myself tragic!"

When the demand for luggage inspection shocks Xiaohong, it is as if the blindfold of self-development drops, and Xiaohong sees the specter of class. The final smile, the luggage inspection, and her employer's businesslike explanation that "whoever [read: domestic workers] leaves will be checked" throws Xiaohong back into her class position. Xiaohong does not perceive this experience as a case of individual humiliation; instead it links her to the collective dagongmei in her agonized reflection. She reflects that working within cells of society, especially the intimate realm of urban homes, domestic workers have a deeper awareness of the violence of "clashes" and "the process of pain and awakening" than dagongmei working in restaurants and stores. What sorts of clashes? To what does one awaken? Xiaohong's reflections in the article remain vague and general; she mimics the enlightenment language circulating in Chinese media by invoking the "civilization and benightedness" and the "beauty and ugliness" of humanity in general. By not adhering to the acceptable city equals civilization and countryside equals benightedness equation, Xiaohong nevertheless subtly transposes civilization and benightedness to a space located between city and countryside. The relationship between a rural woman perceived as lacking in suzhi and the wife of a saintlike writer in the capital city is now rearticulated as "beauty and ugliness between people." Awakening for Xiaohong is a process of dialectical return to the collective. By invoking a "we," Xiaohong negates the previous negation of her cohort, from whom she had tried to distance herself. Xiaohong's dialectical return is not merely a return to her native-place-based cohort; it situates her within the whole dagongmei collective who share her material and discursive predications in postsocialist development.

Xiaohong ends her essay by imaging her hometown Wuwei as a hopeful space: "My home [county] Wuwei is far different today than it was before. The old street leading from the small town [where Xiaohong is from] to the county seat used to be very narrow, but now it has been turned into a broad street. The thatch-roofed houses belong to the history of the old days. Multistoried houses are no longer a novelty. Peasants who have been isolated and enclosed for thousands of years finally have a chance to enter the outside world. Having endured much hardship and difficulty, they are trying to change their lives. Reality has proven that we are right to have come out bravely" (1999: 31).

Xiaohong's essay ends on a hopeful note that resembles the tone of the *Biweekly Forum* article about Wuwei girls, bringing closure to Xiaohong's painful experiences. The specter of class seems to have disappeared in the concluding paragraph of her essay (which should be considered as a negotiated text between herself and the editorial staff at the magazine). However, if read in reverse order, Xiaohong's article uncovers a crucial question: what has happened since "we" bravely came out? Although she envisions her home county Wuwei as a hopeful space, she does not make it an imaginary locus of her future identity; instead, she ends her article by affirming an open-ended "coming out." After sixteen years of experience as a migrant, Xiaohong is still a dislocated migrant traveling between Beijing and Wuwei. Her agony still penetrates beneath the skin of closure and will have no social redress as long as "we don't stand up for ourselves." The term *stand up* (*zhan qi lai*) obliquely harkens back to Mao's 1949 pronouncement "Henceforth the Chinese people will stand up!" In the conditions of postsocialist Development Xiaohong's agony does not allow her to rise up and invoke "the Chinese people"; instead, it compels her to invoke the dagongmei collective from *within* her predicated position.

On her visit to my Beijing apartment in the fall of 1999, Xiaohong told me and two other migrant domestic workers that an employer had claimed that she did not consider her baomu as a baomu. "But will a baomu really cease to be a baomu simply because you don't call her such? She still is!" Xiaohong's critique of the employer in question insists on unmasking the material and discursive predication of domestic workers. This insistence on material and discursive predication of a sign and an identity, born of Xiaohong's own haunting agony, in fact contradicts the free mobility of the signs "dagong" and "labor" propelled by ACFTU and the young enterprising journalists of *Dagong Weekly*. The reality of material and discursive subjection and immobility cannot be displaced or liberated by the mobility of signs.

Coda

Since James Scott's critical work on everyday resistance as a weapon for the weak, "everyday resistance" has become an important terrain where researchers seek to locate subaltern resistance and agency. However, much of the everyday-resistance literature posits autonomous and self-determined individual subjects standing behind acts of resistance. In this kind of analytic exercise, where subaltern subjectivity has an autonomous presence and responds knowingly and suavely to an "external" hegemony, we run the risk of treating subaltern subjectivity as a "thing" rather than "a social and cultural formation arising from processes" (Thompson 1963: 10–11). In her lucid review of the Subaltern Studies Group Rosalind O'Hanlon (1988) points out that in their project of restoring the "suppressed histories" of the subaltern and retrieving "their own" specific and distinctive histories and consciousness, the group calls for an originary presence of the subaltern and risks smuggling the unitary subject through the backdoor.

How should we understand subaltern agency? Can the subaltern speak? Gayatri Chakravorty Spivak distinguishes positivist speaking from discursive speaking. The subaltern can certainly speak, but can it speak discursively? Spivak proposes that "all speaking, even seemingly the most immediate, entails a distanced decipherment by another, which is, at best, an interception. That is what speaking is" (1999: 309). Such a definition of speaking does not allow a transparent representation of the speaking subaltern through unquestioned mediation of the investigating subject, and it renders any deciphering and representation interested and situated. The question is not to abstain from representation, as Spivak writes, but to abstain from an "essentialist utopian politics" that drives representations of "self-knowing and politically canny subalterns" (ibid.: 257) and effaces the itinerary of the subaltern subject (ibid.: 261). History and contemporary practices of speaking bitterness as a form of subaltern speaking reveal discursive conditionings under which subalterns speak and demonstrate how their speaking, such as the Shandong girl's speaking, is intercepted, deciphered, and rejected. Returning to *The Eighteenth Brumaire of Louis Bonaparte*, Spivak suggests, "Marx is obliged to construct models of a divided and dislocated subject whose parts are not continuous or coherent with each other" (ibid.: 258).

Xiaohong's disavowal of what we might call an "everyday resistance" act complicates the celebration of everyday resistance. Indeed, it calls for the need to track the itinerary of how the power of discourse works its way through subjectivity and agency, so that we can better grasp the implications of individual actions and possibilities for social change.

The migrant women who struggle for self-development most often do not cohere as individual subjects of Development or as subjects of resistance. They face the yawning gap between the mobility of signs (suzhi, dagong, self-development) and the subterranean reality of their subjection and predication. This gap has produced varied responses and symptoms and scattered articulations of resistance. Such social schizophrenia produces individual schizophrenia in a few extreme cases, in which the migrant women compulsively spin tales about themselves as someone else. The researchers Tang Can and Feng Xiaoshuang report one such case: "Ten years have passed. She has lived in a predicament of immobility and seen a future with slimmer and slimmer hopes. These, woven with other contradictions, are so hard for her to bear that she sometimes uses illusions to substitute for reality. For example, she has told strangers that she works as a secretary in a prestigious state agency in Beijing, often meets foreigners, and goes abroad. She has told some acquaintances that a certain man wants to destroy her face with sulphuric acid. Sometimes she says that she would like to enter a convent" (1996: 54). A similar case of a compulsive storyteller was also reported by members of the Home for Migrant Women.

Some migrant women have taken issue with the state's claim to socialism. Xiao Cai, a veteran migrant domestic worker, sees the gap as a social failing for a society that calls itself "socialist": "On their lips, employers might say, 'We won't look down on you, and your work is needed by our society.' They say it nicely on their lips, but there is nothing in their action. Their action shows that they don't really place you in an important position. [Since we] live in this socialist environment, every one should be able to enjoy it."

What about familialism? Can the rhetoric of the family make up for the failed hope of self-development? Juju, whose labor experiences contrasted with the story of the "ideal baomu" in chapter 2, was commended by her company as an "excellent domestic service worker [*youxiu jiating fuwuyuan*]" each year for four years in a row, based on the recommendation of the second family she worked for. Having no illusion about her own "coolie" destiny, Juju both rejected and embraced familialism.

That really sounded nice: "One of the family!" But then when they would bring goodies back from their daughter's home, they would share the goodies among themselves and urge each other to eat more. They would never ask me to eat, even if they couldn't finish it. Sometimes when fruit began to rot, then they would ask me to eat it. The fact that they were intellectuals didn't change anything. Intellectuals too can do things that chill one's heart [*yao ren xin han*]. So I felt like I was no more than one who labored for them [*zuo huo de ren*]. If they really wanted to treat me as one of the family, they would have to show it with their actions. . . . The child that I looked after said to me, "Auntie, your hands are like an uncle's hands." I thought to myself: there is so much work that I have to do everyday; isn't everything done by these two hands of mine?

My family has a heavy burden: my father and mother are not in good health and my younger brother and sister are in school. I would like them not to be like me who sells physical labor power [*mai tili*]. I would like them to do mental labor, not like me, a coolie [*kuli*] doing manual labor, not like me without a future. What else can I become in the future? I will probably remain like this for the rest of my life.

Juju's narrative implicitly compares two families, the affluent employers' family and Juju's own poor family, both of which are sustained by her labor. Juju's work produces the quality life of the employers and hence their class identity; however, the employers' self-representation, although predicated on her labor, disarticulates her social value. The same structure of power that valorizes the employers' value and class identity reduces Juju to no more than a coolie. It is in Juju's own family, to which she has been sending almost all her earnings, that her value is honored (by her parents) and that her diligence serves as a model (for her siblings). Juju's hope that her hard labor will nurture a better future for her siblings is also a hope that they will embody and avow the value of her identity and her labor.

While rejecting familialism in one context, Juju embraces it in another. Her sacrifice for her siblings is not unlike the sacrifice of the elder sister in the popular TV series *Jiemei* (Sisters) (Yuan Jun 1999), in which the rural migrant sister sends money to support her younger sister's college education and fervently dreams of a different future for her. At the end of the story, the entrepreneurial younger sister's grand success in business, assisted by the elder sister and her friends in no small ways, would demolish the neighborhood where the elder sister and her friends have built their lives and livelihood. The theme song, however, sentimentalizes the sister's sacrifice based on consanguinity and familialism.

> Connected [are we] by the same blood thicker than water
> If you are in need
> Open your heart to me
> I will give you everything
> My good sister.

Jiemei can be read as a national allegory that celebrates the social mobility of migrants and envelops the migrant working class and the bourgeoisie in the sentimentality of familialism based on national consanguinity. In post-Mao China consanguinity has been strategically mobilized by the state to construct a homogenous national imaginary to sublate political differences between the mainland and Taiwan and to build a greater Chinese national family linking overseas Chinese capital and the vast resource of the mainland's cheap labor pool.[22] One might raise an open-ended question for Juju: if her siblings indeed grow up to be professionals or intellectuals in the future, how will they represent Juju's coolie labor in a way that she will feel her value avowed? Or might they, like many intellectuals and professionals of rural background, look at their elder sister and her migrant labor as a necessary but embarrassing condition of their success and the nation's modernity, whose inappropriate presence will have to be constantly disavowed by modernity?

A Baomu's Diary and Her Employer's Response

On 18 November 2004, *China Youth Journal* (Zhongguo qingnian bao) published a report from Xi'an, capital of Shaanxi Province, about the controversy surrounding a baomu's diary. Coming from rural Shaanxi, nineteen-year-old Xue'er worked for a wealthy family in Xi'an and recorded her grievances about the job in her diary. The diary was accidentally discovered by her employer, causing Xue'er's unexpected dismissal. The employer confiscated the diary and withheld the 700 yuan owed to Xue'er. Xue'er's new employer, a retired journalist and writer in her eighties, was outraged at Xue'er's experiences. She took the issue to the media and encouraged Xue'er to sue her former employers. Later Xue'er won back her diary and the back pay, only to discover that her former employer had inserted comments into her diary. The lawsuit did not go forward due to a variety of interventions.

Below is an excerpt of the diary and the employers' comments (EC) based on the *China Youth Journal*'s article.

DIARY: I have never experienced this kind of humiliation. So what if you are rich? You can ignore another's feelings? Before I had five or six mouthfuls of food during my meal, you told me to go feed the child. Your family members are human beings and are well fed. But have you ever thought that I had not eaten anything since last night? Even dogs and cats have people to care for them. What about me? I have to work while my stomach is empty. I'm simply worse off than dogs and cats! I miss home and I want to go home immediately. This place is sheer hell. I can no longer suffer this suffocating, devilish place.

EC: What if you're hungry? Did you actually imagine that the granny looks after the child so you get to eat? Will you pay the granny? Being rich is being rich! What's wrong with making you look after the child when you're not yet full? Remember, you're not one of our family. You are only a baomu. We have paid you and you have to work!

DIARY: How much have I been wronged. I don't want to talk about it. Let it become dust and disappear! But I'll forever remember what you said, "Rich people can treat you like a dog. [If we] tell you go east, you cannot go west." I almost threw up on hearing this. Can this be true? I want to seriously respond to you, "Wrong! The reason to take your order is because one needs to make a living. But if you don't respect someone else's person-hood, then it's as if you don't respect yourself. You can kick someone and someone may not return the kick. But you actually get kicked, too, even though it's a silent one. Leave. No more working here.

EC: What if [you are treated like] a dog? You know what treatment you've got! You *are* a baomu employed by our household! [Yet] you don't know self-reflection! Being rich *is* good! Are you actually thinking of rebellion while getting paid? Psycho!!

DIARY: Mom, I miss you. You are still the one who's good to me. Someone else's mom has no conscience. She has no heart for me. For two days in a row, I have blood in my stool and something is wrong in my belly. But they still drive me hard. Mom! If it were you, surely you wouldn't let me work when I'm sick. Mom! I want to go home.

EC: [What's wrong with] you working and being sick? Are we supposed to give you a sick leave and pay you at the same time? Are we out of our minds? From tomorrow on, ten yuan will be deducted for each day off.

"Twelve Months of Dagong"

A song entitled "Dagong shi'er yue" was circulating through roadside karaoke machines in Wuwei County in 1998 when I was conducting research there. Composed, written, and sung by an obscure singer named Chao Yang, this song follows a style of lamenting songs in narrating the self's experiences in a yearly cycle. This song represents the experiences of migrancy as highly un-certain and devoid of teleology.

In January I left my village
Together with my buddy Li Zhiqiang
Two days and nights by train
We would go to Guangzhou to break a new path

In February we met a laoxiang [someone from the same native place]
He was working in a toy factory
Thanks to his help we both had a New Year
After the New Year we were busy looking for jobs

March found us waiting on the street
Waiting with others for hope
They say so-and-so made a fortune
I imagine he must have been like this in the beginning

April brought a foreman who was really fat
He waved his hand at several of us
Then I hurried onto the bus
Only then did I notice Li Zhiqiang was gone

In May I arrived at the worksite
In a construction team to build buildings
Every day I was sweating under the sun
I was so tired I just wanted to lie down

In June my heart was pumping when I got paid
Six to seven hundred a month did I earn
I began to see light on the road to getting rich

In July I wrote a letter to my parents
Together with several hundred bucks
Thinking how happy they would be
I would go on no matter how tired or bitter

Mid-August saw the bright moon hanging in the night's sky
The fat foreman gave us a case of beer
He told us not to be homesick
He said this place is just like home

In September a grave misfortune befell me
A falling brick injured my hand
Didn't think the fat foreman would fire me
He disposed of me with a little cash

In October my heart felt a chill
My laoxiang at the toy factory was nowhere to be found
Walking up and down on Tianhe Road by myself
I almost ran out of the money in my pocket

In November I found Li Zhiqiang
He was doing much better than me as a waiter
Who could have thought he would just give me a few bucks
And leave me with a word that he was busy

In December I returned to my village
Father and Mother cried a good cry
The family had a meal of dumplings
The taste was delicious

6

THE ECONOMIC LAW AND LIMINAL SUBJECTS

On a hot autumn day, two migrant women friends met with me in my Beijing apartment: Xiaohong from Anhui and Hua Min from Sichuan. Then in their mid-thirties, both of them had come to Beijing in the early 1980s and had stayed as migrants, working for some years as domestic workers, then as sales representatives. What follows are excerpts from our discussion about why they could not return home.

> XIAOHONG: When I first came out [to Beijing], I returned home after fifteen days in the city. Then I came out again, returned after three months, and again after five months, then six months. Every time I returned home, I stayed for a while and also worked at home, but after a while, I wanted to come out again. Initially I remembered how many times I had gone back and forth. Now I don't even know.
>
> HUA MIN: Since I left home seventeen years ago, slowly I have become estranged from home. I still go home for visits, but I don't think I could return there [for good]. I don't know why you came back out after returning home.
>
> XIAOHONG: I felt that after going back, my heart just couldn't settle down. I never felt as if I wouldn't go out again, or as if I would just stay at home. Absolutely not! I didn't have that peace of mind. I always felt that I would leave again after a short stay. One time I didn't plan to come back out, thinking that Beijing was not so great. But still I came out again. I seem to feel that Beijing is especially bustling and boiling, like a whirlpool.

At home, I feel lonesome, as if far away from life [*yuanli le shenghuo*]. After you return home, you find there is no change, no way out [*meiyou chulu*], and life is boring. So you come out again. Actually in bustling Beijing, you only have this little room and you don't know people. But only here do you feel settled.

HUA MIN: The first few years, I especially looked forward to going home. Every time before going home I used to get excited and prepare gifts well in advance. Neighbors, relatives, and fellow villagers would also ask my parents when I would come back. On my return, the village bustled with activity [*renao*], and I tasted a simple but thick happiness [*chunhou de huanle*]. But gradually, I found that my native place [*laojia*] had become desolate and dissipated [*xiaotiao*]. The countryside seems dismembered [*jieti*]. Many youngsters have gone out and only the old and the very young stay behind.

XIAOHONG: This change happened later. At first there wasn't much change. Later more and more people leave and it becomes more and more coldly lonesome [*lengqing*] at home. You can hardly see young people at home. This is what happened later. The first few years after I came out, the countryside was still pretty active. Around the New Year and other festivals, it was really bustling. But it's not so any longer. Not everyone returns home for the New Year anymore, and those who return usually leave after the fifteenth day of the New Year.

Ideologically, within the representational scheme of post-Mao modernity, the countryside is appropriated as the sign of "poverty," "backwardness," and "tradition" in relation to the modern metropolis. Materially, the countryside has received very little direct investment from the state since the mid-1980s and has experienced a decline in the limited welfare, medical care, and affordable education provided by now disbanded rural collectivities. The countryside has been turned into a base of cheap flexible labor for the post-Mao era's rapid accumulation. This emaciation of the rural for the telos of the urban reorganizes the imaginary of the future and modernity for rural youth and compels them, through migration to the city, to reterritorialize themselves *in* modernity. Because the majority of them, like Xiaohong and Hua Min, are unable to fully reterritorialize themselves as subjects *of* modernity, they find themselves within a painful, indeterminant space of neither belonging to the city nor being able to return—which, however, can also lead to new political possibilities.

To "return" often implies that the place of origin, to which the detached person goes back, remains unchanged. According to Hua Min's and Xiaohong's conversation, however, both their rural communities, even in the process of "Development," are becoming dismembered, dissipated, and desolate. Home (*jia*) is so deeply embedded in the rural community that the reference of *jia* often slides into that of *laojia*, the collective space of community. The same Development discourse that has incited migration has also emaciated the rural community, making it difficult to speak of "return." Just as Heraclitus remarked that "One cannot step into the same river twice," in the course of post-Mao epistemic transformation, migrant women have found themselves unable to return to the same rural community. In the mid-1980s, the early phase of migration, the gifts and commodities Hua Min brought back to the community functioned as stimuli to social animation. Gift and commodity, which are usually thought of as radically separate, intersect here—the appropriate gift can only be a commodity purchased in the city. Yet this brief burst of social animation cannot sustain itself and must give way to desolation. The commodity-gift brought back to the community via migrant wage labor, which gives social life its ephemeral animation, portends its decline. The vitality of the rural economy, material production, and rural life in the native place has been lost.

The serious deterioration of rural economy and rural life itself spurred Li Changping, a former township party secretary in Hubei Province, to appeal directly to the central government: the peasants are really poor (*zhen qiong*), rural society is really bitter (*zhen ku*), and agriculture is really in danger (*zhen weixian*) (Li Changping 2002). With Li's outcry, the rural unrest of recent years and the continual struggles by researchers for recognition of the "three rural issues" (*sannong wenti*)—namely agriculture (*nong ye*), peasants (*nong min*), and rural society or communities (*nong cun*)—finally came to the focused attention of the central government in 2003, giving rise to a new policy discourse of "constructing new socialist countryside" in the eleventh Five-Year Plan. But how to solve this multidimensional problem has been a subject of heated debate. Despite abolishing agricultural taxes in the last couple years and the central government's pledge to promote "social equality," China's Gini coefficient rose to 4.96 in 2006, according to researchers at the Chinese

Academy of Social Sciences.[1] There are researchers and policymakers within and without the government for whom a solution is to push for a leap from the current arrangement of collective land ownership and household-based land-use rights to a thorough privatization of land.[2] There are also social experiments involving rural cooperatives, based on the current institutionalization of ownership and land-use rights.[3] There are still more radical efforts at the margin to push for recollectivization, based on the experiences of a small number of villages in China that remain collectivized in the post-Mao rural reform.[4]

The severity of the three rural issues continues to present a predicament for migrants. Filomeno V. Aguilar (1999), in his analysis of Filipino international migrants, draws on Victor Turner's theory of *rite de passage* (1967) to describe migrancy as a "transitional stage" during which the migrant, like a ritual initiate, is a liminal subject separated from the community and suspended from his or her pre-ritual habits of thinking and action. After undergoing a ritual self-transformation, the migrant rejoins the community as a post-ritual subject with a new personhood and an elevated cosmopolitan status. Although Aguilar is aware of the many problems accompanying the migration of Filipino international migrants, his analysis frames and affirms migrancy as a process oriented toward a ritual teleology. However, as experienced by Xiaohong, the teleology of self-development has remained elusive for most migrant women. Not being able or desiring to return, yet unable to cohere as subjects of Development in the city, they remain stuck as struggling liminal subjects.

To Be Zero or Not to Be: The Problem of "Returning"

Zhang, a forty-one-year-old man, came to Beijing from rural Wuwei in 1982. It was shortly after his graduation from high school, at a time when few men from his area migrated. Before he left, Zhang's village committee was interested in recruiting him to be one of its cadres. Like many rural high-school graduates who did not make it to college, Zhang was interested in becoming a village teacher to continue his intellectual pursuits. Failing in that attempt, he came to Beijing to work in a restaurant through the connection of a cousin who worked in Beijing as a domestic worker. Zhang, at the time of my interview living with his wife and two daughters in Beijing, had recently bought and sold a restaurant in Shijingshan district and had also set up a grocery stand in a big wholesale marketplace for which he paid 7,000 yuan a month in rent. Financing his two daughters' education in Beijing cost tens of thousands of yuan, about one-tenth of what it would have been in rural Wuwei.[5] But Zhang asked me to mark his words: "No matter what I do, even if I fail, I would not let them [his daughters] go back to our old home [in rural Wuwei]. If you write a book in the future, write my words there." A lull fell on our conversation, as I recalled how his recent business adventure in Shijingshan had failed so quickly, forcing him to sell the restaurant two months after he had bought it. There was a tragic, defiant tone in his voice. Veteran migrants, such as Xiaohong, Hua Min, and Zhang, who came to the city in the early to mid-1980s, have a more acute feeling about the transformation of the countryside in the reform process than do younger migrants who came of age after rural decollectivization. Zhang acknowledges that some of the early migrants made some money and became relatively prosperous in the village. Yet, echoing Xiaohong and Hua Min, Zhang also perceived a simultaneous emaciation of rural society.

> By working [dagong] outside and doing business, money has accumulated back in the village, but the rural economy *itself*, material production in the countryside, and rural life *itself* are not as thriving as before. Many people don't see this malady [bibing]. I don't know whether you see it. You know that in our countryside, more and more farmland lies to waste [pao huang].[6] On returning, you find cold lonesomeness [lengqing] and desolation [xiao-tiao] at home. Relations among villagers have become distant [shengshu le]. It feels as if the countryside has had its marrow sucked away [gusui bei chou le]. . . . Before the reapportioning of land to individual households, people were very warmhearted [rexinchang]. If you had something to do, others would be happy to help you. You know in our countryside, houses are close to each other and the doors are wide open. So if you had something going on in your family, others would surely know, and they would come to help. Nowadays, it's all about money. If you have something in your family and need help to take care of some work, you have to pay. No money, no help, unless you're close relatives. Nowadays it's not easy to borrow money anymore, because people think if I can get interest by saving money in the bank, why should I lend it to you? This was unimaginable before.

In Zhang's description the countryside is deeply sick and has lost its vitality and substantiality in recent years. Similar to Hua Min who saw the transformation as dismemberment, Zhang experiences the process as a "sucking away" of the countryside's "marrow." Both of them use corporeal metaphors to describe the problems of the countryside as sickness and malady.[7] One cannot hold migrants themselves as primarily responsible for the countryside's emaciation. The discourse and practices of post-Mao modernity and development strategies have produced an epistemic violence against the countryside that has both reorganized the rural-urban relationship according to a spatial division of labor and pushed rural youth onto the path of migration.

In the 1990s agriculture and the rural economy in general was significantly sustained by remittances from migrants.[8] On average, rural households in Wuwei acquire at least one-third of their income through remittances. It is not uncommon that a household depends almost solely on the income sent back by its migrant sons or daughters. Villagers often complain that farming has turned out to be a losing effort. The situation is worsening since cheaper imports have begun to enter the market for agricultural products after China's World Trade Organization accession.[9] Migrants make money in various ways in the cities, and households are increasingly reticent and vague in communicating to each other about specific sources and amounts of money for fear of envy or competition. Villagers still routinely ask each other how much money they make in a year, but the answer is now often evasive: "Not much. Just getting by." Two-story or even three-story glistening, white-tiled houses arise in the midst of modest single-story brick houses and shabby mud-walled shacks. Some of the new multistory houses are unoccupied, their owners now living and working year-round in Beijing or other cities, or having acquired permanent urban residency and apartments in the county seat. These locked, vacant houses, sometimes with broken windows, stand as empty shells signifying a hollow prosperity in an emaciated place. In rural Wuwei in the late 1990s, it was not difficult to borrow money, but interest rates were prohibitively high. The common interest rate in rural communities in 1998 was 2 percent per month or 24 percent per year—significantly higher than the bank rates, which were inaccessible to most rural residents. To these observations, Juju from Sichuan added, "People have generally become more reticent, not as gregarious or intimate as before." The change in communal intersubjectivity is perhaps most telling during the time of lunar New Year gatherings: "You can see the change especially during the New Year. Previously, the youngsters of our village would gather together to play—jumping rope, kicking the shuttlecock, or going somewhere for fun. Sometimes there were almost a hundred of us. Now it's not like that. Now just a few youngsters get together—only three or five, at most seven or eight. Previously, it was [the youngsters of] the whole village together and we would not go back home until past mealtime. Now during the New Year [the village] is not as bustling as before. People are not together anymore. Only family members spend time together, chat, and visit relatives. This is the biggest change."

None of the migrants I interviewed invoked in their narratives the rural as a place of essential characteristics, but they instead pointed to what Doreen Massey calls an "alternative conceptualization of place: that the characteristics of any place are formed in part through the location and the role of that place within a wider structuring of society . . . a wider *spatial division of labor*" (1994: 115). In doing so, their understanding of the rural as a process forms a sharp contrast with the representations of the rural by the Fifth Generation film-makers, who seized on the rural as an embodiment of an immutable culture cut off from any national or global relations or processes. Migrants' choice to stay in the city, then, cannot simply serve as an affirmation of their embrace of the urban as a universal teleology, nor is their narrative a supporting contribution to this teleology. Instead, their choices are specific expressions of a shift in structures of feeling articulated with the larger picture of how rural communal life and intersubjectivity has been organized and transformed in the processes of reform.

Yet for many labor migrants, the countryside must serve as a last base for the retreat of bodies injured, souls trampled, and hopes lost in the city. Their return most often will not be an enactment of a ritual teleology of the pilgrim subject expected to declare, "Mission accomplished!" Instead, the village becomes more of a refuge from the painful class position that many see as over-determined for them in the city. In 1999, while working for an elderly intellectual couple in Beijing, the migrant worker Xiang mused about her future: "My biggest contradiction [*maodun*] is that I don't know whether I should stay in the city or return to the countryside. . . . Even if I stay, I think I'll remain at the bottom level of society. So, slowly, I come to think I might return to the countryside after all." Several months later, Xiang made an adventurous trip to Tibet to look for a different place to remold herself and her life opportunities. When she arrived in Shanghai in 2001, she wrote, "I will try to be strong. I will struggle to live on in order to prove that I cannot possibly be just a zero."

"To be zero or not to be" is not a matter of choice. To desire a job in the city is not to desire exploitation; it is a struggle to keep one's "zero-ness" at bay insofar as the self's worth is determined by whether and how one serves as a cog in the capitalist Development machine. Xiang's struggle is echoed in two poems authored by a returned migrant from Hebei and circulated to me by a friend.[10]

我依然	I'm Still . . .
其实我明白	Actually I understand
在这世界上	In this world, I'm
我是一棵被遗忘的小草	A stem of grass neglected
被丢弃的小鸟	A bird abandoned
被有钱人鄙视的穷鬼	A poor wretch despised by the rich
被有文化人不耻的文盲	An illiterate ridiculed by the cultured
不管是什么	No matter what I am, I'm still trying to
我都努力在唱出一种属于我的风景	Grow into a scene that I can call mine
飞上属于我的蓝天	Fly into a space of blue sky that is mine
尽管我依然	Even though I'm still
贫穷和低贱	Poor and degraded
我依然	I'm still . . .

告别北京	Farewell Beijing
告别北京	Farewell Beijing
告别文明与现代	Farewell civility and modernity
带着欢笑而来	I came with smiles and cheer
带着泪水而归	Now I leave in tears
为什么文明与现代的都市	Why does this civil and modern metropolis
给我们这一群来自农村的打工妹	Inflict on us dagongmei
深深的伤害	Such deep hurt and injury
告别了北京	Farewell Beijing

告别了梦想与美丽	Farewell my dreams and youthful beauty
我要回乡疗伤	I want to go home to treat my wounds
在经历了自尊和自由的伤害后	Not until after my dignity and freedom have been injured
才知家乡是治愈一切伤口最好良药	Have I learned that my native place is the best cure for all wounds

These two poems speak powerfully against the teleology of the self-development through pilgrimage to the site of civilization and modernity. The central theme of the poem "I'm Still . . ." is the author's coming to grips with what "I" is in this world. The author opens the poem by defining her self through its value-equivalents: neglected grass, an abandoned bird, a despised wretch, a ridiculed illiterate. With the first two images, the poem seems to open in the style of an abandoned lover's song of lament. Reading it against the second poem, one wonders whether the author is implicitly invoking herself as an unrequited lover of modernity which, rather than love her back, reciprocates with abuse. Lest the reader really take this poem to be a love poem, the poet immediately continues the chain of value-equivalents of the self into the social field. The naturalist images of the self as grass and bird connects to the images of the self as a class subject defined in relation to the rich and cultured: a poor wretch despised and an illiterate ridiculed. The fact that this former migrant woman happens to be quite literate suggests that she is speaking from the persona of more common dagongmei (migrant woman workers), who could be illiterate or semiliterate.[11] This self-positioning is clearer in the second poem where the language specifically invokes dagongmei as a group. The ending of the first poem is ambivalent: "Even though I am still / poor and low" suggests that this condition and this realization—the aftermath of her encounter with the city—now serves a new starting point for the self's continuing struggle. But does the ending of "I'm still . . ." suggest that "I" is still perhaps in love (with modernity)?

In "Farewell Beijing" the trope of self-development is a bankrupt dream from which the author awakens to her self's lack of value as a dagongmei in the city. It more directly and indignantly questions the power of civility and modernity to consume the youth and dreams of dagongmei on the one hand, and to inflict pain and agony in return on the other. A series of contrasting nouns suggests that the exchange is anything but equal: dagongmei have exchanged smiles and cheer for tears, dreams for disillusion, and youth for wounds, all in the context of urban "civility and modernity." In the end, the author bids the abusive modernity and civility farewell and retreats to her native place for recuperation. Can her former home really heal her wounds?

One migrant in Shenzhen, as expressed in a letter, refused to be cheered and encouraged by her more optimistic college-educated correspondent and marked herself off as part of a different class of migrants destined for a different future than her correspondent.[12]

I was glad to receive your letter. But after reading it, my heart is very heavy.

Can you really understand how I feel? You can't. At least not completely. Yes, you and I are both thousands of miles away from home. But the natures of our migrations are as different as heaven from earth. You're studying in Beijing, for a diploma that is not accessible to others. All your sorrows and unhappy experiences will melt away when you see that your hard work will bring you great achievements. For there will be returns for your efforts and you will not disappoint yourself or your parents. You will walk on a life path accompanied by flowers and sunshine. But we live at the bottom of society. Perhaps we will never raise ourselves above the water. All that our expended efforts can bring are a low and insignificant wage, abuse and scolding from the managers, and scorn from the local people. What can we do about this? There is no other choice but to bear it. Every one of us came down [to Shenzhen] with a beautiful dream, but how many can really realize the dream after which they chase? In the end we are empty-handed, but we're still unwilling to go home.

As a dagongmei, [I] have expended [*hao jin*] all I have, but what I get in return is zero. Nobody would like this outcome. But this [outcome] is not for me to decide. You're right that no matter how much I miss home and how much I want to return, the path home has become indistinct and vague. I feel especially so. I want to return to my mother's side, but I don't feel content to just go back like this. But I'm also very clear—if not like this, what else? . . .

Perhaps when I return home this winter for the New Year, I will not be able to come back out again. But after I go home, I will certainly try to persuade my mother that next year will be the last year of my dagong life. I know that after the next year, I will enter a different life [read: marriage], whether I'm willing or not. It's not up to me to decide.

What this letter signifies is a profound perception of the overdetermination and alienation for dagongmei as a collective subject position. In the current structure of development most migrants are both incited and condemned to find in wage labor the only means to struggle for recognition, self-expression, and self-realization as modern subjects. Yet the letter writer suggests that this only means of struggle turns out to be a process in which they have given all they have and from which what they still "get in return is zero." It echoes and reinforces the migrant poet's words that self-development proves to be a bankrupt dream. While "getting zero in return" and exchanging smiles for tears, hope for injury, migrants still struggle to be more than zero. The prospect of self-valuation is haunted by a constant danger of liquidation. However, even this unfortunate condition is only temporarily available to women migrants who often have to go back to the countryside to get married. As they reach their early to mid-twenties, young migrant women are racing against time in hope of a change in their life opportunities. Hua Min sketches the struggles facing many migrant women in Beijing.

Many who come out need a place to stay. So they become domestic workers. Some others work in hair salons to wash hair for customers; still others go to small restaurants to be waitresses. So they have a place to stay. Then they begin to think: I can't be a domestic worker all my life; I can't be holding plates all my life. I need a change. So now she begins to try different things and keeps trying because she wants to find a better job. But here and there, she finds that she can't jump out of the confines and she cannot escape the environment she's in. Domestic workers, vegetable vendors, janitors, waitresses. Some of them go to school part time and hope that will give them new opportunities. But, most of the time, that won't happen, because the employment opportunities available to us are those dirty, tiring, and bitter jobs. When she's twenty-three or twenty-four and still cannot find a job she can settle into, she's pressed to think about the problem of marriage. Should she leave or stay? What about her marriage? She can't stay on in the city [as it becomes increasingly difficult to find a job as she passes her late twenties], but she feels too discontent to just go home. So she becomes agonized and anxious. . . . Eventually, even after she returns to the countryside, her heart doesn't settle down there. She will wants to come out again, if she has a chance.

The Shenzhen letter writer has to persuade her mother and possibly her future husband and parents-in-law to allow her to wait another year. Once she is married, the possibility of her coming out to the city again is even more circumscribed, depending as it does on a family decision involving parents-in-law, husband, and, to an indeterminate extent, herself. Certainly it is very rare that a married woman can come out to the city without being in the company of her husband or other relatives. She explains that she cannot embrace the city as a telos, because in the city: "We live at the bottom of [urban] society" and "as a dagongmei, [I] have given all I have, but what I get in return is zero." Yet the letter writer wants to prolong her experience even in this limbo. The emaciated rural home constitutes such a discontinuous other reality that her return seems to amount to her falling over the edge of modernity, to her disappearance into what is perceived as an abject state of nonbeing. In Xiaohong's words, once in the countryside, one is "far away from life" itself. In the scheme of post-Mao Development, the telos of the city monopolizes not only civility and modernity but also the meaning of life itself. The women who have returned to the countryside, but whose "hearts," or subjectivity, can no longer settle down there, experience a double alienation. As Hua Min sighed, "The city is not ours, but there is no way out in the countryside." Even if the countryside may be the dwelling place for returned migrant women's bodies, it is less likely to be the dwelling place for their subjectivities, for their hearts.

The Economic Law, Theology, and Sublation

In the boiling, bustling, whirling development of the cities that is producing both immense wealth and immense poverty, the "economic law" (*jingji guilü*) in post-Mao market reform is invoked as the true, natural, objective, and necessary science of historical Development. Literally, this law is not a law in the legal sense (*falü*), in the sense of expressing the will of the state; it is, rather, a universal law (*guilü*) of the science of economic development, the will of History that dictates the outcome of societal input. The economic law is said to have taught China a lesson: due to Maoist China's defiance or ignorance of the economic law, China lost the opportunity for normal Development and has been punished, and this is why China remains a developing country in dire need of catching up. Ironically, the authority of the universal economic law is aided and certified by a long-standing, official, textbook Marxism that hails Marx as the discoverer of "a universal law in the development of human history."[13] In this linear teleology, the evolution of human society, powered by the dialectic between productive forces and relations of production, unfolds through stages of development: primitive, feudal, capitalist, socialist, and finally communist. While Maoist China had asserted China's "leap" from feudalism directly to socialism, theoretically through Leninism and empirically through the success of the Russian Revolution, some elites in post-Mao China, in the context of global neoliberalism and the collapse of the Soviet Union, could justify the market reforms as going back to the truth of the "stage theory" of vulgar Marxism and as "making up a lesson" of capitalism that China had missed—we cannot beat History.[14] Therefore, liberal economics, which asserts that the market is central to the construction of a rational and normative system of economy, and vulgar Marxism, which endorses History as linear development through stages, converge in their support for the hegemony of the market economy as a natural (for liberal economics) or historical (for vulgar Marxism) necessity.

In this context the economic law, which gathers forces and endorsement from both liberal economics and vulgar Marxism, uses liberal-economic categories to describe and inscribe the history of the People's Republic's political economy as truth-effects of the economic law. The frequent solemn invocation of the economic law by state media and economists speaks in liberal-economic categories and the Marxian terminology of "productive forces" in the same breath, and hence perhaps stitches together the discontinuities of party leadership in separated realms of economy and ideology.[15] As this truth is inscribed, corroborated by the ubiquitous images of a glamorous capitalist modernity, the desire to "catch up" has become hegemonic. At times the problem of ideological baggage is openly cast aside—as the late pragmatist leader Deng's "cat theory" famously encouraged, "It doesn't matter if the cat is a black or white cat, as long as it catches mice."[16] As the landscape of political economy is entrenched and articulated through the framework of liberal-economic categories, the burden of judging truth is shifted from doubting and critiquing these categories themselves to the deep play of empiricism: "Practice is the only criterion by which to judge truth." It should come as no surprise that Shenzhen, an avant-garde city engaged in the deep play of the market economy, should reify the image of Deng and his pronouncement of the truth of empiricism in a gigantic board in the center of the city as a site/sight for the pilgrimage of tourists from all over the country. In this truth of empiricism, the economic law is held to be true, objective, and external, and thus can only be obeyed. The economic law is not itself to be critiqued and transcended; it is itself transcendental.[17]

How is the economic law invoked and represented in relation to dagong-mei? And how do such invocations produce hope and suture the fractured and troubled process of self-development together with national Development? I commented in my fieldnotes about a talk on urbanization given at the Home for Rural Migrant Women by an economist from the Chinese Academy of Social Sciences.

October 17, 2000   Home for Rural Migrant Women

Today is the Home for Rural Migrant Women's bimonthly activity day. The main activity was a talk on urbanization given by Professor Yu, an economist from the Chinese Academy of Social Science. . . . There were about twenty-five people at the talk, with a few male migrants amid the majority of migrant women. Professor Yu spoke calmly and emphatically, yet not without emotion.

Professor Yu, who appeared to be in his mid-fifties, opened his talk by telling the audience that he complained at the meeting of the Beijing municipal government, "How many of you are really from Beijing yourself? Yet you still try to exclude outsiders!" Then he continued:

"What is 'urbanization'? Urbanization is a process and an inevitable outcome of the transition from a backward, traditional rural society to a modern and advanced urban society. Urbanization is a Necessity of History [*lishi de biran*] and cannot be obstructed. . . . Industrialization requires a great amount of labor, but it also renders rural labor power surplus. A high level of urbanization indicates a developed state of economy and an advanced level of society. China is carrying out modernization. Modernization cannot possibly rely on the countryside.

Urbanization is an important index of the level of modernization. Your behavior—rural-to-urban migration—corresponds to the laws of economic development!"

A question came from the audience: "Must national development rely on urbanization?" Another added, "Now there are college graduates going to the countryside to develop their careers."

Professor Yu replied:

"Yes, the newspaper propaganda says that one can get rich by doing agriculture. But in our country per capita farmland is a little more than one mu. Can we get rich by this little land?"

He followed: "I used to eat one-and-a-half *jin* [one *jin* is 500 grams] of grain a day, but now I only eat half a jin a day [implying that one can get nutrition from a diversified diet, including abundant meat, fish, etc.]. By relying on agriculture, our country cannot get rich, nor can it get strong. There is no way that our country can modernize by relying on the "sunrise to sunset" mode of production [associated with traditional agriculture]. Urbanization is an objective law [*keguan guilü*]. In the future, you will probably be citizens of the city rather than villagers in the countryside. . . .

"According to the World Bank's report for 1993, the level of urbanization of low-income countries is 28 percent—these are poor places; the level of urbanization of middle-income countries is 60 percent; advanced countries like the United States, Japan, Germany are above 80 percent. The goal of the state-planning commission is to reach 34.03 percent by the year 2000.[18] Scholars call for an even faster pace of urbanization. . . .

"Recently in a document issued by the Central Party Committee there was this sentence: 'We need to establish *a unified labor market* throughout the country.' This is an idea that has not been talked about in many years. This means two things: first the urban-rural barrier will be broken down; second, barriers among regions will be broken down. Actually, although there are still local regulations that make you ineligible for certain jobs in the city, enterprises like to use rural migrants and do not like to use Beijingers. Beijingers are lazy and prone to troublemaking, while rural migrants are docile and also ask for lower wages. If we have a unified labor market, there will be competition. If there is competition, there is vitality. Policymaking cannot be done by leaders simply patting their own heads. Policies produced in this way are not good policies. Good policies come from below, from your practices. We should have confidence. Policies will develop in a wholesome direction. The migrant population will accelerate economic development. The subject of urbanization is rural people [*nongcun ren*]. Nowadays, the city cannot function without migrants. During the Spring Festival, I cannot find buns to buy and cannot find bean curd to buy, because migrants have all gone home [for the holiday]. My estimate is that the current ratio of urban-to-rural population will be reversed in the next twenty years."

Professor Yu then told the audience a joke:

"The [former] British [Prime Minister] Heath asks God, 'There are many problems in the U.K. As you see it, how many years will it take for them to be solved?' God says, 'Eighty years.' [Former U.S. President] Clinton asks God, 'There are many problems in the U.S. As you see it, how many years will it take for them to be solved?' God says, 'Fifty years.' Deng Xiaoping asks God, 'There are many problems in China. As you see it, how many years will it take for them to be solved?' God says, 'Thirty years.' Yeltsin asks God, 'There are many problems in Russia. As you see it, how many years will it take for them to be solved?' God exclaims, 'I don't think I will live to see it!'"

The punch line, as Professor Yu pointed out: China is the most hopeful country. We all should have confidence! The room rippled with the excitement generated by Professor Yu's talk. The audience was unusually engaged. One participant in the audience commented, "All of our previous speakers have taken the standpoint of urbanites. They hoped that after a few years in the city, we migrant women would go back to the countryside to build our native places. But why should we go back? Did we cause rural poverty? If urbanites are more cultured and more knowledgeable, why don't they go to the countryside and build it?" Another comment from the audience: "The media often express concern about urban laid-off workers. So even I felt sorry that we migrants had snatched the rice bowl from urbanites. But now we can feel justified." But one audience member called for fellow migrant women to return home: "I hope all of us go back to build our native places [*jiaxiang*], because I work in a wholesale market and I encounter people of the lowest level [of society] everyday. Sometimes I see a migrant being beaten up by seven or eight people. The onlookers include both migrants and Beijingers. So I'm angry: we must build our native places well; if we had money, who would be able to bully us like this?" This last comment, stated vehemently, was nevertheless a lone position, and the speaker herself knew that her opinion did not fly well among her fellow migrants (this was not the first time she had raised the idea). The excitement was palpable and even infectious, the migrant audience genuinely agitated. Even though I disagreed with the gist of Professor Yu's talk, I nevertheless found the audience's animation remarkable, as it was rare. What was flowing in the air was a sense of hope, which Professor Yu's talk had generated.

The Chinese Academy of Social Science, where Professor Yu works, is a highly prestigious national research institute, which has contributed members to the Chinese government's top-level think tanks. Professor Yu himself is one of the growing number of liberal economists who are active and vocal in shaping, interpreting, legitimating, prescribing, propagating, and pushing for steady but faster-paced market reform and economic liberalization. Professor Yu's talk centered on a cluster of three interlinked keywords authorized in the name of the economic law: urbanization, unified labor market, and agency of migrants. This cluster of keywords constructs a web of relationships in which migrants are supposed to find the location of their agency, ordained by the economic law as historical necessity. "Urbanization" is defined as "a process and an inevitable outcome" of social development that advances from the city to the country. Placing it in the realm of necessity, Professor Yu uses the language of vulgar Marxism to lend a force of History to the liberal economic category. As History and Nature is unified in Engels's *Dialectics of Nature* (one of the core textbooks on Marxism in China), what is called "Necessity of History" thus acquires the force associated with Nature. What lends force and authority to Yu's liberal economics is not only the fragmented and hallowed Marxian vocabulary but also the World Bank reports that correlate level of development to rate of urbanization, taking the nation-state as the natural unit of world economy.[19] This linear process of development relegates the countryside to the past tense and rural labor power to surplus. The relocation of the agency of rural laborers is thus in their contribution to the development of the city and the nation as the most favored laboring subjects: cheaper and more competitive, docile, mobile. What excited the audience was the legitimization of their migration as "corresponding to the laws of economic development" and thus the predication of themselves as rightful subjects of urbanization — they will have a future in the city and a hope of being citizens of the city.

At a meeting organized by the Beijing municipal government, Professor Yu opened his talk by positioning himself as a champion for the rights of migrants. The exclusionary policies practiced by the Beijing municipal government, which Professor Yu criticized, are not unique to Beijing. Many municipal governments of large cities, troubled by the rising level of urban unemployment and threatened by labor unrest, have employment policies in which "city residents have priority over rural residents; locals have priority over non-locals" (xian chengshi, hou nongcun, xian bendi, hou waidi). While propaganda and government policies promoting free movement of talents (*rencai*) — intellectuals and professionals — began in the mid-1980s, in the 1990s both Beijing and Shanghai instituted policies to exclude labor migrants from over one hundred kinds of low-skilled jobs that require local residency as a necessary condition for employment.[20] The discriminatory "Beijing Municipal Regulations on Migrant Workers and Migrant Business People in Beijing" (Beijing shi waidi lai jing wugong jingshang renyuan guanli tiaoli), passed by Beijing Municipal People's Congress in April 1995, was abolished in 2005.[21] The dam which has functioned to keep migrants from accessing many urban-based benefits has now finally been lifted. While the media celebrates this abolition as an instance of progress, one should note three caveats. First, before the dam was removed, the state had already drastically lowered the level of benefits enjoyed by urban workers. In the process of the reform, urban workers have had many welfare entitlements stripped through structural adjustment of state-owned enterprises; the stripping and devaluation of the urban citizenship of ordinary urban workers have leveled the playing field and paved the road to the "equal citizenship" now offered to migrant workers. Second, discrimination against migrants will continue to exist as long as post-Mao modernity relies on cheap labor for its market-oriented, urban-based development. One can hardly miss the irony that Professor Yu's persona as the honorable champion of the rights of migrant workers is conditioned on these workers' highly prized cheapness. Social cheapness, expressed as discrimination, and the economic cheapness of migrant labor power will continue to articulate through each other and reinforce each other. Third, these regulations have not been very effective in determining hiring decisions, as employers have various means for bypassing such policies and thus pick who they want. Therefore, it is doubtful that the abolition of inequitable policies will bring forth a fundamental change in the employment opportunities of migrant workers.

However, the ways in which such discriminatory regulations were established and abolished have allowed municipal governments to exacerbate the tension between urban workers and migrant workers by pitting one group against the other. To a significant extent this has worked: there has been little social connection and empathy between the two groups of workers. It is not uncommon to hear two groups of workers deriding each other. Urban workers share the general urban prejudice and look down on migrants. Migrants complain that urban workers are spoiled, lazy, and picky, and are not as hardworking and competitive as migrants. Local municipal governments, through the establishment of restrictions on migrant workers, acted as protector of urban workers. Liberal intellectuals have favored and championed migrant workers and have not spared their efforts in criticizing state-owned enterprises and urban workers. The rights of migrants that Professor Yu champions are set in the agenda of establishing a unified national labor market where all boundaries and barriers to labor mobility will be eradicated and labor will be completely unfettered, individual, and free for hire. The underlying assumption is that the market economy in China cannot function properly without a free labor market. The promotion of migrants' rights discourse is thus located within the free-market paradigm.

It is within this paradigm that migrants are called on to fulfill their historical agency, as they are told that their labor mobility is "correspondent with the laws of economic development." With the migrants' advantage of being cheaper, more mobile, and more docile, the agency of migrants lies in inciting competition on the labor market and generating vitality [read: profit] for Development.

In addition to wielding his scientific authority, Yu also borrowed force from a metaphysical authority by telling a joke involving theology. In the joke, God as personified History speaks to the leaders of four nation-states and predicts the resolution of many problems in China—including the distress of migrant workers—within the lifetime of the migrants. History doubles as theology and speaks as God. History as God has spoken and all that remains is empirical practice. Just like the World Bank report, this joke reinforces the nation-state as the natural subject of History and as the Subject that subsumes the agency, destiny, and future of migrants.[22] It is hard to speculate how much the optimism and hope generated by Yu's talk would be sustained after the audience stepped out of the meeting room and into the harsh realities of the everyday devaluation of their being. But almost everywhere migrants look, they encounter texts of the economic law, some produced by state and intellectual elites, some produced by migrants themselves.

Essays by the migrant women Yang Tao and Chunzi contributed to the proliferation of texts on the economic law. Both essays were published in a 2000 issue of *Dagongmei* magazine, which advertises itself as "by and for dagongmei" (*dagongmei ban, dagongmei kan*).[23] The image of a young, vibrant, and modern-looking woman on the cover of the magazine is an advertisement of fables of self-development. Yang Tao was the cover heroine and her essay, "The City Has Changed My Life" (Chengshi gaibian le wo de shenghuo), appeared in the magazine's column "A Star among Dagongmei."

> This is Beijing. This is the ancient and modernizing Beijing. This is a luxurious and magnificent office building. This is a famous design company. This is a young and fashionable white-collar miss [*bailing liren*]. She sits graciously in front of an Apple computer, adeptly revising the plans designed yesterday by her customers. Her gentle and cultivated comments win constant approval from her customers. Soon another of her revisions is approved. Colleagues all commend her intelligence and talent. . . .
>
> Nobody knows that this girl is me, a dagongmei from a small town in the south. When colleagues look at me with admiration, the image surfacing in my mind is about another girl. Then she was only eighteen, at an age that is filled with nothing but dreams. She wanted to go to the capital Beijing that she often saw on TV. She wanted to give herself a try. . . .
>
> I'm very tired every day, rushing about in the city. The pressure from work always puts one's brain in an extremely tense state. But at the same time, I feel that I've benefited and I'm a fuller being. Perhaps youth should be equated with struggle! Looking back at the "me" from yesterday, I know that I'm progressing every day. (Yang Tao 2000, 16)

Yang Tao's essay opens with a series of images that introduce the readers to her new identity in the post-Mao Chinese cultural and economic landscape of modernity. Her narrative opens like a film, with the camera scanning the city, closing in on the office building and then zeroing in and focusing on a young woman inside the building in front of a computer. Her metamorphosis from a dagongmei into a fashionable white-collar miss leaves no traces, except that in her mind's eye, the old self lives on only to function as the benchmark of her success today. The image of modernity as the capital city on TV incited her early dreams, and now she herself seems to have been absorbed by and become part of that image rebroadcast for dagongmei readers.

In contrast, Chunzi's essay, entitled "There Will Be Bread" (Mianbao hui you de), describes a series of events that took place during her ten-year migrant life in Beijing, a life which brought her not wealth and success, but illness and poverty. Chunzi left her native place with dreams. She proved herself by working as a staff member at *Rural Women Knowing All*, as editor of a column called "Sister Chunzi's Mailbox," answering mail and giving advice to many rural young women who wrote in. Unfortunately, she was injured by a vehicle and later developed an eye disease. In 1998 her rental home was burglarized. The only bright events in her migrant life seemed to be her marriage to a Beijing urban worker and the birth of their daughter in 1999. Yet Chunzi remained ill after the Caesarean birth, and she and her husband had no money for her treatment. The couple's attempt to open a restaurant failed completely, which wiped out all their savings. Yet woven into her narrative of these unfortunate events is her surprising faith: "Misery *is* wealth!" (*kunan jiu shi caifu*). Chunzi concludes the essay: "Look, we've got nothing to our name, but we are still happy. We still believe: there will be bread; there will be everything" (2000, 31).

Chunzi's readers will probably not miss the allusion in both the essay's title and its conclusion. "There will be bread; there will be everything" is a well-known phrase from the Soviet film *Lenin in 1918*, which was widely shown in China during the Mao era. Those whose childhood was spent in the Mao era or even in the early years of the reform era would probably remember this expressed optimism and conviction that the newborn Soviet State in 1918 would pull through the drastic food shortage and deliver its socialist promise to its citizens. In the Chinese imagination at the beginning of the twenty-first century, it is no longer socialism that will guarantee bread in the future; it is, rather, continued Development according to the economic law (of the market). Chunzi's experience can hardly constitute a dagongmei success story. Hardship and misfortune run through her migrant life, making it difficult to be subsumed and translated according to the economic law. Yet perhaps because of the difficulty of subsumption and translation, the moral of having faith in the economic law is all the more worth telling and publishing, as it might touch many others like her who find success so far beyond their reach. Chunzi's essay not only adds to the proliferation of texts on the economic law but also contributes to their discursive expansion, for her narrative seems to demonstrate the functionality of the law at its own border, in spite of counter-evidence.

Chunzi's experience, including her present state of poverty and illness, has its meaning transformed when it is subsumed as yet another text of the economic law. Neoliberal logic, manifested as the economic law, frames the meaning of her experience and structures her imagination of the future. The economic law does not just subsume her experience; the very process of this subsumption is also a process of translation and transposition. *Transpose* means "to transfer to a different place or context" and, derivatively, "to write or play (music) in a different key," "to translate into another language" or "a new form," or, as used in mathematics—better befitting our concern with economics here—"to transfer (a term), with its sign changed, to the other side of an equation" (*New Oxford English Dictionary* 1998: 1971). By such a transposition, *misery*, transferred from one side of the equation to the other, and with its sign changed, becomes *wealth*. What has enabled this transposition is the magic formula of the economic law. Although Yang Tao and Chunzi fare quite differently in their migrant experiences, they both appear in their writings as models of *homo oeconomicus* for the reform era, representing a new form of economic moralism.[24]

The analysis cannot just stop here. It would be simplistic to attribute Chunzi's writing of her experience to her naïve faith in the future. Struggling for over ten years as a migrant, Chunzi, perhaps like many other migrants, knows very well how unstable her present is and how uncertain her future. To probe deeper into the politics of representation is to understand a series of linkages between writing, translation, alienation, and the value of the self.

Liminal Subjects and Subterranean Accumulation

> It took advanced countries over a hundred years to complete urbanization and primitive accumulation. Now these countries begin to view human rights as the highest good. This [emphasis on human rights] has become a trend. Within this trend, China begins its urbanization and primitive accumulation. If we completely abide by these human-rights requirements, eight-hour workday, and so on, will we be able to accomplish primitive accumulation? Will our enterprises be able to develop? This problem is a big contradiction for China. We would like to avoid some of the paths traveled by advanced countries and [go through the process with] less cost, blood, and sweat, but we also feel that the economic law is hard to bend.
>
> China used to have a very good social system, admired around the world. But the result was that our economy moved very slowly, far below the world average. . . . What we should do is to do our best to reduce the negative side during this stage [of primitive accumulation]. The situation we see today is surely better than that in Marx's days. . . . Our task is to clear the path for the historically irresistible tide and reduce the cost of development to a minimum.
>
> XIE LIHUA, CONCLUDING REMARKS AT FIRST "NATIONAL FORUM ON ISSUES ABOUT WOMEN MIGRANT WORKERS' RIGHTS AND INTERESTS," 1999[25]

Like Professor Yu's talk, Xie's speech, invoking the economic law as the universal law of Development, and the nation-state as its sovereign subject, is representative of the dominant discourse of Development at the turn of the millennium. Sharing a similar paradigmatic foundation with China's liberal critics, Xie, chief editor of *Rural Women Knowing All* and founder of the Home for Migrant Women, also locates rights within the liberal paradigm of Development and the economic law.[26] It is within this dominant discourse that Chunzi's essay acquires its ideological value and that Hua Min, another veteran migrant woman and a dagongmei activist, struggles for an articulation of her subaltern experiences and vision. Coming to Beijing in the early 1980s and working for nearly ten years as a baomu, Hua Min acquired a vocational college diploma (*dazhuan wenping*) through an adult self-study program, married an urban Beijing resident, and acquired urban residency, all of which are admired as markers of success by many dagongmei. After meeting with her a few times, I began our first long conversation, in July 1999, with a question about how she regarded her success. Hua Min sighed and replied, "My 'success' has many contingencies [*ouran*]. Success is not a necessary [*biran*] result of your struggles. It's not that you expend so much effort and then you have success. I feel that the hardship I have experienced cannot be subsumed [*gaikuo*] or counterbalanced [*dixiao*] by these markers of success. Having a diploma from a vocational college doesn't mean that you can find a job. There are too many people who have such diplomas and yet cannot find jobs. I'm able to stay in Beijing mostly because of my husband. And this matter [love or marriage] itself is a very contingent thing."

Hua Min said she knows that she can use her own experiences to "stir-fry" herself (*chao* or *chaozuo*), to sensationalize herself a model or a "beautiful bubble" story of success to show others. But she is unwilling to do so, precisely because she thinks of her "success" as contingent. She has avoided many interviews by journalists who are avid collectors of such stories (for that reason, she avoided me initially) and deliberately evades being made over into a fable of self-development. Hua Min once submitted an essay to the column "Dagong in Beijing" (Dagong Beijing) of the *Beijing Youth Journal* (Beijing qingnian bao), writing about the experiences of her first year in Beijing. The essay was rejected, with the column editor's suggestion that if she could write an essay like "Married with a Beijinger," it would be published the next day.

In the late 1990s chao or "stir-frying" something or somebody is a process of packaging and salesmanship to make something hot, more attractive, more saleable, and more consumable on the market. This novel use of *chao*, coming to the mainland perhaps from Taiwan, is most frequently associated with speculative maneuvering on the stock and real-estate markets. Now, a news story, a pop star, or stocks, a brand name, and so on can all be "stir-fried" to increase their values. In the judgment of the column editor a love story involving a migrant woman and a Beijinger is more attractive and saleable than a story about the bitter experiences of a new migrant. If Hua Min tried to stir-fry herself or encouraged journalists to stir-fry her, she could produce a representation of herself as a model of success in Beijing, just as the famous Anzi has made herself a star of dagongmei in Shenzhen, attracting thousands of migrants as avid admirers and gaining economic, cultural, and political capital. To stir-fry is to link representation with the dominant regimes of value—economic, cultural, and political. To stir-fry a migrant woman's experience is to engage in writing and representation so as to translate and transpose her experience, with its sign changed to a positive value, to the other side of the equation, to the side of Development or the economic law.

The linkage between chao and the speculative economy of stock and real-estate markets can help one understand the dynamic relationship between representation and the volatile value of the self. If Hua Min were to stir-fry herself as though she were a stock, she could create a bubble of herself, thereby increasing her value and attracting positive speculations and hence investment in her future. She would be invited to give talks, write articles, and maybe even gain one or two political honors. This practice of self-representation resembles the valuation of stocks on the stock market. The more one appears to have value through representation, the more value, investment, and opportunities one will attract and accrue. Therefore, one cannot simplistically attribute Chunzi's writing to a naïve faith and confidence of the author in her future. Chunzi's writing and translation of her experience must be understood as a struggle for recognition as a body of value enmeshed in this economy and politics of writing and representation. Indeed, Chunzi has been informally praised by a prominent elite woman activist and official for having the "correct mindset" (*zhengque de xintai*) and thus being worthy of help. If she has nothing else to her name and therefore no value in any other sense, her writing lets it be known that she has a correct mindset, or valuable subjectivity.

With regard to whether and how the subaltern may speak, what happens when Hua Min covertly refuses to participate in this representation, but continues to speak? The Home for Rural Migrant Women has invited Hua Min, along with other veteran dagongmei, to speak on several occasions, including at meetings with funding agencies and overseas women groups. Hua Min said, "I tell it like it is—migrant women do the dirtiest, bitterest and most tiring work in Beijing. Later cadres from the Women's Federation think that there is some problem with the way I speak. But basically they have forgiven me. They just think it's because my suzhi is low and I'm unable to stand at a higher level to see things [*zhan zai yi ge gaodu kan wenti*]. There is some complaint that my mindset is not good, too narrow-minded, that I can only see things as they stand, and that I'm in need of improvement."

When Hua Min and dagongmei like her speak, what is required of them is not only a subsumption of their experiences into the narrative of the nation-state's Development; there is also an expectation that migrant women's experiences will achieve sublation. *Aufhebung*, often translated as "sublation" in English, means in its common German usage (1) lifting, or the raising of something to a higher level, and (2) preservation. In the Hegelian sense Auf-hebung or sublation is a dialectical process of both overcoming and preserving a thesis at a higher level. To qualify for a "good" mindset, Hua Min would have to "stand at a higher level," that of the nation-state, and to narrate her experience in sublated form such that her experience would be both preserved and overcome by becoming part and parcel of the nation-state's Development. Extending the Hegelian logic, truth is totality, while any part or moment is only partial, thus partially untrue. Hua Min would thus be unable to see the truth of things if she did not stand at a higher level to see her experience as only a moment, as necessary to the totality of the nation-state that is developing. Her refusal to think like the nation-state and to participate in this politics of representation is forgiven and dismissed as a manifestation of her low suzhi. Her politics of resistance is written off as another justification of her subordination. The subaltern indeed cannot speak discursively.

To refuse to "stand at a higher level" is to disallow subsumption and sublation in the politics and economy of representation. For sublation is also a negation, the "structural emergence of alienation."[27] Alienation here is not only capital's appropriation of migrant women workers' surplus labor but also the sublation of their experiences into the language of the economic law of Development, a discourse that enhances their own subordination. It is no coincidence that the subaltern politics Hua Min presently envisions is not a politics of *voice*—she refuses to speak with reporters—but a politics of *presence*: "Now the situation of dagongmei can be summarized in a single character: *hao* [to consume, expend, exhaust, use up, lose, be drained]. We hao time, hao youth, and hao life in the city. It is like saying that unless there is a real change in living conditions in the countryside, we will not go back. We will stick around and hao in the city. You have to give us *shuofa* [answer, accountability].[28] Every time the city police catch migrants [without certificates] and truck them home, migrants make their way back to the city before the police. We cannot be driven out; we cannot be exterminated [gan bu jin, sha bu jue]. . . . About the future, I say this: if we do not break out of the silence, we will perish in this silence."

At a time when consumption sweeps the nation and is said to be good for the national economy, Hua Min represents migrant women practicing consumption of a different kind: hao. Hao is self-depletion, depletion of one's time, labor power, youth, energy, and life itself. The subject of this hao is being consumed, leading to her emaciation, dissolution, and eventual absence, opposite of the usual subject of consumption, who consumes for the reproduction and enhancement of the self. Yet hao has another related use, which Hua Min also invokes when she says, "We will stick around and hao in the city," meaning a conscious assertive tactic of slowly and persistently, through the expenditure and depletion of one's time and energy, wearing away an obstacle (a person or an institution) in order to get something done, to induce a change or a transformation. The tactic of hao is to create a presence, a persistent presence that refuses to go away, but it is a presence enabled by a stubborn yet desperate act of self-depletion in a bid for time to allow one to hold on long enough for the obstacle to finally give way. The first meaning of *hao* refers to a process of being depleted, which was also used by the migrant woman in Shenzhen who wrote about "[having] expended all I have." But the second meaning refers to a tactical process of persistently producing a presence at the expense of self-depletion. It is a struggle in the hope that the obstacle will be forced to give way before "we" is completely consumed and depleted, and in the hope that "we" is not reduced to zero in the end. In Hua Min's representation the objectified process of being consumed and depleted into absence can be turned into a conscious political act of making a presence, a presence that demands and pressures.

Hao may be the most apt figure for the ambiguous state of dagongmei. Between absence and presence, the act of hao is a liminal politics, and a politics of liminal subjects. I return to Turner's terminology, but displace its meaning from a Turnerian ritual teleology to something much more indeterminate. Migration is a process with no guarantee of a ritual teleology; often, migrants are not reunited with the community as elevated postritual subjects. The politics of the future is to break out of the silence in which migrant women are being consumed and depleted. "If we don't break out of the silence, we will perish in this silence" is a well-known nationalist adage in Lu Xun's 1926 essay "In Memory of Miss Liu Hezhen."[29] The context of the event that gave rise to Lu Xun's writing was the crisis of the nation as the subject of history. In Hua Min's refusal to be sublated the subject in crisis is not the nation-state, but the collective subjectivity of dagongmei. While the discourse of development used by middle-class liberal organizers and scholars tries to create a sense of nationhood to displace "class" consciousness, Hua Min tries to retool Lu Xun's nationalist adage for struggles of class subjectivity. And the crisis of this class subjectivity is that it has yet to make a demanding presence. At this historical moment, dagongmei are liminal subjects, between the city and the country-side, between disposable and necessary, between possibilities of absence and those of presence, and between disarticulation and articulation. "Silence" here is an undetermined liminal state that may point to a process of vanishing, depletion, emaciation, and becoming zero, or that may give birth to an explosive presence. Yet, to defy a total depletion, to break out of the silence, and to emerge into a presence, Hua Min does not merely call for voice. A conscious tactic of hao implies a concerted force that determines to persist. The politics of voice alone cannot be the adequate answer to the crisis of subjectivity of which Hua Min warns.

Hua Min wonders, "What will become of us, the migrant women?" Only in mainstream discourse, which casts the contentious and disparate present in terms of a phantasmic coherence of the future, are migrant laborers subsumed into the nation's imagined community. The discourse of Development, unable to transform the vast reality of contradiction, subjection, damaging, and depletion, inflicts pain and frustration on those who struggle for having a future. By doing so, the discourse creates its own critics, its own debt, its own possible negation. Class (*jieji*), as a specter, exists between absence and presence, as migrant women are liminal subjects. It is constantly denied a presence by the dominant discourse of keywords, but it haunts them, revealing them to be catachreses. It inhabits the subterranean "much more enormous real reality" that Xiang describes. Dagongmei's subterranean experiences of this reality keep accumulating. From time to time, the experiences become such an overwhelming and crushing burden that dagongmei must forget in order to live; from time to time they appear scattered between the countryside and the city, hard to piece together. It may be difficult to say what the accumulation will amount to and what kind of quantitative-to-qualitative transformation will give it meaning. But as the reforms continue, these subterranean experiences accumulate in a spectral relationship with the accumulation of gross domestic product. In the unceasing process of daily experiences, possibilities for new forms of consciousness take shape. Hua Min's question and migrant women's poems and letters demonstrate a possibility for critique and self-critique, and for the imagining of a new collective identity in the open-ended process of struggle.

NOTES

Introduction

1. Hao Jian 1996, quoted in Liu 1999: 780.
2. Derrida explains *catachresis* in his dialogue with Richard Kearney: "The term metaphor generally implies a relation to an original 'property' of meaning, a 'proper' sense to which it indirectly or equivocally refers, whereas catachresis is a violent production of meaning, an abuse which refers to no anterior or proper norm" (Kearney 1984: 123).
3. On the political performance of subalterns speaking bitterness, see Anagnost 1997b, chap. 1, and Rofel 1999, chap. 1.
4. Xu Ke 1997, quoted in Chi Zihua, "'Dagongmei' de lishi kaocha" (A Historical Investigation of "Dagongmei"), *Guangming ribao*, 9 July 1999, 7.
5. Chi Zihua's article "Dagongmei de lishi kaocha" (A Historical Investigation of dagongmei) cites a number of historical documents about the late-nineteenth- and early-twentieth-century migration of women from the countryside to the city, from agricultural work to industrial labor (*Guangming ribao*, 9 July 1999, 7). The special issue of *Xin qingnian* (New Youth) in 1920 (vol. 7, issue 6), dedicated to the commemoration of Labor Day, provided investigations of labor conditions in a number of cities, including Shanghai, Nanjing, Tangshan, and Tianjin. Women migrant workers in the special issue were called not dagongmei, but *nügong*.
6. See Amin 2004 for a critique of how the separation of these two spheres is differently articulated and implemented in liberal ideology and social formations.
7. See the *positions* special issue "Chinese Popular Culture and the State" (9.1) and the 2001 roundtable entitled "Globalization, Postsocialism, and the People's Republic of China" hosted by *Signs* (26.4). In labor studies Pun Ngai 2005 and Ching Kwan Lee 2002 are pioneering analyses of postsocialist conditions and politics of resistance.
8. See Rowland 2001, 946n18.
9. "The employment at will rule was the natural offspring of the capitalist economic order, reflecting the value of individualism, the growth of competition, and the mobility of labor" (Freed and Polsby 1989: 558, quoted in Feinman 1991: 739–40).

10. Nick Squires, "Revamp of Labour Laws Draws Mixed Reactions," *South China Morning Post*, 27 May 2005, 12.

11. In these last words one hears the echo of the Haitian Revolution in Hegel's text on the master-slave dialectic. See Buck-Morss 2000 for the long-ignored influence of the slave revolts in Santo Domingo on Hegel's conception of the master-slave dialectic in *Phenomenology of the Mind*.

12. Chu Gansheng's *Nubi shi* (History of Servants) (1995) provides a detailed account of historical categories and treatments of bondservants, as well as fascinating accounts of servant resistance and uprisings. The largest uprising took place at the end of the Ming Dynasty, sweeping over a dozen provinces, and had a close relationship with the peasant uprising, led by Li Zicheng, that toppled the Ming Dynasty. See Yan Hairong 2006 (8–10) for a more detailed briefing on the history of the system of bondservants.

13. See Watson 1994 and Jaschok 1988 for writings on bonded servants in Hong Kong; also see Lu Deyang and Wang Naining 2004 for a survey of female servants in early modern times.

14. The term *baomu* in the early imperial period referred to women in the imperial court whose responsibilities included "nursing, protection, and instruction" of children (Jen-Der Lee 2000). Before 1949, this term had already been adopted in the communist area around Yan'an (see Ding Ling, "San ban jie you gan" [My Thoughts on March 8th], *Jie fang ri bao*, 9 March 1942).

15. Chu Gansheng (1995) wrote in the preface to his book on the history of the bondservant system that he was prompted to write it when he found that, much to his surprise, the teenage son of a friend did not even know what the term *jiading* (a type of male house servant) meant.

16. For rich analyses on gendered and sexualized meanings of domestic-service work, see Ding Naifei 2002, Jaschok 1988, and Watson 1994.

17. E. P. Thompson (1963) asserted that class consciousness must be examined as a cultural and historical process. Dipesh Chakrabarty takes issue with Thompson and points to "the irreducible place that subjectivity occupies both inside and outside the relations of production" (1989: 219). Gayatri Chakravorty Spivak arrives at the differential between representation of the ideal worker and the irreducible heteroclite world of living labor by opening Marx's theory of value to deconstruction. She analyzes use-value or concrete labor as heterogeneous and as "both outside and inside the system of value-determinations" (1988: 162). As Noel Castree reads Spivak, it follows that "value is a chiasmatic (mis)representation of concrete labor ('the working class') but is also, epistemologically, simultaneously a concept that constitutes or worlds this referent and constituency while surreptitiously disavowing this worlding by ignoring the texuality of theory" (1996–97: 73). In the disavowal of the differential between use-value and value lies the weight of a tragic error of socialist representations of the ideal working class. The recognition of this differential does not absolve one of the difficult task of representation, but should urge one to declare one's interests whenever one practices this strategic essentialism.

1. The Emaciation of the Rural

1. Gayatri Chakravorty Spivak's ghastly phrase "the spectralization of the rural," a comment on urban-centered global development (2000), inspired the title of an earlier version of this chapter: "Spectralization of the Rural: Reinterpreting the Labor Mobility of Rural Young Women in the Post-Mao Era" (Yan Hairong 2004). As I use the word *spectralization* in a somewhat different sense in chapter 5, I have changed the title of this chapter to avoid potential confusion.

   One may argue that Xiazi is drawing on traditional Chinese women's rhetoric in using a death threat as an expression of grievances. As Anne E. McLaren observes, "Death is a common metaphor in female grievance genres and threats of suicide not uncommon" (2000: 11). Yet recent statistics show that suicide as an expression of grievance or protest is more than metaphorical. Based on World Health Organization reports, a New York-based human rights group criticized China for having 21 percent of the world's women, but 56 percent of the world's female suicides ("China's Reforms Hit Women Hardest: U.S.-based Rights Group," Agence France Presse, 27 January 1999). Among rural women aged fifteen to thirty-four, suicide is the leading form of death, accounting for nearly one-third of all deaths in this age group ("Rural Suicides Show China's Pit of Despair, Says Study," Agence France Presse, 8 March 2002). See Danyu Wang 2000 for an analysis of rural female suicide in China.

2. In *The Condition of Postmodernity* (1989a), David Harvey analyzed "flexible accumulation" as a specific regime of capitalist accumulation that displaced the previously dominant Fordist regime. It is characterized by freer-floating currency exchange rates, hyper global mobility of capital, decentralized production (e.g., outsourcing, subcontracting), and flexible forms of labor relations. It therefore roughly corresponds to neoliberal ideology and policies; "neoliberalism" and "flexible accumulation" are two different analytics (one at the level of ideology, the other at the mechanics of accumulation) for changes in global capital since the 1970s. See also Harvey's *A Brief History of Neoliberalism* (2005).

3. The mode of accumulation in Mao-era China remains a subject of debate and is not the focus of my project here. By discussing changes in rural-urban relations in part of this chapter, I touch on the mode of accumulation in the Mao era, including its categorization of rural and urban populations through the household-registration system. For studies on the household-registration system and its impact on post-Mao migration, see Kam Wing Chan 1994, Solinger 1999, and Li Zhang 2001. On economic policies in the Mao era and their historical context, see relevant chapters in Gray 1990. The recent discussions on Maoist development policies organized by the *China Quarterly* demonstrate in some way the nature of the debate (Gray 2006; Selden 2006; Bramall 2006).

4. I use *historicity* as opposed to *historicism*. My use of *historicity* follows a historical materialist approach as described by Walter Benjamin: "Where thinking suddenly stops in a configuration pregnant with tensions, it gives that configuration a shock, by which it crystallizes into a monad. A historical materialist approaches a historical subject only

where he encounters it as a monad" (1992: 254). Benjamin criticized historicism as a narrative historiography that "culminates in universal history" (ibid.). Historicism and historicity differ radically in their cultural implications. Historicity defies historicism's assumption of a holistic culture, instead focusing on practices, discontinuities across time and space, and tensions within and between histories: "[A historical materialist] takes cognizance of . . . a revolutionary chance in the fight for the oppressed past. He takes cognizance of it in order to ballast a specific era out of the homogeneous course of history" (ibid.).

5. Of 104 women I interviewed, only sixteen had never migrated. Although some of them had family reasons, most cited illiteracy as the major obstacle to their migration.

6. According to Wuwei Xianzhi Bangongshi 1993, before 1949 frequent floods often caused men and women to seek livelihood as hired hands in cities like Shanghai. Women often worked as maids. Zhu Xiaoyang (1987) states that there was already a tradition of Wuwei women going to Beijing to work as maids in the Ming (1368–1644) and Qing (1644–1911) Dynasties. I have not been able to verify this statement in Beijing or Wuwei.

7. Migration between the cities and the countryside had been very strictly planned by the government until the early to mid-1980s. The number of migrants going to the cities on their own was very small. Rural women migrants, whose migration was mostly outside the state plan, worked mainly as domestic workers before and during the 1970s.

8. To seriously call the double postponement into question, it is necessary to link the specific practices of political economy with the discursive trajectory of the categories of "peasant" and "woman." See Cohen 1994 for an analysis of the Chinese term *nongmin* (peasant) as a loanword from Meiji Japan's pool of neologisms and as a recent political invention. The notion of peasants emerged in the context of an epistemic shift in the rural-urban relationship in the early decades of the twentieth century, shown in Fei Hsiao-tung's study (1968) as a relationship of opposition between the countryside and colonial treaty-port cities. It was in this historical shift, which reorganized the flow of goods, wealth, talents, and power between the country and the city, between China and the outside world, that the notion of peasants emerged in the discourse of China's modernizing intelligentsia (Barlow 1991b), who looked to the countryside and the "peasants" as a repository of China's age-old backwardness and stagnation, as well as of untapped potential for enlightenment. This emergent notion of the Chinese "peasant" found its way into the relationship between the Chinese Communist Party (CCP) and its peasant base. It enabled CCP thinkers, who themselves emerged from the modernizing intelligentsia, to leave their rural roots to spend their formative years in the cities, as well as to adopt with Marx, Lenin, and other modernist thinkers an essential suspicion of the peasantry as a class of small producers prone to backward beliefs. The party developed a theory of the "dual nature" (*liang chong xing*) of the peasants (Kelliher 1994): on the one hand, the severe oppression piled on the backs of the peasants drives them to revolution; on the other hand, their peasant economy engenders "small peasant consciousness" (*xiaonong yishi*), that is, a set of backward beliefs and a petit-bourgeois tendency toward "absolute egalitarianism," found in their desire for an equal share of land as the

ultimate goal of historical peasant rebellions. The dual character of the sign "peasant" is split and distributed onto images represented by two kinds of peasants: the poor peasant that embodies the progressive rural proletariat and the rich peasant that epitomizes the backward small-scale capitalist or aspiring capitalist. In the socialist period the state hailed the newly liberated poor peasant subject as an enthusiastic producer contributing to the industrialization of the new nation-state and to the ultimate industrialization of agriculture. Later, in the late 1970s, it was the individualistic "smallholding" character of the peasantry that was given ideological ascendancy by the post-Mao regime as the peasantry's real and rational nature, which was seized on for economic liberalization, including agricultural decollectivization.

9. See Kirkby 1985 for the context in which industrialization took precedence in the national economy.

10. Although a low price for grain enforced through the unified procurement system is responsible for the near stagnation of the rural sector, Tim Oakes (2000) notes that in the Mao era up to one-third of the state's procurement of grain was transferred to grain-deficient rural areas at subsidized prices. Oakes argues that "China's remarkable success in reducing its mortality rate by more than half in less than two decades—three times as fast as comparable countries—can largely be attributed to the success of its egalitarian grain redistribution policies" (2000: 308).

11. Perkins and Yusuf 1984 shows that in the late 1970s value flow into the countryside exceeded outflow, thereby beginning to reverse the trend in the previous decades of agriculture heavily subsidizing urban industrialization.

12. Some feminist scholars thus concluded that gender revolution in China had been postponed (see Margery Wolf 1985). See Anagnost 1989 and Barlow 1991a for critiques that call into question the assumption in Western feminist scholarship of such "postponement." The relationship between women's liberation and Chinese revolution and socialism has been the subject of ongoing debate. In a roundtable on "Globalization, Postsocialism, and the People's Republic of China," organized by the journal *Signs*, Lin Chun criticized "a recent revisionist trend in scholarship and politics that makes 'women's liberation' under socialism seem nothing more than an ideological metanarrative of the past, to be ridiculed, discarded, and replaced" (2001: 1282). Tani Barlow took issue with "international feminism" and posed the question "Is it possible that, in the minds of some, any Chinese feminism would prove to be too statist or too socialist to qualify legitimately as a 'feminism'?" (2001: 1288).

13. See Andors 1983, Johnson 1983, and Diamond 1975 for detailed examinations of gender ideologies and politics in the Mao era. See Young 1989 for a concise review of gender politics in the Mao decades as "an intimate variable of the overall revolutionary process" (254). For a more recent work that links gender with collective labor and public heroism in 1950s China, see Hershatter 2000.

14. It is noteworthy that Mao spoke of a more profound transformation of Chinese women in an episteme yet to come that would specifically unlink gender equality from mechanization. In his conversation with Andre Malraux, Mao reflected on the revolution of

women as part of the general meaning of revolution: "It isn't simply a question of replacing the Tsar with Khrushchev, one bourgeoisie with another, even if it's called communist. It's the same as with women. Of course it was necessary to give them legal equality to begin with. But from there on, everything still remains to be done. The thought, culture, and customs which brought China to where we found her must disappear, and the thought, culture, and customs of proletarian China, which does not yet exist either, must appear. The Chinese woman doesn't exist yet either, among the masses; but she is beginning to want to exist. And then, to liberate women is not to manufacture washing machines" (Malraux 1968: 373–74).

15. Phyllis Andors (1983: 125) credited the party-state's campaign against Lin Biao and Confucius in 1973 with inspiring more explicit and concerted efforts to campaign for women's equality, including efforts by rural women to gain parity in work points with men.

16. See Honig 2000 for a critique that, even at the height of the Cultural Revolution, when the Iron Girls were national heroes, the question of gender was still marginalized in ideological discussions and practices.

17. Drawn from my own fieldnotes and Gao 1999.

18. In the collective period, even though the traditional stricture of "women–inside–men–outside" was loosened and women generally participated in collective labor, labor assignment often incorporated gender segregation, and women often worked in women's groups.

19. See Lisa Rofel's 1999 ethnography, which shows how, before socialist liberation, the labor of factory women performed under male gaze marked such women as similar to prostitutes ("broken shoes").

20. Migrants who find that farming does not pay often rent the use-right of their land to others, so it is possible now for this woman and her husband to farm land for several families—their relatives or fellow villagers. The current practice in Wuwei, however, is that "tenants" do not need to pay rent and can keep the harvest for themselves, or are even compensated by the "landlords" for taking care of their land. I place "tenants" and "landlords" in quotation marks, because these are problematic terms insofar as no household, in theory, actually owns its land and the rental transaction is viewed only in terms of usufruct.

21. Despite the reputation of Wuwei as a source of baomu, there was an almost equally large presence of young baomu from Jiangsu and Zhejiang during the 1980s. For a time there were 20,000 baomu from Liyang County of Jiangsu Province, according to my informants.

22. Jin Yuanju and Xu Deyuan, "Baomu xiaoying: Laizi Wuwei de diaocha baogao" (Baomu Effect: An Investigative Report from Wuwei), *Anhui ribao*, 15 May 1994, 2.

23. David B. Clarke speaks of the contradiction posed by the "stranger" for modernity: "The entry of the stranger into the spaces of modernity was on the one hand entirely necessary, yet on the other necessarily fraught with anxiety" (1997: 223). Rural migrants are perhaps more alarming than Clarke's abstract "stranger" in that, in the context of

post-Mao anxiety over the quality of the Chinese population and its negative consequences for national competitiveness in the global economy, they are seen by urban Chinese as the embodiment of "low quality" (Anagnost 1995).

24. The Great Leap Forward has become singularly represented as a massive death toll in the mainstream media and scholarly works. For critiques of the politics of representing the Great Leap Forward, see Ball 2006 and Patnaik 1999. For works that debate mainstream representations, see Gao 1999 (chapter on the Great Leap Forward), Han Dongping 2003, and Patnaik 2004.

25. Although limited, efforts were made by the state to introduce medical care to villagers in the 1960s and 1970s, especially through the collectively funded barefoot-doctor system, which resulted in significant improvements in rural health (Gao 1999: 72–91; Knight and Song 1999: 157–58). Access to basic education was also improved through the barefoot-teacher system (Gao 1999: 92–122).

26. To maximize the surplus of industrial output for rapid accumulation, the party-state attempted to reduce the cost of reproduction of the urban-worker population by greatly reducing commercial activities in the cities and minimizing the prices for and limiting consumption of agricultural products via the *hukou* (household registration)-based system of rationing.

27. Rural and suburban industry in the coastal areas was the most important engine of growth in the 1980s. Rural enterprises, most collectively owned, could effectively compete with state-owned enterprises in the 1980s for a number of reasons. There was a massive investment in rural small industry (fertilizer, farm machinery and tools, steel and iron, cement) to support agriculture in the Mao era, especially during the Cultural Revolution period (for the connection between Maoist legacies and post-Mao rural enterprises, see Gao 1999: 203–6; Granick 1990; Perkins 1977; Perry and Wong 1985; Riskin 1971, 1987). Unlike state-owned enterprises, rural enterprises were not held responsible for establishing welfare systems for their employees, who were flexibly recruited and dismissed; and, unlike state-owned enterprises, rural enterprises enjoyed significant tax breaks. Yet the post-Mao state provided little direct investment support for rural enterprises and did not undertake long-term planning with regard to rural industry. The state's development strategy has focused on the city since the late 1970s. The 1990s saw a general decline of rural industry in coastal areas and widespread recognition of the environmental damage that such industry has caused. Even in the 1980s, most interior provinces, including Anhui, did not see much development of rural industry.

28. See Anagnost 1997b: 75–97.

29. It is difficult to compare policies for rural development in the Maoist and post-Mao periods simply in financial terms. There was massive investment during the Maoist period in small rural industry to support agriculture as well as urban industry designed to support agriculture. The rural communes and collectives financed much of the rural industry, but the state subsidized and facilitated this semipublic investment. The massive land reclamation, water control, and irrigation projects were also state-backed projects, even if they were based on peasant labor that was not compensated by the state. The massive

investment in schools and clinics also facilitated rural and agricultural development. None of these investments can be captured in financial terms. My comparison of the two periods in terms of state capital investment is only indicative of changes in support for rural and agricultural development but should not be taken as a comprehensive evaluation of the two periods in terms of support for rural development. I owe thanks to Joel Andreas for this point.

30. See Gao 1999 (177–79) for a detailed discussion of how the reform has influenced rural income. Gao argues that the increase in agricultural production and rural income should be attributed to the government's raising of agricultural prices and relaxation of the procurement system rather than to the much-hailed "household responsibility system." When the government lowered the procurement prices and tightened the monopoly of state procurement in 1985, production significantly dropped.

31. The rough Chinese-U.S. currency exchange rate in the late 1990s was 8.3 yuan: 1 dollar. The following is a typical calculation that I was given in Wuwei's rice-growing villages: 1,200 jin rice/mu x 60 yuan/100 jin = 720 yuan/mu (1 jin = 1.1 pound). Production costs: 70 yuan to rent oxen for plowing, 100 yuan for pesticide and fertilizer per mu, 15 yuan for water pump, 270 yuan for taxes and fees. Net income: 265 yuan/mu. A yield of 1,200 jin/mu is considered a bumper harvest. Harvests usually hover around 1,000 jin/mu. I was given slightly different figures for harvest yields, production costs, and fees in different villages. But the net income of 200–300 yuan/mu for rice growing is widely confirmed.

For cotton growing, I was given the following figures by a township accountant: 500–600 jin unginned cotton/mu x 300 yuan/100 jin unginned cotton = 1,500–1,800 yuan. Production costs (seeds, fertilizer, and pesticide): 300–400 yuan/mu; taxes and fees: 200 yuan/mu. Net income: 1,000–1,200 yuan/mu. A village accountant provided a much lower estimate: 160 jin ginned cotton/mu x 670 yuan/100 jin = 1,072 yuan/mu. Estimates of production costs, taxes, and fees remained the same. Net income: 472–572 yuan/mu. The cotton price was lowered 10 percent in 1998. Although there is a set of criteria for measuring the quality of cotton and each grade of cotton is given a fixed price, local cotton collection stations vary in their assessment of the quality of the fiber turned in by peasants. That directly affects the prices peasants get for their cotton and may account for the different estimates. Villagers tend to support the second estimate, especially because they were hit hard by a widespread pest attack on their cotton in 1998. Cotton growing is much more labor intensive than rice farming. In Wuwei, townships that are located near the Yangtze River and that have sandy land typically grow cotton, whereas inland townships grow rice. Cotton-growing townships have generally been better off than rice-growing townships.

32. Josephine Ma, "Rural Cash Crunch Taxes Reformers," *South China Morning Post*, 8 January 2002, 8.

33. See Potter and Potter 1990 (132–34) and Gao 1999 (72–79) on the function of the village-level medical-care system before the rural reform. Gao's work also makes a comparison of rural health before and after the rural reform.

34. See Hayford 1998 for a good analysis of the Orientalist discourse of "peasant China."

35. Yan'an, a poor rural area in northwest China, was the base from which the CCP fought against the Japanese invasion in World War II and against the Nationalist Party led by Chiang Kai-shek. In what later became known as the Yan'an period, the CCP reformed policies that began in the Jiangxi Soviet and experimented with many new policies. During that period, many left-wing young urban intellectuals went to Yan'an to join the revolution.

36. The term "773861" is not limited to Wuwei or Anhui Province but has a very wide circulation in rural China. The reality it reflects is found in rural areas in a number of provinces, such as Sichuan, Anhui, Shangdong, and Hubei.

37. De facto land abandonment reached peaks in 1984 and 1992. In 1984, 1.2 percent of total arable land in Chaohu Prefecture, Anhui, (50,000 mu) was left unfarmed (Chen Sanle, "Renzhen jiejue gengdi paohuang wenti" [Seriously Handle the Problem of Farmland Abandonment], *Anhui ribao*, 31 January 1984, 2; Wang Jiayan et al. 1993). This statistic still understates the problem, as it does not include the land that was underfarmed and underused (Zhonggong Hexian 1998).

38. According to *Nanfang zhoumo* (Southern Weekend), 12,189 people were injured in 1998 in Shenzhen, the capital of overseas investment and migrant labor ("Zhou Litai dai min-gong qixue shangshu, jinbaiqi gongshangan luxu kaiting" [Zhou Litai Sues on Behalf of Migrants, Hundreds of Work-Injury Cases Gradually Make It to the Court], *Nanfang zhoumo*, 26 November 1991, 1). Ninety percent of the injured lost their fingers, hands, or even arms. The work-related death toll in 1998 numbered more than eighty. This amounts to thirty-one persons injured every day and one death every four and a half days in the city. A survey in Beijing reveals that 70 percent of migrant women working in the city are not covered by any insurance ("Bohushanxia' nan chengliang" [Hard to Enjoy the Cool under the Protective Umbrella], *Zhiye daokan*, 18 August 1999, 2).

39. Foreign direct investment in China in 1999 totaled $40 billion. China's share of the total capital flowing into Asia has gone up from 18 percent in the early 1990s to 42 percent in 1999 ("US Businessmen Tell ASEAN It Risks Losing Out to China and India," Agence France Presse, 15 October 2000).

40. This is not to say that the specifics of their local cultural and gender dynamics do not matter in shaping their experiences of migration. From my interviews in Beijing, I found that women from provinces throughout China, whether Anhui, Sichuan, Henan, Shandong, or Gansu, share many important problems as migrants. It is the connection and commonality of migrant women that I am interested in exploring here.

41. Liu Li is the eldest in her family and has two younger teenaged brothers. She is from a mountainous county in Henan, where the main product is wheat. Because of deterioration in the management of water controls and the irrigation system (a not uncommon problem after decollectivization), they are visited by alternating droughts and floods, which reduces wheat productivity by half. To subsidize their meager agricultural income, her father and a younger brother who quit school engage in the backbreaking labor of loading and transporting rocks to a construction site.

42. According to Liu Li, villagers stereotype migrant women on the basis of representations in government campaigns against licentious activities and through soap operas on TV involving migrant women and their rich male patrons.

43. *Feudal* attained common currency in the countryside in the Mao era to label certain thoughts or people who constituted obstacles to establishing gender equality or a more democratic familial relationship in which women and the younger generation are supposed to have some say.

44. To find a woman a "mother-in-law's family" is to marry her off. This expression, which is often used in rural areas, manifests a patrilineal principle that is mediated by the senior figure of mother-in-law.

45. See Han Dongping, n.d.

46. During my entire stay in rural Wuwei, I saw only one young woman working in the fields.

47. Mao analyzed the layers of oppression experienced by peasants in semicolonial Chinese society, pointing out that rural women, in addition to bearing the mountains of oppression also experienced by their menfolk (articulated through political, clan, and religious systems of authority), were also subjected to the power of their husbands (*fuquan*, the patriarchal system of authority) (1967 [1927]).

48. This gendering practice bears resemblance to the gender discourse in nineteenth-century England that marked working-class women as insufficiently gendered (Armstrong 1987; McClintock 1995: 100–104).

49. The editor, Xie Lihua, recalled her encounter with this young woman: "It is not because of poverty that she fled home. Her native place is not poor and may even be said to be well-off. But material wealth does not imply spiritual enrichment. She came to Beijing because she was hungry but could not find food for her spirit. She said that her failure at the entrance exam for college was a fatal blow to her. She could no longer mingle with those girls and married women of her own age. She felt that if she had to repeat the old path of her parents, she would rather choose death itself" (1995: 5). This woman expected to lose her job because of housing difficulties. The house or apartment in which her employers lived was provided to them by their work unit. Work units sometimes adjust housing distribution among their employees by increasing or reducing the sizes of accommodations provided.

50. Becoming hegemonic since the 1960s and offering an increasingly unrestrained freedom of capital (domestic and international), pro-market developmentalism finds its supporters among the political and business elites in China and other countries in the South. Escobar 1995a and Crush 1995 provide incisive critiques of the discourse of development.

51. This Manichean logic, constitutive of the rise of the post-Mao regime, which based its legitimacy on "totally negating" (*quanpan fouding*) the Cultural Revolution, often plagues discussion and debates in China about problems of Maoist social projects and the post-Mao reform. Affirmation of certain socialist values of the Maoist era is immediately taken and criticized as a total endorsement of everything in that era. The 1980s

"New Enlightenment" trend within the intelligentsia supported the post-Mao reform's claim to modernity and represented the Maoist era, especially the Cultural Revolution, as a feudal dark age, to be negated by post-Mao development. By assuming a notion of universal capitalist modernity (albeit inflected by Chinese characteristics), such a logic obstructs the emergence within post-Mao Chinese society of detailed, nuanced, or multivalenced reflections on socialist experiments. Such critical reflections of the past are much needed for imagining alternative visions of social justice. One strategy employed by left-leaning intellectuals in China has been to examine the contradictions and disjunctures within modernity itself and argue that Maoist socialism was both an ideology of modernization, with problems inherent to modernization as such, and a critique of Euro-American capitalist modernity (Wang Hui 1998).

Standing in apparent opposition to this Manichean logic is a multiculturalist argument about modernity. I agree with Fredric Jameson's criticism of the latter position.

How then can the ideologues of "modernity" in its current sense manage to distinguish their product—the information revolution, and globalized, free-market modernity—from the detestable older kind, without getting themselves involved in asking the kinds of serious political and economic, systemic questions that the concept of a postmodernity makes unavoidable? The answer is simple: you talk about "alternate" or "alternative" modernities. Everyone knows the formula by now: this means that there can be a modernity for everybody which is different from the standard or hegemonic Anglo-Saxon model. Whatever you dislike about the latter, including the subaltern position it leaves you in, can be effaced by the reassuring and "cultural" notion that you can fashion your own modernity differently. (2002: 12)

The competing social visions of Maoist and post-Mao modernities challenge such a relativist vision of modernity. The relationship between socialism and modernity is a question to be further explored, rather than ignored or disavowed. Here I beg to disagree with Jameson's statement that "the only satisfactory semantic meaning of modernity lies in its association with capitalism" (ibid.: 13).

2. Mind and Body

1. Another version of this complaint is that "to find a good baomu is harder than to find a good daughter-in-law."

2. It is very difficult officially to tally the number of domestic helpers, as many of them come on their own and may not register themselves as temporary residents. Wang Shanping (1992) gave the figure of 50,000–60,000 domestic workers in Beijing between 1982 and 1988. The total number of households in the eight urban districts of Beijing (Dongcheng, Xicheng, Chongwen, Xuanwu, Chaoyang, Fengtai, Shijingshan, and Haidian), which constitute the city proper, was 1.8 million, according to the 1990 national census (Beijing shi 1992). Assuming that one domestic worker worked for one household, then approximately 2.7 percent to 3.3 percent of the total households in the city proper employed domestic workers in the 1980s. The actual percentage of households employing domestic service is most likely significantly higher, because some domestic workers

worked for more than one household. In my interview with him in 1999, Mr. Zhang Xianmin, founding manager of the biggest domestic-service company in Beijing, estimated the number of domestic workers to be around 100,000, and in 2004 he estimated the figure to have reached 150,000 (Lin Hongmei and Liu Yangyang 2004). Based on the 2000 national census, the total number of households in the city proper was 2.6 million (Guowuyuan renkou pucha bangongshi 2003). Assuming one household per domestic worker, the percentage of households employing domestic workers would be 5.7 percent, but, again, the actual percentage should be significantly higher. Li Dajing, deputy head of the Beijing Municipal Home Economics Association, estimated in 2003 that about 200,000 households (about 7.6 percent) in the eight downtown districts of Beijing had hired domestic workers ("Beijing in Need of Housemaids," Xinhua News Agency, 13 December 2003). This is the basis for the figure "less than 10 percent" that I provide in the text. It is estimated in the same report that 223,000 households will require full-time domestic workers and another 225,000 will require part-time domestic workers in 2005. If the estimate is accurate, then the percentage of households using full-time or part-time domestic service would increase to 17 percent. It was reported in 2003 that more than 10 percent of families in Shanghai employ domestic workers ("More Shanghai Families Are Employing Maids," *South China Morning Post*, 18 September 2003, A6).

3. The differences relevant to the analysis here in part echo the "three big differences" (*san da cha bie*) that the Mao-era state recognized to be problems: differences between the city and the countryside, between mental and manual labor, and between workers and peasants.

2, Part I: "Intellectuals' Burdens"

4. The neologism *zhishifenzi* (intellectuals or knowledgeable elements) emerged in the 1920s to name a new subject-position that claimed knowledge of universal truth adopted from the West for the good of China, against the now degraded tradition (later including Mao-era communism). For details, see Barlow 1991b.

5. Jacques Donzelot (1979) in his *The Policing of Families* analyzes family life as a "moving resultant" of social processes.

6. Gail Hershatter's study of woman-labor models in the 1950s shows that "the state did not so much create a new gendered division of labor as valorize, propagate, and remunerate one that already existed among many poor households in rural Shaanxi" (2000: 81). She also points out that while women embraced with enthusiasm the state's recognition, honor, and remuneration of their labor and creativity, many of them consciously observed and conformed to normative expectations for women (ibid.: 88).

7. Delphy's analysis of domestic work shows that a domestic mode of economy with patriarchal relations of production exists alongside capitalist relations (1984, 71–73). She defines this familial relation of production as the household head's domination and appropriation of the value created through domestic work.

8. Marxist feminist debates in the 1970s on the question of domestic work focused on

whether and how nonpaid domestic labor performed by housewives creates surplus value and relates in value terms to industrial production (e.g., Seccombe 1974, 1975; Coulson, Magaš, and Wainwright 1975). Succeeding waves of the women's movement certainly have not solved the problem of gender inequality in many spheres of social life, including domestic life (see Hochschild and Machung 1989). Mechanization of domestic work has not reduced the need for paid domestic labor. In fact, hiring domestic workers has become an important global phenomenon in the last two decades, with an increasing number of transnational migrant women employed in domestic service in North America and Europe (e.g., Anderson 1997; Momsen 1999; Parrenas 2001). For example, Bridget Anderson reports, "Increasingly, European families depend on migrant labour to carry out basic subsistence and reproductive tasks that cannot be moved elsewhere" (1997, 37). Blaine Harden informs that, with the number of American households worth $10 million or more quadrupling in the last decade, the statistics of the new rich "scream for good [domestic] help" and the demand for butlers "has no precedent in the country's history, except perhaps in the boom years of the 1920s" ("Molding Loyal Pamperers for the Newly Rich," *New York Times*, 24 October 1999, 1). Recent literature on the global migration of nannies, maids, and sex workers from the Third to the First World has generated new discussions of the transnational circulation of affective labor and the meeting of women from the North and South as employers-mistresses and employees-maids in the global market of domestic labor. Barbara Ehrenreich and Arlie R. Hochschild argue that the First and Third World are taking on traditional male and female roles in the global transfer of women's traditional work and "a division of labor feminists critiqued when it was 'local' has now, metaphorically speaking, gone global" (2002, 12).

9. Disputes over the domestic division of labor were the most frequent cause for divorce in Beijing in the early 1980s (Jiang Xia 1986).

10. According to this survey's random sample of 19,449 persons—among which 45.6 percent were men and 54.4 percent were women, 49.5 percent rural and 50.5 percent urban—women spend 254.1 minutes each day on domestic work, while men spend 93.1 minutes; urban women spend 214.1 minutes daily on housework, while urban men spend 86.3 minutes; rural women spend 267.4 minutes daily on housework, while rural men spend 95.1 minutes.

11. See Barlow 1994 for a detailed discussion of the unmaking of the Maoist woman, the losing battles waged by the Women's Federation, and the ascendancy of woman as "the female sex" in 1980s reform China.

12. For example, this view was alluded to in Fang Fang 1998.

13. The four modernizations are the modernization of industry, agriculture, defense, and science and technology. Among the four, modernization of science and technology is considered to be the most important. Lao Tian, in his sharply critical essay "Why Was the 'Deng Xiaoping Process' Possible," examines the process of how the elite stratum (*jingying jieceng*) has made its interests central to national political and fiscal policies guiding resource distribution in the reform era (2004a).

14. Here I borrow Gayatri Chakravorty Spivak's reading of Marx on capital (1987b: 52). For my analysis, the agent that appropriates the mind of one class and the body of another is not only capital but also the state, which engineers its development on the basis of a specific division of the mind and the body.

15. See Hoffman 2001 for a careful examination of the valuation of professionals through the discourse of rencai, and Anagnost 1997a for the linkage between child nurturing and modernity.

16. In a way this is a mirror opposite of the twist in George Bernard Shaw's "Pygmalion" in which the flower girl Liza's demonstration of accent and social demeanor was so perfect that she was suspected to be other than what she appeared. The mirror opposite is also found as a frequent theme in English literature in the persona of the "gentleman's gentleman," the perfect butler who is a good imitation and not a "proper" gentleman. Yet here the situation is a reverse and a paradoxical one: because Xiao Ling is a struggling urban intellectual in her true identity and not a "proper" baomu, she can appreciate and abide by the labor standard and thus be a perfect baomu.

2, Part II: The Proper Baomu

17. The income of intellectuals in the early to mid-1980s seemed stagnant when compared with the income increases for peasants and urban workers, and with profits made by some street vendors in that period. This is reflected in the rhyme "Laoda xiao, lao'er le, bu san bu si cun chaopiao, zhishifenzi guang zhe pigu zuo huajiao" (Elder brother smiles; the second brother is happy; dubious characters have money to save; the intellectual sits on his sedan chair bare-bottomed). A number of factors, including the adjustment of state grain-procurement prices, contributed to the growth of peasant income in the first several years of the 1980s. The wage reform introduced in factories following the rural reform allowed some income increase for many urban workers in the form of bonuses. It was widely ridiculed at the time that those producing missiles did not make as much as those selling tea eggs (a play on the homophone *dan* in *daodan* [missiles] and *chayedan* [tea eggs]) and that those wielding surgical knives did not make as much as those brandishing haircut knives (scissors). As the economist Han Deqiang observed (2000), the "gold-collar class" (intellectuals, high-level bureaucrats, entrepreneurs, and white-collar managerial staff for foreign businesses) has greatly benefited from the second phase of reform since the early 1990s, while peasant income has stagnated and workers' income has sorely declined in relative and absolute terms.

18. The rapid commercialization and privatization of residential apartments and houses, supported and encouraged by government policies (see Fraser 2000), has wrought changes in neighborhood dynamics even in neighborhoods constructed during the Mao era. In newly developed, guarded, private, luxurious apartment complexes, affordable to the upper echelon of urban society, the relationship among neighbors and the notion of collectivity and entitlement are radically different.

19. "China to End Govt Bailout for Bankrupt SOEs," *China Daily*, 3 February 2005, http:// www.chinadaily.com.cn/.

20. Nancy Armstrong's argument about the eighteenth-century emergence of domesticity in England is relevant here, in that modern domesticity was constructed "as the only haven from the trials of a heartless economic world" (1987: 8).

21. Among the employers I interviewed, some who had very young children believed that good-looking nannies would be conducive to the psychological development of their children.

22. It is instructive to recall Gillian Brown's analysis of the relationship in nineteenth-century America between the market and domestic sentimentalism, in which objects must be "purified of their market origin" before they can be transformed into domestic possessions (1990: 47).

23. Thought work, most often carried out through didactic conversation, is a process of initiating ideological change in an individual and is part of ideological work of the Communist Party. See Louis Althusser's "Ideology and Ideological State Apparatuses" (1972) for an analysis of ideological practices in capitalist society.

24. Zhang Meirong's and Nan Song's discussion of the value of domestic labor is linked with the question of women's liberation: "In a strict sense, the women's liberation movement and women's liberation are two different concepts. The former is women's liberation in its narrow sense . . . but the real women's liberation is a liberation of all women that enables the whole female population to be freed from unjust social systems, including class exploitation, oppression, and bondage, as well as patriarchy and unequal gender relations. . . . The Western feminist movement played a positive role in improving women's economic and social status, but it has also avoided the fundamental problem of class exploitation within the system of private ownership of means of production. Therefore, it only improved the situation and status for a minority of women, but is not a liberation of women in general" (1994: 81). However, my analysis does not allow me to agree with their assessment of the emergence of baomu in China: "The baomu phenomenon that has recently emerged [in China] is completely different from that under the system of private property. It is a substitute plan that is in between the domestic labor of working people's households and social labor. . . . It acknowledges objectively that domestic labor is a necessary social division of labor" (ibid.: 55). This cheerful appraisal elides the unequal class relationship that exists at the heart of domestic-worker employment in contemporary China. (I thank my friend Shao Shan and her brother for taking great trouble to photocopy *Jia wu lao dong jia zhi lun* for me.)

Intermezzo 1

1. For more information, see http://www.cctv.com.cn/.

3. *Suzhi* as a New Human Value

1. This company is one of many "economic bodies" (*jingji shiti*) that sprang from state institutions in the post-Mao economic reform. As hybrids, they challenge the conventional categories of "state" and "private" organization. This company, attached to the Women's Federation, is only partially a state institution—the top management includes

cadres from the Women's Federation who are on the state payroll, but its lower-level staff are contract workers. A number of scholars of China's political economy have described a variety of institutional models to analyze a market socialism with "Chinese characteristics." See Blecher 1991 for "local developmental state," Oi 1995 for "local state corporatism," and Duckett 2000 for "state entrepreneurialism."

2. The word *suzhi* or *zhisu* was associated with population quality in the discourse of eugenics and national character in the early twentieth century. It reemerged in the post-Mao economic reforms in the late 1970s and progressively gained density in its articulation of a new social economy in the 1980s and 1990s. For an exploration of its link with the politics of modeling and social control, see Bakken 2000.

3. "Remin Ribao Carries Editorial Entitled 'Concentrate Efforts on Improving the Quality of the People of the Nation,'" Xinhua News Agency, 20 October 1997, FBIS-CHI-97-293.

4. Susan Greenhalgh provides rich, sensitive analyses of how "population" has become the domain for national modern aspirations, scientific management, policy interventions, and power exercises in post-Mao China (2003a, 2003b). However, her analysis ignores the earlier global circulation of Malthusian and eugenic discourses and their connections with aspirations for national rejuvenation among Chinese intellectuals of varied political inclinations—royalists, republicans, socialists, liberals, and conservatives—in the late nineteenth century and early twentieth. Without examining the earlier global historical connection and influence, her studies fail to address the historical deposits in the idea of population, appearing to ascribe the processes of thinking and making national policies on population in China, particularly in the post-Mao era, to a "Marxist-Leninist-Maoist approach to population control" (Greenhalgh 2003a, abstract). While debates about Marxism, socialism, and the legacy of Maoism in China have been ongoing since the 1980s and have particularly surged since the late 1990s, to describe post-Mao birth-planning policies as "Marxist-Leninist-Maoist" risks confirming the official ideology at its face value. See Sakamoto 2004 for an important historical analysis of the circulation and impact of eugenics discourse among Chinese intellectuals at the beginning of the twentieth century.

5. See Anagnost 1995 for an analysis of suzhi discourse in the representation of bodies in post-Mao China that is centrally focused on the problem of productivity. See Murphy 2004 for the impact of the Suzhi discourse on rural education.

6. Xiaoyong, "Burang tigao suzhi" (Not Allowed to Improve Quality), *Nanfang zhoumo*, 11 May 1999, 11.

7. Walden Bello (1994) offers a very detailed and statistical analysis of the global effects that developmentalism has produced, specifically through a policy package called "structural adjustment" promoted by the IMF and the World Bank. Some intellectuals in China have also begun to adopt a critical stance toward Development (Han Shaogong et al. 2004). The power of developmentalism constrains imaginations of alternative development so that rescuing development from Development has become an increasingly critical task.

8. For example, Shao Yanxiang, a well-known intellectual himself, quotes the prominent liberal intellectual Li Shenzhi in his call for a curriculum in citizenship: "Mr. Shenzhi has suggested that the phrase 'the quality of the Chinese is too low' has become generally acknowledged. How can we improve the quality of the Chinese?" ("Huhuan gongmin ke" [Calling for Citizenship Curriculum], *Xinmin wanbao*, 10 April 1999, 12). Shao argues that a citizenship class in junior high school, which would teach civil behavior, knowledge of the constitution, law, ethics, and so on, would be a good beginning.

9. "Development is the indisputable truth" are the exact words pronounced by late paramount leader Deng Xiaoping when he visited Shenzhen in 1992, the city bordering Hong Kong, a special economic zone for overseas capital and an advanced model for China's market transition. After the suppression of the social movement in 1989, the talks given by Deng Xiaoping following his "southern tour" gave the go-ahead to China's further marketization.

10. Hu Angang, Zou Ping, and Li Chunbo (2001) analyze the growth of regional economic disparities since 1978 and argue that a structure of Four Worlds now exists in China. High-income and advanced areas such as Shanghai, Beijing, and Shenzhen constitute the First World, with per capita consumption reaching above the average level of upper-middle-income countries (US$8,320). The 1999 per capita gross domestic product (GDP) in Pudong, a new economic zone in Shanghai, reached US$25,472 (measured by purchasing power parity equivalents). This figure is 83.2 percent of the per capita GDP in the United States. The Second World includes large and medium-sized cities throughout the country, small cities in coastal areas, and some rural areas in wealthy provinces like Guangdong and Fujian. The GDP in the Second World is below the upper-middle-income countries, but above lower-middle-income countries (US$3,960). The Third World covers the vast rural areas. The Fourth World encompasses ethnic minority rural areas, border areas, and areas where the income levels are extremely low.

11. The recent publication *Zhongguo ren suzhi yanjiu* (Research on the Quality of Chinese People), which systematically surveyed *Renmin ribao* (People's Daily) from 1993 to 1999 for publications on suzhi, categorized these publications by specific suzhi topics and compared the distribution of suzhi topics in the newspaper with those in magazines during the same time period (Sha Lianxiang et al. 2001). Other recent book publications on suzhi include *Zhongguo nongmin suzhi lun* (On the Quality of Chinese Peasants) (Chen Qingli 2002), *Guomin suzhi yousilu* (Worried Thoughts about the Quality of the People of the Nation) (Xie Sizhong 1997), *Renlei suzhi xue* (The Science of Human Quality) (Lu Xun 2002), and *Guomin suzhi xue* (National Quality as a Branch of Learning) (Shan Peiyong 1997).

12. For example, among popular books on display, one can find a Chinese translation of the book *Test Yourself/Test Your IQ* by Jim Barrett, Ken Russell, and Philip Carter, titled in Chinese *Suzhi ceshi shouce* (A Manual for Suzhi Testing), with the subtitle "Testing Your Talent and Character and Predicting Your Career and Future" (Liu Xiangya 2001).

13. Suzhi education as a critique and corrective of exam-oriented education (*yingshi jiaoyu*)

became a hot issue first with regard to middle- and high-school education. With the institutionalization of suzhi education in university curricula after 1995, universities have been given special funds to support suzhi education. I thank Meng Dengying, a professor at Beijing Youth Politics College, for this information. See Kipnis 2001 and Thogersen 2000 for discussions and debates on the concept and practices of "suzhi education."

14. "Nanjing daxuesheng chi 'wenhua suzhi' zhengshu mouzhi" (University Students in Nanjing Look for Jobs with "Cultural Suzhi" Diploma), Xinhua News Agency, reprinted in *Jinpin gouwu zhinan*, 6 June 1999, C1. This suzhi diploma consists of graded evaluations of student performance in cultural suzhi courses, campus cultural and athletic activities, internship experience, and examinations on suzhi, computer skills, and English. The Xinhua report on this new practice stated, "The quantified data [reported on the suzhi diploma] brought a smile of satisfaction to middle-school principals looking for qualified teachers for their schools" (ibid.). In 1999 a private company marketed its services to college students who wanted to improve their suzhi qualifications, offering suzhi evaluation and testing, role playing, lectures, practical training, conversations with successful individuals, and so forth (Yin Wei, "Beida yingjiesheng ziban gongsi, zhili suzhi jiaoyu" [Beijing University Graduate Establishes His Own Company Dedicated to Suzhi Education], *Jingpin gouwu zhinan*, 6 July 1999, C1).

15. "Zhonggong zhongyang guowuyuan guanyu shenhua jiaoyu gaige, quanmian tuijin suzhi jiaoyu de jueding" (A Resolution of the Central Committee of the Chinese Communist Party and the State Council Regarding the Deepening of Educational Reform and Pushing forward Suzhi Education), Xinhua News Agency, reprinted in *Bejing qingnian bao*, 17 June 1999, 2.

16. Here one recalls Foucault's analysis of the notion of "humanity" in eighteenth-century penal reform: "Punishment must have 'humanity' as its 'measure,' without any definitive meaning being given to this principle, which nevertheless is regarded as insuperable" (1979: 75).

17. For example, "Enshrining Human Rights," published by *China Daily*, has as its lead sentence, "China's 1982 Constitution will be amended for the fourth time, further clarifying the country's stance on the protection of human rights, with a particular emphasis on private-property rights," while insisting that "the draft amendment [to the constitution] also incorporates the theory of 'Three Represents' into the constitution's preamble as one of the guiding principles of the nation, together with the heritage and further development of Marxism, Leninism, Mao Zedong Thought and Deng Xiaoping Theory" ("Enshrining Human Rights," *China Daily*, 23 December 2003, http://www.chinadaily.com.cn/).

18. My analysis of suzhi here benefits from Gayatri Chakravorty Spivak's discussions of Marx's writing on value (1990: 96; 2007: 445–46) and Ann Anagnost's theorization of suzhi (2004).

19. I draw the notions of "deterritorialization" and "reterritorialization" from Deleuze and Guattari (1983) and from Brian Massumi's (1992) reading of their work. My reading

of Massumi is that the process of deterritorialization and reterritorialization is also a process of decoding ("a change in the pattern of actions affecting [the subject]") and recoding ("the imposition of new patterns of connection with itself and its surroundings") (1992: 51).

20. Zi Ye, "Nongmin de yanguang" (Peasants' Vision), *Renmin ribao*, 6 December 1983, 1, reprinted in *Anhui ribao*, 8 December 1983, 1.

21. Xue Bian, "Nongcun guannian bianqe yu fan fengjian yishi" (The Reform of Rural Thought and Anti-feudal Consciousness), *Anhui ribao*, 10 October 1986, 4.

22. Ibid. *Chi dahu* (literally, eating the big household) was a form of popular rebellion, practiced before the establishment of the People's Republic, in which poor peasants would seize and redistribute the food reserves of wealthy landlords during famine times.

23. During my fieldwork in rural Wuwei County, I discovered a strong dislike among peasants for the late reform leader Deng Xiaoping. More than a few middle-aged cadres use their nostalgia for Maoist egalitarianism to critique problems arising in the market economy—the disruption of rural communities, increasing disparity between rich and poor, and the attendant problems of alienation among rural individuals and households. See also Dorfman 1996; Josephine Ma, "Rural Cash Crunch Taxes Reformers," *South China Morning Post*, 8 January 2002, 8.

24. Wang Zhaoyao, "Ba nongmin yin xiang shichang" (Leading the Peasantry to Market), *Anhui ribao*, 4 October 1992, 3.

25. Ibid.

26. Similar titles proliferated in the 1980s in the provincial party newspaper: Xue Dazhen, "Help Peasants Enhance Their Consciousness of Commodity Production" (Bangzhu nongmin zengqiang shangpin shengchan yishi), *Anhui ribao*, 16 March 1985, 2; Cao Shaoping, "Ten Years of Reform Have Changed the Image of Peasants" (Shinian gaige gaibian le nongmin de xingxiang), *Anhui ribao*, 6 December 1988, 3; Zhang Chuanyu, "There Has Been a Great Change in Peasant Consciousness" (Nongmin de guannian qi le henda de bianhua), *Anhui ribao*, 7 May 1988, 2; "Ten Great Changes in Contemporary Peasant Consciousness" (Dangdai nongmin guannian de shi da biange), *Anhui ribao*, 10 February 1987, 4.

27. Cheng Fengjun, "Zhengque chuli yu nongmin de guanxi" (On the Correct Handling of Our Relationship with the Peasantry), *Anhui ribao*, 14 May 1996, 5.

28. "Wenhua fuping yu cunmin zizhi de xin tansuo" (A New Exploration of Cultural Poverty Relief and Village Autonomy), *Anhui ribao*, 25 August 1998, 7.

29. This Chinese phrase could be translated literally as "poverty in humans themselves." Here poverty is no longer an external condition. The external condition of poverty is a reflection and result of poverty, backwardness, and lack within human subjectivity itself, either individual or collective. It may refer to a population in the context of regional poverty, but it may also be understood as referring to individuals in terms of their ability to recognize their individual self-interest. It is this process of "recognition" that is constituted as the problem, one that is not unlike the thesis of "cultural poverty"

of the 1970s and 1980s in the United States. Poverty is a problem of values orientation, rather than of more material economic forces.

30. "Wenhua fuping yu cunmin zizhi de xin tansuo," 7.

31. In the Mao era cultural centers, as part of the state ideological apparatus, provided reading rooms for the public, organized performances, art exhibits, and so forth.

32. Yu Fengbin, "Jintian de wenhua, mingtian de jingji" (Today's Culture, Tomorrow's Economy), *Anhui ribao*, 29 March 1995, 5.

33. Cultural work is becoming reoriented towards a market sensibility through "short courses" (*duanqi ban*), which have become a lucrative sideline for increasingly entrepreneurialized university professors who go to the countryside and small towns to give lectures, or who teach rural and small town cultural workers sent to university campuses to raise their suzhi. These relationships exemplify how restructuring is affecting all levels and bringing them into alignment with the new logic. I thank Ann Anagnost for this point.

34. Wu Yongyun, "'Wenhua xiaxiang' qianyi" (Preliminary Comments on "Taking Culture down to the Countryside"), *Anhui ribao*, 21 March 1997, 1.

35. "'Shuxue,' 'zaoxue,' 'zaoren': Guanyu fuping de jidian sikao" ("Transfusing Blood," "Producing Blood," "Producing Human Beings": Several Points on Poverty Relief), *Anhui ribao*, 9 May 1995, 6. The author observes, "There are new development projects every year, which are often spectacular at the moment of opening, but become desolate in their implementation and dismal in their output." The cause of these failures is coded as the low suzhi of peasants and their apparent lack of interest in leaving poverty.

36. Jin Yuanju, "Tigao nongmin suzhi de shehui daxue" (A Social University that Improves the Quality of Peasants), *Anhui ribao*, 16 June 1998, 7.

37. Ibid.

38. The Law on Compulsory Education issued in 1986 charges parents and families with the responsibility of ensuring nine years of basic education for their children, but exonerates the state from any obligation of having to provide resources for this.

39. Sun Yuchun, "Huangtudi de liebian" (Fissures in the Yellow Earth), *Anhui ribao*, 1 September 1995, 5.

40. This association is certainly not confined to the city of Tianjin. A survey in Shanghai from 1995 revealed that "the perception of criminality is the most important reason for mutual wariness and mutual separation" between migrants and urban residents (Ding Jinhong and Stockman 1999: 126).

41. The classic twelfth-century Chinese novel about rebels in the Song Dynasty (960–1279) is titled *Shui hu zhuan* (The Water Margin) (Shi Nai'an 1996), and Ding Ling's 1933 novel about peasants is titled *Shui* (Water) (Ding Ling 1954); in both cases water symbolizes a force of resistance and rebellion. The imagery of "flow" (*liudong*) in describing the migrant population today (*liudong renkou*) refers to the unmooring of the household-registration system that had formerly checked movement from the country to the city. As Development now demands the labor power of the migrant population,

good governance and control lies in the proper channeling (*dao*) of the migrant population, rather than in blocking it up (*du*), a strategy used by the legendary sage Yu to stop the frequent flooding of the Yellow River. Some economists speak about the flow of migrant labor as if it were water in a reservoir that could be released or dammed up according to market needs. Like the consumption of rural women as domestic labor power, the consumption of bottled water has also become a marker of class distinction (Boland 2001). Occasional scandals about where bottled water is sourced raise alarms about the quality and safety of its consumption, echoing scandals about the quality and history of domestic workers.

42. The selection process requires recommendation letters from employers about their domestic workers and from domestic workers about their employers. Photo displays and videos were produced from the award ceremonies. The practice was later dropped by the Tianjin company because the new director found it to be too much of a bother.

43. *Bu heshi* literally means "not suitable or appropriate," which can give rise to multiple interpretations: the workload was too heavy, the work environment was too demeaning, she had bad relations with her employer, or she was sexually harassed. The company did not explain to me the precise reason why she had found her working conditions to be unsuitable—either they had not bothered to ask her or she had refused to give a reason.

44. The manager herself was not clear and could not tell me what might have happened to this woman. Her intention was to use the story as a demonstration of how effectively their network functions as a security system. However, given the widespread representation of migrant criminality, especially petty theft, I suspect the runaway woman may have been prosecuted for theft. During my interviews with domestic workers, they often complained bitterly that they were immediately suspected when things were missing or misplaced in the homes where they worked. Many of these workers were also aware that employers often tested whether their "hands and feet were clean" by leaving purses or cash behind as bait.

45. There is another reason why the local labor bureau is unwilling to engage in organizing labor migration. With the reform of the state-owned enterprises leading to massive layoffs of urban workers nationwide in the 1990s, the central and provincial governments instructed labor bureaus to center their work on helping laid-off workers by signing them up for minimal welfare and registering them at reemployment centers. Labor bureaus also had to ensure a certain reemployment rate (50 percent in 1998), as related to me by a cadre at Wuwei County's labor bureau. With the labor bureau having to focus on laid-off workers, it does not have the resources to organize rural migrants for labor export.

46. Jin Yuanju, "Tigao nongmin suzhi de shehui daxue" (A Social University that Improves the Quality of Peasants), *Anhui ribao*, 16 June 1998, 7.

47. This reading of the mark of rurality in this woman's transformed bodily habitus can be read in relation to Pun Ngai 2003, which shows how urbanites are able to "recognize"

migrant workers as rural, even when they "dress up" as urbanites to perform leisurely consumption in the theme park Splendid China. For these women, cosmetics and fashion are more than superficial; they are the material markers of what Development comes to mean—to be a knowing consuming subject.

48. For some people, state ownership of enterprises and state mediation of the market reform seem to contradict the thesis that China can be characterized as neoliberal. Leong H. Liew thus characterizes the relationship between China and neoliberalism as a "loose hug" (2005: 349). Some others seriously doubt whether an authoritarian state could practice neoliberalism. Wang Hui addresses this question.

> Chinese society did not undergo the same disintegration as the Soviet Union and the East Europe, and the social transformation in China was therefore characterized by a certain continuity. Were we to sum up this process in a simple and thus incomplete fashion, we could say that under the continuation of the system of state political power, Chinese society has pushed forward a process of market extremism. . . . The dual nature of this combination of continuity and discontinuity has defined the nature of Chinese neoliberalism. Neoliberalism depends on the force of national and supranational policy and economic power. . . . [T]o use the existence of state interference as a way to avoid recognizing the hegemony of neoliberalism is completely beside the point. The hegemonic status of Chinese neoliberalism took shape as part of the process by which the state used economic liberalization to overcome its crisis of legitimacy. (2003: 43–44)

Reflecting on the genealogy of social thought in the urban-reform process of the 1980s and 1990s, Han Yuhai also points out the function of critical state-policy designs in shaping the process of market liberalization and in promoting social disparities (2004: 30–32). Han reminds one that it was the neoconservatism and neo-authoritarianism of the 1980s that mobilized the power of the state and the elites to push for the expansion of the market and privatization. Therefore, "neoliberalism consists of 'neo-authoritarianism,' 'neo-conservatism' and liberalization of capital" (Han Yuhai 2005: 32). See Han Deqiang 2003 for his analysis of how neoliberalism is embedded in the assumptions and articulations of national economic policies formulated by the third plenum of the sixteenth Party Congress. For a class analysis of the reform process, see Lao Tian 2004a.

Yet the thesis of a *specific* Chinese neoliberalism that stresses the function of the state does not make the case of China exceptional. In "Neoliberalism and the Restoration of Class Power" David Harvey (2006) traces the earliest neoliberal experiment to the neoliberal state formation in Chile after Augusto Pinochet's coup on the "little September 11th" of 1973, facilitated by U.S. forces, and the subsequent military suppression of democratic labor movements. According to Harvey, "The nation-state remains the absolutely fundamental regulator of labor. The idea that it is dwindling or disappearing as a center of authority in the age of globalization is a silly notion. In fact, it distracts attention from the fact that the nation-state is now more dedicated than ever to creating a good business climate for investment, which means precisely controlling and repressing labor movements in all kinds of purposively new ways: cutting back the social wage, fine-tuning migrant flows, and so on" (2001: 14).

49. For most urban residents at the time, domestic service was still a novel idea and a sensitive topic. When the Beijing company was established in 1983, making paid domestic work a service for purchase, it became a nationwide news story. Most urban working-class families were (and still are) unable to afford domestic helpers. However, an emergent affluent class—who may "not be able to reach the level of the high [as high-level cadres and elite], but are unwilling to stoop to the low [*gaobucheng, dibujiu*]," in the words of the director of the company in Beijing—have contributed to a growing demand for domestic labor. Thus, there was apparently a great demand for domestic workers in the 1980s.

50. I thank Delia Davin for making Wang's thesis available to me. The number of migrant women working as domestic workers is very hard to pin down. My estimate based on my interviews with domestic-worker recruitment agencies coincides with Wang Shanping's study (1992). According to *A Collection of Data on Population Migration in China* (Zhongguo renkou qianyi shuju ji) (Zhuang 1995: 101), the total number of domestic workers migrating to Beijing between 1 July 1985 and 30 June 1990 was 4,802 from within the Beijing area and 34,117 from other provinces. The total number was thus 38,199. Given the difficulty in surveying migrants, this was a rather conservative count.

51. The exchange rate between Chinese currency and U.S. dollars during 1975–82 was about US$1 to 1.5–1.97 yuan.

52. Wang Shanping also briefly mentions that Wuwei migrants often tried to force women from other provinces out of the neighborhoods dominated by Wuwei women (1992: 83).

53. Also see the work of Li Zhang (2001) for an analysis of how migrants have constructed networks of mutual support based on shared native-place identity.

54. My analysis of neoliberal governmentality draws on the late lectures of Foucault as translated and discussed in Gordon 1991. Neoliberal ideology and policy is associated with emergence of the New Right in the North Atlantic economies during the Reagan and Thatcher administrations of the 1980s. In the neoliberal vision the economy furnishes the model for a global organization of the social (Gordon 1991: 43). Neoliberalism has two contradictory sides. As Belsey summarizes, "In its liberal guise, neoliberalism is the politics constructed from the individual, freedom of choice, the market society, laissez-faire, and minimal government. Its neoconservative component builds on strong government, social authoritarianism, disciplined society, hierarchy and subordination, and the nation" (Andrew Belsey 1986: 173, quoted in Overbeek and van der Pijl 1993: 15). Saskia Sassen also cautions that language such as "deregulation," "financial and trade liberalization," and "privatization" only captures the consequence of struggles and negotiations, but not the process "in which the state participates in setting up the new frameworks through which globalization is furthered; nor do they capture the associated transformations inside the state" (1999: 158).

55. Michael Perelman (2000) shows that Adam Smith and other classical political economists were, in their more practical writings, strong advocates of government interventionist policies to force peasants into factories during the process of primitive capital accumulation, despite their economic theories advocating laissez-faire policies toward the market.

56. Xuan Zhongguang, "Rencai shi qiye de diyi ziben" (Quality Persons are the Number One Capital Resource for Enterprise), *Anhui ribao*, 17 August 1994, 5.

57. Jean Comaroff and John L. Comaroff (1999) deal intricately with the question of abstraction in their analysis of an imagined zombie production as the brutal form of extraction and abstraction of pure surplus value in the encounter of rural South Africa with global neoliberalism.

58. Diane Elson's elaboration of Marx's value theory of labor and the subsumption of labor under capital clarifies what characterizes labor under capitalism. Elson argues that in a capitalist society "other aspects of labour [individual, private, heterogeneous, social, etc.] are subsumed as expressions of abstract labour. The form of the universal equivalent reflects only abstract labor" (1979: 165). Hence, "The real subsumption of labour as a form of capital is a developed form of the real subsumption of the other aspects of labour as expressions of abstract labour in the universal equivalent, the money form of value" (ibid.: 166).

59. Arif Dirlik (2002) argues that the passing of socialism and the rise of East Asian societies as a new center of capitalist power in the late 1970s and early 1980s have contributed to a decentering of capitalism. Dirlik's analysis links this decentering of capitalism with the now popular discourse of "multiple modernities."

60. See Sonntag 2005 and Krishnamurthy 2005 about call centers in India.

Intermezzo 2

1. Xue Yong, "Meiguo de Den Xiaoping zhi lian" (America's Love for Deng Xiaoping), *Nanfan renwu zhoukan* (Southern People Weekly), no. 14 (2004), www.nanfandaily.com/cn/nfrwzk/.

4. A Mirage of Modernity

1. The provincial media typically estimate the number of migrants from Anhui to be five million, although in my interview the director of the Population Institute at Anhui University estimated the number to be around three million.

2. I was told of the following breakdown of the 180 yuan charged in Quanyang: 10 yuan for a physical examination at the township hospital for hepatitis, 50 yuan for obtaining a work card from the township government, 80 yuan for the bus ride to Beijing, and 40 yuan for other expenses. The 110 yuan charged by the Beijing company included 50 yuan for a security deposit, 20 yuan for job introduction, 10 yuan for a copy of *The Handbook of a Family Attendant* (Jiating fuwuyuan shouce), 20 yuan for a worker card, and 10 yuan for medical fees.

3. The business trip involved negotiating about supplying domestic workers to Shenzhen. On learning about conditions of employment in Shenzhen, Xiumei decided not to pursue the opportunity. The starting wage in Shenzhen was 350 yuan and increased to 400 yuan in two months; afterwards, there were no raises. Wages were paid once every two months by the company, rather than by the family served. Xiumei's mother complained about not knowing how much the family paid the company. Furthermore, the company in Shenzhen did not allow migrant women to return home within the first year and also forbade migrant women to use the telephone in the homes they work for, thus making it hard for families in Quanyang to contact their daughters and wives working in Shenzhen. Although the Jiao family considered these rules excessively rigid, Xiumei's mother admired the company for its cleanliness and was impressed to see workers scrubbing the floor on their hands and knees.

4. "NPC Deputies Concerned over Income Disparities," Foreign Broadcast Information Service, 12 March 2001, FBIS-CHI-2001-0312. This article is the English translation of the news issued by the official Xinhua News Agency (domestic service). Another study shows that less than 5 percent of citizens owned almost half of the nation's sum of personal savings ("China's Income Disparity Grows," *People's Daily*, 12 July 2000, http://english.peopledaily.com.cn/). Research by the Chinese Academy of Social Science shows the income disparity still growing ("China Suffers Widening Income Gap: Report," Xinhua News Agency, 7 January 2007).

5. The sociologist Sun Liping sheds some light on how labor was rewarded in China's 2002 gross domestic product (GDP). The total sum for wages and salaries was 12 trillion yuan, only 12 percent of GDP, 21.4 percent of the total disposable income of rural and urban residents, and 33 percent of the total disposable income of urban residents. Twenty-four trillion yuan—67 percent of the total disposable income of urban residents—came to urban individuals in forms other than salary or wages. See Sun Liping, "Shouru fenpei chaju shi ruhe kuoda de?" (How Has Income Disparity Widened?), *Nanfang zhoumo*, 10 April 2003, http://www.nanfangdaily.com.cn/.

6. I thank Liang Xiaoyan for this information.

7. Pun Ngai makes a parallel argument (2003).

8. During Premier Zhu Rongji's tenure (1998–2003), the Chinese government pursued an active fiscal policy that aimed to boost the economy by vastly increasing government spending. In order to ensure a 7 percent growth rate in 2002, the government pushed the budget deficit to an unprecedented $37 billion, 19 percent more than that of the previous year. Some Chinese economists warn that China has accumulated a dangerous amount of debt ("China's Future: A Dampened Blaze," *Economist*, 15 March 2002, 71). Yet analysts claim that in order to "deter social upheaval," the government must ensure a 7 percent growth rate to generate sufficient jobs. With intensified competition following China's entry into the World Trade Organization, the situation will degenerate further and unemployment will rise (Erik Eckholm, "Premier Defends China's Economic Policies but Notes Rural Poverty," *New York Times*, 15 March 2002, 4).

9. For example, the mass media promoted a new concept with regard to consumption:

"Spend tomorrow's money today" (jintian hua mingtian de qian) or "consumption in advance" (*tiqian xiaofei*), encouraging people to consume on credit. The masses are not easily transposed into the expected level of consumption in this increasingly stratified society. When dealing with the problem of insufficient consumption and deflation, economists have tackled and critiqued the problem from various aspects: stock-market analysis, relations between savings and consumption, urban-rural relations that could potentially endanger a market economy, and so on. (For example, see Hu Shuli, "Yuan mu yan neng qiu yu?" [How Is It Possible to Find Fish in the Tree?], *Nanfang zhoumo*, 25 June 1999, 23; Zhou Hong, "Gongwuyuan yinggai jiaxin?" [Should Civil Servants Get a Pay Raise?], *Nanfang zhoumo*, 25 June 1999, 23; and Dang Guoying, "Xiaofei nan kuoda, zhengjie zai tizhi" [The Difficulty of Expanding Consumption Lies in the System], *Nanfang zhoumo*, 25 June 1999, 23.) A letter from a reader to *Southern Weekend*, entitled "Lowering Interest Rates Cannot Incite Me to Consume," offers a more critical perspective on the problem. The letter states, "Nowadays the question of how to consume seems to be a hot topic. Many media have been instructing and advising people on how to consume. The banks have lowered interest rates again and again, to persuade people to adopt a new consumption attitude. Banks have lowered interest rates for the seventh time. Not only has this not incited people to spend money, but banks witnessed even more savings than before. What could be the reason behind this?" The letter then analyzes which groups of people can and cannot afford to consume, and suggests that the problem of economic insecurity and anxiety facing the working-class population is responsible for wage-earners' fear of spending money (Zhang Xiaofei, "Lower Interest Rates Cannot Incite Me to Consume," *Nanfang zhoumo*, 2 July 1999, 8).

10. According to a World Bank report (2002), the Gini coefficient in China, based on 1998 economic data, was 0.40. However, the official Xinhua News Agency, reporting on the meetings of the National People's Congress in March 2001, stated that the Gini index had already reached 0.45 ("NPC Deputies Concerned over Income Disparities," Xinhua News Agency, 12 March 2001, FBIS-CHI-2001-0312). *People's Daily* acknowledges that "the Gini Coefficient of China's individual income was 0.424 in 1996, 0.456 in 1998, 0.457 in 1999 and 0.458 in 2000. According to international standards, China has entered the stage of 'absolute disparity' and the gap is still widening" ("How Wide Is the Gap of China's Individual Income?" *People's Daily*, 31 August 2001, http://english .peopledaily.com.cn/).

11. The gendering of consumption may be traced to the spatial division of production and consumption that emerged during European industrialization. Before industrialization, production was more often carried out in the household and involved both men and women, old and young. In the industrial era, production was relocated from the household to the factory, and male workers dominated factory production. The household became more associated with consumption. Hence our modern stereotype: men are producers and women consumers. Feminist scholars have examined the long-established equation of women and consumers (Donohue 1999; Armstrong 1987; Willis 1991; Spigel and Mann 1992). The coupling of "women" and "consumption"—femininity of con-

sumption and consumption of femininity—has mutually reinforced the subjugation of both to men and (waged) "production." As part of enlightenment thinking, the gender ideology that associated women's identity with consumption also traveled to the margins of the modern (European) world, where industrial capitalism was not yet a dominant form of social production. During the American Revolution, for example, women were identified as consumers, and such an identity threatened republican virtue (Kerber 1980). Similarly, during national rejuvenation efforts in the late Qing and early Republic, Chinese reformers such as Liang Qichao also argued that women as consumers weakened the state (Orliski 2003). The rising prominence of the consumer through the emergence of consumerism since the 1970s should instead be linked to an intensified pressure on consumption to realize surplus value (Haug 1986; Storper 2000). Today the continued equation of consumers with women, combined with the new assertion of "consumption as the vanguard of history," has led Daniel Miller, an anthropologist of consumption, polemically to argue that the housewife is a "global dictator" (1995: 34). For an analysis of gender, youth, and consumption in contemporary China, see Zhang Zhen 2000.

12. For a fine analysis of media images of femininity, see Evans 2000. Harriet Evans suggests that the explosion of media images of femininity occurred in the 1980s following the establishment of the first Special Economic Zones in the south as the vanguard of the growing market economy. For the removal of urban women from the labor force, see Rosen 1994 and Cartier 2001. Both studies cite rich data to delineate how working-class and professional women are disproportionately laid-off or forced into retirement or extended maternity leave during enterprise or business restructuring. Women constitute 65 percent of layoffs in the state sector, while they represent only 40 percent of the workforce (Beech 2003). Workers who are women and thirty-five years or older are less desired by the labor market (*Women's International Network News* 1999).

13. Migrant women in Thailand (Mills 1999: 136) feel more obliged than men to send money home, and factory women in 1920s and 1930s Shanghai (Honig 1986: 168) and 1950s–1980s Taiwan (Margery Wolf 1972: 98–99; Kung 1983: 17–27) faced considerable parental control over their labor and wages. Diane Wolf (1992: 174–75) compares parental involvement in daughters' labor and remittance decisions in Java and Taiwan, and finds much tighter parental control in Taiwan. In mainland China, while earlier generations of migrant women, who were almost all married, sent their earnings to their rural homes, most unmarried migrant women I interviewed in Anhui and Beijing reported that their parents did not expect money from them, though some of them did send remittances once in a while. In Hunan, while parents expected sons to send money home, they did not expect the same of their daughters ("Wailai nülaogong yanjiu" ketizu 1995: 82).

14. See Tang 2003 for an incisive analysis of how Guilian and Ermo, two rural women characters in the films *In the Wild Mountains* (Yeshan) and *Ermo*, respectively, became desiring subjects through contacts with post-Mao consumption on their trips to the city.

15. See Tang 1998 for an analysis of a middle-class subject's attempts to master the language of sign-objects while reconfiguring and re-presenting his own subjectivity in the process.

16. This story states that before going out one weekend morning, a couple told their baomu not to forget to wash the laundry and the baby. (Colloquial Chinese uses the same verb [xi] for washing clothes and bathing.) So, after the domestic finished the laundry, she put the baby in the washing machine. Also alluding to this story, Li Tao, an activist for a Beijing-based nongovernmental organization, asserted that "improving migrant women's suzhi is the most important task of employing units and customers" (1999).

17. Bridget Anderson (2000) analyzes the tension between body as personhood and body as property and argues that it is not only labor power but also the personhood of the domestic worker that is commodified.

18. Huang Jianguo, "Lingren guanzhu de 'baomu weiqu jiang'" (A Notable "Baomu Grievance Award"), *Yangzi wanbao*, 21 October 1999, 3.

19. Sun Wanning (2004) analyzes the overwhelming attention and honor shown by the Women's Federation and provincial leaders in both Guangdong and Anhui to the Anhui migrant woman Hong Zhaodi, who crippled herself in Guangdong when she resisted forced prostitution. The Sichuan migrant woman Tang Shengli, who for a similar reason jumped from a building in Chengdu, the capital of Sichuan Province, received similar official attention and free medical help from prestigious hospitals (*Jiedao* 1998: 6). Compared to the attention shown to these two migrant women, the deep-rooted structural problems that lead to their plight and continue to produce daily abuse and violence against women are very much ignored. Many other cases of serious physical abuse and rape of migrant women receive little media attention or interest even after the abuse is exposed (Li Tao 2000; "Beijing Man Hired Then Raped Four Teen Maids," *Straits Times*, 9 August 2002, www.straitstimes.com). The attention to and approval of these women protecting their sexual purity at all costs sends a conservative message: sexual purity underlies the value of migrant womanhood. It implies that though migrant women may have little control over work conditions, labor exploitation, and physical abuse, they do have control over their sexual purity and are responsible for protecting it. In fact, raped migrant women who have "failed" in protecting their sexual purity have difficulty in obtaining official media attention and support, and find it difficult to sue the perpetrators.

20. My analysis is not unrelated to the notion of "emotional labor" in the field of service work explored by the sociologist Arlie Hochschild (1983) and others (e.g., Steinberg and Figart 1999), but I stress here how migrant domestic women enter into a specific class position.

21. See Guang 2003 for a detailed description and analysis of the dispute about fashion and taste in terms of rural-urban relations. It also examines the use of nationalism in this clash and demonstrates its failure as a counterdiscourse in this debate. My effort here is to situate this debate in the context of contemporary relations between production

and consumption and to examine the role played by provincial elites in Anhui in both defending the name of "Anhui" and distancing "Anhui" from migrant women. Despite the clash, provincial elites, like the Shanghai author, ended up disavowing migrant women.

22. Wang Weiming, "Chuan lizhi tuoxie mangjie pao de nurenmen" (Women in Cheap Sandals Running Amok on the Streets), *Qingnian bao*, 27 July 1996, reprinted in *Xin'an wanbao*, 7 August 1996, 1.

23. For a critique of how culture rises as capital, see Jing Wang 2001.

24. Wang Weiming, "Chuan lizhi tuoxie mangjie pao de nurenmen."

25. See Haiyan Lee 2006 for a perceptive analysis of a television fantasy of domestic workers' transformation.

26. Wang Weiming, "Chuan lizhi tuoxie mangjie pao de nurenmen."

27. See Sun Wanning 2002 on the discourse of poverty and provincial identity of Anhui.

28. Zhang Kun, "Yu 'chuan' wen zuozhe Wang Weiming de duihua" (A Dialogue with the Author Wang Weiming), *Xin'an wanbao*, 14 August 1996, 1.

29. Bi Xiaojian and Lu Liejia, "Huishang de houdai, ni zenmela?" (Progeny of the Hui-shang, What Has Happened to You?), *Anhui ribao*, 17 May 1992, 1.

30. Ji Jiahong, "Kua shiji de zhaohuan: Jianshe Anhui xin xingxiang" (A Cross-century Call: Constructing a New Image of Anhui), *Anhui ribao*, 29 July 1999, 5.

31. Ibid.

32. Ibid. In Anhui there are certainly perceptions about regional differences (city vs. countryside, north vs. south). These internal differences are often obscured in representations of Anhui, both by Anhui people themselves who travel outside the province and by outsiders.

33. Qiu Zhengping, "Dianshi lianxuju 'Hui Shang' kanpian yantaohui" (A Seminar on the TV Series *Huishang*), *Anhui ribao*, 16 May 1997, 7.

34. Sun Bangkun, "Sheng lingdao he zhuanjia xuezhe shengzhan dianshi xiliepian 'Anhui ren zai tequ'" (Provincial Leaders, Experts, and Scholars Highly Praise the TV Series *Anhui People in the Special Economic Zone*), *Anhui ribao*, 7 August 1997, 1.

35. Wang Shanggai, "Ren de xingxiang: Quyu xiangxiang de linghun" (A People's Image: The Soul of a Region's Image), *Anhui ribao*, 10 March 1998, 8.

36. Kong Fanqing, "Wo de Anhui qingjie" (My Feelings for Anhui), *Xin'an wanbao*, 4 November 1994, 3.

37. Ibid.

5. The Specter of Class

1. Foucault defines technologies of the self as those which "permit individuals to effect by their means or with the help of others a certain number of operations on their own bodies and souls, thoughts, conduct, and way of being, so as to transform themselves in order to attain a certain state of happiness, purity, wisdom, perfection or immortality" (1988: 18). Technologies of the self are closely linked to governmentality, which

he defines as "this contact between the technologies of domination of others and those of the self" (ibid.: 19).

2. Catherine Gallagher (1987) carefully examines the notions of the body and the connections between the physical bodies of the masses and the social body (of society) in the works of Thomas Malthus and Henry Mayhew. The Victorian loathing of "mere life" is a Mayhewian extension of Malthus's logic (ibid.: 104).

3. My argument about the relationship between survival and Development is inspired by Nancy Armstrong's writing on the distinction between nature and culture: "The difference between nature and culture is always a function of culture, the construction of nature being one of culture's habitual tropes of self-authorization" (1987: 262n6).

4. See Lü Xiaobo and Perry 1997 for a historical examination of the work-unit system.

5. Hua Rui, "Sandai baomu: Jiongran butong renshenglu" (Three Generations of Baomu: Radically Different Life Paths), *Xin'an wanbao*, 10 December 1998, 12.

6. Brian Hammer's (n.d.) critique of the discourse of poverty in China shows the continual link between self-development, regional development, and national development, as often stressed in official poverty-relief speeches.

7. In recent years, the neoclassical economist Friedrich Hayek has enjoyed popularity among certain Chinese intellectuals, particularly prominent economists. However, as I have argued in my analysis of neoliberalism, there are complex connections between the political and the economic. The very reconstruction of the meaning of *economy* is political. Wang Hui's analysis (2003) also insists that the economic reform has always been a political process.

8. In various media discussions of the effects that China's entry into the World Trade Organization has had on the domestic economy, economists and pundits seldom examine how specific treaties will influence domestic industry. In fact, treaties are seldom revealed to the public. Instead, much of the discussion has been based on a belief in market economy ("Seize Opportunities and Meet Challenges from WTO Entry," Xinhua News Agency, 28 February 2000). For example, in order to assuage doubts and worries about the domestic economy after the World Trade Organization accession, a *China Daily* article simply argues that "progress is motivated by competition, a fact which has been proven by twenty years of reform and opening up," and "the problem of state enterprises can be solved only through structural adjustment. Competition from the outside might be a catalyst to the process" ("More Gains than Losses in Long Term," *China Daily*, 13 October 1999, 4).

9. For a review of various understandings of *jieji* (class) and *jieceng* (strata) in the late 1980s, see Zhang Wanli 1990.

10. Although Liang does not touch on the Chinese Communist revolution, it remains implicit as a part of the past he has generalized.

11. For a critical review of this book, see Yan Ming 2002.

12. Liu Shi, former vice-chairman of ACFTU, lists and details four profound changes concerning the working class: (1) a rising wage labor form of employment (*guyonghua*); (2)

impoverishment (*pingkunhua*); (3) disempowerment (*wuquanhua*); and (4) fragmentation (*fensanhua*) (2003).

13. "China: New Rich Are Communist Party's New Role Models," Inter Press Service, 3 May 2002.

14. "Jingjiao nonghu baomu qun" (A Group of Baomu Serving Rural Households in a Beijing Suburb), *Beijing qingnian bao*, 17 December 1995, www.chinainfobank.com.

15. For the influence of *Self-Help* in colonial Egypt, see Mitchell 1988. See Bailey 1990 for the influence of Smiles in China in the early decades of the twentieth century.

16. The traditional English version of these verses is: "No saviour from on high delivers / No faith have we in prince or peer / Our own right hand the chains must shiver / Chains of hatred, greed, and fear." The lyrics cited in the text are my translation of the Chinese version that appears on the cover of *Self-Help*.

17. See Anita Chan 1985 (231n20) for a discussion of tempering young people during the Maoist era.

18. I do not intend to imply that, as an advocate and champion for migrant women, Xie was not concerned with the well-being of migrant women. It was perhaps her principal concern with their survival and success in the market economy that motivated her efforts to instill such discipline in migrant women through pedagogical "lessons."

19. Judith Butler uses "citation" to refer to "the process of that sedimentation or what we might call materialization . . . the acquisition of being through the citing of power, a citing that establishes an originary complicity with power in the formation of the 'I'" (1993: 15). See Smith 1996 for a critique of Butler's "citation" and "performativity," which Smith claims reduce social processes of interpellation to a monist performance (179–80).

20. The Chinese original is "wo bu neng gan ziji kanbuqi ziji de shi." Here, Xiaohong uses *ziji* as both observer and observed. Since this is preceded by "because my self is always keeping watch over myself," I take the first *ziji*, the observer, to mean "my self" and the second *ziji* to mean "myself."

21. I do not intend to use the Freudian frame in all its detail; my borrowing of the framework is only provisional.

22. See Sautman forthcoming.

6. Economic Law and Liminal Subjects

1. Geoff Dyer, "Income Gap in China Widens," *Financial Times*, 27 December 2005, 5.

2. Not surprisingly, the Internet, rather than the print or visual media, is the most active medium for such debates. For an example of advocacy for land privatization, see section 3 of Du Guang 2002, titled "Jianchi gaige de shehuizhuyi fangxiang" (Insisting on a Socialist Orientation for the Reforms), which proposes marketization and corporatization of agriculture based on private ownership of land. The commentary on Du's essay, posted by Xu Sheng on the same web page and entitled "Shenme shi shehuizhuyi?" (What Is Socialism?), expressed a diametrically opposed view against Du's version of socialism.

3. See Day and Hale 2007 on China's "New Rural Reconstruction" current of alternative-development activism. A prominent institutional base for this current is the recently established James Yen Rural Reconstruction Institute (see http://www.yirr.ngo.cn/) led by Wen Tiejun and Lau Kin Chi. See Wen Tiejun 2001 for an example of his perspective.

4. Such viewpoints are expressed by some contributors to the left-leaning website of Utopia Salon (Wu you zhi xiang) (see http://www.wyzxsx.com). Lao Tian is a leading contributor on this issue. His published essay "'Sannong' yanjiu zhong de shiye pingbi yu wenti yishi juxian" (The Restricted Vision and the Limited Problem-consciousness in "Sannong" Studies) is a trenchant analysis (2004b). For a more concentrated advocacy of the rural collective economy, see the regular "Rural Investigation" section of the online-journal *Zhongguo yu shijie* (China and the World), http://www.zgysj.com/main.htm.

5. Students without Beijing residency are charged much higher tuition and fees for their education in Beijing public schools, and most migrants could not afford to send their children to Beijing schools even at the regular tuition. Some leave their children with relatives in the countryside so that they can go to local schools, while others bring them to the city and send them to unofficial, unregistered schools for migrant children, themselves run by educated migrants. There may be two hundred such schools in Beijing, although there is no official statistic. Because these schools are often harassed or may be ordered to close for providing substandard education, they must play hide-and-seek with local authorities. One school I know moved five or six times within half a year. While the number of elite private schools is growing in Beijing, most schools for migrant children cannot afford the fees required for official registration. On the difficulties and problems that children of migrant parents encounter while trying to receive an education in Beijing, see a detailed investigation by Han Jialing 2001.

6. With little income generated from farming, Zhang allowed his six-mu "responsibility" land to lie fallow, but he continued to pay all agricultural taxes and fees, which amount to 1,800 yuan a year. Agricultural taxes and fees have been comprehensively abolished since 2006, at least in policy.

7. I thank Chris Brown for pointing out this metaphor to me.

8. See Croll and Huang 1996 on the contradictory effects of migration on rural agriculture.

9. Once a net exporter of agricultural products, China became a net importer in 2005, with a deficit of US$8.3 billion. Agricultural production is predicted to diminish 5 to 10 percent in the next five to ten years (Yang Fangyi and Li Bo 2006).

10. This poem and another three were submitted by their author to a magazine in Beijing for publication, but were rejected.

11. The 1990 census offers an approximate educational profile of migrants, of whom rural-to-urban migrants are the overwhelming majority and urban-to-urban migrants the minority. Among migrants, 11.2 percent have no or little education; 30.8 percent have a primary-school education; 43.2 percent have a junior-middle-school education; 9.6

percent have a senior-middle-school education; and 2.2 percent have a college education (quoted in Kam Wing Chan 1999). Feng Xiaoshuang reports on a survey of 48 rural-to-urban migrant women in Beijing that one-third of the women are illiterate, one-third have a primary-school education, and another third have a junior-middle-school education ("Liudong de xiaoyong he daijia" [The Effect and Cost of Migration], in *Shoujie quanguo dagongmei quanyi wenti yantaohui lunwenji* [The Collected Works of the First Forum on Issues about Women Migrant Workers' Rights and Interests], 1999: 9–12, unpublished typescript). A survey of 395 members of the Home for Rural Migrant Women reveals that 2 are illiterate, 68 (17 percent) have a primary-school education, 254 (64 percent) have a junior-middle-school education, and 71 (18 percent) have a senior-middle-school education or above (Li Tao, "Lun 'dagongmei zhi jia' de renwu he qiantu" [On the Task and Future of the Home for Rural Migrant Women], in *Shoujie quanguo dagongmei quanyi wenti yantaohui lunwenji*, 1999: 73–78, unpublished typescript). ·

12. I thank the friend who shared this letter with me. The identity of the writer and the receiver, however, cannot be revealed here.

13. Friedrich Engels was instrumental in popularizing a certain version of Marxism which has had a long legacy in Mao-era China. His *Dialectics of Nature* (1972) unifies the laws of history and nature. In his "Speech at the Graveyard of Karl Marx," delivered in 1883, Engels compared Marx with Charles Darwin and interpreted Marxism as a discovery of "the law of development of human history" (1978: 681). See Oishi 2001 for a studious analysis of the difference between Marx and Engels. In a letter, written in 1877 and addressed to Nikolaion (N. F. Danielson), Marx rebutted the attempt to universalize his theory about capitalism as a general thesis of human history.

> Now, what application to Russia could my critic draw from my historical outline? Only this: if Russia tries to become a capitalist nation, in imitation of the nations of western Europe, and in recent years she has taken a great deal of pains in this respect, she will not succeed without first having transformed a good part of her peasants into proletarians; and after that, once brought into the lap of the capitalist regime, she will be subject to its inexorable laws, like other profane nations. That is all. But this is too much for my critic. He absolutely must need metamorphose my outline of the genesis of capitalism in western Europe into a historico-philosophical theory of the general course, fatally imposed upon all peoples, regardless of the historical circumstances in which they find themselves placed, in order to arrive finally at that economic formation which insures with the greatest amount of productive power of social labor the most complete development of man. But I beg his pardon. He does me too much honor and too much shame at the same time. (Marx 1934: 111)

14. V. I. Lenin explicitly and famously developed a theory that socialist revolution may not be initiated in the most advanced capitalist countries, but may break out in the weakest link in the chain of imperialist powers (1964: 519–20).

15. For a good critique of taken-for-granted notions of "the economy," see Buck-Morss 1995. John Rajchman, too, argues that "the economy" is a "space of constructed visibility" (1991: 81).

16. For a cogent analysis of the "cat" theory and the contradictions in post-Mao market reform, see Weil 1996.

17. In analyses by liberal observers, the prevalence of corruption, fraud, and counterfeiting in the financial market, and the collusion of political and economic powers to carve up public property and state assets only signify an ever-more-urgent need to reify the economic law. In their eyes, these shocking misbehaviors and criminalities are considered a baneful legacy of the authoritarian regime and therefore factors external to the idealized market economy. For example, the prominent Chinese author He Qinglian's relentless and insightful analysis of corruptions and China's political and economic system is based on such assumptions (1998, 2000). Yet as Nancy Holmstrom and Richard Smith (2000) point out, these misbehaviors and criminalities constitute the secret of "primitive accumulation" in the postsocialist world, much as they did for the historical origin of capitalism in Europe and the United States.

18. The level of urbanization in 2000, calculated as the percentage of the total national population that was urban residents, reached 36.22 percent. See Wu Li's research paper (2003) for a detailed display of urbanization statistics and his explanation on what criteria have been used to define "urban population."

19. The nation-state as the natural subject of international law and world economy has been challenged by world-systems scholars such as Immanuel Wallerstein, Andre Gunder Frank, Giovanni Arrighi, and Samir Amin.

20. On February 14, 1995, the Shanghai-based newspaper *Wen Hui Bao* published the municipal labor bureau's No. 1 Circular (*tonggao*) of the year, specifying which professions and which types of work are not open to migrants. Migrant workers are not allowed to work in the fields of finance and insurance, and are not to be hired as administrative clerks, dispatchers, department store sales persons, receptionists for starred hotels, telephone operators, etc. In the same year, the Beijing Municipal Labor Bureau also publicized its circular, announcing a similar list of professions and types of jops open and closed to migrant workers (Wang Jiayan et al. 1996). A migrant worker pointed out with irony and bitterness that among the two hundred and six types of jobs available to migrant workers, the first one is beautician work on corpses, a kind of job that is generally considered especially inauspicious and degrading.

21. "Beijing quxiao wailai wugong xianzhi" (Beijing to Abolish Restrictions on Migrants), *People's Daily* (overseas edition), 26 March 2005, 1.

22. My use of *subsume* or *subsumption* is drawn from Marx's theorization of the subsumption of labor under capital (1977: 1021) and Diane Elson's elaboration of this concept: "The domination of the abstract aspect of labour, in the forms of value, is . . . not in terms of the obliteration of other aspects of labour, but in terms of the subsumption of these other aspects to the abstract aspect. That subsumption is understood in terms of the mediation of the other aspects of labour into money form" (Elson 1979: 174). While both Marx and Elson use *subsumption* when discussing labor processes under capitalism, here I explore the discursive subsumption of subjectivity.

23. *Dagongmei* is edited and published by the *Rural Women Knowing All* magazine. The year 2000 issue was the first issue and also a trial issue.

24. My analysis here draws on Antonio Gramsci: "Every social form has its *homo oeconomicus*, i.e. its own economic activity. . . . To expect that civil society will conform to the new structure as a result of propaganda and persuasion, or that the old *homo oeconomicus* will disappear without being buried with all the honours it deserves, is a new form of economic rhetoric, a new form of empty and inconclusive economic moralism" (*Il materialismo storico e la filosofia di Benedetto Croce* 1948: 266–67, quoted in Gramsci 1971: 208–9).

25. The conference took place in Beijing, 16–18 June 1999, and was sponsored by *Rural Women Knowing All* (affiliated with the official newspaper *China Women's News* [Zhongguo funü bao]) and Oxfam, Hong Kong. Xie Lihua is the chief editor of the *Rural Women Knowing All* and vice-chief editor of *China Women's News*. The translation is based on the notes that I took during Xie Lihua's speech. The printed text of her speech in *The Collected Works of the First National Forum on Issues about Women Migrant Workers' Rights and Interests* has somewhat different wording, but carries the same theme and keywords (*Shoujie* 1999).

26. Civil society, as represented by this nongovernmental forum, is instrumental in shaping and charting a new economic moralism.

27. This is taken from Spivak in "Feminism and Critical Theory": "Simply put, alienation in Hegel is that structural emergence of negation which allows a thing to sublate itself" (1987a: 278n3).

28. The word *shuofa* came into a wider circulation with Zhang Yimou's film *The Story of Qiuju*, in which the character Qiuju takes numerous expeditions to pursue a shuofa for an injury inflicted by the village head. As explained by the director Zhang Yimou, the meaning of *shuofa* "does not mean an 'apology' but an answer, an explanation, a clarification" (quoted in Anagnost 1997b: 138).

29. Liu Hezhen, a student of the National Beijing Women's Normal College, was killed in a demonstration on 25 March 1926 by the Duan Qirui government.

REFERENCES

Aguilar, Filomeno V. 1999. "Ritual Passage and the Reconstruction of Selfhood in International Labor Migration." *Sojourn* 14.1: 98–139.

All-China Women's Federation and the State Statistical Bureau. 2001. "Dierqi zhongguo funü shehui diwei chouyang diaocha zhuyao shuju baogao" (Data Report on the Second Random-Sample Survey of the Social Status of Chinese Women). Women's Study Institute of China, http://www.wsic.ac.cn/.

Althusser, Louis. 1972. "Ideology and Ideological State Apparatuses (Notes towards an Investigation)." In *Lenin and Philosophy, and Other Essays*, trans. Ben Brewster, 127–86. New York: Monthly Review Press.

Amin, Samir. 2004. *The Liberal Virus*. New York: Monthly Review Press.

Anagnost, Ann. 1989. "Transformations of Gender in Modern China." In *Gender and Anthropology: Critical Reviews for Research and Teaching*, ed. Sandra Morgan, 313–42. Washington: American Anthropological Association.

———. 1995. "A Surfeit of Bodies: Population and the Rationality of State in Post-Mao China." In *Conceiving the New World Order: Local/Global Intersections in the Politics of Reproduction*, ed. Faye Ginsburg and Rayna Rapp, 22–41. Berkeley: University of California Press.

———. 1997a. "Children and National Transcendence in China." In *Constructing China: The Interaction of Culture and Economics*, ed. Ernest Young et al., 195–222. Ann Arbor: University of Michigan Center for Chinese Studies.

———. 1997b. *National Past-times: Narrative, Representation, and Power in Modern China*. Durham, N.C.: Duke University Press.

———. 2004. "The Corporeal Politics of Quality." *Public Culture* 16.2: 189–208.

Anderson, Bridget. 1997. "Servants and Slaves: Europe's Domestic Workers." *Race and Class* 39.1: 37–49.

———. 2000. *Doing the Dirty Work? The Global Politics of Domestic Labor*. New York: Zed Books.

Andors, Phyllis. 1983. *The Unfinished Liberation of Chinese Women, 1949–1980*. Bloomington: Indiana University Press.

Andreas, Joel. Forthcoming. "'Mass Recommendation' of 'Worker-Peasant-Soldier' Students during the Chinese Cultural Revolution." In *Rise of Real Engineers: The Chinese Cultural Revolution and the Origins of China's New Class*. Stanford, Calif.: Stanford University Press.

Armstrong, Nancy. 1987. *Desire and Domestic Fiction: A Political History of the Novel*. New York: Oxford University Press.

Bailey, Paul. 1990. *Reform the People: Changing Attitudes towards Popular Education in Early Twentieth-Century China*. Edinburgh: Edinburgh University Press.

Ba Jin (Pa Chin). 1972. *Family*. New York: Anchor Books.

Bakken, Børge. 2000. *The Exemplary Society: Human Improvement, Social Control, and the Dangers of Modernity in China*. Hong Kong: Oxford University Press.

Ball, Joseph. 2006. "Did Mao Really Kill Millions?" *Monthly Review*, September, http://www.monthlyreview.org/.

Barlow, Tani E. 1991a. "Theorizing Women: *Funü, Guojia, Jiating* [Chinese Women, Chinese State, Chinese Family]." *Genders* 10: 132–60.

———. 1991b. "*Zhizhifenzi* [Chinese Intellectuals] and Power." *Dialectical Anthropology* 16.3–4: 209–32.

———. 1994. "Politics and Protocols of Funü: (Un)making National Woman." In *Engendering China: Women, Culture, and the State*, ed. Christina K. Gilmartin et al., 339–59. Cambridge, Mass.: Harvard University Press.

———. 2001. "Globalization, China, and International Feminism." *Signs* 26.4: 1,286–91.

Baudrillard, Jean. 2001. *Selected Writings*. Ed. Mark Poster. Oxford: Polity Press.

Beech, Hannah. 2003. "The Sky Is Falling." *Time*, 21 July. http://www.time.com/.

Beijing shi ren kou pu cha ban gong shi. 1992. *Beijing shi 1990 nian ren kou pu cha zi liao* (The 1990 Beijing Population Census Data). Beijing: Zhongguo gong ji chubanshe.

Bello, Walden. 1994. *Dark Victory: The United States, Structural Adjustment and Global Poverty*. London: Pluto Press / Food First and Transnational Institute.

Belsey, Andrew. 1986. "The New Right, Social Order, and Civil Liberties." In *The Ideology of the New Right*, ed. Ruth Levitas, 169–97. Cambridge: Polity Press.

Benjamin, Walter. 1992. "Theses on the Philosophy of History." In *Illuminations*, ed. Hannah Arendt, 245–55. London: Fontana Press.

Bi Shumin. 1996. "Zihua buman" (Purple-Flowered Curtain). In *Bi Shumin wenji* (A Collection of Bi Shumin's Works), 419–506. Beijing: Qunzhong chubanshe.

Blackstone, William. 1765–69. *Commentaries on the Laws of England*. Oxford: Clarendon Press.

Blecher, Marc. 1991. "Development State, Entrepreneurial State: The Political Economy of Socialist Reform in Xinju Municipality and Guanghan County." In *The Chinese State in the Era of Economic Reform*, ed. Gordon White, 265–91. London: Macmillan.

Bodman, Richard. 1991. "From History to Allegory to Art." In *Deathsong of the River: A Reader's Guide to the Chinese TV Series* Heshang, ed. Su Xiao Kang and Wang Luxiang, trans. Richard W. Bodman and Pin P. Wan, 1–62. Ithaca, N.Y.: East Asian Program, Cornell University.

Boland, Alana. 2001. "Transitional Flows: State and Market in China's Urban Water Supply." Ph.D. diss., Department of Geography, University of Washington.

Boydston, Jeane. 1990. *Home and Work: Housework, Wages and the Ideology of Labor in the Early Republic*. New York: Oxford University Press.

Bramall, Chris. 2006. "The Last of the Romantics? Maoist Economic Development in Retrospect." *China Quarterly* 187: 686–92.

Brown, Gillian. 1990. *Domestic Individualism: Imagining Self in Nineteenth-century America*. Berkeley: University of California Press.

Buck, David D. 1984. "Changes in Chinese Urban Planning since 1976." *Third World Planning Review* 6.1: 5–26.

Buck-Morss, Susan. 1995. "Envisioning Capital." *Critical Inquiry* 5: 13–30.

———. 2000. "Hegel and Haiti." *Critical Inquiry* 26: 821–65.

Burns, Richard. 1757. *Justice of the Peace and Parish Officer*. 4th ed. Vol. 3. [London]: A. Millar.

Butler, Judith. 1993. *Bodies That Matter: On the Discursive Limits of "Sex."* New York: Routledge.

Cartier, Carolyn. 2001. "Gendered Industrialization." In *Globalizing South China*, 176–204. Oxford: Blackwell.

Castree, Noel. 1996–97. "Invisible Leviathan: Speculations on Marx, Spivak, and the Question of Value." *Rethinking Marxism* 9.2: 45–78.

CCTV (Department of Economics). 1999. "Er shi nian, er shi ren" (Twenty Years, Twenty Individuals). In *Jing ji ban xiao shi* (Economic Half an Hour), 49–58. Beijing: Zhongguo jing ji chubanshe.

Chakrabarty, Dipesh. 1989. *Rethinking Working Class History: Bengal 1890–1940*. Princeton: Princeton University Press.

———. 2000. "Universalism and Belonging in the Logic of Capital." *Public Culture* 12.3: 653–78.

Chan, Anita. 1985. *Children of Mao: Personality Development and Political Activism in the Red Guard Generation*. Seattle: University of Washington Press.

Chan, Kam Wing. 1994. *Cities with Invisible Walls*. Hong Kong: Oxford University Press.

———. 1999. "Internal Migration in China: A Dualistic Approach." In *Internal and International Migration: Chinese Perspectives*, ed. Frank Pieke and Hein Mallee, 49–72. Richmond, Surrey: Curzon Press.

Chen Qingli. 2002. *Zhongguo nongmin suzhi lun* (On the Quality of Chinese Peasants). Beijing: dangdai shijie chubanshe.

Chen Shaogong. 1999. *Jieceng: Zhongguo ren de gediao yu jieceng pinwei fenxi* (Class: An Analysis of Chinese Styles and Taste). Beijing: Dazhong chubanshe.

Chen Xiaoqing, dir. 1993. *Yuan zai Beijing de jia* (A Home Far Away from Home). Chinese Central Television and Anhui Provincial Television.

Chen Xin and Huang Ping. 2003. "Xiaofei zhuyi wenhua zai zhongguo shehui de chuxian"

(The Emergence of a Consumerist Culture in Chinese Society). Chinese Sociology Website, http://www.sociology.cass.cn/.

Chi Li. 1992. "Taiyang chushi" (The Birth of a Sun). In *Taiyang chushi*, 51–116. Wuhan: Changjiang wenyi chubanshe.

———. 1999. *Lai lai wang wang* (Back and Forth). Beijing: Zuojia chubanshe.

Chu Gansheng. 1995. *Nubi shi: Zhongguo nubi wenti de lishi sikao* (A History of Servants: A Historical Examination of the Servant Question in China). Shanghai: Shanghai wenyi chubanshe.

Chunzi. 2000. "Mianbao hui you de" (There Will Be Bread). *Dagongmei* (supplement): 31.

Clarke, David B. 1997. "Consumption and the City, Modern and Postmodern." *International Journal of Urban and Regional Research* 12.2: 219–37.

Cohen, Myron L. 1994. "The Cultural and Political Inventions in Modern China: The Case of the Chinese 'Peasant.'" In *China in Transformation*, ed. Tu Wei-ming, 151–70. Cambridge, Mass.: Harvard University Press.

Comaroff, Jean, and John L. Comaroff. 1999. "Occult Economies and the Violence of Abstraction: Notes from the South African Postcolony." *American Ethnologist* 26.2: 279–309.

Coulson, Margaret, Branka Magaš, and Hilary Wainwright. 1975. "'The Housewife and Her Labor under Capitalism': A Critique." *New Left Review* 89: 59–71.

Croll, Elizabeth. 1983. *Chinese Women since Mao*. Armonk, N.Y.: M. E. Sharpe.

Croll, Elizabeth, and Huang Ping. 1996. "Migration against and for Agriculture in Eight Chinese Villages." *China Quarterly* 149: 128–47.

Crush, Jonathan, ed. 1995. *Power of Development*. London: Routledge.

Dai Jinhua. 1999. "Rewriting Chinese Women: Gender Production and Cultural Space in the Eighties and Nineties." In *Spaces of Their Own: Women's Public Sphere in Transnational China*, ed. Mayfair Mei-Hui Yang, 191–208. Minneapolis: University of Minnesota Press.

Davin, Delia. 1975. "Women in the Countryside of China." In *Women in Chinese Society*, ed. Margery Wolf and Roxane Witke, 243–73. Stanford, Calif.: Stanford University Press.

———. 1976. *Women and the Party in Revolutionary China*. Oxford: Clarendon Press.

Davis, Deborah. 2000. "Introduction." In *The Consumer Revolution in Urban China*, ed. Deborah Davis, 1–22. Berkeley: University of California Press.

Day, Alexander, and Mathew A. Hale, eds. 2007. "New Rural Reconstruction." Summer issue, *Chinese Sociology and Anthropology* 39.4.

de Brauw, Alan, and Scott Rozelle. 2003. "Household Investment through Migration in Rural China." Department of Economics Working Papers, no. 200, Williams College, Williamstown, Mass. http://www.williams.edu/economics/.

Defoe, Daniel. 1724. *The Great Law of Subordination Consider'd; or the Insolence and Unsufferable Behavior of servants in England Duly Enquir'd into*. London: n.p.

Deleuze, Gilles, and Felix Guattari. 1983. *Anti-Oedipus: Capitalism and Schizophrenia*.

Trans. Robert Hurley, Mark Seem, and Helen R. Lane. Minneapolis: University of Minnesota Press.

Delphy, Christine. 1984. "The Main Enemy." In *Close to Home*, trans. Diana Leonard, 57–77. Amherst: University of Massachusetts Press.

Diamond, Norma. 1975. "Collectivization, Kinship, and the Status of Women in Rural China." In *Toward an Anthropology of Women*, ed. Rayna Reiter, 372–95. New York: Monthly Review Press.

Ding Jinhong and Norman Stockman. 1999. "The Floating Population and the Integration of the City Community: A Survey on the Attitudes of Shanghai Residents to Recent Migrants." In *Internal and International Migration: Chinese Perspectives*, ed. Frank N. Pieke and Hein Mallee, 119–33. Surrey, England: Curzon.

Ding Ling. 1954. *Shui* (Water). Hong Kong: Xindi chubanshe.

Ding Naifei. 2002. "Seeing Double, or Domestic and Sex Work in the Shade of the Bondmaid-Concubine." *Taiwan* 48 (December): 135–68.

Dirlik, Arif. 1989. "Postsocialism? Reflections on Socialism with Chinese Characteristics." In *Marxism and the Chinese Experience: Issues in Contemporary Chinese Socialism*, ed. Arif Dirlik and Maurice Meisner, 361–84. Armonk, N.Y.: M. E. Sharpe.

———. 1997. "Chinese History and the Question of Orientalism." In *The Postcolonial Aura: Third World Criticism in the Age of Global Capitalism*, 105–28. Boulder, Colo.: Westview Press.

———. 2002. "Modernity as History: Post-revolutionary China, Globalization and the Question of Modernity." *Social History* 27.1: 16–39.

Donald, Stephanie Hemelryk, and Christina Lee. 2001. "Mulan Illustration? Ambiguous Women in Contemporary Chinese Cinema." In *Images of the "Modern Woman" in Asia: Global Media, Local Meanings*, ed. Shoma Munshi, 123–37. Surrey: Curzon Press.

Dong, Yueling. 1999. "Chaidui Beijing" (Migrating to Beijing). *Qingnian wenzhai* 4: 3–6.

Donohue, Kathleen G. 1999. "What Gender Is the Consumer? The Role of Gender Connotations in Defining the Political." *American Studies* 33.1: 19–44.

Donzelot, Jacques. 1979. *The Policing of Families*. Baltimore: Johns Hopkins University Press.

Dorfman, Diane. 1996. "Spirits of Reform: The Power of Belief in Northern China." *positions* 4.2: 253–89.

Dryden, Gordon, and Jeannette Vos. 1999. *The Learning Revolution*. Los Angeles: The Learning Web.

Duckett, Jean. 2000. "Bureaucrats in Business, Chinese-style: The Lessons of Market Reform and State Entrepreneurialism in the People's Republic of China." *World Development* 29.1: 23–37.

Du Guang. 2002. "Jianchi gaige de shehuizhuyi fangxiang" (Insisting on a Socialist Orientation for the Reforms). Wuliucun, http://www.taosl.net/duguang01.htm.

Ehrenreich, Barbara, and Arlie R. Hochschild, eds. 2002. *Global Woman: Nannies, Maids, and Sex Workers in the New Economy*. New York: Metropolitan Books.

Elson, Diane. 1979. "The Value Theory of Labour." In *Value: The Representation of Labour in Capitalism*, ed. Diane Elson, 115–80. London: CSE Books.

Engels, Friedrich. 1972. *Dialectics of Nature*. Moscow: Progress Publishers.

———. 1978. "Speech at the Graveside of Karl Marx." In *The Marx-Engels Reader*, ed. Robert C. Tucker, 681–82. New York: W. W. Norton.

Escobar, Arturo. 1995a. *Encountering Development: The Making and Unmaking of the Third World*. Princeton: Princeton University Press.

———. 1995b. "Imagining A Post-development Era." In *Power of Development*, ed. Jonathan Crush, 211–27. London: Routledge.

Evans, Harriet. 2000. "Marketing Femininity: Images of the Modern Chinese Women." *China Beyond the Headlines*, ed. Timothy B. Weston and Lionel M. Jensen, 217–43. New York: Rowman and Littlefield.

Fang Fang. 1998. "Yuan mengxiang cheng zhen" (Wishing a Dream to Come True). *Jiangting* 11: 27.

Fei Hsiao-tung. 1968. *China's Gentry: Essays on Rural-Urban Relations*. Chicago: University of Chicago Press.

Feinman, Jay M. 1991. "The Development of the Employment-at-Will Rule Revisited." *Arizona State Law Journal* 23: 733–40.

———. 2004. "Unmaking Law: The Classical Revival in the Common Law." *Seattle University Law Review* 28: 1–59.

Foucault, Michel. 1979. *Discipline and Punish*. New York: Vintage Books.

———. 1988. *Technologies of the Self: A Seminar with Michel Foucault*, ed. Luther H. Martin, Huck Gutman, and Patrick H. Hutton. Amherst: University of Massachusetts Press.

———. 1991. "Governmentality." In *The Foucault Effect: Studies in Governmentality*, ed. Graham Burchell, Colin Gordon, and Peter Miller, 87–104. Chicago: University of Chicago Press.

Fraser, David. 2000. "Inventing Oasis: Luxury Housing Advertisements and Reconfiguring Domestic Space in Shanghai." In *The Consumer Revolution in Urban China*, ed. Deborah Davis, 25–53. Berkeley: University of California Press.

Frazier, Kimberly J. 2004. "Legislative Note: Arkansas's Civil Justice Reform Act of 2003: Who's Cheating Who?" *Arkansas Law Review* 57: 651–96.

Fussell, Paul. 1998. *Ge diao: She hui deng ji yu sheng huo pin wei* (Class: A Guide Through the American Status Stystem). Trans. Liang Lizhen, Yue Tao, and Shi Tao. Beijing: Zhongguo shehui kexue chubanshe.

Gallagher, Catherine. 1987. "The Body Versus the Social Body in the Works of Thomas Malthus and Henry Mayhew." In *The Making of the Modern Body: Sexuality and Society in the Nineteenth Century*, ed. Catherine Gallagher and Thomas Laqueur, 83–106. Berkeley: University of California Press.

Gao, C. F. Mobo. 1999. *Gao Village: A Portrait of Rural Life in Modern China*. London: Hurst.

Gordon, Colin. 1991. "Governmental Rationality: An Introduction." In *The Foucault Effect:*

Studies in Governmentality, ed. Graham Burchell, Colin Gordon, and Peter Miller, 1–51. Chicago: University of Chicago Press.

Gramsci, Antonio. 1971. *Selections from the Prison Notebooks of Antonio Gramsci*. Ed. and trans. Quintin Hoare and Geoffrey Nowell Smith. New York: International Publishers.

Granick, David. 1990. *Chinese State Enterprises: A Regional Property Rights Analysis*. Chicago: University of Chicago Press.

Gray, Jack. 1990. *Rebellions and Revolutions: China from 1800s to 1980s*. New York: Oxford University Press.

———. 2006. "Mao in Perspective." *China Quarterly* 187: 659–79.

Greenhalgh, Susan. 2003a. "Planned Births, Unplanned Persons: 'Population' in the Making of Chinese Modernity." *American Ethnologist* 30.2: 196–215.

———. 2003b. "Science, Modernity, and the Making of China's One-Child Policy." *Population and Development Review* 29.2: 163–96.

Guang, Lei. 2003. "Rural Taste, Urban Fashions: The Cultural Politics of Rural/Urban Difference in Contemporary China." *positions* 11.3: 613–46.

Guo Chuanhuo. 1997. *Zhongguo Baomu* (Baomu in China). Beijing: Zuojia chubanshe.

Guowuyuan renkou pucha bangongshi. 2003. *2000 ren kou pu cha fen xian zi liao* (2000 Census Materials Divided by County). Beijing: Zhongguo gong ji chubanshe.

Hale, Matthew. 1713. *Analysis of the Law*. London: In the Savoy: John Nutt.

Hammer, Brian. n.d. "The Discursive Construction of Poverty in China." Unpublished manuscript.

Han Deqiang. 2000. *Peng zhuang: Quanqiuhua xianjin yu zhongguo xianshi xuanze* (Collision: The Trap of Globalization and China's Realistic Choices). Beijing: Jingji guanli chubanshe.

———. 2003. "Paichu xin ziyouzhuyi ganrao, wanshan shehuizhuyi hunhe jingji tizhi" (Getting Rid of the Interference of Neoliberalism, Improving Socialist Mixed Economic System). China Study Group, http://www.chinastudygroup.org/.

Han Dongping. 2003. "The Great Leap Famine, the Cultural Revolution and Post-Mao Rural Reform: The Lessons of Rural Development in Contemporary China." China Study Group, http://www.chinastudygroup.org/.

———. n.d. "Professional Bias and Its Impact on China's Rural Education." China Study Group, http://www.chinastudygroup.org/.

Han Jialing. 2001. "Beijing shi liudong ertong yiwu jiaoyu zhuangkuang diaocha baogao" (A Report on the Situation of Compulsory Education of Migrant Children in Beijing). *Qingnian yanjiu* 8: 1–8; 9: 10–18.

Han Shaogong et al. 2004. "Why Must We Talk about the Environment? A Summary of Nanshan Seminar." *positions* 12.1: 237–46.

Han Yuhai. 2004. "Dangdai zhongguo de shehuizhuyi chuantong ji xiangguan wenti" (Contemporary Chinese Socialist Legacy and Related Issues), part 3. *Pipan yu zaizao* 14 (December): 29–38.

———. 2005. "Dangdai zhongguo de shehuizhuyi chuantong ji xiangguan wenti" (Contemporary Chinese Socialist Legacy and Related Issues), finale. *Pipan yu zaizao* 15 (January): 27–35.

Hao Jian. 1996. "Yihetuan being de shenyi" (Moaning from the Boxer Syndrome). *Dushu* 3 (March): 8.

Harootunian, Harry. 2000. *History's Disquiet: Modernity, Cultural Politics, and the Question of Everyday Life*. New York: Columbia University Press.

Harrell, Stevan. 2000. "Changing Meanings of Work in China." In *Re-drawing Boundaries: Work, Households, and Gender in China*, ed. Barbara Entwisle and Gail E. Henderson, 67–76. Berkeley: University of California Press.

Harvey, David. 1989a. *The Condition of Postmodernity*. Cambridge, Mass: Blackwell.

———. 1989b. "From Managerialism to Entrepreneurialism: The Transformation in Urban Governance in Late Capitalism." *Geografiska Annaler* 71B.1: 3–17.

———. 2001. *Spaces of Capital*. New York: Routledge.

———. 2005. *A Brief History of Neoliberalism*. Oxford: Oxford University Press.

———. 2006. "Neo-liberalism and the Restoration of Class Power." In *Spaces of Global Capitalism*, 1–62. London: Verso.

Haug, W. F. 1986. *Critique of Commodity Aesthetics: Appearance, Sexuality and Advertising in Capitalist Society*. Minneapolis: University of Minnesota Press.

Hayford, Charles. 1998. "The Storm over the Peasant: Orientalism and Rhetoric in Constructing China." In *Contesting Master Narrative: Essays in Social History*, ed. Jeffrey Cox and Shelton Stromquist, 150–72. Iowa City: University of Iowa Press.

Hegel, G. W. F. 1980. *Lectures on the Philosophy of World History: Introduction*. Trans. H. B. Nisbet. Cambridge: Cambridge University Press.

He Qinglian. 1998. *Xiandaihua de xianjing* (The Pitfalls of Modernization). Beijing: Jinri zhongguo chubanshe.

———. 2000. "China's Listing Social Structure." *New Left Review* 5 (September–October): 69–99.

Hershatter, Gail. 2000. "Local Meanings of Gender and Work in Rural Shaanxi in the 1950s." In *Re-drawing Boundaries: Work, Households, and Gender in China*, ed. Barbara Entwisle and Gail E. Henderson, 79–96. Berkeley: University of California Press.

Hochschild, Arlie Russell. 1983. *The Managed Heart: Commercialization of Human Feeling*. Berkeley: University of California Press.

Hochschild, Arlie, with Anne Machung. 1989. *The Second Shift: Working Parents and the Revolution at Home*. New York: Viking.

Hoffman, Lisa. 2001. "Guiding College Graduates to Work: Social Constructions of Labor Markets in Dalian." In *China Urban: Ethnographies of Contemporary Culture*, ed. Nancy Chen et al., 43–66. Durham, N.C.: Duke University Press.

Holmstrom, Nancy, and Richard Smith. 2000. "The Necessity of Gangster Capitalism: Primitive Accumulation in Russia and China." *Monthly Review* 51.9: 1–11.

Honig, Emily. 1986. *Sisters and Strangers: Women in the Shanghai Cotton Mills, 1919–1949*. Stanford, Calif.: Stanford University Press.

———. 2000. "Iron Girls Revisited: Gender and Politics of Work in the Cultural Revolution, 1966–76." In *Re-drawing Boundaries: Work, Households, and Gender in China*, ed. Barbara Entwisle and Gail E. Henderson, 97–110. Berkeley: University of California Press.

Honig, Emily, and Gail Hershatter, eds. 1988. *Personal Voices: Chinese Women in the 1980's*. Stanford, Calif.: Stanford University Press.

Hooper, Beverley. 1985. *Youth in China*. Victoria, Australia: Penguin Books.

Hu Angang, Zou Ping, and Li Chunbo. 2001. "1978–2000 nian: Zhongguo jingji shehui fazhan de diqu chaju" (1978–2000: Regional Disparity in China's Economic and Social Development). In *2001 Nian: Zhongguo shehui xingshi fenxi yu yuce* (2001: Analysis and Forecast of China's Social Profile), ed. Ru Xin, Lu Xueyi, and Shan Tianlun, 167–84. Beijing: Shehui kexue wenxian chubanshe.

Hua Guoshun. 1999. "Gao duzhe: Jiu cong ni kaishi" (To the Readers: It Begins with You). *Jiaodian* 41 (September): inside cover.

Huo Da. 1983. "Baomu." *Dangdai* 1: 55–62.

Jacka, Tamara. 1997. *Women's Work in Rural China: Change and Continuity in an Era of Reform*. Cambridge: Cambridge University Press.

Jameson, Fredric. 2002. *A Singular Modernity: Essay on the Ontology of the Present*. New York: Verso.

Jaschok, Maria. 1988. *Concubines and Bondservants: A Social History of a Chinese Custom*. London: Zed.

Jiang Xia. 1986. "Zhede changdao de jiawu laodong fuwu gongzuo" (A Model of Domestic Labor Service Work Worth Propagating). *Hongqi* 3: 38–39.

Jiedao. 1998. "*Lienü Tang Shengli*" (Chaste Woman Tang Shengli). *Jiedao* 2: 6.

Johnson, Kay Ann. 1983. *Women, the Family and Peasant Revolution in China*. Chicago: University of Chicago Press.

Johnston, Claire. 1974. "Women's Cinema as Counter-cinema." In *Notes on Women's Cinema*, ed. Claire Johnston, 28–29. London: Society for Education in Film and Television.

Judd, Ellen R. 2002. "The Meaning of Quality." In *The Chinese Women's Movement between State and Market*, 19–32. Stanford, Calif.: Stanford University Press.

Kearney, Richard. 1984. *Dialogues with Contemporary Continental Thinkers: The Phenomenological Heritage*. Manchester, U.K.: Manchester University Press.

Keenan, Thomas. 1993. "The Point Is to (Ex)change It: Reading Capital, Rhetorically." In *Fetishism as Cultural Discourse*, ed. Emily Apter and William Pietz, 152–85. Ithaca, N.Y.: Cornell University Press.

Kelliher, Daniel. 1994. "Chinese Communist Political Theory and the Rediscovery of the Peasantry." *Modern China* 20.4: 387–415.

Kerber, Linda. 1980. *Women of the Republic: Intellect and Ideology in Revolutionary America*. New York: Norton.

Kipnis, Andrew. 2001. "The Disturbing Educational Discipline of 'Peasants.'" *China Journal* 46: 1–24.

Kirkby, Richard. 1985. *Urbanization in China: Town and Country in a Developing Economy, 1949–2000 A.D.* London: Croom Helm.

Knight, John, and Lina Song. 1999. *The Rural-Urban Divide: Economic Disparities and Interactions in China*. Oxford: Oxford University Press.

Kojève, Alexandre. 1980. *Introduction to the Reading of Hegel*. Ithaca, N.Y.: Cornell University Press.

Krishnamurthy, Mathangi. 2005. "Outsourced Identities: The Fragmentation of the Cross-border Economy." *Anthropology News* 46.3: 22–23.

Kung, Lydia. 1983. *Factory Women in Taiwan*. Ann Arbor: University of Michigan Press.

Lacan, Jacques. 1977. *Ecrits: A Selection*. Trans. Alan Sheridan. London: Tavistock.

Lao Tian. 2004a. "'Deng Xiaoping duo cheng' wei shen me shi ke neng de" (Why Was "Deng Xiaoping Process" Possible). *Pipan yu zaizao* 14: 1–20.

———. 2004b. "'Sannong' yanjiu zhong de shiye pingbi yu wenti yishi juxian" (The Restricted Vision and the Limited Problem-consciousness in "Sannong" Studies). *Kaifang shidai* 4, http://www.opentimes.cn/.

Lee, Ching Kwan. 1998. *Gender and the South China Miracle*. Berkeley: University of California Press.

———. 2002. "From the Specter of Mao to the Rule of Law: Labor Insurgency in China." *Theory and Society* 31.2: 189–228.

Lee, Haiyan. 2006. "Nannies for Foreigners: The Enchantment of Chinese Womanhood in the Age of Millennial Capitalism." *Public Culture* 18.3: 507–29.

Lee, Jen-Der. 2000. "Wet Nurses in Early Imperial China." *Nan nü* 2.1: 1–39.

Lefebvre, Henri. 1995. "Renewal, Youth, Repetition." In *Introduction to Modernity*, trans. John Moore, 157–67. London: Verso.

Lenin, V. I. 1964. *Lenin Collected Works*. Vol. 24. Moscow: Progress Publisher.

Levy, Marion. 1968. *The Family Revolution in Modern China*. New York: Atheneum.

Li Changping. 2002. *Wo xiang zongli shuo shihua* (I Speak the Truth to the Premier). Beijing: Guangming ribao.

Li Cishan. 1920. "Shanghai laodong zhuangkuang" (Labor Conditions in Shanghai). *Xin qing nian* 7.6: 621–703.

Li Hang. 1996. "Jiawu laodong yu gongzuo quanli de baohu" (Domestic Labor and the Protection of the Right to Work). *Funü yanjiu luncong* 1: 7–10.

Li Hong, dir. 1997. "Hui dao fenghuang qiao" (Returning to Phoenix Bridge). Pre-release version of documentary film in possession of author.

Li Shuqing. 1988. "Nongcun renkou suzhi yanjiu gaishu" (A Review of the Study of Quality of Rural Population). *Renkou yanjiu* 2:59–61.

Li Tao. 1999. "Tigao suzhi, mouqiu fazhan" (Improving Suzhi, Striving for Development). In *Chengshi li ni you duo yuan?* (How Far Is the City from You?), Li Jianyong and Li Tao, 145–61. Shanghai: Shanghai kexue puji chubanshe.

———. 2000. "Ta weishenme aida?" (Why Was She Beaten?). *Dagongmei* supplement: 40–42.

Li Xiaojiang. 2001. "From 'Modernization' to 'Globalization': Where Are Chinese Women?" *Signs* 26.4: 1,274–78.

Li Zuojun. 2000. *Zhongguo de genben wenti: Jiuyi nongmin hechuqu?* (China's Fundamental Problem: Where Would Nine Hundred Million Peasants Go?). Beijing: Zhongguo fazhan chubanshe.

Liang Shiqiu. 1993. "Di liu lun" (The Sixth Relationship). In *Liang Shiqiu mingzuo xinshang* (Appreciating the Famous Works of Liang Shiqiu), 42–45. Beijing: Zhongguo heping chubanshe.

Liang Xiaosheng. 1997. *Zhongguo shehui ge jieceng fenxi* (An Analysis of the Strata in Chinese Society). Beijing: Jingji ribao chubanshe.

Liew, Leong H. 2005. "China's Engagement with Neoliberalism: Path Dependency, Geography, and Party Self-reinvention." *Development Studies* 41.2: 331–52.

Lin Chun. 2001. "Whither Feminism: A Note on China." *Signs* 26.4: 1,281–86.

Lin Hongmei and Liu Yangyang. 2004. "Jiazheng fuwuye: Shei lai kaifa wubaiwan ren de jiuye gangwei?" (Domestic Service Sector: Who Will Create Five Million Jobs?). http://www.southcn.com/.

Litzinger, Ralph. 2002. "Theorizing Postsocialism: Reflections on the Politics of Marginality in Contemporary China." *South Atlantic Quarterly* 101.1: 33–55.

Liu, Lydia H. 1993. "Translingual Practice: The Discourse of Individualism between China and the West." *positions* 1.1: 160–93.

———. 1999. "Beijing Sojourners in New York: Postsocialism and the Question of Ideology in Global Media Culture." *positions* 7.3: 764–97.

Liu Shi. 2003. "Dangqian zhongguo gongren jieji zhuangkuang" (Current Conditions of Chinese Working Class). China Study Group, http://www.chinastudygroup.org/.

Liu Xiangya, trans. 2001. *Suzhi ceshi shouce* (A Manual for Suzhi Testing). Haikou: Nanhai chuban gongsi.

Liu Xiuming. 1996. "Nongmin wenti: Dongfang shehui fazhan de guanjian" (Peasant Problem: The Key to the Development of East Asian Societies). *Qiushi zhazhi* 9:37–41.

Lo, C. P. 1986. "Socialist Ideology and Urban Strategies in China." *Urban Geography* 8: 440–58.

Lu Deyang and Wang Naining. 2004. *Shehui de youyichengmian: Zhongguo jindai nüyong* (Another Dimension of Society: Female Servants in China's Near-modern Times). Shanghai: Xuelin chubanshe.

Lü Xiaobo and Elizabeth Perry, eds. 1997. *Danwei: The Changing Chinese Workplace in Historical and Comparative Perspective*. Armonk, N.Y.: M. E. Sharpe.

Lu Xueyi, ed. 2002. *Dangdai zhongguo shehui jieceng yanjiu baogao* (Research Report on Contemporary Chinese Social Strata). Beijing: Shehui kexue wenxian chubanshe.

Lu Xun. 1926. "In Memory of Miss Liu Hezhen." In *Lu Xun: Selected Works*, trans. Yang Xianyi and Gladys Yang, 2:267–72. Beijing: Foreign Languages Press.

———. 1956. "My Old Home." In *Lu Xun: Selected Works*, 1:90–101. Beijing: Foreign Languages Press.

Lu Xun. 2002. *Renlei suzhi xue* (The Science of Human Quality). Beijing: Zhongguo dang'an chubanshe.

Ma, Laurence J. C., and Yehua Dennis Wei. 1997. "Determinants of State Investment in China, 1953–1990." *Tijdschrift voor Economische en Sociale Geografie* 88.3: 211–25.

Magnet, Myron. 1986. "The Decline and Fall of Business Ethics." *Fortune*, 8 December, 65–72.

Malraux, Andre. 1968. *Anti-memoirs*. New York: Holt, Rinehart and Winston.

Mao, Zedong (Mao Tse-tung). 1967 [1927]. *Analysis of the Classes in Chinese Society*. Peking: Foreign Languages Press.

———. 1967 [1937]. "On Practice." In *Selected Works of Mao Tse-Tung*, 1:295–309. Peking: Foreign Languages Press.

Marx, Karl. 1934. "A Letter on Russia." New International 1.4 (November): 110–11.

———. 1973. *Grundrisse*. Trans. Martin Nicolaus. New York: Random House.

———. 1977. *Capital: A Critique of Political Economy*. Vol. 1. Trans. Ben Fowkes. New York: Vintage.

———. 1994. *The Eighteenth Brumaire of Louis Bonaparte*. New York: International Publishers.

Massey, Doreen. 1994. "Double Articulation: A Place in the World." In *Displacements: Cultural Identities in Question*, ed. Angelike Bammer, 110–21. Bloomington: Indiana University Press.

Massumi, Brian. 1992. *A User's Guide to Capitalism and Schizophrenia: Deviations from Deleuze and Guattari*. Cambridge, Mass.: Massachusetts Institute of Technology Press.

Mayle, Peter. 1998. *You guan pinwei* (Expensive Habits). Trans. Song Weihang. Beijing: Xinshijie chubanshe.

McClintock, Anne. 1995. *Imperial Leather: Race, Gender and Sexuality in the Colonial Contest*. New York: Routledge.

McLaren, Anne E. 2000. "The Grievance Rhetoric of Chinese Women: From Lamentation to Revolution." *Intersections* 4: 1–17.

Miller, Daniel. 1995. "Consumption as the Vanguard of History." In *Acknowledging Consumption: A Review of New Studies*, ed. Daniel Miller, 1–57. New York: Routledge.

Mills, Mary Beth. 1999. *Thai Women in the Global Labor Force: Consuming Desires, Contested Selves*. New Brunswick, N.J.: Rutgers University Press.

Min Xiaohong. 1999. "Chenzhong de huaji" (My Heavy-hearted Youth). *Nongjianu baishi tong* 2: 28–31.

Mitchell, Timothy. 1988. *Colonising Egypt*. Berkeley: University of California Press.

Mo Ru. 1920. "Nanjing laodong zhuangkuang" (Nanjing's Labor Conditions). *Xin qing nian* 7.6: 1,063–78.

Momsen, Janet Henshall, ed. 1999. *Gender, Migration and Domestic Service*. New York: Routledge.

Murphy, Rachel. 2004. "Turning Chinese Peasants into Modern Citizens: 'Population Quality,' Demographic Transition, and Primary Schools." *China Quarterly* 177: 1–20.

Naughton, Barry. 1995. "Cities in the Chinese Economic System: Changing Roles and Conditions for Autonomy." In *Urban Spaces in Contemporary China: The Potential for Autonomy and Community in Post-Mao China*, ed. Deborah S. Davis, Richard Kraus, Barry Naughton, and Elizabeth J. Perry, 61–89. Washington: Woodrow Wilson Center Press / Cambridge University Press.

Ni Wei. 1999. "Xujia zhuti de shenhua ji qiantaici" (A Myth of an Illusory Subject and Its Unspoken Words). *Shanghai wenxue* 4: 79–80.

Oakes, Tim. 2000. "China's Market Reforms: Whose Human Rights Problem?" In *China Beyond the Headlines*, ed. Timothy B. Weston and Lionel M. Jensen, 295–326. New York: Rowman and Littlefield.

O'Hanlon, Rosalind. 1988. "Recovering the Subject: Subaltern Studies and Histories of Resistance in Colonial South Asia." *Modern Asian Studies* 22.1: 189–224.

Oi, Jean. 1995. "The Role of the Local State in China's Transitional Economy." *China Quarterly* 144.1: 132–49.

Oishi, Takahisa. 2001. *The Unknown Marx: Reconstructing a Unified Perspective*. London: Pluto Press / Takushoku University, Tokyo.

Orliski, Constance. 2003. "The Bourgeois Housewife as Laborer in Late Qing and Early Republican Shanghai." *Nan nü* 5.1: 43–68.

Overbeek, Henk, and Kee van der Pijl. 1993. "Restructuring Capital and Restructuring Hegemony: Neo-liberalism and the Unmaking of the Post-war Order." In *Restructuring Hegemony in the Global Political Economy: The Rise of Transnational Neo-liberalism in the 1980s*, ed. Henk Overbeek, 1–27. London: Routledge.

Parrenas, Rhacel Salazar. 2001. *Servants of Globalization: Women, Migration, and Domestic Work*. Stanford, Calif.: Stanford University Press.

Patnaik, Utsa. 1999. "On Measuring 'Famine Deaths': Different Criteria for Socialism and Capitalism?" *Akhbár* 6 (November–December), http://www.indowindow.com/akhbar/.

———. 2004. "The Republic of Hunger." IDEAS, http://networkideas.org/.

Perelman, Michael. 2000. *The Invention of Capitalism: Classical Political Economy and the Secret History of Primitive Accumulation*. Durham, N.C.: Duke University Press.

Perkins, Dwight. 1977. *Rural Small-scale Industry in the People's Republic of China*. Berkeley: University of California Press.

Perkins, Dwight, and Shahid S. Yusuf. 1984. *Rural Development in China*. Baltimore: Johns Hopkins University Press.

Perry, Elizabeth, and Christine P. W. Wong. 1985. *Political Economy of Reform in Post-Mao China*. Cambridge, Mass.: Harvard University Press.

Pheng Cheah. 2000. "Universal Areas: Asian Studies in a World in Motion." *Traces* 1: 37–70.

Phillips, Kevin. 2002. *Wealth and Democracy: A Political History of the American Rich*. New York: Broadway Books.

Potter, Sulamith Hein. 1983. "The Position of Peasants in Modern China's Social Order." *Modern China* 9: 465–99.

Potter, Jack, and Sulamith Hein Potter. 1990. *China's Peasants: The Anthropology of a Revolution*. Cambridge: Cambridge University Press.

Pun Ngai. 1999. "Becoming *Dagongmei* (Working Girls): The Politics of Identity and Difference in Reform China." *China Journal* 42: 1–18.

————. 2003. "Subsumption or Consumption? The Phantom of Consumer Revolution in 'Globalizing' China." *Cultural Anthropology* 18.4: 469–92.

————. 2005. *Made in China*. Durham, N.C.: Duke University Press.

Qingnian xinxiang (Youth Letterbox). 1980. "Rensheng, xinyang, qiantu" (Life, Faith, and Future). *Qingnian xinxiang* 3: 1–2.

————. 1982. "Xingfu zhi lu zai hefang?" (Where Is the Road to Happiness?). *Qingnian xinxiang* 7: 30.

Quanyang zhen Beijing jiating fuwuyuan zhaosong zhan. 1997. "97 niandu laowu shuchu gongzuo zongjie" (Work Summary on Labor Export in 1997). Quanyang, Anhui, 11 December, unpublished manuscript.

Rajchman, John. 1991. *Philosophical Events*. New York: Columbia University Press.

Riskin, Carl. 1971. "Small Industry and the Chinese Model of Development." *China Quarterly* 46: 245–73.

————. 1987. *China's Political Economy*. New York: Oxford University Press.

Rofel, Lisa. 1989. "Hegemony and Productivity: Workers in Post-Mao China." In *Marxism and the Chinese Experience: Issues of Socialism in a Third World Socialist Society*, ed. Arif Dirlik and Maurice Meisner, 235–52. Armonk, N.Y.: M. E. Sharpe.

————. 1994. "Yearnings: Television Love and Melodramatic Politics in Contemporary China." *American Ethnologist* 21.4: 700–722.

————. 1999. *Other Modernities*. Berkeley: University of California Press.

Rosen, Stanley. 1994. "Chinese Women in the 1990s: Images and Roles in Contention." In *China Review 1994*, ed. Maurice Brosseau and Lo Chi Kin, 17:1–28. Hong Kong: Chinese University Press.

Rowland, Joshua. 2001. "'Forecasts of Doom': The Dubious Threat of Graduate Teaching Assistant Collective Bargaining to Academic Freedom." *Boston College Law Review* 42: 941–66.

Sakamoto, Hiroko. 2004. "The Cult of 'Love and Eugenics' in May Fourth Movement Discourse." *positions* 12.2: 329–76.

Sassen, Saskia. 1999. "Embedding the Global in the National." In *States and Sovereignty in the Global Economy*, ed. David A. Smith, Dorothy J. Solinger, and Steven C. Topik, 158–71. London: Routledge.

Sautman, Barry. Forthcoming. *Relations in Blood: Chinese Racial Nationalism*. Seattle: University of Washington Press.

Schein, Louisa. 2001. "Urbanity, Cosmopolitanism, Consumption." In *China Urban: Ethnographies of Contemporary Culture*, ed. Nancy N. Chen et al., 225–41. Durham, N.C.: Duke University Press.

————. 2002. "Notes for Discussion." Paper presented at "Anthropology in and of China: A Cross-Generation Conversation," Center for Chinese Studies, University of California, Berkeley, 8–9 March.

Seccombe, Wally. 1974. "The Housewife and Her Labour under Capitalism." *New Left Review* 83: 3–24.

————. 1975. "Domestic Labour: Reply to Critics." *New Left Review* 94: 85–96.

Selden, Mark. 2006. "Jack Gray, Mao Zedong and the Political Economy of Chinese Development." *China Quarterly* 187: 680–84.

Sha Lianxiang et al. 2001. *Zhongguo ren suzhi yanjiu* (Research on the Quality of Chinese People). Zhengzhou: Henan renmin chubanshe.

Shan Peiyong. 1997. *Guomin suzhi xue* (National Quality as a Branch of Learning). Zhengzhou: Henan yike daxue chubanshe.

Shen Rong. 1980. "Ren dao zhongnian" (At Middle Age). *Chinese Literature* 10: 3–63.

———. 1986. "Yongyuan shi chuntian" (Eternal Spring). In *Shen Rong ji* (A Collection of Shen Rong's Works), 1–148. Fuzhou: Haixia wenyi chubanshe.

Shi Nai'an. 1996. *Shui hu zhuan* (The Water Margin). Beijing: Guangming ribao chubanshe.

Shoujie quanguo dagongmei quanyi wenti yantaohui lunwenji (The Collected Works of the First National Forum on Issues about Women Migrant Workers' Rights and Interests). 1999. Beijing, 16–18 June, unpublished typescript.

Skinner, William G. 1985. "Presidential Address: The Structure of Chinese History." *Asian Studies* 44.2: 271–92.

Smiles, Samuel. 1999. *Ziji zhengjiu ziji* (Self-help). Trans. Liu Shuguang et al. Beijing: Beijing yanshan chubanshe.

Smith, Dorothy E. 1996. "Telling the Truth after Postmodernism." *Symbolic Interaction* 19.3: 171–202.

Sobchack, Vivian. 1999. "'Is Anybody Home?' Embodied Imagination and Visible Evictions." In *Home, Exile, Homeland: Film, Media, and the Politics of Place*, ed. Hamid Naficy, 45–61. London: Routledge.

Solinger, Dorothy J. 1993. "The Place of the Central City in China's Economic Reform: From Hierarchy to Network?" In *China's Transition from Socialism*, 205–22. Armonk, N.Y.: M. E. Sharpe.

———. 1999. *Contesting Citizenship in Urban China: Peasant Migrants, the State and the Logic of the Market*. Berkeley: University of California Press.

———. N.d. "Images of Chinese Peasant Migrants." Unpublished manuscript.

Sonntag, Selma K. 2005. "Appropriating Identity or Cultivating Capital." *Anthropology News* 46.3: 22.

Spigel, Lynn, and Denis Mann. 1992. *Private Screenings: Television and the Female Consumer*. Minneapolis: University of Minnesota Press.

Spivak, Gayatri Chakravorty. 1987a. *In Other Worlds: Essays in Cultural Politics*. New York: Routledge.

———. 1987b. "Speculations on Reading Marx: After Reading Derrida." In *Poststructuralism and the Question of History*, ed. Berek Attridge, Geoff Bennington, and Robert Young, 30–62. Cambridge: Cambridge University Press.

———. 1988. "Scattered Speculation on the Question of Value." In *In Other Worlds: Essays in Cultural Politics*, 154–75. New York: Routledge.

———. 1990. "Practical Politics of the Open End." In *The Post-colonial Critic: Interviews, Strategies, Dialogues*. New York: Routledge.

————. 1999. *A Critique of Postcolonial Reason: Towards a History of the Vanishing Present.* Cambridge, Mass.: Harvard University Press.

————. 2000. "From Haverstock Hill Flat to U.S. Classroom, What's Left of Theory?" In *What's Left of Theory? New Works on the Politics of Literary Theory*, ed. Judith Butler, John Guillory, and Kendall Thomas, 1–39. New York: Routledge.

————. 2007. "A Position without Identity." *positions* 15.2: 429–48.

Steinberg, Ronnie J., and Deborah M. Figart. 1999. "Emotional Labor since *The Managed Heart.*" *Annals* 561: 8–25.

Storper, Michael. 2000. "Lived Effects of the Contemporary Economy: Globalization, Inequality, and Consumer Society." *Public Culture* 12.2: 375–409.

Sun Wanning. 2002. "Discourse of Poverty: Weakness, Potential and Provincial Identity in Anhui." In *Rethinking China's Provinces*, ed. John Fitzgerald, 55–177. New York: Routledge.

————. 2004. "Indoctrination, Fetishization and Compassion: Media Constructions of the Migrant Woman." In *On the Move: Women and Rural-to-Urban Migration in Contemporary China*, ed. Arianne M. Gaetano and Tamara Jacka, 109–30. New York: Columbia University.

Sun Xiaomei. 1993. "Yiqun wailaimei zai jingcheng" (A Group of Migrant Women in Beijing). *Nüxing yanjiu* 1.

Tan Shen. 1997. "Nongcun laodongli liudong de xingbie chayi" (Gender Differences in Rural Labor Mobility). *Shehuixue yanjiu* 1: 42–47.

Tang Can and Feng Xiaoshuang. 1996. "Lao baomu yu xiao baomu: Liangbei ren de shidai xinji" (Old Baomu and Young Baomu: The Trajectories of Two Generations). *Dongfang* 6: 49–54.

Tang, Xiaobing. 1996. "New Urban Culture and the Anxiety of Everyday Life in Contemporary China." In *In Pursuit of Contemporary East Asian Culture*, ed. Xiaobing Tang and Stephen Snyder, 107–22. Boulder, Colo.: Westview Press.

————. 1998. "Decorating Culture: Notes on Interior Design, Interiority, and Interiorization." *Public Culture* 10.3: 530–48.

————. 2003. "Rural Women and Social Change in New China Cinema: From Li Shuangshuang to Ermo." *positions* 11.3: 647–74.

Thogersen, Stig. 2000. "The 'Quality' of Chinese Education and the New Ideal Student." *Nordic Newsletter of Asian Studies* 4: 4–7.

Thompson, E. P. 1963. *The Making of the English Working Class.* New York: Vintage Books.

Tomlins, Christopher. 1992. "Law and Power in the Employment Relationship." In *Labor Law in America*, ed. Christopher L. Tomlins and Andrew J. King, 71–98. Baltimore: Johns Hopkins University Press.

————. 1995. "Subordination, Authority, Law: Subjects in Labor History." *International Labor and Working Class History* 47: 56–90.

Trouillot, Michel-Rolph. 1991. "Anthropology and the Savage Slot: The Poetics and Politics of Otherness." In *Recapturing Anthropology: Working in the Present*, ed. Richard G. Fox, 17–44. Santa Fe, N.M.: School of American Research Press.

Turner, Victor. 1967. *The Forest of Symbols: Aspects of Ndembu Ritual*. Ithaca, N.Y.: Cornell University Press.

"Wailai nülaogong yanjiu" ketizu. 1995. "Waichu ladong yu nongcun ji nongmin fazhan" (Labor Migration and Development of the Countryside and Peasantry). *Shehuixue yanjiu* 4: 75–85.

Walker, Timothy. 1837. *Introduction to American Law*. Philadelphia: n.p.

Wang, Danyu. 2000. "Violence against Themselves: Suicide in Rural China." Paper presented at the annual meeting of the American Anthropological Association, San Francisco, 15–19 November.

Wang, Jing. 1996. "*Heshang* and the Chinese Enlightenment." In *High Culture Fever: Politics, Aesthetics, and Ideology in Deng's China*, 118–36. Berkeley: University of California Press.

———. 2001. "Culture as Leisure and Culture as Capital." *positions* 9.1: 69–104.

Wang Hui. 1998. "Contemporary Chinese Thought and the Question of Modernity." *Social Text* 16.2: 9–36.

———. 2000. "Fire at the Castle Gate." *New Left Review* 6: 69–99.

———. 2003. "The 1989 Social Movement and China's Neoliberalism." In *China's New Order*, 46–77. Cambridge, Mass.: Harvard University Press.

Wang Jiayan et al., eds. 1996. *Beijingshi waidi laijing renyuan bibei shouce* (An Indispensable Manual for Non-local Personnel in Beijing). Compiled by Beijingshi gong'an ju (Beijing Municipal Public Security Bureau), Beijingshi laodong ju (Beijing Municipal Labor Bureau), Beijing jingji xingxi zhongxin (Beijing Economic Information Center), and Beijingshi wailai renkou guanli gongzuo lingdao xiaozu (Office of the Work Team Managing Migrant Population in Beijing). Beijing: Xinhua chubanshe.

Wang Qimin and Sun Yu, dir. 1982. *Ren dao zhongnian* (At Middle Age). Changchun Film Studio.

Wang Shanping. 1992. From Country to the Capital: A Study of Wuwei-Beijing Female Migrant Group in China. Master's thesis, Oxford Polytechnic.

Wang Shucheng and Li Renhu. 1996. "Wuwei: Baomu xiaoying" (Wuwei: The Baomu Effect). *Ban yue tan* 8: 23–25.

Wang Xiaoming. 1999. "Banzhangnian de shenhua" (The Myth of a Half Face). *Shanghai wenxue* 4: 71–74.

Watson, Rubie S. 1994. "Girls' Houses and Working Women: Expressive Culture in the Pearl River Delta, 1900–41." In *Women and Chinese Patriarchy: Submission, Servitude and Escape*, ed. Maria Jaschok and Suzanne Miers, 25–44. Hong Kong: Hong Kong University Press.

Weber, Max. 1978. *Economy and Society*. Berkeley: University of California Press.

Weil, Robert. 1996. *Red Cat, White Cat: China and the Contradictions of Market Socialism*. New York: Monthly Review Press.

Wen Tiejun. 2001. "Reflections at the Turn of the Century on 'Rural Issues in Three Dimensions.'" *Inter-Asia Cultural Studies* 2.2: 187–295.

Wilk, Richard. 1995. "Learning to be Local in Belize: Global Systems of Common Difference." In *Worlds Apart: Modernity through the Prism of the Local*, ed. Daniel Miller, 110–33. London: Routledge.

Williams, Raymond. 1976. *Keywords*. London: Fontana / Croom Helm.

Willis, Susan. 1991. *A Primer for Daily Life*. London: Routledge.

Wolf, Diane. 1992. *Factory Daughters: Gender, Household Dynamics, and Rural Industrialization in Java*. Berkeley: University of California Press.

Wolf, Margery. 1972. *Women and the Family in Rural Taiwan*. Stanford, Calif.: Stanford University Press.

———. 1985. *Revolution Postponed: Women in Contemporary China*. Stanford, Calif.: Stanford University Press.

Women's International Network News. 1999. "China: Women over 35 'Unemployable.'" *Women's International Network News* 25.1: 57.

Wood, H. G. 1877. *A Treatise of the Law of Master and Servant: Covering the Relations, Duties and Liabilities of Employers and Employees*. Albany, N.Y.: John D. Parsons.

World Bank. 1997. *Sharing Rising Incomes: Disparities in China*. Washington: World Bank.

———. 2002. *World Development Report 2002*. Oxford: Oxford University Press.

Wu Li. 2003. "1978–2000 Zhongguo chengshihua jincheng yanjiu" (A Study of the Progress in Urbanization from 1978–2000). China Economic History Forum, http://economy .guoxue.com/.

Wu Peimin, dir. 1999. *Tian Jiaoshou jia de ershiba ge* baomu (Twenty-eight Baomu at Professor Tian's). Shanghai dianying zhipian chang (Shanghai Film Studio).

Wuwei xianzhi bangongshi (Office of Wuwei Annals). 1993. *Wuwei xianzhi* (Wuwei Annals). Beijing: Shehui kexue wenxian chubanshe.

Xie Lihua. 1995. "Guniang, ni weishenme jincheng?" (Girl, Why Do You Come to the City?). *Nongjianü baishitong* 1: 4–6.

Xie Sizhong. 1997. *Guomin suzhi yousilu* (Worried Thoughts about the Quality of the People of the Nation). Beijing: Zuojia chubanshe.

Xu Ke. 1997. "Zai yue zhi dagongmei" (Dagongmei in Guangdong). In *Kangju biji huihan* (The Collected Notes of Kangju). Taiyuan: Shanxi guji chubanshe.

Xu Xue. 1995. "Mingtian, wo hui gen xiang ge ren" (Tomorrow, I Will Be More Like a Human Being). *Zhongguo qingnian* 2: 11.

Xun Da. 1996. "'Jiawu laodong baochou hua' shi tiaobo fuqi guanxi" ("Remunerating Domestic Labor" Is Fomenting Discord in Conjugal Relations). *Xiandai jiating* 10: 30.

Yan Hairong. 2001. "Suzhi, ziwo fazhan, he jieji de youling" (Suzhi, Self-Development, and the Specter of Class). *Dushu* 3: 18–26.

———. 2004. "Spectralization of the Rural: Reinterpreting the Labor Mobility of Rural Young Women in the Post-Mao Era." *American Ethnologist* 30.4: 478–596.

———. 2006. "Rurality and Labor Process Autonomy: The Question of Subsumption in the Waged Labor of Domestic Service." *Cultural Dynamics* 18.1: 5–31.

Yan Ming. 2002. "Ping *dangdai zhongguo shehui jieceng yanjiu baogao*" (Review of *Research Report on Contemporary Chinese Social Strata*). China Education and Research Network, http://www.edu.cn/.

Yang Fangyi and Li Bo. 2006. "Miandui WTO, zhongguo gongmin shehui neng zuoxie-shenme?" (Facing the WTO: What Can Chinese Civil Society Do?). *Zhongguo fazhan jianbao* 30 (June), http://www.chinadevelopmentbrief.org.cn/.

Yang, Gladys. 1980. "A New Woman Writer Shen Rong and Her Story 'At Middle Age.'" *Chinese Literature* 10: 64–70.

Yang Tao. 2000. "Chengshi gaibian le wo de shenghuo" (The City Has Changed My Life). *Dagongmei* (supplement): 16.

Ye Jingde. 1996. "Jiawu laodong, nanu pingdeng yu qiye zhengce" (Domestic Labor, Gender Equality, and Enterprise Policies). *Funü yanjiu luncong* 4: 40–43.

Yin Yiping. 1999. *Gao ji hui: Zhong guo cheng shi zhong chan jie ceng xie zhen* (High-class Gray: A Portrait of the Chinese Urban Middle Class). Beijing: Zhongguo qingnian chubanshe.

Young, Marilyn. 1989. "Chicken Little in China: Some Reflections on Women." In *Marxism and the Chinese Experience*, ed. Arif Dirlik and Maurice Meisner, 253–67. Armonk, N.Y.: M. E. Sharpe.

Yu Jie. 1998. "Sandai baomu" (Three Generations of Baomu). *Lian'ai, hunyin, jiating* 10: 1.

Yu Jie and Wang Lei. 1998. "Sandai baomu de meng: Hukou, zhuanqian, chuang shiye" (Dreams of Three Generations of Baomu: Make a Living, Make Money, and Make an Enterprise). *Anhui huabao* 3: 46–48.

Yuan Jun, dir. 1999. *Jiemei* (Sisters). Guangzhou Television Station.

Zeng Min. 1989. "Guangxi renkou de wenhua suzhi yu shangpin shengchan de guanxi" (The Relationship between the Cultural Quality of Guangxi's Population and Commodity Production). In *Zhongguo xinnanbu renkou xianzhuan yanjiu* (Studies of the Present Situation of China's Southwestern Population), ed. Yunnan Provincial Census Office and Yunnan Provincial Research Center for Population Development Strategies, 165–72. Kunming: Yunnan renmin chubanshe.

Zhang, Li. 2001. *Strangers in the City: Reconfigurations of Space, Power, and Social Networks within China's Floating Population*. Stanford, Calif.: Stanford University Press.

———. 2002. "Spatiality and Urban Citizenship in Late Socialist China." *Public Culture* 14.2: 311–34.

Zhang Lixi. 1998. "Fuqi chongtu: Jiating xingbie fengong moshi chonggou guocheng zhong de yige biran xianxiang" (Conflict between Husband and Wife: An Inevitable Phenomenon in the Process of Restructuring Gendered Division of Labor within Family). *Funü yanjiu luncong* 3: 4–8.

Zhang Meirong and Nan Song. 1994. *Jia wu lao dong jia zhi lun* (On the Value of Domestic Labor). Taiyuan: Shanxi ren min chubanshe.

Zhang Wanli. 1990. "Jinqi woguo shehui jieji, jieceng yanjiu zongshu" (A Review of Recent Studies of Class and Strata in China). *Zhongguo shehui kexue* 5: 173–81.

Zhang, Xudong. 2001. "The Making of the Post-Tiananmen Intellectual Field: A Critical Overview." In *Whither China: Intellectual Politics in Contemporary China*, ed. Xudong Zhang, 1–75. Durham, N.C.: Duke University Press.

Zhang Zhen. 2000. "Mediating Time: The 'Rice Bowl of Youth' in Fin de siècle China." *Public Culture* 12.1: 93–113.

Zhonggong Hexian Xianwei Zhengce Yanjiushi. 1998. "Guanyu nongcun laoli shuchu, gengdi paohuang ji tudi liuzhuan qingkuang de diaocha" (An Investigation on Labor Migration, Land Wasting, and Land Circulation). *Chaohu gongzuo tongxun* 8: 11–13.

Zhu Xiaoyang. 1987. "Mangliu zhongguo" (The Blind Wanderers of China). *Zhongguo zuojia* 4: 349–86.

Zhuang, Ya'er. 1995. *Zhongguo renkou qianyi shuju ji* (A Collection of Data on Population Migration in China). Beijing: Zhongguo renkou chubanshe.

Brauw, Alan de, 152–53
Burn, Richard, 16
Butler, Judith, 199–200

Cao Yu, 19
capital accumulation, 2
capitalism: as despotic, 14; globalization, 2; market economy and, 12
Castree, Noel, 252 n. 17
catachresis, 5
Chakrabarty, Dipesh, 14, 252 n. 17
chao. See stir-frying
chastity, 33
Cheah, Pheng, 2
Cheng Fengjun, 121–22
chenggong renshi, 153–54
Chen Qingli, 119
Chen Shaogong, 156
Chen Xin, 153
Chen Xiuchen, 146
chiku. See eating bitterness
Chi Li, 154, 157
chuan, 205–6
Chunzi, 240, 241–42
cities: coastal, 38, 39; development strategies, 41; rise of, 36–44; transformation of, 37–38; urbanization and, 36, 234–35
Clarke, David B., 256–57 n. 23
class: backwardness and, 195; consciousness, 195, 252 n. 17; equalization, 196–97; gender and, 53, 59, 77–78, 107; identity and, 19–20, 153–54; injustice, 54; *jieji* consciousness, 195; language of, 155; mobility, 102, 129; narrative, 204–12; oppression, 5; reform, 98–102; self-development and, 188; specter of, 202–12, 248; wealthy, 153; worker identity and, 19–20
collective labor. *See under* labor
commodity economy, 120–21
consumption, 67; culture of, 156, 158–59; depletion and, 247; domestic labor and, 168; domestic life and, 81–82; education and, 117; gender and, 159, 161; gender value and, 159; image and, 172; migrant women and, 146–48, 152–53, 160–62, 168, 180, 182, 246–47; narrative, 148–65; vs. production, 148, 153, 158, 162, 165, 178–80, 183; semiotic value and, 176–78; women as consumers, 67, 146, 276 n. 11. *See also* production
Croll, Elizabeth, 83
Cultural Revolution (1966–1976): on Chinese tradition, 42–43; on domestic servants, 19; vs. high-ranking officials, 33; mass line policies, 68; post-Mao regime on, 260–61 n. 51; women's liberation and, 31

dagong, 6, 189, 196–97, 201, 203, 212, 218, 225
dagongmei: collective, 210–12, 248; consciousness of, 204, 210–11; consumption and, 246–47; defined, 6; discrimination against, 9; economic law and, 234; education and, 6–7; life as, 6–10; narratives, 228–32; transformation and, 145–46, 147
Darwin, Charles, 283 n. 13
Dazhai Brigade, 38, 49
decollectivization, 35, 47, 120, 151, 225, 254–55 n. 8
Defoe, Daniel, 15
Deleuze, Gilles, 119
Delphy, Christine, 65
Deng Xiaoping, 11, 118, 233–34
Derrida, Jacques, 5
Development: culture of, 122–23; economic law of, 246; power of, 200; *suzhi* and, 115–16, 119, 120. *See also* self-development
Dirlik, Arif, 11–12, 52, 274 n. 59

discrimination: against *dagongmei*, 9; gender, 28, 107

domestic service: bondservant system and, 17–18; consumption and, 168; demand for, 36; domestic labor and, 31, 33, 34, 91, 106–7; domestic life and, 81–84; *dagongmei* account of, 3–10; employer survey, 109–10; feminization, 62; first-time servants and employers, 54–55; gender and, 55–57, 67–68; integration and, 33; intellectuals and, 67–69; in Mao era, 18–19; mobilization and, 21, 66; in post-Mao era, 19; productivity in, 65; propriety, 34, 55–56, 70, 74, 79, 83, 89, 91–93, 106; sociality/socialization and, 66, 103–7; subjectivity and, 98–102, 171; surveys, 65–66; time/value management and, 80–83, 84. See also *baomu*

Dryden, Gordon, 81

duixiang, 22–23

Dundes, Alan, 140

eating bitterness, 100, 151, 197–204, 210

economic law, 232–42, 246

economy, market. *See* market economy

education and cheap labor, 6–7

Ehrenreich, Barbara, 262–63 n. 8

elite youth, 48–49

Elson, Diane, 274 n. 58

emaciation of rural, 39, 43–44, 45, 222–23, 225–26, 247–48

employers: complaints by, 54–55, 89, 132, 170; consumption and, 168–69; growth of, 80; interviews with, 53–54; propriety and, 34, 55–56, 70, 74, 79, 83, 89, 91–93, 106; semiotic value and, 176–78; survey of, 109–10

employment: employment-at-will, 17; master-servant relationship and, 15–17

Engels, Friedrich, 283 n. 13

equality, in Mao era, 20, 30–31, 85

Evans, Harriet, 161, 277 n. 12

familialism, 213–16

family service company, 111–12, 113, 125, 132, 134, 149

Feinman, Jay, 17

femininity, 49, 161, 276–77

feminization of domestic service, 62, 63, 67

Feng Xiaoshuang, 213

Fifteenth Party Congress, 112, 113, 114

folklore, urban, 139–43

food shortages, 29

forgetting, 5, 8, 24

Foucault, Michel, 40, 131, 135, 268 n. 16, 279 n. 1

Four Worlds, 116

freedom: accumulation and, 36; bourgeois view of, 15; violence and, 26

Fukuyama, Francis, 15

funü, 6, 30–31. *See also* rural migrant women

Fussell, Paul, 156

fuwuyuan, 20

Gao, Mobo C. F., 48

gaze: disciplinary, 198, 207–8; employer's, 51, 173; evaluative, 177, 192–93; mirroring, 207–9; patriarchy's, 34; voyeuristic, 181

gender: class and, 53, 59, 77–78, 107; consumption and, 159, 161; discrimination, 28, 107; disorder and, 67; division of labor and, 30, 58, 64–66, 68; domesticity and, 24; domestic work and, 67–68; equality, 30–31, 255–56 n. 14, 260 n. 43; guilt and, 58; politics, 30–31, 62–64, 67; praxis, 30; production and, 159; roles, 48; subjugation, 19. *See also* women

globalization: capitalist market, 2, 116;

globalization (*continued*)
China's place and, 2–3; terminology and, 1

Gramsci, Antonio, 285 n. 24

Great Leap Forward, 38, 64

Greenhalgh, Susan, 266 n. 4

Guattari, Félix, 119

guilt, gendered, 58

Guo Chuanhuo, 80

Hale, Matthew, 16

Han Deqiang, 264 n. 17, 272 n. 48

Han Dongping, 257 n. 24, 260 n. 45

Han Yuhai, 272 n. 48

Harden, Blaine, 262–63 n. 8

Harootunian, Harry, 46

Harvey, David, 39, 253 n. 2

Hegel, G. W. F., 2, 14

Heraclitus, 223

Hershatter, Gail, 58

Heshang (TV series), 42

heterogeneity, 119, 136–37

Hochschild, Arlie R., 262–63 n. 8

Home for Rural Migrant Women, 9, 190, 196, 200, 214, 234, 245

home ownership, 82–83

Honig, Emily, 58

hope, 26

household responsibility system, 26

housing reform, 81–82

Hua Min, 9, 22, 243–49

Huang Ping, 153, 282 n. 8

Huo Da, 72, 75, 78

identity: class and, 19–20, 153–54; cultivation of, 138; memory and, 5; rural women and, 28, 35–36, 44, 102, 161, 176, 180–85, 191; rural youth and, 48, 51

illiteracy. *See* literacy of rural women

industrialization: as emancipation, 30; national, 29

intellectuals: burdens of, 55, 56–57, 68–70, 78–79, 81; domestic life narrative of, 82–83; mental work and, 68–69; professionalization of, 80; student recruitment by, 56

Iron Girls, 31, 44, 47, 49, 62

Jacka, Tamara, 31, 64

Jiangxi Soviet, 30

Jiang Zemin, 112, 118, 195

jianmin, 17–18

jieji. See under class

jiemei, 215

jilei, 202

Jin Yuanju, 111

Judd, Ellen, 120

Keenan, Thomas, 137

keywords, 1–2, 3, 112; catachresis of, 5, 13; global, 13; meaning and, 5; postsocialism and, 3–13; reality beneath, 4–5; truth and, 10–11

kinship networks, 133

Kirby, Richard, 38, 40

labor: affect, 75, 99, 100, 105–6; agricultural, 17, 28, 32, 34–35, 43; bureaus, 92; cheap, 6–7, 36, 75, 159, 216, 238; collectives, 29–31, 124; as commodity, 103–4; conditions, 55; demands of, 17; diligent, 74; in discipline, 15; division of, 18, 30, 58, 64–66, 68, 194, 227; domestic, 34, 55–57, 67–69, 70, 81–84, 91, 106–7; emancipation of, 26; exporting counties, 36; flexibility, 37; gender and, 58, 64–66, 68; market, 88, 90–91, 93; master-servant relationship of, 17; mental, 55, 69, 106; migrant, 10, 13, 27, 36, 43, 51, 96, 123–31, 134; mobility, 51, 124, 129, 149, 239; motivation of, 79, 94; peasant, 32, 40;

neoliberalism, 131–38; urban folklore in, 139–43

new women, 49

nomenclature. *See* keywords

nongcun funü, 28. *See also* rural migrant women

nügong, 6, 30–31. *See also* rural migrant women

O'Hanlon, Rosalind, 212

old society, 19–20, 33–34, 42, 49, 54–55, 168

party-state, 10, 49–50, 122

patriarchy, 28, 30, 32, 33, 34, 36, 260 n. 47

peasants: land reform and, 6, 26; mobilization of, 5, 124; new, 120–23. *See also* rural migrant workers; rural migrant women

People's Commune, 38

Perelman, Michael, 274 n. 55

personhood, 25, 34, 113; rural women and, 50–51; youth and, 44–52

petit-bourgeois, 9, 254–55 n. 8

place-based networks, 133

political economy, and subjectivity, 26–27

population planning, 114

postsocialism, Chinese: economy and, 11; keywords and, 3–13; structural conditions, 12

poverty: relief, 113–14, 122–23, 134; subjectivity and, 122, 136

Pratt, Edmund, 15

price controls, 29

privatization, 41, 43–44

production: agricultural, 41, 43; city and, 37–38, 39, 181; class and, 9; collectives, 41; vs. consumption, 148, 153, 158, 162, 165, 178–80, 183; education and, 117; gender and, 159; household-based, 124; migrant women and,

148; patriarchal relationship of, 65; relations, 14–15, 17, 33; responsibility, 29; in rural areas, 37–38, 43, 223, 225; sociality and, 13, 63–64; *suzhi*, 130, 137. *See also* consumption

professionalization, 46

propriety, 34, 55–56, 70, 74, 79, 83, 89, 91–93, 106

Pun Ngai, 6, 251 n. 7, 271–72 n. 47, 275 n. 7

qingnian, 48

quality. See *suzhi*

Reagan, Ronald, 140–43

reality, and keywords, 4–5, 24

refeminization. *See* feminization of domestic service

rice rations, 38–39

rights of workers, 17

Rofel, Lisa, 189

Rozelle, Scott, 152–53

rural, appropriation of by city, 42

rural migrant women: as backward, 182; as *baomu*, 88–90; as consumers, 146–48, 152–53, 160–62, 168, 180, 182; grievance letter of, 50; identity and, 28, 35–36, 44, 102, 161, 176, 180–85, 191; industrialization and, 30; literacy and, 32; marriage and, 31–33, 160, 162; migration from Wuwei County, 27–36; patriarchy and, 28, 30, 32, 33, 34, 36; personhood and, 50–51; production and, 148; recruitment of, 70, 91–93, 124–27, 131, 132, 138; returning, 124, 147–48, 163–64, 180, 182, 221–32; self-development and, 190; social integration of, 33–34; sociality and, 70–72, 74, 103–7; subjectivity of, 37, 92, 98; transformation of, 145–47, 190–91; as transgressors, 34. *See also dagongmei* rural migrant workers, 12, 13; emancipation of, 25–52; manual labor and, 69; market economy and, 10; mobilization of, 75, 93; view of, 37

rural-urban relations: appropriation and, 42; economic law and, 235–36; income disparity and, 41; shift in, 39; subjectivity and, 27

rural youth: domestication, 48; grievance letter of, 50; identity and, 48, 51; migration account, 45–46; personhood and, 44–52

Said, Edward, 22
Schein, Louisa, 40, 156
Schultz, Theodore, 118
Scott, James, 212
self-development: class and, 188, 194, 196; defined, 192; desire and, 187; eating bitterness and, 197–204, 210; market economy and, 10; migrant-urban workers and, 190, 213; narratives, 199–204; poems, 228–29, 231; speaking bitterness and, 179; subjectivity and, 210, 213, 224; *suzhi* and, 129, 188–94; transformation and, 188, 192
servants: consciousness of, 87, 88; old society and, 54–55. *See also* domestic service; master-servant relationship
shame, 32–34, 64
Shen Rong, 66–67; "At Middle Age," 56–59, 69, 72; "Eternal Spring," 59–62, 69–70
Smith, Adam, 118, 135, 274 n. 55
Smith, Dorothy, 205–6
Sobchack, Vivian, 163
sociality and socialization, 33–34, 66, 70–72, 74, 79, 103–7, 152
social revolution and peasants, 6
social welfare, 189, 257 n. 27
Solinger, Dorothy, 128
speaking bitterness: domestics and,

179; practice of, 5, 13, 54, 202; rural women and, 34–35; self-development and, 179, 202–3; subjectivity and, 213
Special Economic Zones, 39
spending habits, 157–58
Spivak, Gayatri Chakravorty, 24, 129–30, 213, 252 n. 17, 253 n. 1
Steedman, Carolyn Kay, 1
stir-frying, 244–45
subalternity: agency and, 212, 213; domestic workers and, 95–96; migrant women and, 24, 49, 50, 200; speaking and, 202, 213, 243, 245–46; subjectivity, 3, 24, 27, 212; transformative power of, 22, 203
subjectivity: body and, 93–98; death and, 26; of domestic workers, 98–102, 171; interiority and, 163; migration and, 25–26; modernity and, 50, 102; narrative, 98–101; poverty and, 122, 136; rural women and, 50; self-development and, 210, 213, 224; self-representation and, 5; subaltern, 3, 27, 212; subjection, 16; transformation and, 163–64; urban modern, 46; value and, 137
subjugation, gender, 19
sublation, 246
suku. See speaking bitterness
Sun Liping, 275 n. 5
Sun, Wanning, 278 n. 19
surplus value, 113, 124, 129, 137, 178, 182, 188–94, 198, 201–2, 262–63 n. 8
surveys: on domestic work and gender, 65–66; of employers, 109–10; on level of modernization, 117
suzhi: defined, 75, 113, 119, 207; development and, 115–16; education and, 99, 117–18, 130; as human value, 111–43; improvement of, 98–99, 102, 104, 111–13, 115–16, 118, 130, 135; labor migration and, 123–31; labor power and,

suzhi (*continued*)
197, 199; of laid-off women workers, 84; language of, 119; national, 114; as neohumanism, 131–38; origins, 114; as political keyword, 112; in post-Mao era, 114; poverty and, 120–23; responsiveness and, 96; statistics on, 117–18; subjectivity and, 94, 207; as surplus value, 113, 188–94, 198, 201–2

Tang Can, 213
Tang, Xiaobing, 164
Tan Shen, 48
Tao Yuanming, 74
technologies of the self, 279 n. 1
terminology, regulative. *See* keywords
Thompson, E. P., 252 n. 17
time management, 80–81
Tomlins, Christopher, 15, 64
tradition: backwardness and, 42, 121, 222, 234; death of, 42–43
Trouillot, Michel-Rolph, 23
truth: keywords and, 10–11; self-development and, 199–200, 202; as totality, 246
Turner, Victor, 224
Twenty-eight Baomu at Professor Tian's (TV series), 53

union exclusions, 17
urban reforms, 36, 234–35
urban-rural relations. *See* rural-urban relations
urban workers, 10, 12, 37, 80, 84–85, 189, 190, 238–39

violence: class and, 195; discursive, 51; freedom and, 26; history of, 26; rural emaciation and, 44; symbolic, 183
Volosinov, Valentin, 205
Vos, Jeannette, 81

wage labor. *See dagong*
Walker, Timothy, 16
Wangfujing, Grandma, 134
Wang Hui, 136
Wang, Jing, 42
Wang Weiming, 181
Wang Xiaoming, 153, 154
Wang Zhaoyao, 121
welfare systems, 189, 257 n. 27
Wilk, Richard, 152
will, appropriation of, 14–15
Williams, Raymond, 1–2
women: in Chinese women's movement, 188; as consumers, 67; elderly, as *baomu*, 86–88; gender value of, 159–60; labor and, 29, 32, 53; new, 49; socialist, 67; status and value of, 120. *See also* femininity; gender; rural migrant women
women's liberation: Cultural Revolution and, 31; public labor and, 62; on rural women, 34; socialist discourse, 33
Wood, H. G., 16

xiao zi, 9, 254–55 n. 8
Xie Lihua, 200–201, 243
Xing Xianman, 146
Xu Ke, 6

Yang Tao, 240–41
Yin Yiping, 156–57
youth. *See* elite youth; rural youth
Yu, Professor, 234–39

Zhang, Li, 12
Zhang Meirong, 265 n. 24
Zhao Ziyang, 39
Zhu Rongji, 275 n. 8
ziwo fazhan. *See* self-development
zuoren. *See* personhood

Chapter 1 previously appeared as "Spectralization of the Rural: Reinterpreting the Labor Mobility of Rural Young Women in Post-Mao China," *American Ethnologist* 30.4 (2003). A previous version of chapter 3 was published as "Neo-liberal Governmentality and Neo-humanism: Organizing Value Flow through Labor Recruitment Agencies," *Cultural Anthropology* 18.4 (2003). I thank *Cultural Anthropology*, *American Ethnologist*, the American Anthropological Association, and the University of California Press for permission to include these materials here.

Yan Hairong is an assistant professor of applied social sciences at Hong Kong Polytechnic University.

Library of Congress Cataloging-in-Publication Data
Yan, Hairong.
New masters, new servants : migration, development,
and women workers in China / Yan Hairong.
p. cm.
Includes bibliographical references and index.
ISBN 978-0-8223-4287-8 (cloth : alk. paper)
ISBN 978-0-8223-4304-2 (pbk. : alk. paper)
1. Women domestics—China—Social conditions.
2. Rural women—Employment—China.
3. Rural-urban migration—China. I. Title.
HD6072.2.C6Y36 2008
331.40951—dc22   2008028456